D1572747

phenomenology and treatment of ANXIETY

phenomenology and treatment of ANXIETY

Edited by

William E. Fann, M.D.
Ismet Karacan, M.D., (Med) D.Sci.
Alex D. Porkorny, M.D.
Robert L. Williams, M.D.

all of the

Department of Psychiatry
Baylor College of Medicine
Houston, Texas

SP MEDICAL & SCIENTIFIC BOOKS

New York • London

SPECTRUM PUBLICATIONS, INC.
175-20 Wexford Terrace, Jamaica, N.Y. 11432

Library of Congress Cataloging in Publication Data

Main entry under title:

Phenomenology and treatment of anxiety.

   Proceedings of a symposium sponsored by the Dept. of Psychiatry and the Office of Continuing Education, Baylor College of Medicine, held in Houston, Tex., Dec. 1-2, 1977.
   Includes index.
   1. Anxiety—Congresses. I. Fann, William E., 1930- II. Baylor College of Medicine. Dept. of Psychiatry. II. Baylor College of Medicine. Office of Continuing Education. [DNLM: 1. Anxiety—Congresses. 2. Anxiety—Therapy—Congresses. WM172 P541 1977]
RC531.P45   616.8'522   78-32092
ISBN 0-98335-070-2

Contributors

GEORGE L. ADAMS, M.D.
Department of Psychiatry
Baylor College of Medicine
Houston, Texas

ROBERT E. ALLEN, M.D.
Department of Psychiatry
University of Southern California Medical
School
Los Angeles, California

HAROLD BROWN, M.D.
Department of Medicine
Baylor Colege of Medicine
Houston, Texas

HILDE BRUCH, M.D.
Department of Psychiatry
Baylor College of Medicine
Houston, Texas

NORMAN DECKER, M.D.
Department of Psychiatry
Baylor College of Medicine
Veterans Administration Hospital
Houston, Texas

JORGE DE LA TORRE, M.D.
Department of Psychiatry
Baylor College of Medicine
Houston, Texas

CARL EISDORFER, PH. D., M.D.
Professor and Chairman
Department of Psychiatry
University of Washington School of Medicine
Seattle, Washington

JACK R. EWALT, M.D.
Department of Psychiatry (Emeritus)
Harvard University Medical School
Boston, Massachusetts
Director
Mental Health and Behavioral Science Service
U.S. Veterans Administration
Washington, D.C.

MAX FINK, M.D.
Department of Psychiatry
Health Sciences Center
School of Medicine
State University of New York
Stony Brook, New York

FRED FRANKEL, M.B., CH.B., D.P.M.
Department of Psychiatry
Harvard Medical School
Beth Israel Hospital
Boston, Massachusetts

ROBERT M. GILLILAND, M.D.
Department of Psychiatry
Baylor College of Medicine
Houston-Galveston Psychoanalytic Institute
Houston, Texas

DAVID GREENBLATT, M.D.
Department of Medicine
Harvard Medical School
Massachusetts General Hospital
Boston, Massachusetts

ROBERT L. ILARIA, M.D.
Department of Psychiatry
Baylor College of Medicine
Veterans Administration Hospital
Houston, Texas

HOWARD B. KAPLAN, PH. D.
Department of Psychiatry
Baylor College of Medicine
Houston, Texas

ISMET KARACAN, M.D., (MED) D.SC.
Department of Psychiatry
Baylor College of Medicine
Veterans Administration Hospital
Houston, Texas

DAVID W. KRUEGER, M.D.
Department of Psychiatry
Baylor College of Medicine
Houston, Texas

JERRY W. LESTER, PH. D.
Department of Psychiatry
Baylor College of Medicine
Houston, Texas

HAROLD LIEF, M.D.
Department of Psychiatry
University of Pennsylvania School of
Medicine
Philadelphia, Pennsylvania

WILLIAM T. MCKINNEY, M.D.
Department of Psychiatry
University of Wisconsin Medical School
Madison, Wisconsin

ROY B. MEFFERD, JR., PH. D.
Departments of Psychiatry and Physiology
Baylor College of Medicine
Department of Psychology
Graduate School
University of Houston
Department of Behavioral Science
University of Texas School of Public Health
Veterans Administration Hospital
Houston, Texas

ELAINE C. MORAN
Primate Laboratory
University of Wisconsin
Madison, Wisconsin

FERRIS N. PITTS, JR., M.D.
Department of Psychiatry
University of Southern California Medical
School
Los Angeles, California

ALEX D. POKORNY, M.D.
Department of Psychiatry
Baylor College of Medicine
Houston, Texas

D. EUGENE REDMOND, JR., M.D.
Departments of Psychiatry
and Pharmacology
Yale University School of Medicine
New Haven, Connecticut

KARL RICKELS, M.D.
Department of Psychiatry
University of Pennsylvania School of
Medicine
Philadelphia, Pennsylvania

ROBERT L. ROESSLER, M.D.
Department of Psychiatry
Baylor College of Medicine
Houston, Texas

LAURENCE R. SCHWEITZER, M.D.
Department of Psychiatry
Baylor College of Medicine
Houston, Texas

RICHARD I. SHADER, M.D.
Department of Psychiatry
Harvard Medical School
Massachusetts Mental Health Center
Boston, Masachusetts

LARRY B. SILVER, M.D.
National Institute of Mental Health
Rockville, Maryland
Piscataway, New Jersey

J. CATESBY WARE, PH.D.
Department of Psychiatry
Baylor College of Medicine
Houston, Texas

ROBERT L. WILLIAMS M.D.
Department of Psychiatry
Baylor College of Medicine
Houston, Texas

JOSEPH WOLPE, M.D.
Department of Psychiatry
Temple University School of Medicine
Eastern Pennsylvania Psychiatric Institute
Philadelphia, Pennsylvania

WILLIAM W.K. ZUNG, M.D.
Department of Psychiatry
Duke University Medical Center
Veterans Administration Hospital
Durham, North Carolina

Partial financial support of the symposium on the Phenomenology and Treatment of Anxiety, conducted at Baylor College of Medicine on December 1-2, 1977, was provided by the following pharmaceutical manufacturers:

Boehringer Ingelheim
Hoechst-Roussel Pharmaceuticals
Hoffmann-LaRoche
Lederle Laboratories
McNeil Laboratories
Pfizer
Sandoz Pharmaceuticals
Schering
Smith Kline & French Laboratories
The Upjohn Company
USV Laboratories
Warner/Chilcott
Wyeth Laboratories

The editors and conference participants are most grateful to these organizations for their valuable assistance and for their dedication to the continuing education of physicians and other health care professionals.

Acknowledgments

This volume originated in a symposium on the Phenomenology and Treatment of Anxiety, held at Baylor College of Medicine in Houston, Texas, December 1-2, 1977. The symposium was one in the College's annual series of conferences devoted to the study of major psychiatric disorders.

The success of the conference, and the strength of the present volume, are largely attributable to the hard and competent work of several individuals whose enormous contributions are not necessarily apparent from scanning the table of contents or the list of invited guests.

Dr. Fred Taylor, Mss, Margaret Klug, Evalyn Wasson, and Jimmie Winzeler of the Baylor Office of Continuing Education arranged and administered the conference impeccably; we are most grateful for the efforts and expertise of this outstanding group.

Mrs. Tommie Brackendorff worked on arrangements and conference registrations. Ms. Marsha Kracht operated the audio-visual equipment. Mss. Nancy Berry and Katie Destouet prepared the manuscript for publication. Ms. Elaine Miller indexed the volume.

Bruce Richman, M.A., Adjunct Assistant Professor in the Department of Psychiatry at Baylor and the Houston Veterans Administration Hospital, served as managing editor of the volume.

To each of these individuals the editors express their sincere gratitude.

Preface

This volume represents the proceedings of a symposium on the Phenomenology and Treatment of Anxiety, held in Houston, Texas on December 1-2, 1977. The conference was sponsored by the Department of Psychiatry and the Office of Continuing Education of Baylor College of Medicine in Houston, and was the third in the College's series of annual symposia devoted to study of the major psychiatric disorders.

Our intention in conducting the conference and publishing the papers and scholarly discussions presented there was to bring together scientists and clinicians of established reputation for a mutual exchange of ideas concerning the nature and treatment of anxiety. Pathological anxiety in its protean manifestations is confronted by practitioners in every medical discipline and intrudes upon virtually every aspect of clinical psychiatry. Anxiety can be both a precipitant and a complication of characterologic, neurotic, and psychotic disorders, and can be completely disabling in its severity. Pharmacological treatment of anxiety symptoms accounts for the largest class of medical prescription in the United States. Although much has been learned about the psychodynamic and biological factors influencing anxiety, diagnosis and effective treatment of this complex medical condition is a continuing medical problem; the mounting evidence of pandemic incidence in our culture is rather compelling testimony to the incomplete state of the art.

The present volume is not a comprehensive text book; instead, it is directed toward a series of special questions which may have been less adequately addressed in general discussions of anxiety. The book is roughly divided in four sections, the first of which is directed toward matters of clinical and theoretical assessment of the condition. Dr. Zung, the originator of some of the most widely used diagnostic instruments in clinical psychiatry, discusses the identification and quantification of significant anxiety symptoms. Drs. Schweitzer and Adams, psychiatrists with extensive interest in community medicine, address the important issue of how the non-psychiatric physician recognizes and deals with anxiety in the large group of patients who present to family and general practitioners. Dr. Eisdorfer discusses the special problems of anxiety in geriatrics, a population at unusually high risk medically and socially for development of anxiety and anxious depression. Dr. Jack Ewalt discusses in some detail an anxiety symptom complex widely seen among his patients in the Veterans Administration but somehow overlooked by the compilers of the DSM II, the traumatic neuroses. Dr. Roy Mefferd, who has specialized in quantification of psychological events for application in the nation's space program, attempts to identify distinctions between anxiety as a normal adaptive mechanism and as a clinical syndrome requiring medical intervention. Dr. Pokorny examines the implications of extreme and potentially intolerable anxiety as a possible element in suicide. Dr. Silver, a noted child psychiatrist, reviews the nature and management of anxiety among the young, and, as Dr. Eisdorfer discussed with the old, the circumstances under which this group can be at special risk.

Eight chapters concentrate upon biological, or, more strictly, physiological elements of anxiety. Dr. Mefferd reviews the concept that the psychological event can have a physiological basis. The chapter by Drs. Pitts and Allen proceeds toward this course from a different tack, reviewing Dr. Pitts' now-famous lactate studies and some of the controversial attention the work has drawn. Dr. McKinney details some of the human implications of his extensive studies of psychological effects in primates, and Dr. Eugene Redmond presents what is surely the most comprehensive consideration in the medical literature of the influences of brain norepinephrine in anxiety responses. Dr. Harold Brown, a well-known internist, reviews some of the physiological ailments which can present with primarily anxious symptomatology, and suggests the importance of the sometimes neglected physical examination in the psychiatrist's diagnostic procedures. Drs. Williams, Karacan, and their colleagues in the Baylor Sleep Disorders Center review the literature on the effects of anxiety upon sleep patterns and report their own study comparing medicated and non-medicated anxious insomniacs to controls. Drs. Roessler and Lester report the results of their innovative studies of the relationships between anxiety and human vocal function, and Dr. Fink, the renowned psychopharmacologist and electroencephalographer, discusses the effects of antianxiety agents upon clinical symptoms and the EEG record.

Five chapters examine psychodynamic elements of anxiety. Dr. Gilliland discusses the important analytic issues which have remained current from Freud's time until our own. Dr. Hilde Bruch reviews the contributions of Harry Stack Sullivan, the great theoretician who considered the influence of anxiety to be central to the nature of the individual's emotional development and personality. Dr. Krueger applies the dynamics of anxiety to psychological development and the emergence of characteristic maladaptive responses. Dr. Decker, a psychiatrist who specializes in psychiatric liaison work in a large general hospital, discusses the nature and effects of anxiety among people who are confronted with the combined trauma of illness and institutionalization. Dr. Howard Kaplan considers the developmental effects of chronic early anxiety upon the individual's self-esteem and subsequent social adjustment.

Advances in treatment approaches are examined in a concluding section. Dr. Harold Lief explains the diagnostic and therapeutic techniques which he has developed for alleviation of sexual dysfunction associated with anxiety. Dr. Karl Rickels reviews the pharmacological management of anxiety symptoms, and Drs. Greenblatt and Shader discuss pharmacokinetics of the benzodiazepine anxiolytics and their sub-groups. Drs. Pitts and Allen review the evidence for significant antianxiety activity of the beta-adrenergic blocking agents, a compound class developed for use in cardiovascular disorders but now widely prescribed as anxiolytics. Dr. Joseph Wolpe discusses clinical techniques for the systematic desensitization of individuals who are impaired by anxious or phobic response habits, and Dr. Jorge de la Torre explains the use of specialized short-term psychotherapeutic modalities for relief of targeted anxiety symptoms. In the concluding chapter Dr. Fred Frankel considers the definition and clinical application of hypnotic techniques in treatment of anxiety states.

The energetic reader who spends time with all of the twenty-seven papers will find that each author, writing independently, has found it necessary to re-articulate a definition of anxiety in the context of the work presented. This urge toward constant adjustment and reconsideration of the matter at hand does not bespeak fundamental theoretical disagreements among medical practitioners, but rather the remarkable breadth and inexhaustible interest of the subject. By confronting some of the important current issues in the study of anxiety from theoretical and clinical vantages, we hope to have compiled a significant contribution to the ongoing process of definition and understanding.

William E. Fann, M.D.
Ismet Karacan, M.D., (Med) D. Sc.
Alex D. Pokorny, M.D.
Robert L. Williams, M.D.

Contents

phenomenology and treatment of ANXIETY

CHAPTER 1

Assessment of Anxiety Disorder: Qualitative and Quantitative Approaches

William W. K. Zung

Familia sic putant omnes quae jam factor nec de salebris cogitant, ubi via strata.

The topic of this chapter is the assessment of anxiety, a job that, by the nature of the definitional vagueness of the term, is perhaps second in difficulty only to the definition of depression. Anxiety is a word used to mean many things, such as: 1. An affect; a dysphoric mental feeling state (He feels anxious). 2. Etiologic: the underlying cause of behavior (He overeats because of his anxiety). 3. Motivator: a drive (He is anxious to please you). 4. Situational response: a specific stimulus-response (He is anxious to please you). 4. Situational response:a specific stimulus-response (He is anxious over his new job). 5. Personality trait: an inherent and habitual mode of response (He is an anxious person). 6. Emotional disorder: variously called an anxiety disorder, anxiety neurosis, anxiety reaction, or anxiety state.

Assessment methods for anxiety have reflected these various usages of the word. Cattell and Scheier surveyed test procedures for anxiety and reported that at least 120 specific measures had been developed as of 1961 (1), reflecting the large diversity by which anxiety as a word had been defined. McReynolds surveyed the available techniques for the assessment of anxiety as of 1967 and reviewed a total of 88 formal anxiety measurement procedures (2). DeBonis performed a systematic analysis of 27 anxiety inventories and scales in 1974 (3). A more recent review of the assessment of anxiety was performed by Borkovec in 1977, containing 191 references to rating instruments (4). The large number of assessment procedures testifies not only to the centrality of anxiety as a concept, but also to the less-than-satisfactory status of anxiety assessment technology.

Of the various ways in which the word anxiety is used, the use of it in the context of a trait-state has been most frequently elaborated upon (1,5). The anxiety-trait concept includes describing an individual as having a global, trans-situational personality trait, in which anxiety is his or her habitual mode of responding, a characteristic which the person brings to any given situation, and/or which makes him anxiety-prone. The anxiety-state concept is that of a condition which is a phenomenon of distress as the current state, an entity at a particular time period. A further distinction of the anxiety-state is made between anxiety states that are free-floating nonsituational, generalized, and nonspecific, as distinguished from anxiety-states that result from specific stimulus-response situations, which are induced and usually phobic in nature. Our focus in this paper will be on the use of the word "anxiety" in the context of an anxiety-state as a generalized clinical disorder.

For a clinical entity to be diagnosed, treated, or investigated as an experimental variable, adequate techniques for its identification and measurement must be available. Because of the multidimensional and multidisciplinary use of the word "anxiety," there has been no simple or satisfactory method of measuring anxiety. The operational definition approach is one way of reaching common agreement. In turn, operational definitions that are used as the basis of rating scales are valuable for their ability to identify, to stratify, and to be predictive. Controlled studies of response to treatment intervention and other forms of therapeutic outcome analysis can only be as good as the measurements of change used in the methodology.

In the application of a biometric approach to the study of anxiety disorders, I have proposed the following formula as one approach to put into perspective the various procedures for measuring anxiety:

$$I = i_1 + i_2 + \ldots + i\text{-}n + x + r$$

I stands for the indicator of psychopathology that the procedure(s) purports to measure. It can be the smallest of units, such as an individual sign or symptom, or it could be a larger unit where the I is that of anxiety as a trait or state. The small i's in the formula indicate the actual measurements made, whether it be one (i_1) or many $(i\text{-})$. For example, I could be the indicator of psychopathology for anxiety as a disorder. In this hypothetical definition are included the sleep disturbance associated with anxiety, and the presence of nightmares. These then would be i_1 and i_2, respectively. If the sleep disorder found in anxiety itself is chosen as the I, then the number of minutes it takes to fall asleep, and the total number of minutes asleep would be designated as i_1 and i_2, respectively. Each assessment procedure has an objective and the number of items used and selected should reflect and should be sufficiently inclusive with respect to its primary objective: the indicator of psychopathology.

The actual assessment techniques used can range from the most subjective to the most objective. The usual *subjective* approach is that of the clinical global impression, where values are assigned based upon an overall impression of the patient in an unstructured interview. Global ratings of anxiety by clinicians represent a combination of observational data and interpretation of the patient's self-report. However, it must be kept in mind that the set a clinician has before actually seeing a patient frequently determines his diagnosis, which in turn reflects the severity of illness of the patient (6). At another level, rating procedures could be all-inclusive and include anxiety as one of many measures in a *systematic* approach. An example of this would be the Multiple Affect Adjective Check List, which uses mood words that measure anxiety in addition to other moods (7). Rating devices such as the Fear Thermometer (8) use a *focused* approach and choose only one aspect of anxiety. In the assessment of anxiety, *nonspecific* approaches have been used, such as projective testing using ink blots. *Semi-objective* rating scales have been developed in which specific cues for ratings of specific signs and symptoms are given, as well as instructions on how to rate quantitatively. Examples of these are the Hamilton Anxiety Scale (9) and the Anxiety Status Inventory (10). Lastly, *objective* measurements using laboratory instrumentation to determine psychophysiological variables have been used to measure somatic reactivity associated with anxiety. Specific physiological measurements for the various organ systems of the body have been developed for the quantification of a specific biological event. Examples include: 1. central nervous system—electroencephalogram, average evoked responses; 2. cardiovascular system—electrocardiogram, blood pressures; 3. respiratory system—respiration rate and depth; 4. gastrointestinal system—stomach motility, and pH; 5. genito-urinary system—penile circumference in males, and vaginal blood volume in females; 6. musculoskeletal system—electromyogram; and 7. skin—skin potential response, palmar sweat response.

During and before the time that these measurements are made, there are experimental noises or the x in our formula that enters into every measurement, and cannot always be controlled. These include: 1. intellect—the intelligence of the subject; 2. affect—the emotional set of the subject at the time of testing; 3. motivation—the amount of cooperation given; 4. adaptation—the practice effect of repeated measurement, the amount of learning, habituation and satiation; 5. introspection—the effect of cognitive elaboration by the subject during the test period; 6. arousal level—differences in attention levels as influenced by age, drug effects; 7. test construction *a*. if there is a lack of specific target signs and symptoms for the subject to rate; *b*. if the items are inexact or confusing; *c*. if there is lack of familiarity with the test format, making it difficult to determine the meaning of each response; and *d*. if the responses asked to be made are forced with no appropriate alternate choice. In addition to these experimental noises, other variables that influence assessment outcome include: 1. the subject's premorbid personality; 2. cultural background. 3. course of the anxiety disorder; and 4. external environment, such as associated events, social relations, physical functional capacity, and test environment.

Even after all attempts have been made to take into account the experimental noises, using the best state-of-the-art test construction, there is always a small residue, or *r* left. This is the unmeasured and untapped reaches which remain unaccounted for and defy explanation. In reviewing the basic formula for establishing a measurement of psychopathology for *I*, it is evident that the better the choice of *i*'s, the better *I* approaches the variable chosen to be measured. In addition, the smaller the *x* and *r*, the more accurate is our indicator of psychopathology.

Like other diagnostic labels we use in medicine, the term "anxiety disorder" is a shorthand term that describes a complex set of variables characterized by several dimensions. Research on anxiety measurements such as those described above have shown that data from such various aspects of anxiety as the affective-subjective, motor-behavioral, and physiological measures do not corelate well with one another (4). It is clear that any measure of affective, motor, and physiological responses are interrelated, but not in a simple linear fashion. More important, the lack of high correlation reflects the role of individual differences in patterns of anxiety responses, and the multidimensional aspect of anxiety as a disorder.

Rating scales themselves can be divided into those which are observer-rated and self-rated. Several authors have addressed themselves to this issue with the observations that: 1. It has never been convincingly demonstrated that clinician observer ratings are more accurate than self-report procedures (6); and 2. Self-ratings are not inferior to the more complex methods simply because they are relatively simple and straightforward. On the contrary, they may often represent the technique of choice, particularly in the measurement of current or state anxiety (2).

Although different results may be obtained by using observer-rated and self-rated scales, these differences should be viewed as mutually inclusive rather than jointly exclusive. For example, differences between observer-rated and self-rated results may be the result of one or another of the following differences: 1. Differences in the content of the two rating instruments. 2. The ability to perceive and report specific symptoms are different, with some easier for an observer, while others are easier for the subject to rate. 3. Differences may be due to interpretation of the existing clinical state. Observer ratings are usually performed by experienced clinicians who rate individuals based upon a continuum of severity of illness as evolved from seeing many patients in many settings, while self-ratings by subjects are based upon a continuum based upon himself or herself as the normative baseline in a limited setting. 4. Differences in role of the rater. This can be illustrated by looking at the different raters used in studies: The physician as a rater is looking at the core of the disorder and interpreting the psychopathology in terms of signs and symptoms. The nurse as a rater is looking at the patient as a member of her nursing unit or ward. Although the checklist of variables to be rated may ask for psychopathology, the nurse is interpreting this in terms of the patient as a model patient. What is his appearance, hygiene, habits? How cooperative is he as a patient? How does his behavior affect ward routine? Such reported differences are useful as additional data, rather than detrimental as conflicting data, if we can understand and know the source of these differences.

OPERATIONAL DEFINITION OF ANXIETY DISORDER AND CONSTRUCTION OF THE SCALE

Rating scales that are direct attempts to translate the operational definition of psychopathology, be it a symptom, trait, or syndrome, into a measurement that can be both qualitative and quantitative will help to increase both the precision and power of the observation of the variable(s) recorded.

The first problem in planning an operational definition or classification is that of choosing the measurement characteristics that are going to be used as a basis for the empirical identification of the underlying population. The variables chosen are such that they are: 1. relevant for distinguishing between different types of psychiatric patients (anxious or not anxious); 2. relevant for distinguishing between psychiatric patients and normals; 3., productive of homogeneity within groups so defined that patients who are grouped together are similar enough that for most practical purposes they can be treated as if they are all alike (all anxious); and 4. useful in assigning individuals according to the definition developed so that the operational definition will have some general applicability.

In the construction of the present rating instrument the symptoms of the illness were delineated by using the descriptive approach, since the basis of definition and classification in psychiatric nosology continues to be based upon presenting symptomatology (11).

Anxiety as a disorder is defined in the *Diagnostic and Statistical Manual,* second edition, or DSM-2, as a neurosis characterized by anxious overconcern extending to panic and frequently associated with somatic symptoms (12). More detailed definitions and descriptions of anxiety and its characteristic symptoms are described by the following authors and are summarized in Table 1: Kolb in *Noye's Modern Clinical Psychiatry* (13), Lief

6

Table 3. The Self-rating Anxiety Scale (SAS)

Name _____

Age _____ Sex _____

Date

	None OR A Little of the Time	Some of the Time	Good Part of the Time	Most OR all of the Time
1. I feel more nervous and anxious than usual.				
2. I feel afraid for no reason at all.				
3. I get upset easily or feel panicky.				
4. I feel like I'm falling apart and going to pieces.				
5. I feel that everything is all right and nothing bad will happen.				
6. My arms and legs shake and tremble.				
7. I am bothered by headaches, neck and back pains.				
8. I feel weak and get tired easily.				
9. I feel calm and can sit still easily.				
10. I can feel my heart beating fast.				

Gastrointestinal System			
Nausea and vomiting	Nausea, vomiting, diarrhea, anorexia	Nausea, vomiting, diarrhea	Vomiting and diarrhea Anorexia
Genitourinary System			
Increased desire to urinate	Urinary frequency, urgency	Urinary frequency	Frequency
Skin			
Face flushed, perspiration	Flushing of face, sensation of heat	Flushing or pallor, cold, wet extremities	Flushing Sweating
Central Nervous System			
Mind in constant daze, absent-minded	Lack of concentration, decreased memory, perceptual defects, irritability		
Difficulty in falling asleep, fearful dreams	Difficulty in falling asleep, fitful sleep, unpleasant dreams	Sleep disturbances	Insomnia Nightmares

in *Comprehensive Textbook of Psychiatry* (14), Portnoy in the *American Handbok of Psychiatry* (11), and a report on anxiety neurosis by Wheeler, White, Reed and Cohen (15).

In devising our rating instrument, diagnostic criteria used were comprised of the most commonly found characteristics of an anxiety disorder, such as those listed in Table 1. From this list of criteria, an observer-rated Anxiety Status Inventory (ASI) and a patient Self-rating Anxiety Scale (SAS) were constructed.

Table 2 contains the diagnostic criteria for anxiety as a psychiatric disorder (five affective and fifteen somatic symptoms).

For the purpose of constructing the SAS, illustrative verbatim records were made from patient interviews and those examples most representative for the particular symptom were selected for inclusion. Table 3 is the actual form of the SAS as it is used and to be filled out by the patient, and is based on the twenty diagnostic criteria listed in Table 2.

So that the patient is less able to discern a trend in his answers, the scale was devised so that of the twenty items used, some of the items were worded symptomatically positive, and others symptomatically negative, depending upon their suitability and usage. In addition, an even number of columns were used to eliminate the possibility of a patient checking middle and extreme columns.

Table 2. The operational definition of an anxiety disorder

Affective symptoms of anxiety

1. Anxiousness, nervousness
2. Fear
3. Panic
4. Mental disintegration
5. Apprehension

Somatic symptoms of anxiety

6.	Tremors	14.	Paresthesias
7.	Body aches and pains	15.	Nausea and vomiting
8.	Easy fatiguability, weakness	16.	Urinary frequency
		17.	Sweating
9.	Restlessness	18.	Face flushing
10.	Palpitation	19.	Insomnia
11.	Dizziness	20.	Nightmares
12.	Faintness		
13.	Dyspnea		

Table 1. A comparison of symptoms found in anxiety disorders as reported by various authors

	Kolb (13)	Lief (14)	Portnoy (11)	Wheeler et al. (15)
AFFECTIVE SYMPTOMS	Apprehension, worried, inexpressible dread, painful uneasiness of mind	Apprehension, fearfulness, feeling of impending death, helplessness, mental disintegration	Apprehension, uneasiness, anticipation of danger, helplessness	Apprehension, Fear of death, Nervousness
SOMATIC SYMPTOMS				
Musculoskeletal System	Tremor, tension headache	Muscle tightness, tremors, spasms painful movements, headaches, neck and back pains	Increased tension, tremors, stiffness	Trembling, Shakiness
	Weakness	Weakness		Headache, Tires easily, Weakness, Fatigued all the time
	Restlessness	Restlessness		
Cardiovascular System	Palpitation, rapid heartbeat	Palpitation, throbbing pain in chest	Palpitation, rapid pulse, increased Blood Pressure	Palpitation
Respiratory System / Hyperventilation:	dizziness, fainting, shortness of breath, feeling of choking, pressure on thorax, paresthesias	Dizziness, shortness of breath, constriction in chest, paresthesias	Rapid or irregular breathing	Dizziness, Faintness, Breathlessness, Breathing unsatisfactory, Paresthesias

11. I am bothered by dizzy spells.				
12. I have fainting spells or feel like it.				
13. I can breathe in and out easily.				
14. I get feelings of numbness and tingling in my fingers, toes.				
15. I am bothered by stomachaches or indigestion.				
16. I have to empty my bladder often.				
17. My hands are usually dry and warm.				
18. My face gets hot and blushes.				
19. I fall asleep easily and get a good night's rest.				
20. I have nightmares.				

In using the scale, the patient was asked to rate each of the twenty items as to how it applied to him within the past week in the following four quantitative terms; none *or* a little of the time, some of the time, good part of the time, most *or* all of the time. The SAS is constructed so that the less anxious patient will have a low score on the scale, and the more anxious patient will have a higher score. In scoring the SAS, a value of 1, 2, 3, and 4 is assigned to a response depending upon whether the item was worded positively or negatively.

An index for the SAS was derived by dividing the sum of the values (raw scores) obtained on the 20 items by the maximum possible score of 80, converted to a decimal and multiplied by 100. The SAS index is a total indication of how anxious the patient is in terms of the operational definition and expressed in percentage. Thus, an SAS index of 55 may be interpreted to mean that the patient has 55% of the anxiety measurable by the scale.

Self-rating scales have the following advantages: 1. They provide information on some variables that only the subject himself or herself can provide. 2. They do not involve the use of trained personnel to administer. 3. They take a short time for the patient to complete. 4. They are easy to score. 5. They provide objective data. 6. They can be used as a separate measurement to document change over time. 7. They can be used in any clinical setting, including mail returns by subjects. 8. They are inexpensive.

The fact that self-rating scales can define a disorder for clinical purposes should not distract us from our efforts as clinicians or research investigators, but rather should spur us on to develop better psychometric approaches toward the understanding of the underlying psychiatric disorder so defined.

VALIDITY AND RELIABILITY OF THE SAS

The validity of any rating instrument—i.e., its ability to measure what it is supposed to measure—can be determined by expert opinions that confirm that the signs and symptoms described in the scale represent a recognizable clinical condition, and demonstration that the results of the scale can distinguish patients with the disorder under consideration, and correlate with other scales conceded to be valid.

The first criterion was fulfilled when the scale was constructed based upon the literature available. We want to stress that the diagnostic criteria were not meant to be all-inclusive, and it does not encompass all schools of psychiatric orientation, or all theories about anxiety. Rather, the list was chosen in order to delineate the essential core symptoms. As for the second criterion, several studies performed by us have shown consistently that the SAS is able to discriminate patients with anxiety disorders from other diagnostic categories at a statistically significant level (10, 16). A study was performed to demonstrate the correlation between the Hamilton Anxiety Scale (HAS) and the Self-rating Anxiety Scale. Results of this study, based upon data obtained from 548 separate HAS and SAS ratings, were analyzed using the Pearson Product-Moment Correlation for calculation of the coefficient r, which was 0.75 (p = < 0.01).

Since the original publication of the article on a rating instrument for anxiety disorders in 1971 (10), the SAS has been used in a number of studies by us, and Table 4 is a summary of our data to date. We were interested in: 1. developing baseline data for normal subjects in order to answer the question "How normal is anxiety?" and 2. developing baseline data for subjects with varying degrees of "risk," ranging from patients seen in a family practice setting to patients seen with known cardiac disease to psychiatric patients with and without diagnoses of anxiety disorders. Using the total data base available, a morbidity cutoff score was developed in order to establish the level at which individuals might be viewed as "well and not sick" and "sick and not well". Statistical analyses using analysis of variance showed that the mean SAS index from the normal adults was significantly lower than those obtained from all patient groups (p = < 0.01). There was no significant difference for the SAS indices obtained from anxious out- and inpatients. Lastly, mean SAS indices between psychiatric patients with and without diagnoses of anxiety disorders were significantly different (p = < 0.01).

Several cross-national studies using the SAS have been reported, and their results are in basic agreement with those we have reported. Miao (17) studied over 900 college students in Taiwan, and reported a mean (S.D.) SAS index of 42.3 (8.3).

Table 4. Comparison of the Self-rating Anxiety Scale (SAS) indices among various groups tested, using a morbidity cut-off SAS index of 45

| | | SAS Index | | | SAS Index | | | |
| | | | | | 44 and Under | | 45 and over | |
Group	N	M	(s.d.)	N	(%)	N	(%)
Normal Adults	196	34.4	(6.9)	178	(91)	18	(9)
Patients Family Practice	101	41.8	(9.7)	69	(68)	32	(32)
Cardiac Service	567	45.5	(9.8)	281	(50)	286	(50)
Psychiatry Service Not Anxiety Disorder	1,111	48.8	(12.7)	327	(29)	784	(71)
Anxiety Disorder	403	58.8	(11.9)	46	(11)	357	(89)
Outpatients	(351)	58.7	(11.6)				
Inpatients	(52)	59.8	(14.3)				

Jegede (18) reported a study performed in Nigeria in which the SAS was administered to 206 normal subjects and 142 psychiatric outpatients. He reported that the mean scores for these two groups were significantly different, and based upon his methodology, the SAS had sufficient reliability and construct validity to justify further use in Nigeria.

Since the publication of the initial description of the SAS in 1971 (10), several authors have dealt with the issue of defining anxiety as a disorder. Feighner, Robins, Guze, Woodruff, Winokur, and Munoz (19) published diagnostic criteria for fourteen psychiatric illnesses, and their diagnostic criteria for an anxiety neurosis is summarized in Table 5. In this and the tables following (Tables 5–8), I have attempted to match the items that measure the same sign or symptom between the SAS and the respective work to be compared. The identifying numbers of the SAS and the identifying number or letter as they appear in the original works makes it easier to refer to each source as needed. We can see by referring to Table 5 that there are items in one operational definition that are not in the other.

Table 5. Comparison of the Zung and Feighner operational definitions for anxiety disorders

Scale Item	Zung: ASI and SAS	Feighner et al.	Scale Item
1.	Anxiousness and nervousness	anxious, nervous	(A.2)
2.	Fear	Fearfulness	(A.2)
3.	Panic		
4.	Mental Disintegration		
5.	Apprehension	Apprehension	(A.2)
6.	Tremors		
7.	Body aches and pains		
8.	Fatigue and weakness		
9.	Restlessness		
10.	Palpitation	Palpitations	(A.2b)
11.	Dizziness	Dizziness	(A.2e)
12.	Faintness		
13.	Dyspnea	Dyspnea, chest pain/discomfort	(A.2a,c)
14.	Paresthesias	Paresthesias	(A.2f)-(A.2f)
15.	Nausea and vomiting		
16.	Urinary frequency		
17.	Sweating		
18.	Face flushing		
19.	Insomnia		
20.	Nightmares		

Items not in Zung
Age of onset prior to 40 (A.1)
Choking or smothering sensation (A.2d)

Table 6. Comparison between diagnostic criteria used in the ASI and SAS, with the 40 most frequent themes selected in 27 anxiety rating scales

Scale Item	Zung: ASI and SAS	Most Frequent Themes	Rank Order
1.	Anxiousness and nervousness	Anxiety; nervousness	(9; 1)
2.	Fear	Vague fears	(18)
3.	Panic		
4.	Mental Disintegration	Lack of self-confidence	(12)
5.	Apprehension	Worry; uneasiness	(11; 24)
6.	Tremors	Trembling	(4)
7.	Body aches & pains	Aches; headaches	(13; 19)
8.	Fatigue & weakness	Fatigue	(7)
9.	Restlessness	Agitation	(2)
10.	Palpitation	Palpitations	(5)
11.	Dizziness		
12.	Faintness		
13.	Dyspnea	Respiratory troubles	(33)
14.	Paresthesias	Paresthesia	(25)
15.	Nausea and Vomiting	Troubles in the stomach; nausea	(10; 15)
16.	Urinary frequency		
17.	Sweating	Sweating	(3)
18.	Face flushing		
19.	Insomnia	Difficulty in sleeping	(6)
20.	Nightmares	Nightmares	(8)

		Most Frequent Themes	Rank Order
		Themes not in Zung	
		Troubles in,	
		concentrating	(14)
		Unhappiness	(15)
		Dependency on others	(16)
		Crying	(17)
		Precise fears	(20)
		Irritability	(22)
		Ruminations of past	(23)
		Appetite problems	(26)
		Constipation	(27)
		Shyness	(28)
		Indecision	(29)
		Self-efficiency problems	(30)
		Fear of lower intelligence function	(31)
		Life-death problems	(32)
		Sensibility	(34)
		Fear of others	(35)
		Sadness	(36)
		Obsessional ideas	(37)
		Guilt	(38)
		Exhilaration	(39)
		Energy problems	(40)

DeBonis (3) performed a systematic analysis of item content of twenty-seven anxiety inventories and scales. These included four rating scales specific for anxiety and filled out by the clinician, and twenty-three rating scales filled out by the subject as a self-rating scale. The results showed a large consensus in the choice of scale items, and Table 6 summarizes in rank order, the forty most frequent themes selected in the twenty-seven anxiety rating scales reviewed. By referring to Table 6, we can see that the SAS contains the first thirteen of the most frequent themes used. In addition, there are items in the SAS that are not in the list of most frequent themes.

The oldest and most often used interviewer-rated scale specific for an anxiety disorder was published in 1959 by Hamilton (9). Table 7 compares the SAS with the Hamilton Anxiety Scale with respect to their item contents. We can see that they are very similar, except for two items that measure panic and mental disintegration in the SAS, and four items in the HAS with different conceptual contents.

Table 7. Comparison of the Zung and Hamilton operational definitions for anxiety disorders

Scale Item	Zung: ASI and SAS	Hamilton	Scale Item
1.	Anxiousness and Nervousness	Anxious mood	(1)
2.	Fear	Fearful	(1)
3.	Panic		
4.	Mental disintegration		
5.	Apprehension	Anticipation of the worst	(1)
6.	Tremors	Tenson	(2)
7.	Body aches and pains	Somatic: muscular	(7)
8.	Fatigue and weakness	Tension: fatigability	(2)
9.	Restlessness	Tension: restlessness	(2)
10.	Palpitation	Palpitations	(9)
11.	Dizziness	Giddiness	(9)
12.	Faintness	Fainting feelings	(9)
13.	Dyspnea	Dyspnea	(10)
14.	Paresthesias	Somatic: sensory	(8)
15.	Nausea & vomiting	Nausea, vomiting	(11)
16.	Urinary frequency	Frequency of micturition	(12)
17.	Sweating	Tendency to sweat	(13)
18.	Face flushing	Flushing	(13)
19.	Insomnia	Insomnia	(4)
20.	Nightmares	Nightmares	(4)
		Items not in Zung	(3)
		Fears; phobias	(5)
		Intellectual: difficulty in concentration	(5)
		Depressed mood	(6)
		Behavior at interview	(14)

Table 8. Comparison of the Zung and FDA Guidelines operational definitions for anxiety disorders

Zung: ASI and SAS Scale Item		FDA Guidelines, June 1974	Scale Item
1.	Anxiousness and nervousness	Nervous; anxious	(1; 2)
2.	Fear	Fearful	(2)
3.	Panic	Panicky	(2)
4.	Mental disintegration	Losing control	(3)
5.	Apprehension	Apprehensive; disaster, death	(2; 3)
6.	Tremors	Trembling, Shaking	(7)
7.	Body aches and pains	Tense, aching muscles	(6)
8.	Fatigue and weakness	Weakness	(14)
9.	Restlessness	Restless, fidgeting	(8)
10.	Palpitation	Heart beating fast	(9)
11.	Dizziness	Dizziness	(14)
12.	Faintness	Faintness	(14)
13.	Dyspnea	Trouble catching breath	(10)
14.	Paresthesias	Tingling feelings in hands or feet	(15)
15.	Nausea and vomiting	Stomach "gas", nausea	(16)
16.	Urinary frequency	Frequency of bladder	(17)
17.	Sweating	Sweating; cold clammy hands	(11; 12)
18.	Face flushing		
19.	Insomnia		
20.	Nightmares		
		Items not in Zung	
		Avoiding certain places, things (4)	(4)
		Feeling tense or keyed up	(5)
		Dry mouth	(13)

Because we diagnose in medicine in order to treat, it is worth noting what diagnostic criteria are used when antianxiety agents are investigated. Table 8 compares the SAS with the Food and Drug Administration (FDA) guidelines for psychotropic drugs, published as a draft in 1974 (20), in defining the anxiety state. By referring to the table, we can see that the FDA guidelines for and definition of an anxiety disorder are almost identical to the item contents of the SAS. The guidelines omitted the sleep disturbances found in anxiety states, and have three items not found in the SAS.

We can assess anxiety as a disorder qualitatively by measuring one or all of its parts, and we can assess one or all of its component parts quantitatively by using the simplest to the most sophisticated of methods. If we are to take a giant step toward understanding anxiety as a disorder, we must first take that one small step. When the road is paved, it will be easier to look back and consider how rough the way used to be.

REFERENCES

1. Cattell, R.B., and Scheier, I.H. *The Meaning and Measurement of Neuroticism and Anxiety.* New York: Ronald Press, 1961.
2. McReynolds, P. The assessment of anxiety: A survey of available techniques. In P. McReynolds, ed., *Advances in Psychological Assessment.* Palo Alto, Calif.: Science and Behavior Books, 1968.
3. DeBonis, M. Content analysis of 27 anxiety inventories and rating scales. In P. Pichot, ed., *Psychological Measurements in Psychopharmacology. Modern Problems in Pharmacopsychiatry,* Vol. 7, Basel, Karger: 1974.
4. Borkovec, T.D., Weerts, T.C., and Bernstein, D.A. Assessment of anxiety. In A. Ciminero, K. Calhoun, and H. Adams, eds., *Handbook of Behavioral Assessment.* New York: Wiley, 1977.
5. Spielberger, C.D. *Theory and research on anxiety.* In C.D. Spielberger, ed., *Anxiety and Behavior.* New York: Academic Press, 1966.
6. Temerlin, M.K. Suggestion effects in psychiatric diagnosis. *J. Nerv. Ment. Dis.* 147:349-353, 1968.
7. Zuckerman, M. The development of an affective adjective checklist for the measurement of anxiety. *J. Consult. Clin. Psychol.* 24:457-462, 1960.
8. Walk, R.D. Self-ratings of fear in a fear-provoking situation. *J. Abnorm. Soc. Psychol.* 52:171-178, 1956.
9. Hamilton, M. The assessment of anxiety states by rating. *Brit. J. Med. Psychol.* 32:50, 1959.
10. Zung, W.W.K. A rating instrument for anxiety disorders, *Psychosom.* 12:371-379, 1975.
11. Portnoy, I. The anxiety states. In S. Arieti, ed., *American Handbook of Psychiatry,* Vol. 1. New York: Basic Books, 1959.
12. *Diagnostic and Statistical Manual of Mental Disorders,* 2nd ed. Washington, D.C.: American Psychiatric Association, 1968.
13. Kolb, L. *Noyes' Modern Clinical Psychiatry,* 7th ed., Philadelphia: Saunders, 1968.
14. Lief, H. Anxiety reaction. In A. Freedman and H. Kaplan, eds., *Comprehensive Textbook of Psychiatry,* Baltimore: Williams & Wilkins, 1967.
15. Wheeler, E., White, P., Reed, E., and Cohen, M. Neurocirculatory asthenia (anxiety neurosis, effort syndrome, neurasthenia). *J.A.M.A.* 142:878-888, 1950.
16. Zung, W.W.K. The differentiation of anxiety and depressive disorders: A biometric approach. *Psychosom.* 12:380-384, 1971.
17. Miao, E. An exploratory study on college freshmen mental health status. *Acta Psycholog. Taiwanica* 18:129-148, 1976.
18. Jegede, R.O.: Olukayode Psychometric attributes of the Self-rating Anxiety Scale. *Psycholog. Rep.* 40:303-306, 1977.
19. Feighner, J.P., Robins, E., Guze, S.B., Woodruff, R.A., Jr., Winokur, G., and Munoz, R. Diagnostic criteria for use in psychiatric research. *Arch. Gen. Psychiat.* 26:57-63, 1972.
20. Guidelines for the Conduct of Clinical Trials—FDA Guidelines for Psychotropic Drugs. *Psychopharm. Bull.* 10 (4): 70-91, 1974.

CHAPTER 2

The Diagnosis and Management of Anxiety for Primary Care Physicians

Laurence Schweitzer and George Adams

INTRODUCTION

Acute anxiety is a paralyzing state of emotional anguish that has proved to be an enduring aspect of human existence. Its subjective qualities have been richly chronicled by many philosophers, physicians, psychologists and social historians. One of the most penetrating and clinically precocious descriptions of this state was provided by Ali ibn-Hazm, an Arab philosopher (994-1064) who noted that: "No one is moved to act or resolves to speak a single word who does not hope by means of this action to ward off or to release anxiety from the spirit" (1).

This insight touches precisely on those dual qualities of anxiety that modern behavioral scientists find so fascinating. First, anxiety promotes both adaptive and maladaptive behavior, a characteristic that has served to play a central role in the development of psychoanalytic concepts of psychopathology. Second, the affect of anxiety and the remembrance of past experiences are regarded as a vehicle for developmental change and general ego development. Thus anxiety has been tied to general ego development as well as to the origin of psychopathology.

After decades of study, however, a scientific understanding of anxiety is incomplete. Its origins and the processes involved in modifying this uncomfortable emotion remain a mystery. Although anxiety is ubiquitous, one cannot measure its true prevalence in health or illness; nor is it clear how individuals differ in their subjective experience and regulation of anxiety. Finally, there is need to know more about the natural course and treatment of anxiety. The following discussion attempts to address these issues in a manner helpful to the physicians practicing in a primary care setting.

DEFINITION

Anxiety appears in two clinically recognized forms. The first is known by a variety of terms: acute anxiety state, free-floating anxiety, or panic states. The second, a chronic state, is variously called anxiety neurosis, neurasthenia, neurocirculatory asthenia, effort syndrome, cardiac neurosis, and other names (2, 3, 4).

Acute Anxiety

Acute anxiety is an emotional state characterized by subjective feelings of dread, apprehension, and/or impending disaster. Often the patient reports a fear of sudden death *(angor animi)* or imminent insanity, or a fear of losing control and becoming disoriented and/or committing an aggressive or destructive act. The anxiety state is to be differentiated from a phobic neurosis, since anxiety occurs under a variety of conditions and is not restricted to a particular situation, person, or object. Sexual concerns appear not to be prominent or particularly distressing features of this syndrome.

In addition to its psychological content, acute anxiety is usually accompanied by one or more physiological signs, although their presence is not necessary to make a diagnosis. These signs include palpitations, tremulousness, and diaphoresis. Hyperventilation is common and may lead to paresthesias of the lips and fingers, carpopedal spasms, and in extreme cases, generalized convulsions. Some patients experience diarrhea or genitourinary frequency. Faintness and dizziness are common, and a general sympathetic reaction can occur, manifested by dilation of the pupils, flushing of the skin, and excessive perspiration over the face and palms. Other physical symptoms include shortness of breath, tightness in the throat, and/or feelings of acute helplessness accompanied by the patient's plaintive appeals for help.

An individual's particular symptomatology appears characteristic and constant over time and reflects in its manifest content the operation of many interacting factors. These include a physiological diathesis, early emotional experiences, and social or cultural norms characteristic for that individual. Thus, the expression of anxiety is the resultant of several forces and will differ from individual to individual according to age, sex, socioeconomic status, and culture. The role of these different factors in acute and chronic anxiety will be dealt with in later sections of this discusison.

Chronic Anxiety

A large group of patients experience unremitting episodes of anxiety. These episodes, in contrast to acute anxiety attacks, are relatively frequent and prolonged. Often a carefully obtained past history is sufficient to delineate two categories of such patients. The first is characterized by prior good health, strength, and vigor, whereas the premorbid history in the second group suggests a lifelong pattern of easy fatigability, inability to do hard work, tension, nervousness, and fear of crowds. The former group of patients are deemed to suffer from a chronic anxiety neurosis, while the latter group have been categorized as having neurocirculatory asthenia or more simply neurasthenia. (Other terms commonly associated with this syndrome are effort syndrome, Da Costa's syndrome, cardiac neurosis, soldier's heart, irritable heart, and vasomotor instability [4].) The importance of distinguishing between chronic anxiety neurosis and neurasthenia will be clarified when the rationale of management is discussed.

The consequence of sustained or repetitive anxiety—that is, anxiety that does not lead to the development of a neurotic symptom—are identical. The patient most frequently complains of fatigability, breathlessness, nervousness, palpitations, chest pain, and sighing. In addition, one or more of the following symptoms (in order of frequency) is present in over 50% of patients: dizziness, faintness, apprehension, headaches, paresthesias, weakness, trembling, halitosis, insomnia, and unhappiness (2, 4).

PREVALENCE OF ANXIETY

Anxiety is a ubiquitous, often normal and useful experience differing in degree among individuals. When severe—i.e., maladaptive—we term it pathological. Unfortunatley, diagnostic reliance on such differences in degree of severity creates fundamental difficulties in determining its true prevalence. Where is the line to be drawn between normal and pathological? In practice, physicans have generally diagnosed anxiety in those patients whose distress was sufficiently great to bring them to seek medical attention for the symptoms described above. However, when these practical criteria are used to define anxiety, one is left with an illness characterized by a surfeit of symptoms and a relative paucity of signs. Obviously, the limitations of diagnostic reliance on subjective criteria are self-evident in any strictly scientifc protocol. Yet this type of prevalence data contains useful scientific information about the way doctors in clinical practice spend their time.

Indeed, if such prevalence findings lack clinical precision, perhaps their greater value lies in what they tell us about the utilizaiton of medical expertise.

Prevalence within Psychiatric Practice

In private psychiatric practice and outpatient clinics, anxiety states have been reported as a primary diagnosis in 6% to 15% of all treated cases (5, 6). Lader noted that the diagnosis of anxiety neurosis was made in 8% of the Maudsley Hospital Outpatient Services, and that this rate was constant over a period of nine years (7). Rees determined that the prevalence of anxiety was somewhat higher, estimating that 7% to 16% of all psychiatric patients in Great Britain suffered primarily from anxiety (8).

Occurrence in General Practice

Data limited to a psychiatric population does not provide the best estimate of the prevalence of pathological anxiety. Certainly there must be many individuals suffering from anxiety who are seen and treated by family practitioners or within primary care facilities.

In the United States White and Jones (9) reviewed 3,000 civilian patients with cardiac signs or symptoms and found that 302 (10%) suffered neurocirculatory asthenia alone. Gross (10) surveyed a rural area in England and arrived at a somewhat lower estimate of about 2%. More recent data is available on the prevalence of neurotic states, but this information lacks specificity, since it does not deal with anxiety per se. For example, Primrose (11) reported that 13.2% of patients treated by general practitioners in England suffered primarily from emotional disorders. Similarly, Shepherd et al. (12) found a mean annual prevalence rate of 12.5% for neurosis in the practices of physicians in London. (Other estimates of the proportion of time spent in general practice dealing with emotional disorders range up to 76% [13].) Studies of psychopharmacologic prescribing practices suggest that functional disorders comprise at least 10% to 20% of the general practitioner's consultations (14).

Recently Marsland et al. (15) carefully compiled a data bank for patient care within the state of Virginia. A statewide sample of 526,196 patient visits to 118 family practitioners were recorded between July 1, 1973, and August 1, 1975. These data were based on approximately 88,000 different patients, or 2.3% of the poulation of Virginia. Table 1 summarizes the psychiatric diagnoses provided by these family physicians.

Depressive and anxiety neuroses constituted the vast majority of psychiatric problems (86.8%) seen by family practitioners. All other neurotic disorders accounted for less than 3% of the total psychiatric illness. This proportion appears to underestimate the true prevalence of the remaining

Table 1. State of Virginia data bank sample of 526,196 patient visits to family practitioners
Psychiatric illness: Proportion of total visits by diagnostic category

Diagnosis*	No. of Visits	% of Total	% of Psychiatric Total	Ratio of Male to Female
1. Depressive neurosis	7833	1.49	46.97	1:4.27
2. Anxiety neurosis	6645	1.26	39.84	1:2.93
3. Schizophrenia	904	0.17	5.42	1:1.65
4. Organic psychoses	571	0.11	3.42	1:1.56
5. Obsessive-compulsive neurosis	305	0.06	1.83	1:2.80
6. Hysterical neurosis	143	0.03	0.86	1:4.30
7. Affective psychoses	111	0.02	0.67	1:0.95
8. Phobic neuroses	69	0.01	0.41	1:3.93
9. Delusions and hallucinations	57	0.01	0.34	1:0.78
10. Psychosomatic disorders	39	0.01	0.23	1:0.95
TOTAL	16.677			

*526 diagnostic categories

neurotic conditions, and suggests that neuroses other than anxiety and depression are largely self-referred to specialized psychiatric facilities. By way of contrast, anxiety and depressive neurotics, experience a considerable degree of physical symptomatology, and appear to find their way to medical practitioners for consultation and treatment. This impression is supported by the data in Table 2.

Here, the ten most common symptoms of anxiety and neurasthenia are tabulated after these symptom categories were culled from the general data bank. This well-known group of anxiety symptoms accounted for 1.4% of all visits made to family physicians. When cases of neurasthenia proper are included, the proportion becomes almost 1.5% of all visits. The addition of anxiety per se brings the total to 3.3% of all visits and 3.8% of all patient visits that were for symptomatic complaints (i.e., exclusive of periodic checkups and preventive care visits). While this figure may not appear particularly

Table 2. State of Virginia data bank sample of 526,196 patient visits* to family practioners

Diagnosis†	No. of Visits	% of All Visits	Ratio of Male to Female
1. Dizziness	1845	0.35	1:1.93
2. Headache	1467	0.28	1:3.99
3. Syncope	965	0.18	1:0.87
4. Chest pain and Arrythmias	611	0.12	1:1.98
5. Weakness	563	0.11	1:1.92
6. Sweating	480	0.09	1:1.14
7. Insomnia	294	0.06	1:0.99
8. Paresthesias	215	0.04	1:1.42
9. Trembling	78	0.01	1:1.11
Subtotal	6518	1.24	
10. Neurasthenia (Chronic fatigue)	283		1:2.68
Subtotal	6801	1.29	
11. Physical disorders (nonpsychophysiological)	3923		1:2.68
12. Neurasthenia total	10,724	2.04	
13. Anxiety	6,645		
14. Total: Anxiety + Neurasthenia	17,369	3.30	1:2.33

*July 1, 1973—August 1, 1975
†526 diagnostic categories

Table 3. Comparative frequency of diagnoses, State of Virginia data bank and Casa de Amigos Clinic, Houston, Texas

A. Ten most common diagnoses in the Virginia sample

Diagnoses	% of Total	Cumulative %
1. Preventive Exams	8.35	8.35
2. Hypertension—all forms	5.74	14.09
3. Lacerations and trauma	4.02	18.11
4. Pharyngitis and tonsilitis	3.83	21.94
5. Anxiety (anxiety + neurasthenia)	3.30	25.24
6. Bronchitis	2.57	27.81
7. Sprains and Strains	2.44	30.25
8. Diabetes mellitus	2.36	32.61
9. Comon cold	2.08	34.69
10. Obesity	2.03	36.72

B. Ten most common diagnoses in sample* of Casa de Amigos Clinic, Houston Texas

1. Upper respiratory infections	8.75	8.75
2. Pregnancy	5.54	14.29
3. Diabetes mellitus	5.28	19.57
4. Hypertension—all forms	4.40	23.97
5. Anxiety	2.90	26.87
6. Obesity	2.85	29.72
7. Pains and aches	2.69	32.41
8. Vaginitis (all forms)	2.48	34.89
9. Dermatologic	2.17	37.06
10. Urinary-tract infections	2.07	39.13

*Total of all visits for November 1973 = 1,932 problems.

impressive, Table 3A demonstrates that anxiety is the fifth most common diagnosis overall. Indeed, the diagnosis of hypertension (the most common finding) exceeded anxiety by only 2.25% of the total.

A similar sample (Table 3B) drawn from a municipally supported primary care facility serving a socioeconomically disadvantaged Mexican-American population in Houston, Texas, presents similar findings (16). In this instance the distribution of physical illnesses differed, but anxiety still ranked fifth among conditions for which physicians were consulted; it occupied almost 3% of recorded physician activity by type of problem.

Thus the frequency of anxiety qualifies it as a first-order symptom in patients utilizing family and/or primary care services. If depressive neurosis is aggregated with anxiety, this constellation of closely related emotional disorders contributed 25,202 patient visits—4.8% of the total—in the Virginia sample and would be second ony to hypertension in prevalence.

Simple prevalence figures, however, do not adequately describe the utilization of physician time. Indeed, the fact of the matter is that emotional problems consume a disproportionate share of the medical practitioner's time. Several studies have estimated that primary care physicians actually spend between 20% and 70% (17, 18) of their time evaluating and treating emotional disorders. These problems include diagnoses of mental illness per se, as well as the anxiety, tension, and depression associated with day-to-day living. Borus (17) reported that where mental health services have been added to primary care armamentarium, utilization has been very brisk. One neighborhood center with a mental health program reported a treated incidence rate of 53 per 1,000 population, which represents five times the national rate of utilization for all outpatient services. Moreover, this rate of utilization was twenty times that of free-standing community mental health centers (12).

Again it can be noted that these prevalence data are imprecise. However, the conclusion that psychiatric services place heavy demands on the physician's time, and that these services are particularly sought out when they are imbedded within a comprehensive framework of medical services, seems quite clear. Primary care physicians are well aware of these facts, and Borus (17) has noted that 27% of all articles appearing in *Primary Care* during 1975 were written by psychiatrists (13).

Finally, over and above the considerations presented with respect to the prevalence of anxiety and the demand that this disorder makes on the physician's time, anxiety is a regular concomitant of many physical disorders. Moreover, it plays a preeminent role in many psychiatric illnesses: it is often associated with depression, obsessive-compulsive neurosis, and hysteria, and is an integral element of the syndrome of schizophrenia.

Prevalence in the General Population

A survey of Sterling County, Pennsylvania, suggested that over half of the population (577 per 1,000) needed psychiatric care (19). Again, at least 23% of the sample in the Midtown Manhattan Study suffered from serious psychiatric illness (20). A survey conducted by the Gallup Poll Organization of Great Britain found similar results. Using a well-validated and reliable self-rating scale developed by Salkind and Loldiz with fairly conservative criteria for anxiety, the researchers found that neurasthenia was present in 7.2% of the population and anxiety states occurred in 31%. They also found that anxiety was greater in females, tended to increase with advancing age, and increased with decreasing socioeconomic status (21).

In a prospective study of applicants for driver's licenses, Nystrom and Lindegard (22) followed 3,019 males for six years. At the end of this time they searched hospital and clinical records for evidence of treatment within this group for neurasthenia and/or anxiety states. The rates for treated neurasthenia were 0.866 per 1,000 per year and anxiety 0.866 per 1,000 per year, thus totaling 1.732 per 1,000 per year for acute and chronic states. Since the ratio of females to males is usually on the order of 2 to 1 or 3 to 2, a more realistic incidence of treated anxiety in the general poulation would be in the range of 4 to 5 per 1,000 per year. Depressive neurosis was found to occur at a rate of 1.89 per 1,000 per year. These figures bear a remarkable similarity to those derived from studies of the general practice population and add credence to the notion that anxiety is a major determinant in the utilization of health care services.

CLINICAL FEATURES

Course of Chronic Anxiety

In 1950, Wheeler and coworkers (4) reported a twenty-year follow-up study of 173 patients selected as uncomplicated examples of neurocirculatory asthenia from a case register of 2,799 patients seen prior to 1928. They found that anxiety symptoms had a mild yet persistent course characerized by exacerbations and remissions. Of the 144 patients who responded to a questionnaire, symptoms had continued to bother 62% and had interfered with work in 28%. In 60 patients actually examined, 88% had continuing symptoms, and only 12% described themselves as well. It seems remarkable that despite the 20-year persistence of symptoms, only 11 of the polled sample, or 7.6%, had sought psychiatric assistance. The important therapeutic implications of this behavior will be discussed under the rubric of management.

More recently, Schapira and coworkers (23) and Kerr, Roth, and Schapira (24) have provided additional followup information on 126 patients seen on an average of 3.8 years after discharge from a psychiatric hospital. At the time of discharge, 80% of the depressed group and 56% of the anxiety group were rated as improved. Immediately after discharge, both groups experienced a steep increase in morbidity, so that six months after discharge, only 67% of the depressed and 44% of the anxious patients continued to be improved (p < .025). This difference disappeared by the end of the first year, but thereafter the depressed patients tended to improve while the anxious patients followed a more fluctuating course. By 3.8 years, 62% of the depressed but only 53% of the anxiety group had improved (p < .025). Moreover, 38% of the original anxiety group had experienced subsequent hospitalizations, and in all but one of the cases the diagnosis was anxiety state. By way of contrast only 26% of the depressed group became ill again, with 85% diagnosed as depressed and 15% identified as anxiety states.

Finally, there was a constant tendency for the range of symptoms in the anxiety group to be more frequent and severe.

The constancy and the specificity of anxiety symptomatology has been noted by many authors. The results noted above support the notion that anxiety neurosis is a specific and chronic disorder. They also indicate that in general, 12% of all patients will recover completely, 15% will experience continuous moderate to severe disability, and 73% will be divided about equally between those with symptoms and no disability, and those with symptoms and mild disability.

Physical Health

Despite the symptoms of palpitation, breathlessness, and apprehension, no association between chronic anxiety and increases in the incidence of such diseases as hypertension, peptic ulcer, or arthritis has been demonstrated. Again, Wheeler and coworkers (4) found that anxious patients actually fared better than controls when compared on the mean number of hospitalizations, operations, and deaths per year. These data have been corroborated more recently (25, 26). Indeed, only one report of pathology actually linked to anxiety (i.e., exclusive of stress states or stressful events without manifest anxiety) has emerged from a search of the literature.

Gorsuch and Key (27) reported that anxiety attacks during the first trimester of pregnancy were associated with significant increases in complications at birth. However, states of anxiety prior to conception did not influence outcome, nor did life stress and strain. On the other hand, a number of studies have indicated that life stress and strain may precipitate later physical illness (28, 29)—in particular, cardiovascular and hypertensive disorders (30) and more general illnesses in individuals sustaining stressful life events (31). These data, as intriguing as they are, do not touch specifically on the issue of anxiety. No significant correlations to illness have been observed in studies in which anxiety is clearly documented. Moreover, the data relating stress to physical illness appears shaky as well. Although significant correlations between stress states and a number of illnesses have been observed, the correlates are usually small (usually less than .30) and can account for no more than 9% of the variance in illness. Rahe's correlations were consistently about 0.12 (31).

Sex: Most studies of acute and chronic anxiety have demonstrated a sex bias, with women tending to experience the illness in ratios between 2:1 and 3:2 to men (32). Moreover, Schapira and coworkers (23) found that men did better generally than women over time—i.e., had fewer additional "break—downs" and a generally milder progression of their anxiety symptoms.

Age: It has often been stated that the onset of pathological anxiety rarely occurs before the age of 18 or later than 35 (2). Whereas this has generally been accepted, the Virginia Data Bank offers some evidence that anxiety may occur well past 35. For example, those 35 and older made up 65% of the total treatment visits. By way of contrast, patients between the ages of 0 and 15 contributed 2.3% of the total treatment visits.

Since these data are drawn from treatment visits (i.e., prevalence), one could argue that the onset of anxiety may have been considerably earlier in the group of individuals over 35. The fact that individuals over 35 years of age were represented out of proportion to their numbers in the general population may thus only represent an increase in the frequency of anxiety attacks in an older age group. For the purpose of this discussion, however, it is precisely this high utilization rate in the older group that is important.

The number of elderly persons is currently increasing rapidly in our population. Consequently, one can expect that the demand for medical services within this group will increase correspondingly. Moreover, if anxiety bears a specific relationship to the climacterium and life changes of the elderly, such studies may be a fruitful area of research as well as having important implications for the planning and delivery of services to a potential high-risk group.

Outcome

It was noted earlier than anxiety per se has a persistent and fluctuating course. Ten to 12% of the patients recover spontaneously, 15% deteriorate and experience substantial disability as a result of their symptoms, and the remaining 75% are evenly divided among those who are symptomatic without disability and those with mild disability. Kerr, Roth, and Schapira looked for factors that predispose to a lower morbidity. Using a battery of nine predictor variables, they found two factors were related to improved outcomes. They were male sex and a history of heavy drinking episodes. Such factors as agitation, suicidal tendencies, hysterical features, syncopal episodes, derealization, phobias in childhood, and frank anxiety symptoms were all negatively correlated with improvement. On the other hand, a family history of psychiatric disease, prior psychiatric illness, age, social class, intelligence, mode of onset, and duration of illness were unimportant predictors of improvement (24).

The relationship of symptom improvement to sex appeared due to a somewhat better premorbid adjustment within the male subpopulation, but this factor may actually not be an artifact of sampling. Wheeler and coworkers (4) had previously suggested that the males in their sample fared better overall.

A relationship of excessive alcohol use to improvement was accounted for by a small group of men who developed social anxiety and then used alcohol as a coping mechanism. If this explanation is true, it would identify a small group of alcohol abusers who could be helped by psychotherapeutic and/or pharmacologic treatment available within the hands of the general practitioner. It also suggests that individuals having a form of social or situational anxiety may be profitably differentiated from those patients with more diffuse and vague mode of onset. One would suspect that the primary care physician would prove most successful with the former group (i.e., patients with structured anxiety state: that border on a phobic organization).

Etiology

Hypotheses regarding the source of anxiety range form the biologic through psychologic to sociologic, with good evidence in each of these areas. This discussion will confine its scope to a review of genetic, biochemical, and psychological studies.

Genetic Factors: Studies of families containing anxious patients provide inferential evidence of a genetic predisposition to anxiety. Cohen (33) noted that when one parent was affected, 37.7% of the children also suffered with anxiety. When both parents were anxious, the percentage of children similarly affected rose to 61.9%. When children serve as the index case, and the parents are normal, 27.5% of the other children are affected with anxiety. Several other studies of families tend to support the concept of an intra-family resemblance in the type of neurosis (34, 35, 36).

More recent evidence drawn from studies of monozygotic (MZ) and dyzygotic (DZ) twins provide direct support for a genetic predisposition to anxiety. Young, Fenton, and Lader (37) studied 64 male subjects that included 17 MZ twins and 15 pairs of DZ twins. Intraclass correlations among the MZ twins for the free-floating anxiety and phobic anxiety scales of the Middlesex Hospital Questionnaire were $r = + .56$ and $r = + .60$ ($p < .01$) respectively and $r = .12$ and $r = -.12$ for the DZ twins respectively ($p = NS$). Moreover, scales for neurotic depression and obsessive-compulsive traits were not significant in either DZ or MZ twins.

The implications of these genetic data are important for the primary care physician. They suggest that whenever one member of a family is anxious, it will not be uncommon for the physician to find that other members suffer in a similar manner. Moreover, the primary care physician can best intervene in a primary or early secondary preventive manner to reduce the morbidity of the anxiety process. Since the constitutional predisposition to develop anxiety is only one component of personality, the expression of anxiety will depend on complex interactions with the environment. Changes in the environment can thus have important consequences for the development or suppresison of illness, and proper treatment of the anxious parent with reduction in his or her state of agitation and/or apprehension may serve by way of a general reduction in tension to forestall the expression of anxiety in the children.

Biochemical Features: Studies of Cohen and White (38), Jones and Mellersh (39), Linko (40), and Holmgren and Strom (41) independently demonstrated abnormalities of lactate metabolism associated with anxiety states. Indeed, disproportionate increases in serum lactate were observed when subjects performed maximal exertion or strenuous work. Pitts and McClure (42) extended these findings by demonstrating a strong temporal association between the infusion of sodium lactate and the production of anxiety in susceptible subjects (i.e., those previously diagnosed as having had anxiety attacks). Since the addition of calcium ions to the lactate solution ameliorated these effects, Pitts and McClure (42) suggested that excess lactate in anxious individuals complexed ionized calcium at excitable membranes. By virtue of an undefined defect of anaerobic or aerobic and/or calcium metabolism, anxiety would somehow then occur.

Grosz and Farmer (43) critically examined these conclusions by replicating the experiment done by Pitts and McClure. Using sodium bicarbonate as a control infusion, they found the bicarbonate ion to be as effective as lactate in producing anxiety symptoms and concluded that a state of metabolic alkalosis was the factor common to both studies that could account for the anxiety attacks. Moreover, they demonstrated that all subjects reported paraesthesias just as in the Pitts and McClure study (42), and on this account, dismissed both the lactate ion and calcium depletion as specific precipitants of the anxiety.

The work of Pitts and McClure is now perceived as less of a breakthrough than it was in the late sixties. However, the biochemical study of anxiety continues to hold promise as an experimental model to study this affect. The fact remains that only anxiety-prone individuals respond to a marked metabolic alkalosis by an anxiety attack and this finding continues to await explication. On the other hand, lest enthusiasm overtake reality, one must be clear that at best one is dealing with a biochemical end mechanism for the expression of anxiety symptoms and not a primary cause. Further inquiries at this level of explanation will need to be supported by psychological factors and the nature of the organism's interrelationships with the environment. On the basis of the biochemical studies available, one can only conclude that more fundamental differences among individuals are involved in the production of anxiety than can be accounted for by shifts of pH or changes in concentration of ionized calcium.

Psychological Theories: Perhaps the most comprehensive approach to the study of anxiety has been provided by psychoanalytic practitioners and theorists. Freud drew extensively on the concept of anxiety as an organizing principle in human psychology. In Freud's theoretical structure, anxiety was given a pre-eminent role in the psychology of infants and children as well as adults (44). He divided anxiety into two classes, and designated the first as primary anxiety. This state, an inevitable experience of infancy, was felt to be precipitated by a build-up of tension (i.e., hunger, visceral discomfort) within the organism occurring either too rapidly or in such magnitude that it was not discharged by the homeostatic mechanisms available. Based on infant observations, he postulated that this state of emotional flooding was accompanied by experiences of overwhelming distress, helplessness, and chaos. It was further postulated that such experiences left unconscious memory traces of the dysphoria. Such memories and the wish to avoid the repetition of the primary anxiety subsequently served to promote the development of ego functions related to the mastery of reality and the control of tension states.

Later in the organism's psychological development, the possibility that highly charged unconscious emotional complexes might erupt into consciousness would act to provoke an unconscious reaction called signal anxiety. This signal mechanism, defensive in nature, was theorized to mobilize ego resources, which in turn adaptively discharged the build-up of tension. Whenever the disequilibrium of energy within the mental apparatus was not discharged or bound into a symptom, secondary (conscious) anxiety was experienced. Thus conscious anxiety was prima facie evidence that a breakdown had occurred in the ego's capacity to master tension.

The notion of conflict between unconscious impulses and those aspects of the ego responsible for the maintenance of an organism's relationship to reality has yielded insights into the mental functioning of many neurotic states. However, the efficacy of psychoanalytic treatment of anxiety states per se remains subject to quesiton. A number of studies have failed to show that psychoanalytic psychotherapy produces any greater percentage of remission than supportive management by the primary care physician (45, 46). Again, this may well be a function of the type of anxiety that is treated. One might suspect that structured anxiety states—i.e., socially induced or situationally specific neuroses—might respond well to psychoanalytic psychotherapy or analysis. Such discriminations have not always been reported, but it would seem that psychoanalytic psychotherapy of phobic conditions would be much more successful than the same treatment in anxiety per se.

Other theoretical explanations of the psychological aspects of anxiety include maladaptive responses to disruptive relationships with significant others (47), the physiological state of arousal caused by stimulus conditions in the environment that are misinterpreted by the individual (48), a learned drive that creates a neurotic conflict (49), and a condition of apprehension precipitated by a threat to values characteristic of or basic to an individual's personality (50).

One of the more recent and durable psychological findings regarding anxiety is Spielberger's State-Trait Anxiety Model (51). The research of Cattell and Scheier (52) had demonstrated two distinct anxiety factors: trait anxiety and state anxiety. Trait anxiety was defined as a relatively stable characteristic of the personality of a particular individual, whereas state anxiety was a transitory or acute condition that varied from moment to moment and from day to day. The trait factor was loaded with such characterological variables as ego weakness, guilt proneness, and a tendency to embarrassment, while the state factor was derived from a series of variables that covaried over periods of measurement. These variable fluctuations were found to define a transitory state or condition of the organism that had high loadings on such physiological variables as respiration and systolic blood pressure. The concept of an anxiety state-trait dichotomy is consistent with the findings cited earlier by Wheeler et al. (4), Cohen (2), and Kerr, Roth, and Schapira (24). It will be recalled that these studies demonstrated the stability of the anxiety characteristic over time within individuals and the stability of this symptom across diagnostic groups.

Derogatis and coworkers (53) demonstrated a unitary anxiety dimension that could be isolated in a sample of anxious patients. Moreover, this anxiety dimension was consonant with prevailing notions of this construct and was found to be specific for anxiety, since an analogous and independent dimension of anxiety was absent from the factor structure of the control (depressed) group.

MANAGEMENT

The prevalence of anxiety among patients seen in general practice makes it clear that a substantial amount of physician time is spent dealing with this problem. It is important, then, to determine how this time is actually spent and whether it would be allocated more profitably.

Diagnosis

All rational treatments require a diagnosis. Diagnosis of anxiety can be particularly difficult, however, because the illness has protean pathology and is often accompanied by somatic signs and/or autonomic involvement. Often actual signs of physiological disturbance are present. As examples, changes in the EKG that are concomitants of anxiety include slight to moderate inconstant tachycardia, minor depression of S-T junction, and inversion of T waves. Occasionally, minimal elevation of temperature accompanies these symptoms and can suggest a diagnosis of rheumatic carditis. A normal sedimentation rate as well as a tendency for the tachycardia to disappear rapidly during sleep serves to distinguish the anxiety neurosis from other entities. β-adrenergic receptor blockage (by propranolol hydrochloride) has been demonstrated to ameliorate such autonomically mediated symptoms as palpitations, sweating, and diarrhea (54). The EKG changes in T waves also are easily reversed by sympatholytic drugs such as ergotamine tartrate or ergocoarnine. Studies of peripheral blockade, however, have not demonstrated an actual reduction in the subjective experiences of distress in anxious individuals (54).

The diagnosis of anxiety is further complicated by the fact that the symptoms often suggest physical causation that the physician and patient both have an investment in seeking out. Clancy and Noyes (55) examined the records of 71 classic anxiety neurotics drawn from the clinics of the University of Iowa Hospitals (1967-1971) with an eye to determining the nature of diagnostic procedures employed. They found that 20 different categories of tests were actually carried out upon the 71 patients. If one counted each category of test as one instance, an amazing 358 tests and procedures were performed on the group with a range of 0-11 and a median of more than 5 per patient.

In addition, consultations with other specialists were frequently ordered and the authors note that there were 135 such consultations for the 71 patients. The cost of these procedures ranged from $0 to $450, with an average of $155 per patient. The total cost per patient for diagnostic tests and consultations amounted to an average of $222 per patient.

These data are remarkable, since anxiety can be positively diagnosed and need not depend on the careful exclusion of a host of unlikely causes. However, other factors obviously intervene in what should be a rational process, as Clancy and Noyes (55) make clear. Most of the patients in their study did not consider themselves to be suffering from an emotional disorder. One patient was quoted as saying, "I do not want to be told what I haven't got. I want the doctor to find something." In another case the patient said, "I know I am nervous, I have always been nervous, but don't try to tell me that is what is wrong." Finally, the authors noted that many patients refused to accept a return appointment with a psychiatrist when this was offered.

Thus it would appear that most of the anxiety neurotics in this study were threatened by the prospect of identifying an emotional basis for their distress. Indeed, they openly stated that they would prefer medical consultation rather than accept psychiatric help. Why should this be so?

Possibly there was an unexpected and unusual bias in this study, as both the patients and the doctors clearly denied emotional factors. Obviously the medical staff had collaborated with the patient's denial of psychological factors by participating in a search for organic illness despite the absence of clinical signs. The great number of diagnostic procedures and consultations requested by the physicians bear witness to this conclusion. Moreover, one would speculate that once the physician began to search for organic illness as an explanation of the patient's symptomatology, it became particularly difficult for the patient to give up his or her own denial of emotional factors. Indeed, at that point he or she had his or her physician's denial to support them as well.

The authors do not feel that these data are unusual. Indeed, common experience suggests that these results are rather characteristic of medical practice. Physicians too often use a variety of rationalized diagnostic procedures or referrals to specialized consultants to deny the presence of emotional conflict in their patients. Indeed, such testing and continuous consultation reveal an anxiety in the physician who finds it difficult to recognize emotional conflict. As a corollary and partial corrective, one would recommend that physicians first consider the characteristic symptoms of anxiety as an expression of psychological conflict and reserve diagnostic testing for the evaluation of bona fide signs. Such practice will foster the diagnosis of anxiety on a positive basis and avoid the costly round of procedures and consultations necessary for exclusion. We offer no specific recommendation for the anxious physician.

Treatment in General Practice

Gardner, Peterson, and Hall (56) provide a particularly illuminating picture of the practice of psychiatry in the hands of general practitioners (GPs) today. Surveying referrals by GPs to psychiatric outpatient services in Great Britain, they gathered information about patients' perception of their illness, their treatment in the hands of the general practitioners, their perception of their treatment's efficacy, and any untoward events that the patient experienced during treatment. The actual duration and characteristics of the treatment were also recorded.

A sample of 285 men and 384 women yielded the following facts. Neurotic and character (behavior) disorders were the most common diagnoses. Unfortunately the category of anxiety was not examined directly, so the following characterization is more generally true for neurotic disorders than anxiety per se. Sixteen percent of the males as compared with 31% of the females were seen for more than eight visits (p < .001), with the number of consultations increasing with advancing age of the patient in both sexes. When the actual duration of treatment was studied, the tendency to refer men early persisted. Fifty-one percent of the men but only 31% of the women were seen for less than a month (p < .001). This difference held when age and diagnostic variations between the sexes were taken into account.

In most cases psychotropic medication was used: 57% for men as compared to 76% for women (p < .001). The number of prescribed drugs (not including hypnotics) increased with age for both sexes and the percentage of patients receiving drugs was high in both neurotic and functionally psychotic states. Sixty-three percent of the patients received drugs as their only therapy, and yet 55% of both men and women reported serious noncompliance with the medication regime. The percentage of noncompliance tended to be greater with protocols involving more drugs; in women, noncompliance among cases treated with one drug as opposed to three drugs (18%) was significantly different (P < .001).

Over half the patients reported untoward events—i.e. a worsening in their condition—yet 69% of the males and 65% of the females stated that they were satisfied with their treatment. Paradoxically, 64% of the males and 60% of the females welcomed referral to the psychiatrist. Neither the expertise of the referring general practitioner, the number of consultations prior to referral, nor the diagnosis had any effect on the patients' opinion of their treatment or their attitude toward the referral.

Thus, one draws the following conclusions. General practitioners in England tend to work longer with women and to prescribe medication more frequently for them. Overall, 68% of patients receive some medication, but 55% of this group fail to take their medication as prescribed. Half of the patients experience emotional setbacks during the treatment, but paradoxically, the majority are satisfied with their treatment. An almost equal number welcome psychiatric referrals.

It is perplexing that almost 70% of the patients in this sample received medication (63% as the *only* therapy) and yet over 50% failed to take the medication as prescribed. Studies by Wilcox, Gillon, and Hare (57) and Porter (58) found similar percentages of noncompliance: 48% and 50% in psychiatric and general practices respectively. These findings raise a number of issues. From a therapeutic point of view, it makes sense to question our current strong reliance on neuroleptics as the only modality of psychiatric therapy used by general practitioners. Beyond that, one asks what type of psychotherapy can the general practitioner carry out that will augment our current use of neuroleptics in the treatment of anxiety? In this regard, the following observations and recommendations seem pertinent.

Therapeutic Guidelines

1. Acute anxiety states. Patients are more likely to bring acute symptoms of anxiety to the attention of the general practitioner. Generally the dysphoric state has passed and the patient wishes to obtain some measure of control to ensure that the anxiety will not recur. Alternatively, many wish relief from recurrent episodes of anxiety. These patients often experience premonitory distress when recalling their experiences for the physician and fear that they are becoming crazy or mentally ill.

As a general rule, encouraging some measure of catharsis is effective in establishing the physician as a helpful person. Moreover, the patient profits from an opportunity to discharge some of his or her anticipatory anxiety (the memory of the previous state) while simultaneously assessing the reaction of the physician. It is fundamental to the success of subsequent treatment that the physician encourage the patient to describe in detail the events surrounding the first or most recent episode of anxiety. In such circumstances, it is common for a precipitating event or idea to manifest itself along with some of the original affect. In other cases the patient may not become aware of the precipitant factor but will usually experience an attenuated form of the original anxiety. In either event, the physician should be a source of calm reassurance and objectivity. His attitude should convey a serious interest in the content and meaning of the patient's psychological experience.

If the physician is able to help the patient verbalize feelings during the anxiety state, this simple intervention may have unanticipated and important therapeutic effects. First, the patient will have been enabled to make an acceptable confrontation with this previously unconscious—i.e. conflicted and disagreeable—impulse. (Sexual impulses are unusual precipitants of unmodified anxiety, although they play a central role in the development of phobic, hysterical, and obsessional symptoms.) Second, this verbalized confrontation then serves therapeutically as a partial interpretation in the following sense.

As an emotionally charged and conflicted group of ideas gains greater access to consciousness, the previously described unconscious mechanism known as signal anxiety alerts the ego to this danger. This signal stimulates an inner-directed scanning and concomitantly serves to activate a number of other ego components. These include the individual's characteristic defenses, as well as the autonomous functions of reality testing, the sense of reality, and adaptation to reality. Most important for the purposes of this discussion is the promotion of effective repression. It is this fundamental defense that failed at the time of the original trauma and that allowed the ego to be overtaken in surprise by the emergence of a conflicted impulse. The ego's passive experience of this conflict was central to the experience of anxiety. Thus any circumstance that will subsequently alert the ego to the conflict will place it in an active and anticipatory state. This in turn allows the available defenses to reduce the degree of excitation and in this way strengthens repression in relation to the conflicted material.

Moreover, when signal anxiety provokes a general mobilization of the ego, but anxiety emerges, the presence of the physician facilitates another fundamental defense, that of identification. The mastery of anxiety by identification with one's parents' fantasized omnipotence and omniscience is one of the earliest and most successful devices that remains available to adults for the regulation of anxiety. Since the physician is vested with appreciable amounts of omniscience and omnipotence, he provides a readily available object for this defense. By identifying with the physician's calm and accepting attitude, the patient incorporates these qualities into his own ego. These newly appropriated qualities can then serve to strengthen ego deficiencies in dealing with reality as well as modify superego conflicts related to aggressive impulses.

Over and above these specific alterations in the mental apparatus, the experience of catharsis and abreaction serves to effect a successful repetition and mastery of the traumatic event. The fact that the patient is helped to deal with anxiety from an active position (due to the development of signal anxiety) rather than from the former passive condition of surprise and alarm is central to achieving such mastery. The memory of the successful experience with the physician will then serve to generate an attitude of confidence and self-reliance.

Thus, simple catharsis under properly controlled circumstances can serve to abreact, to strengthen ego defenses, and to provide an experience of successful mastery. These are real therapeutic accomplishments and can be carried out within a treatment visit in the hands of a general practitioner. Often this process is accomplished in no more than fifteen minutes, and the patient can then be reassured via suggestion that he may only experience an attenuated form of the anxiety in the future. In cases where exacerbations do occur, a repetition of this approach may often serve to maintain a homeostatic balance for the patient. The more complicated psychotherapeutic processes that include strengthening of specific ego functions via interpretation of unconscious drives, manipulation of the transference, and the interpretation of resistances and characterological defenses are not to be encouraged—indeed, are strictly contraindicated in the hands of the primary practitioner.

In the hands of the primary practitioner, catharsis, reassurance, reality testing, and above all, the avoidance of the development of secondary gain are extremely important. Indeed, the development of the idea that anxiety symptoms are a reflection of an underlying physical disease is a very common form of secondary gain that should be carefully eschewed. The concept of organic or systemic dysfunction provides false comfort to the patient in the rationalization that his illness is an uncontrollable external event for which he has no responsibility. Therefore, laboratory tests and consultations should be carefully avoided if the history allows the physician to make a clear diagnosis of an acute anxiety state.

2. *Chronic anxiety.* As already noted, many patients experience repetitive states of anxiety. For the most part, those who go on to develop a chronic neurotic condition fail to elaborate their anxiety in the way that a phobic or hysteric might. For example, it has already been noted that in other symptom neurotic states traumata will provoke a degree of anxiety sufficient to cause a regression of the ego to an earlier devellopmental period. In the process, defenses are mobilized that are characteristic of the earlier period to which the regression had occurred. These defenses then elaborate the memory of the experience by unconscious mechanisms including repression, fragmentation, symbolization, and condensation and/or displacement of the mental representation of the experience. Further unconscious elaboration may be necessary in order to maintain repression and avoid anxiety. In any event, it is essential to the production of a neurotic state that the mode of discharge, or more specifically the relationship between the unconscious drives (the system id) and the ego-superego complex, be very much modified in form and appearance. By way of contrast, in anxiety states the simplest possible compromise exists. The affect appears consciously—i.e., the anxiety—while the accompanying fantasy content remains repressed.

Over time, repetitive episodes of anxiety can lead to a more stable and different type of symptom formation in some individuals. In these cases, the affect itself becomes bound to a physical symptom and is experienced as an organic sensation—i.e., palpitations, breathlessness, dizziness, fatigue, and so forth. As noted earlier, there are two types of patients in whom anxiety is transformed into organic sensations, and we refer to these patients as neurasthenics. One group is found to have had prior good health and energy levels and generally prove to have the better prognosis. They tend to experience spontaneous remissions and tend to develop less severe symptoms. In some of these cases a degree of psychological-mindedness may be present, and if the patient is agreeable to psychiatric consultation, he may profit from such a referral.

The second group of neurasthenics have had a lifelong history of easy fatigability and somatic complaints. This group has fully transformed its anxiety into somatic sensations, and because of this requires a somewhat different approach. Because of the early onset of somatic symptoms and sensations, these patients can be thought to have experienced an arrest in their ability to transform anxiety into adaptive behavior or to use it as a stimulus to perform psychological transformations—i.e., defensive operations. Consequently, their repertoire of psychological adaptation is severely limited, and this fact imposes very obvious constraints on the outcomes that can be expected from psychological intervention. Certainly one cannot strengthen defenses that do not exist or profitably attempt to stimulate types of defenses that have not proven useful in the past. Alternatively, reconstructive psychotherapeutic work in a primary care setting is unfeasible. Beyond this, many patients in whom the condition of anxiety is essentially fixed for life are not particularly interested in obtaining psychotherapeutic help.

In these cases it is important for the physician to provide reassurance and patient counsel in order to establish a good working alliance. One aims to establish a good working relationship in order to avoid doctor shopping and the inevitable round of costly diagnostic procedures and consultations that are so much more easily offered than emotional support. Above all, it is important for the patient to feel that his physician can accept his somatic symptoms and his rationalization that the cause of his distress is external (i.e., an illness). Under these circumstances a friendly alliance may be maintained for years. The chronic neurasthenic may respond particularly well to medication as an adjunct in terminating acute episodes of anxiety or in dealing with sustained periods of distress. Taking such medicine PRN effectively lessens his anxiety and further reinforces the patient's sense that the anxiety is not under his control but is in the province of the physician's expertise. In a more fundamental sense such an approach can be considered psychologically supportive, since the physician is indeed aiding a preformed defensive organizaiton—i.e., rationalization and externalizaiton.

Balint's (59) psychoanalytic contributions in the area of general practice should be noted. He points out that many patients frantically search for a diagnosis and in the process offer their physicians a series of illnesses, in the hope that the physician will accept one and allow the patient to be sick. Recently, Scaramella (60) reviewed the treatment of anxiety by primary care physicians. He stressed the fact that reassuring the patient that nothing is very wrong with him often proves to be counterproductive. Indeed, this approach generally increases the patient's anxiety. Thus he once again emphasizes the need for the physician to accept the neurasthenic's symptomatic complaints and for him to convey an attitude of confidence and competence to the chronic neurasthenic. Such an approach will often reassure the patient that the physician is interested—i.e. the physician also feels that something needs treatment and this rationalization will be supportive of the patient's most important defensive operation.

Finally one must note that the chronic neurasthenic can be extremely demanding and childlike. and their capacity to engender aggression can't be underestimated. Indeed, at times the physician's countertransference may provoke him to suggest that a more sinister, perhaps occult process is at work within the patient. Such statements can only serve to aggravate the patient's degree of distress and cause great punishment to the patient and his family. Thus it is always important for the physician to know himself when treating such patients and to be sensitive to his own countertransference reactions.

REFERENCES

1. Lader, M. The nature of anxiety. *Brit. J. Psychiat.* 121:481-492, 1972.
2. Cohen, M. Neurocirculatory asthenia. *Med. Clin. N. A.* 33:1343-1364, 1949.
3. Fenichel, O. *The Psychoanalytic Theory of Neurosis.* New York: Norton, 1945.
4. Wheeler, E.O., White. P.D., Reed, E.W., et al. Neurocirculatory asthenia (anxiety neurosis, effort syndrome, neurasthenia). A twenty-year follow-up study of one hundred and seventy-three patients. *J.A.M.A.* 142:878-889, 1950.
5. Wheeler, E.O., White, P.D., Reed, E., et al. Familial incidence of neurocirculatory asthenia (anxiety neurosis, effort syndrome). J. Clin. *Invest.* 27:562, 1948.,
6. Lader, M. Anxiety: Its nature and treatment. *S. Afr. Med. J.* 49:939-943, 1975.
7. .Lader, M. Research report: Institute of psychiatry and clinical psychopharmacology research team. *Psychol. Med.* 4:110-116, 1974.
8. Rees, W.L. General aspects of anxiety: An introductory survey. In W.L. Rees, ed., *Symposium on Anxiety Factors in Comprehensive Patient Care.* New York: American Elsevier, 1973.
9. White, P.D., and Jones, T.D. Heart disease and disorders in New England. *Am. Heart J.* 3:302-318, 1928.
10. Gross, W.M. Mental health survey in a rural area. *Eugenic Rev.* 40:140-152, 1948.
11. Primrose, E.J. R. Psychological illness: A community study. Mind and Medicine Monograph No. 3. London: Tavistock Publications, 1962.
12. Shepherd, M., Cooper, B., Brown, A.C., et al. Psychiatric Illness in General Practice. London: Oxford University Press, 1966.
13. Borus, J.F. Neighborhood health centers as providers of primary mental-health care. *New Eng. J. Med.* 195):140-145, 1976.
14. Parish. P.A. The prescribing of psychotropic drugs in general practice. *J. Royal Col. Gen. Pract.* (Suppl. 4) 21:1-77, 1971.

15. Marsland. D.W.. Wood. M.. and Mayo. F. Content of family practice: A data bank for patient care. curriculum. and research in family practice—526.196 patient problems. *J. Family Pract.* 3:25-68. 1976.
16. Valbona. C. Monthly Statistical Report—Casa de Amigos Community Health Clinic. November 1973.
17. Borus. J.F. The community mental health center and the medical practitioner: A first step. *Psychiatry* 34:274-288. 1971.
18. Lemere. F.. and Kraabel. A.B. The general practitioner and the psychiatrist. *Am. J. Psychiat.* 116:518-521. 1959.
19. Leighton. D.C.. Harding. J.S.. Macklin. D.B.. et al. The character of danger.*The Sterling County Study III.* New York: Basic Books. 1963.
20. Srole. L.. Langner. T.S.. Michael. S. T.. et al. *Mental Health in the Metropolis: The Midtown Manhattan Study,* Vol. 1. New York: McGraw-Hill. 1962.
21. Shepherd. M.. Cooper. B.. Brown. A.C.. and Kalton. G.W. *Psychiatric Illness in General Practice.* London: Oxford University Press. 1966.
22. Nystrom. S.. and Lindegard. B. Predisposition for mental syndromes: A study comparing predisposition for depression. neurasthenia. and anxiety state. *Acta Psychiat. Scand.* 51:69-76. 1975.
23. Schapira. K.. Roth. M.. Kerr. T.A.. et al. The prognosis of affective disorders: The differentiation of anxiety states from depressive illness. *Brit. J. Psychiat.* 121:175-181. 1972.
24. Kerr. T.. Roth. M.. and Schapira. K. Prediction of outcome in anxiety states and depressive illness. *Brit. J. Psychiat.* 124:125-133. 1974.
25. Lee. R.E.. and Schhneider. R.F. Hypertension and atherosclerosis in executives and nonexecutive personnel. *J.A.M.A.* 1447-1450. 1958.
26. Meltzer. L.E. Anxiety in cardiovascular disease. In W.L. Rees. ed. *Symposium on Anxiety Factors in Comprehensive Patient Care.* New York: American Elsevier. 1973.
27. Gorsuch. R.L.. and Key. M.K. Abnormalities of pregnancy as a function of anxiety and life stress. *Psychosom. Med.* 36:351-362. 1974.
28. Holmes T.. and Masuda. M. Life changes and illness susceptibility. In B.S. Dohrenwend and B.P. Dohrenwend. eds.. *Stressful Life Events* New York: Wiley. 1974.
29. Ratkin. J.G.. and Struening. E.L.. Life events, stress and illness. *Science* 194:1013-1020. 1976.
30. Wolff. H.G. Life stress and cardiovascular disorders. *Circulation* 1:187-203. 1950.
31. Rahe. R.H. Subjects' recent life changes and their near future illness susceptibility. *Adv. Psychosom. Med.* 8:2-19. 1972.
32. Wood. P. Refresher course for general practitioners—cardiac neurosis. *Brit. Med. J.* ii:33-35. 1950.
33. Cohen. M.E. The high familial prevalence of neurocirculatory asthenia (anxiety neurosis. effort syndrome). *Am. J. Hum. Genet.* 3:126-158. 1951.
34. Brown. F.W. Heredity in the psychoneuroses. *Proc. Royal Soc. Med.* 35:785-790. 1942.
35. Cooper. A.J.. Cowie. V.A.. and Slater. E. Familial aspects of "neuroticism" and "extraversion." *Brit. J. Psychiat.* 111:70-83. 1965.
36. Slater. E.. and Shields. J. Genetical aspects of anxiety. *Brit. J. Psychiat.* Special Pub. No. 3:62-71. 1967.
37. Young. J.P.R.. Fenton. G.W.. and Lader. M.H. The inheritance of neurotic traits: A twin study of the Middlesex Hospital Questionnaire. *Brit. J. Psychiat.* 119:393-408. 1971.
38. Cohen. M.E.. and White. P.D. Life situations. emotions. and neurocirculatory asthenia (anxiety neurosis. neurasthenia. effort syndrome). *Res. Nerv.Ment. Dis. Proc.* 29:832-869. 1950.

39. Jones M., and Mellersh, V. Comparison of exercise response in anxiety states and normal controls. *Psychosom. Med.* 8:180-187, 1946.

40. Linko, E., Lactate acid response to muscular exercise in neurocirculatory asthenia. *Ann. Med. Int. Fenniae* 39:161-176, 1950.

41. Holmgren, A. and Ström, G. Blood lactate concentration in relation to absolute and relative work load in normal men, and in initial stress, atrial septal defect, and vasoregulatory asthenia. *Acta Med. Scand.* 163:185-193, 1959.

42. Pitts, F.N., Jr. and McClure, J.N., Jr. Lactate metabolism in anxiety neurosis. *New Eng. J. Med.* 277:1329-1336, 1967.

43. Grosz, H.J. and Farmer, B.B. Pitts and McClure's lactate-anxiety study revisited. *Brit. J. Psychiat.* 120:415-418, 1972.

44. Freud, S. Inhibition, symptoms and anxiety. In *The Complete Psychological Works of Sigmund Freud, Vol XX* trans. J. Strachey. London: Hogarth Press, 1957.

45. Eysenck, H.J. The effects of psychotherapy, an evaluation. *J. Consult. Psychol.* 16:319-324, 1952.

46. Malan, D.H. The outcome problem in psychotherapy research: A historical review. *Arch. Gen. Psychiat.* 29:719-728, 1973.

47. Sullivan, H.S. *The Interpersonal Theory of Psychiatry.* New York: Norton, 1953.

48. Schachter, S., The interaction of cognitive and physiological determinants of emotional state. In L. Berkowitz, ed. *Advances in Experimental Social Psychology* vol. 1. New York: Academic Press, 1964.

49. Dollard, J. and Miller, N. *Personality and Psychotherapy.* New York: McGraw-Hill, 1950.

50. May, R. *The Meaning of Anxiety.* New York: Ronald Press, 1950.

51. Spielberger, C.D. Anxiety as an emotional state. In C.D. Spielberger, ed. *Anxiety: Current Trends in Theory and Research.* Vol. 1 New York: Academic Press, 1972.

52. Cattell, R.B., and Schier, I.H. The nature of anxiety: A review of 13 multivariate analyses comparing 814 variables. *Psycholog. Rep.* (Monograph Suppl.) 5:351-388, 1958.

53. Derogatis, L.R., Lipman, R.S., Covi, L., et al. Factorial invariance of symptom dimensions in anxious and depressive neuroses. *Arch. Gen. Psychiat.* 27:659-665, 1972.

54. Stone W.N., Gleser, G.C., and Gottschalk, L.A. Anxiety and B-adrenergic blockade. *Arch. Gen. Psychiat.* 29:620-622, 1973.

55. Clancy, J., and Noyes, R., Jr. Anxiety neurosis a disease for the medical model. *Psychosom.* 17:90-93, 1976.

56. Gardner, A.O., Peterson, J., and Hall, D.J. A survey of general practitioners' referrals to a psychiatric outpatient service. *Brit. J. Psychiat.* 124:536-541, 1974.

57. Wilcox, P.R.C., Gillon, R., and Hare, E.H. Do psychiatric outpatients take their drugs? *Brit. Med. J.* ii: 790-792, 1965.

58. Porter, A.M.W. Drug defaulting in general practice. *Brit. Med. J.* i:218-222, 1969.

59. Balint, M.L. *The Doctor, the Patient, and the Illness.* New York: International Universities Press, 1964.

60. Scaramella, T.J. Management of depression and anxiety in primary care practice. *Prim. Care.* 4:67-77, 1977.

CHAPTER 3

Anxiety in the Aged

Carl Eisdorfer

Professional interest in the care of the aging has increased rather markedly during recent years for a variety of reasons. Perhaps the most significant of these reasons is the considerable increase in the number and proportion of persons in the United States who have reached the age of 65 and the rather remarkable impact that this has had on our health care system in the United States.

The data indicate that while the population of the U.S. has risen approximately two and a half times during this century, the number of persons aged 65 and over has increased approximately seven-fold, now comprising in excess of 10% of the U.S. population (over 21 million Americans). The proportion of older Americans is continuing to grow in relation to the general population and should reach 12.5% before the turn of the century (1). The aged are a population at risk and are certainly the recipients of a considerable amount of medical care, accounting for some 25% to 30% of the total health care costs of the U.S. (2).

In the aggregate, psychiatrists and other health care professionals and systems have shown a relative paucity of interest in problems of the aged (3). Much of the mental health and psychiatric literature on the aged has been devoted to the cognitive disorders and organic brain syndromes, and only scanty epidemiologic data are available on anxiety, depression, and the other

43

nondementing conditions. This is reflected in the service sector, where only approximately 2% to 3% of all outpatient psychiatric care is devoted to the population over age 65, despite the fact that this group represents over 10% of the population.

Several reasons may exist for this phenomenon: it may indeed be that older persons represent a select cohort of individuals who have survived with generally fewer neurotic and and functional psychiatric difficulties, while their less fortunate (i.e., higher risk) peers have dropped out of the population through differential mortality. Of course, this would signal the importance of good mental health for survival, and while this idea is attractive to those of us in the mental health profession, the data in support of such a hypothesis are hardly compelling. Alternatively, it may be that older persons are less psychologically minded, and therefore tend to somatize more of their minor psychopathology (e.g., anxiety and depression), taking their problems into the physical health sector. In addition, we probably do have a cohort of older persons who are not psychologically minded and who see psychiatric help as being stigmatizing, rather than desirable. Older persons may also think that the mental health community is uninterested in and unresponsive to them, with the result that the target population of older people do not wish to seek help where the helpers are not perceived to be interested in them. It may also be that the social pressures of children, who as surrogate parents do not wish to see their own aging parents labeled as psychiatrically impaired, present a barrier to careful psychiatric evaluation.

Among the young, anxiety is a major symptom and disorder. Among the aged, it has received little attention. It should be recognized that anxiety itself is a complex construct. As Blumenthal has pointed out (4), it is alternatively an affect, a symptom, a psychopathologic state, and a theoretical state.

As an affect, it is of course a subjective event, in which people typically have a sense of dread and/or fear, often without an appropriate basis. Anxiety is also a symptom of other disorders, including depression, certain forms of psychosis, and even certain physical conditions. This is partially out of a concern for survival, a fear of loss of function, or a direct autonomic imbalance. It can be a psychopathologic state, as in an anxiety neurosis. Anxiety is also a hypothetical state, as hypothesized in the concept of "mechanism of defense," an intrapersonal technique designed to avoid the experience of anxiety. It may also be used as a theoretic state, describing a motivational force in a number of psychological theories, or as an intervening interferring state, in complex tasks involving learning or performance situations. In general, anxiety is related to events described as stress-inducing; it is felt to be associated with the physiologic events related to fight or flight (5). It has also been proposed (6) that freezing may be an alternative behavioral maneuver, when fight or flight is perceived to be inappropriate or impossible. This has particular relevance to older people, whose somatic losses make successful fighting more difficult, and of course flight becomes more difficult when the individual moves more slowly. Since loss of speed is a problem particular to the aged (6), anxiety may be associated with acquiescence or compliance on demand, a cognitive state more associated with freezing than with fighting or running. Such a situation may be particularly the case where anxiety is associated with depression, as in the face of major losses or concurrent multiple losses (e.g., death of many friends and relatives, loss of roles, loss of income, loss of physical health, and the like).

In assessing anxiety, we are likely to see its manifestations in three areas: in the behavior reflected in acts of avoidance and an inability to make decisions; in the cognitive subjective area—that is to say, in personal feelings and reports; and in the physiologic area, where autonomic and/or central nervous system activity is heightened and physical manifestations of the anxiety state are present. While these three areas may overlap, they are not perfectly correlated; and in particular persons the correlation among the behavioral, the cognitive, and the physiologic manifestations of anxiety is poor. It is thus possible to have behavioral and/or physiologic manifestations of anxiety without the subjective recognition of an anxiety state. There may also be differential tolerance of anxiety.

Spielberger's concept of (7) trait versus state anxiety is another useful explanatory construct. The trait-state concept separates trait anxiety (i.e., a heightened expectation that an individual will experience subjective anxiety) from state anxiety (the experiential state at a point in time). Persons with trait anxiety show also important qualitative differences in their manifestation of anxiety, in that people who are frightened (i.e., made anxious) by specific events may demonstrate patterns of anxiety different from the patterns exhibited by persons with heightened trait anxiety (i.e., those whose anxiety state often has no clear external cue). We may thus question whether individuals with low trait anxiety who begin to develop fears in later life have somewhat different traits than the young.

On a behavioral level, anxiety is usually seen as agitated avoidance behavior and difficulty with decision-making, particularly as this involves complex phenomena. Usually, long delays and a withholding of response are characteristic of high-anxiety persons in situations requiring a complex response (7). It is of interest to note that this type of behavior also describes what we often see among the normal aged, particularly in the areas of memory, learning, and reaction to complex decision-making situations.

On a subjective level, the experience of anxiety may include the perception of skin changes, tachycardia, early-evening insomnia, a sense of foreboding, and the like. Salzman (8) suggests that fatigue may be a dominant subjective symptom of anxiety among the aged. On the physiologic level, a number of other phenomena have been reported. There is increased muscle tension in the EMG of older anxious patients (9). Heart rates show less variability than among younger subjects (10). The plethysmograph, reflecting cardiovascular integrity, similarly shows less variability in the old.

Electrodermal response has been shown to be perhaps the most consistent measure of anxiety, and it remains active in the old, where an increased proportion of specific electrodermal response, as a percentage of basal activity, increases with age in men more than in women (11). Free fatty acids in the blood have shown heightened elevation in the aged, to a far greater extent than is exhibited in the young, when older men are asked to learn a simple verbal test (12). This pattern is not characteristic of women and again confirms the notion that men are different from women.

Studies of peripheral catecholamine, also associated with stress, indicate that circulating norepinephrine may increase with age (13), in contrast to previous expectations, which suggests that the aged may not be as unresponsive as we have believed.

Clinical management of the anxious patient involves, first of all, a decision to measure anxiety. Rating scales for anxiety seem particularly ineffective with the aged, and Salzman (14) has proposed that his and Shader's use of a 100 mm line (15) asking subjects to assess a variety of events, including fatigue, may be one of the best practical devices to use. Interviewing the aged patient requires no special art, but a set of reasonable interviewing strategies which show respect for the basic integrity of the patient as an individual in his/her own right. Difficulty with older patients arises in three general areas. First the patient may be brought in by his/her own child or some other younger individual who assumes the role of parent surrogate, the infantalization of the older patient has put him/her in a highly vulnerable position vis-a-vis self-esteem. We often see that an older individual is ignored while a physician discusses the patient's condition with his/her son or daughter or even grandchildren. Obviously, this is not designed to maximize the opportunity for interaction between the examiner and the patient. Second, the older person is often not psychologically minded, and he/she is part of a cohort of individuals who did not grow up with positive attitudes toward mental health. This may be complicated by the feeling that examination by a psychiatrist is designed to label them "crazy" and to institutionalize them or at least to get them out of their current living arrangement. This is not a desirable setting for an honest interview. Finally, older persons, either because of the coexistence of brain disease and/or some other illness, may have problems in the somatic realm, and the psychiatrist must bear this in mind when the interview takes place. If in his/her interview of an older person the psychiatrist shows empathy and respect for the older person, uncertainty is reduced and there is more likely to be some feedback from the older person. In the case of some patients, particularly inpatients or patients in long-term care, physical contact by the psychiatrist, speaking loudly and clearly enough, and making sure that the patient understands the language used are important.

When the patient and the physician are not natives of the same country and/or when regional linguistic differences prevail, these basic issues in communication are particularly important. Third, physical illness of a variety of types may be manifested in physiologic states that appear to be anxiety; thus stress may lead to hypersecretion of ADH, leading in turn to hypoatremia, which is anxiety producing (appearing), but which is largely treatable by appropriate electrolyte therapy. Anxiety may also be a variable in a differential diagnosis of depression. This should be kept in mind, particularly where the treatment of anxiety does not result in a lifting of the symptoms. A variety of drugs, particularly the polydrug situation in which older people often find themselves, may lead to anxiety-type syndromes. It is important that the interview and the management of the patient include periodic drug reviews. A review of the life style of the patient, paticularly if he/she has suffered multiple losses, is important—again reflecting the fact that we know relatively little about the psychology of multiple losses.

Anxious older persons may present with hypochondriasis, and this is a particular problem. The pitfalls here are that the physician, often frustrated at not being able to diagnose and treat the complaints presented, may become irritated and may maintain that the patient's problems are "all in his/her head" and that there is "nothing wrong," often doing a physical examination to prove that the patient's concerns are unwarranted. In this regard, sham procedures are to be discouraged and complex psychiatrically worded explanations of psychodynamics are no better; rather, patients with anxiety and hypochondriasis need and deserve support from the physician, who should indicate a willingness to work with the patient on his/her problems. Brief, regular meetings with the patient are helpful. Patient education is valuable, too, in terms of a knowledge of the stress states that may exacerbate the patient's physical problems. Methods of tension reduction can be helpful. Simultaneously, the physician is then in a position to help reestablish certain roles and contexts for the patient to deal with the etiology of the anxiety.

Although it may be somewhat simplistic, it is valuable to note Doerr's (9) proposal that when anxiety is manifested in its cognitive form, psychosocial therapies are much more likely to be helpful. With greater somatization, it is entirely likely that the more successful approach should be more through medication and tension reduction through such physical methods as biofeedback of EMG, relaxation exercises, and the like.

Finally, we should identify the medications useful in anxiety. In terms of prescriptions filled, the benzodiazepines and substituted diols are the most used medications. It has been pointed out that while anti-anxiety medications are probably clearly more effective than placebos, age itself as a variable in pharmacokinetics has not been studied. Salzman and Shader, in 1973 (16), did find sex differences in response to diazepam, and Salzman and coworkers (17) found that the placebo is relatively more effective with older volunteers. The role of anti-anxiety medication in OBS has not been clarified, although it has been clinically advocated in many instances. One study of aged men (18) demonstrated the value of propranolol in reducing autonomic indices of arousal and in improving learning. This study has not been repeated, however, nor its clinical effectiveness assessed.

In summary, it should be pointed out that our knowledge base concerning anxiety in the aged is quite limited. Epidemiologic studies have not been helpful, partly because of difficulties in assessing anxiety in older persons. It is possible that older persons may manifest anxiety in differing ways than the young. The treatment of heightened autonomic activity and/or stress in older persons is not markedly different from that of the young, but it does require clinicians who are comfortable in dealing with aged patients and who are willing to develop a therapeutic relationship with them.

References

1. Myers, GC. Future age projections and society. Paper presented at World Conference on Aging: A Challenge for Science and Social Policy, organized by L.Institute de la Vie, Vichy, France, April 1977, proceedings in press.
2. Kovar, M.G. Health of the elderly and use of health services. *Public Health Reports,* Department of Health, Education and Welfare, 92:1, 197.
3. Kramer M., Taube, C.A., and Redick, R.W. Patterns of use of psychiatric facilities by the aged: Past, present, and future. In C. Eisdorfer and M.P. Lawton, ed. *The Psychology of Adult Development and Aging.* Washington, D.C.: American Psychological Association, 1973.
4. Blumenthal, M.D. Diagnosis and treatment of anxiety in the aged. Paper presented at Symposium on Anxiety in the Elderly, sponsored by Department of Psychiatry. University of Arizona, November 16-17, 1977.
5. Eisdorfer, C., and Wilkie, F. Stress, disease, aging and behavior. In J. Birren and K.W. Schaie, eds. *Handbook of the Psychology of Aging.* New York: Van Nostrand, 1977.
6. Jarvik, L. Anxiety and Stress in the aged. Paper presented at Symposium of Anxiety in the Elderly, sponsored by the Department of Psychiatry, University of Arizona, November 16-17, 1977.
7. Spielberger, C.D., Gorsuch, R.E., and Lushane, R.E. *Manual for the State-Trait Anxiety Inventory.* Tallahassee: Florida State University, 1968.
8. Salzman, C. Psychometric rating of anxiety int he elderly. Paper presented at Symposium on Anxiety in the Elderly, sponsored by the Department of Psychiatry, University of Arizona, November 16-17, 1977.
9. Doerr, H. Psychophysiological assessment of anxiety in the aged. Paper presented at Symposium on Anxiety in the Elderly, sponsored by the Department of Psychiatry, University of Arizona, November 16-17, 1977.
10. Marsh, G.R., and Thompson, L.W. Psychophysiology of aging. In J.E. Birren and K.W. Schaie, eds. *Handbook of the Psychology of Aging.* New York: Van Nostrand, 1977.
11. Eisdorfer, C., Doerr, H., and Follett, W. Age and sex interaction with electrodermal level and response. Paper presented at the 17th annual meeting for the Society for Psychophysiological Research, Philadelphia, Pennsylvania, October 13, 1977.
12. Powell, A.H., Eisdorfer, C., and Bogdonoff, M.D. Physiologic response patterns observed in a learning task. *Arch. Gen. Psych.* 10:192-195, 1964.
13. Lake, C.R., Ziegler, M.G., Coleman, M.D., and Kopin, I.J. Age-readjusted plasma norepinephrine levels are similar in normotensive and hypertensive subjects. *New Eng. Med. J.* 298:208-209, 1977.

14. Saltzman. C.. et al. Psychopharmacologic in elderly volunteers: effect of diazepam in males. *J. Am. Geriatr. Soc.* 23:451-457, 1975.
15. Salzman. C.. and Shader, R.I. Research in geriatric psychopharmacology. *J. Geriatr. Psychiat.* 8:165-184, 1975.
16. Salzman. C.. and Shader, R.I., Responses to psychotropic drugs in normal elderly, In C. Eisdorfer and W.E. Fann, *Psychopharmacology and Aging.* New York: Plenum, 1973.
17. Salzman C.. Shader R.I.. Harnat & J.S. et al. Response of the elderly to psychotropic drugs: predictable or idiosyncratic? Psychopharmacology Bulletin. 11(4):48-50 Oct., 1975.
18. Wilke. F.L. Eisdorfer, C. and Nowlin, J.B. Memory and blood pressure in the aged. Exp. Aging Res. 2 (1) 3-16, 1976.

Phenomenology and Treatment of Anxiety

CHAPTER 4

Traumatic Neuroses

Jack R. Ewalt

The term "traumatic neurosis" is used intermittently in the medical literature and not always to describe precisely the same category of disorder. It is not included in DSM-2.

Following World War I, Freud (1) wrote: "The war neuroses, insofar as they are distinguished from ordinary neuroses of peacetime by special characteristics, are to be regarded as traumatic neuroses whose occurrence has been made possible or has been promoted by a conflict in the ego." And "in traumatic and war neuroses the human ego is defending itself from a danger which threatens it from without or which is embodied in a shape assumed by the ego itself. In the transference neuroses of peace the enemy from which the ego is defending itself is actually the libido whose demands seem to it to be menacing. In both cases the ego is afraid of being damaged— in the latter case by the libido and in the former by external violence."

At times the term is used to describe cases sometimes called post-traumatic syndromes where there has been questionable brain injury. For example, Auerbach and his coworkers (2) made a survey among neurosurgeons and neurologists and found that most felt that the syndrome was due to organic brain trauma with emotional aggravation. There was, among this group, considerable sentiment that litigation and possible compensation also contribute to the disorder. They were equally pessimistic about therapy, feeling that medications and psychotherapy were questionably useful. Selye (3) wrote that the stress syndrome is nonspecific in causation and depends on the conditioning factor which can selectively influence the reactivation of certain organs. Selye further mentions as do Bourne (4) and others, that the same stressor can elicit different manifestations in different individuals. Also, what is a stressor for one person may be a pleasure for another.

Those of you who have seen the earlier classifications of DSM-3 will note that under the section of anxiety reactions, the term "traumatic neurosis" does not occur, but it does occur in Section Q of Chapter 3—309.81 Post-Traumatic Disorder. The description in the current manuscript of DSM-3—note this is not the final version—describes the important factors:

> The essential feature is the development of characteristic symptoms after the experiencing of the psychological traumatic event or events outside the range of human experience usually considered to be normal. The characteristic symptoms involve reexperiencing the traumatic event, numbing of responsiveness to or involvement with the external world and a variety of other autonomic, dysphoric, or cognitive symptoms.

The authors of DSM-3 also point out that while the symptoms of a post-traumatic disorder may begin soon after the traumatic event, it is not unusual for the emergence of characteristic symptoms to occur after a latency period of several days or even months after the original trauma. They further list the operational criteria for the diagnosis:

> (1) A recognizable stressor that would be expected to evoke a significant symptom to distress in almost all individuals.
>
> (2) Reexperiencing the traumatic event by recurrent dreams or suddenly feeling or acting as if the traumatic event is occurring because of an association to some current environmental or ideation stimulus.
>
> (3) Diminished interest in significant activities, feelings of detachment or estrangement or constriction of effective responses, and
>
> (4) Hyperalertness or exaggerated startle response, sleep disturbance, guilt about surviving, memory impairment, avoidance of activities that arouse recollection of the traumatic event, and intensification of symptoms by exposure to events which symbolize or resemble the trauamtic event. At least two of these symptoms must be present to accurately use the diagnosis.

Thus, the traumatic neurosis or post-traumatic disorders are different than the other neuroses in that the external situation is real rather than symbolic. But the situation may have some particular symbolic significance to the individual and may be one of the reasons why some persons in a particular situation develop post-traumatic disorders and others do not. The larger number of these cases tend to come in waves, and follow wars or disasters such as the Texas City explosion of many years ago or the floods in Johnstown, Pennsylvania, in the last few years. The symptoms, when they do come, have a rather specific constellation with allowances for individual variation. Some of the variations such as phobic or compulsive components are probably marks of the pre-illness personality constellation of the individual rather than specific to the disorder itself. Because the disorder tends to occur following wars and other mass traumatic situations, to make this a bit more practical I am going to confine the rest of my remarks to post-traumatic syndromes resulting from wartime experience. I do this because we are currently attempting to cope with the post-traumatic syndromes or neuroses of Vietnam era veterans.

World War I produced a large number of patients diagnosed as suffering from war neurosis or shell shock. Mott (5) wrote rather extensively in this area, as did several psychiatrists from the United States. Mott believed that most of the cases were a form of hysteria and felt that the development of the disorder was a combination of fear, fatigue, and the personality of the individual soldier. He further stated that they were truly states of emotional shock and that removing them from the theater of operation would result in a cure. He also implied that because a large number of men suffering from these functional disabilities were receiving pensions, the disability would remain permanent.

A number of people wrote on psychogenic disorders of one sort or another produced by World War II. Most notable were Grinker and Spiegel, William Menninger, Douglas Bond, and others. These discussions of the post-traumatic syndrome all had an analytic flavor. Several of these authors mention one thing as important for prevention; as Bourne (6) puts it "identification with his group is the most powerful protective device for the soldier and overcomes the individual's feeling of being isolated...Such identification plus the drive toward a fixed, well-known, easily understood and completely accepted goal, is the defense against neurosis." The common reaction of soldiers in World War II was called combat fatigue and was generally assumed to be due to stress, fatigue, exposure to the elements, and danger beyond the individual's ego capacity to cope. It was believed that unit morale and mutual support did much to delay these reactions. It is interesting, however, and somewhat parenthetical to point out that the death rate following imprisonment in World War II for those in the Pacific theater is many times higher than that for those in the European theater, whose postwar death rate is essentially that of the non-veteran population. Brill, Beebe, and Gilbert (7) made a follow-up of the war neurosis of World War II five years following discharge from the military. They found that psychoneurosis of all sort made up just over 3% of the admissions for medical care in World War II and represented 703,000 casualties. They found that the neurotic patients tended to be older. The condition was not related to intellectual level (as measured by the tests in use during World War II); the incidence tended to be lower in the better educated and lower in the group with combat experience (contrary to expectations), but on the other hand, for those in combat it was higher in riflemen and gunners as opposed to those in technical positions. The follow-up data is based on examination of 1,475 cases. Each of these was examined by a psychiatric colleague selected from near the residence of the veteran, but the examinations were according to a fairly specific schedule. The researchers found the suicide rate was approximately three times that of the age-related general population. Only 8.7% were symptom-free. Twenty-four percent had shown symptoms before service; 43% developed symptoms in service, and 4% after discharge. The symptoms present were principally those found in the Vietnam era veteran—post-traumatic syndromes consisting of anxiety, depression, nightmares, insomnia, headaches, psychosocial disorders, irritability, restlessness, and an increased incidence of alcoholism. The researchers found a general tendency toward improvement, and while many had residual symptoms, 67% were making a satisfactory occupational adjustment and 33% were impaired or making a marginal adjustment; 15% were not working; 52% were not on compensation. They also noticed that 16% felt that the compensation helped them in their readjustment; 69% felt that it had no effect, and 16% felt that it had a bad effect. Forty-eight percent of the group were on compensation; the median amount was 20% disability. Of this group on compensation, 18% felt that it had been helpful; 61% felt it had no effect, and 21% (10% of the total sample) felt that it had a bad effect.

The Korean conflict produced no such phrase as "shell shock" or "combat fatigue," although some of the persons were said to have a "zombie reaction." This group also has a high POW and post-discharge mortality rate, similar to that of POWs from the Pacific theater of World War II (8).

The Vietnam era veterans represent the bulk of our current problems of traumatic syndrome or neurosis, and I will now describe the current concepts of the dynamics of the syndrome. Koranyi (9) notes that man must face modern dangers with Stone Age psychological equipment. In modern war he gets his blood pressure up, his endocrine system revs up, his muscles are ready, and then he waits or fires a gun at an unseen object. The commanding officer and the midbrain cortex give conflicting orders, which contribute to his stress. Peter Bourne (6) points out that there are fewer cases of psychiatric casualties while in Vietnam, but that there are many in the readjustment period. "The psychological and social problems of the Vietnam era veteran probably exceed those of any previous conflict, and ironically it is many of the factors which helped to keep psychiatric casualties low in Vietnam, which served to compound the readjustment difficulties of the veteran when he returns." The twelve-month tour held down the zone-of-combat mental health casualities, but took away the group support, so for each man the war was his own. "If all we have in effect done is delay the timing in which the peak incidence of psychiatric breakdown occurs, we have not accomplished very much." It is interesting to note that the Vietnam groups, while they sometimes meet as groups for therapy, do not meet so far as I have become aware in groups made up of members of a single unit. Harry Truman used to speak fondly of the reunion of his World War I artillery unit, and a number of my colleagues have attended the annual reunions of their old World War II outfit. Twelve-month rotation gave the soldier little identify with his group. It would be very difficult to pick any group of Vietnam era veterans who fought through the whole campaign as members of a single unit that had experienced induction, service, rest camps, renewed service, and discharge together.

The lack of popularity or general public support of the Vietnam War also probably contributed to post-discharge adjustment problems. Lifton (10) speak of technical violence and the absurd deaths that have replaced sexual repression as an urgent theme for contemporary man. He thinks "psychic numbing" is a better term than repression to describe the mental dynamics in this group of patients. In other publication (11), he has spoken of the "pornography of death."

Charles Figley (12) describes persons who develop stress reactions and raises the question (but does not answer it conclusively) of whether such individuals are predisposed, or whether the syndrome is due to the severity and nature of the trauma. The data show that those veterans with combat experience exhibit more pathology than noncombat veterans. In some patients there is a considerable delay between the traumatizing event and the reaction. Chaim Shatan has written extensively on the delayed post-catastrophic syndrome in the Vietnam era veterans, in survivors of concentration camps, and others. He has coined the term "post-Vietnam syndrome," and wants DSM-3 to contain a specific diagnosis of post-stress disorder. He believes the disorder is a specific one among post-Vietnam veterans consisting of a constellation of symptoms:

1. Guilt (surviving while friends did not and killing when there was no real justification).

2. Being scapegoated; feeling used, deceived and betrayed by society.

3. Rage. Combat brutalization, dehumanization of the enemy, conflicting identity of civilian and soldier because of the nature of the guerrilla warfare.

4. Alienation; inability to love due to fear of risking positive emotion toward others who might be killed, and fear of trusting them.

The occurrence of psychopathology among Vietnam era veterans may be of interest. There now are 29,900,000 living veterans. Of this number, 8,500,000 or about 28%, are veterans of the Vietnam era. Of this group, 67% were not in Vietnam; 2,800,000, or one-third, were in Vietnam. The average age of Vietnam veterans is 34.3 years. Of veterans, 509,000 have disorders resulting from military service, and 86,000 of these are psychiatric disorders (18%). The last year for which we have data, about 30% of our hospital discharges with psychiatric diagnoses were Vietnam era veterans.

Lifton, Figley, Shatan, and Engendorf, among others, have been conducting group therapy with many elements of a rap session with some of the Vietnam era veterans. For example, Lifton (14) relates: "One veteran somewhat prone to violence in childhood spoke of his post Vietnam experiences as 'struggles to overcome the beast in me,' by which he meant an inclination to attack other people suddenly while in a dream-like state in which he was hardly aware of what he was doing. Another one of the professionals helped the group break through the protective armor by pointing out the profound fear behind each situation of violence the veterans described. To which he quickly responded, 'Yes, sometimes I think I am still back with those thirteen guys in my squad; it's like going out on a mission and waiting for the first shot.' He was, in their words, associating his violent impulses with death anxiety." Lifton further comments on the discussion of joy over alternate transgression: mutilating a corpse and dancing around the corpse (14). Lifton (11) has also referred to the pornography of death. Engendorf (15) has an excellent article on techniques for dealing with Vietnam era veterans of this type and suggests ways of treating them. It is a think-and-do- book describing method as well as background. Some of the techniques are somewhat like those of Wishnie (16) in working with aggressive patients in drug and mental health treatment programs. Both are valuable additions to our understanding and treatment of people with traumatic reactions, as well as persons with problems in controlling aggression.

The patient may not seek help from usual professional sources. He is often embittered and feels he is suspect by the insurance company, the Veterans Administration, the disaster relief agency, or other sources of possible help. Minor and major rebuffs as he toils through the layers of bureaucracy in all such agencies confirm his belief that he is not to be helped. Some form of therapeutic outreach is necessary. Informal interview, examination, and treatment sites are often more successful in attracting these patients. Use of churches, community centers, or nonmedical public buildings for the gathering place have been useful. Colleagues from service (or civilian disaster area) make good contact persons or ombudsmen.

Therapy must be direct, problem-oriented, and face-to-face. For many patients, group therapy with compatriots is more successful than one-to-one forms of therapy.

The patients must be encouraged to talk out their anger, guilt, and sadness. Timid therapists may find such sessions frightening, and such fears may be made known to the patient. The therapist must be active, responsive, and not abundantly analytical in a passive or noncommenting style used with other types of patients. Listening with active response and support are basic.

The patient's complaints about society's response to his complaints and symptoms must be reality-tested in open, frank discussions supporting the real grievance and confronting the fantasies and distortions. Adjustment to his current situation must be supported. His efforts to do for himself are to be encouraged, and growth in coping behavior and responsibility for himself is a major goal.

Our program in the Veterans Administration is to extend services as extensively as possible, with greater emphasis on ambulatory programs, and to teach our staff that veterans are to be treated for the symptoms they present rather than for presumed symptoms that would make them easier to manage in the particular treatment format. The difficulty involved in encapsulating and categorizing the manifestations of traumatic neurosis has been a large factor in its absence from the diagnostic rolls, and therapeutic approaches often must be as varied as the patients and the events that bring them to care.

REFERENCES

1. Freud, S. *Psycho-analysis and War Neuroses Viii,* Vol. 5, International Psychoanalytic library. London: Hogarth Press, 1919.
2. Auerbach, A., Scheflen, N., and Scholz, C. A questionnaire survey of the posttraumatic syndrome. *Dis. Nerv. Sys.* 28:110, 1967.
3. Selye, H. Confusion and controversy in the stress field. *J. Human Stress* 1 (2): 1975.
4. Bourne, P. *Men, Stress and Vietnam.* Boston: Little, Brown, 1970.
5. Mott, F. *War Neuroses and Shell Shock.* London: Oxford University Press, 1944.
6. Bourne, P. *The Vietnam Veteran in Contemporary Society.* Dept. Med. and Surg., Washington, D.C.: U.S. Veterans Administration, 1972.
7. Brill, N., Beebe, G., and Gilbert, *A Follow-up Study of War Neuroses.* VA Medical Monograph, National Research Council, January 1955.
8. Stenger, C. *American Prisoners of War. Washington, D.C.:* U.S. Veterans Administration, 1977.
9. Koranyi, E. Psychobiological corelates of battlefield psychiatry. *Psychiatric J. Univ. Ottowa* 2:3, 1977.
10. Lifton, R. On death and the continuity of life. *Omego* 6(2): 143, 1975.
11. Lifton, R., and Olsen, E. *Living and Dying.* New York: Praeger, 1974.
12. Figley, C. *Stress Disorders Among Vietnam Era Veterans.* New York: Brunner/Mazel, 1978.
13. Shatan, C. Delayed post-catastrophic syndromes in Vietnam veterans, concentration camp survivors and others. (Paper presented at the APA, Toronto, 1977.
14. Lifton, R. *Home from the War.* New York: Simon & Schuster, 1973.
15. Engendorf, A. Suggestions for psychotherapy with Vietnam veterans. In Figley and Figley, eds., *Stress Disorders Among Vietnam Era-Veterans.* New York: Brunner/Mazel, 1978.
16. Wishnie, H. *The Impulsive Personality.* New York: Plenum, 1977.

CHAPTER 5

How Much Anxiety is "Normal"?

Roy B. Mefferd, Jr.

INTRODUCTION

When I say that Mr. X is anxious, what exactly do I mean? He may be anxious *to:* read a book, have a happy marriage, live to an old age. Or he may be anxious *about* his inability to: make good grades, make a good impression in job interviews, relate well with the opposite sex, make ends meet. Or he may be anxious *because he fears* he will never learn to: pass tests or interviews, or write reports. Or he may be anxious *because of a real* or imagined difficulty in coping. On the other hand, he may *need situations to explain* his otherwise inexplicable tension, nervousness, ambivalence, dread. He may be anxious for *no apparent reason* at all. I may ask whether Mr. X is anxious now, is a little or very anxious, is seldom, often, or usually anxious. What state is he in when he is not anxious?

I. DOES ANXIETY FIT THE "NORMAL RANGE" CONCEPT?

Are anxious states temporary "attacks" springing from and returning to a fairly firm trait level, albeit more frequently or more easily in some than in others? Or is anxiety a "normal" state that oscillates about a trait level, more frequently or in larger swings in some than in others? Does unpleasant, clinical anxiety appear only when the attacks or swings are outside some normal range? Or do the attacks or swings become of clinical concern because they arise from such a high trait level that they are often, or even usually, outside this range? Do some people never have unpleasant anxious states? Are there two qualitatively different kinds of anxiety, one "normal" and the other "pathological" (1), or is the difference merely quantitative?

Anxiety is quite different from the situationally related emotions (e.g., anxiety has been differentiated from both fear and arousal [2], or as threats to self-esteem versus harm [3]). Most specific emotions are clearly adaptive in nature—act or withdraw; be open or cautious; be careful or carefree. Anxiety, on the other hand, does not provide such obvious survival advantages, although many theorists (4, 5, 6, 7) argued that some amount of anxiety has survival advantages. One construct (8) allows for oscillations back and forth from fear to excitement through the "protective ambivalence" of anxiety.

If my own conceptualizing has some basis in fact, then the medical concept of a normal range of anxiety has validity. An immediately relevant question is whether or not anxiety (i.e., apprehensive anticipation) is a state that has adaptive value in preparation for stress. We compared the responses of "normal," physically fit young males to the anticipation of, the experience of, and the recovery from a severe environmental stress— reduced atmospheric pressure (9, 10, 11, 12). This stressor elicits both the nonspecific stress response and predictable compensatory responses (13, 14, 15). While some "stressors" prepare the individual for a particular response (e.g., the "ready, " "get set" instructions preceding the "go" of a footrace result in massive anticipatory responses that are adaptive for the actual response following the "go" signal (16); others do not, even though this has been suggested (17). Our idea was that in naive subjects the differences between an apprehensive, anticipatory response to an unfamiliar and possibly traumatic stressor would be quite different form the actual stress itself. Further, this anxiety might intensify during stress (18). If the high level of sympathetic (S) activation in hypoxia (i.e., a highly ergotropically tuned state—EE/t [18, 19]) is overcompensated for by the parasympathetic (PS) activity, an adverse PS-dominant distress (i.e., a highly trophotropically tuned state—e/TT) results (e.g., the vasovagal reaction ranging from headaches to syncope).

Our anticipatory stressor consisted of a procedure to allay fear, but to generate a "healthy" dose of anticipatory anxiety (10). Subjects experiencing large anticipatory responses should be poor risks for stressful situations, and this occurred, but too little anticipation was also maladaptive. Among those subjects who developed very high anticipatory heart rates (HR), 3 fainted when their blood sample was taken and 13 had vasovagal reactions. These over-reacting subjects were in an obvious state of excitement (e.g., agitated, flushed, sweating, talkative) before the sudden reversal to confusion, vomiting, cold sweat, pallor, hyperactivity of gut and/or bladder, loss of muscle tone—the classical triad of an intense trophotropic reversal (19). The adrenal medulla was also activated, augmenting the already elevated norepinephrine. This alone can produce an E/T to e/T reversal (20). Subjects with very low anticipatory HR *also* had difficulty: eight had vasovagal reaction.

Of the 126 original volunteers, 19 percent suffered vasovagal reactions (all of these were at the HR extreme). The morale of these men was very high, and the conditions were such that once into the experiment, peer pressure was very strong to continue. This large number of anomalous responders demonstrated just how maladaptive an apprehensive, anticipatory anxiety may be (21, 22). The 74 subjects who did not become ill maintained their rank order HR positions during anticipation and stress, but their performance decreased with increased HR (10, 23).

States involving excitement, tenseness, or stress (24) need not be accompanied by an unpleasant affect. Likewise, unpleasantness is associated with many states and situations that do not involve anxiety. Just as different physical stressors induce different compensatory patterns, different specific affects probably do so as well (e.g., fight versus flight; fear-terror versus interest-excitement). Unlike these states, however, anxiety is a generalized state that need not be associated with any apparent stimulus. Dozens of objective measures (25) identified only two patterns of anxiety state responses—"anxiety" and "effort stress"—comparable with our work (9). We (10) concluded then that anxiety was evidence of only a part of a broader attention-appraisal-response organization system distinct from various supportive neural and endocrine systems. This view is in basic agreement with that of Tyrer (1). Any given physical stressor may require specific physiological compensatory responses that are antagonistic to the anxiety activation. However, I agree with Costello's view (7) that anxiety, even when unpleasant, is really an adaptive mechanism in that it causes the threatened individual to stop and explore the discrepancies between his capabilities and his aspirations to cope with the situation. In the case of people who experience maladaptive preparatory responses for stress, activation reversals promptly remove them from the danger (11). This concept of normal range is compatible with Spielberger's views (26) on trait-state anxiety.

We measured hundreds of variables of an ex-anxiety reaction patient for 120 consecutive days (27). His anxiety varied asystematically between periods of 1. extreme unhappiness, worry, disgust, nervousness, anger, hostility, irritability, and sympathetic-type complaints, and 2. either "friendly, cheerful, motivated" or "passive, ambivalent, unmotivated" and parasympathetic-type complaints. I shall discuss this negative correlation between unhappiness-anxiety and friendliness-clearheadedness later.

II. WHAT REALLY IS TRAIT ANXIETY (NEUROTICISM)?

Freud (and Kirkegaard before him) and Jung focused their microscopes squarely on two broad universal personality traits—neuroticism (anxiety) and extraversion, respectively. All major theorists today find and describe these same two traits regardless of how they do it or of what they name them. The observed correlations between the scales of various authors vary mainly for methodological reasons (28, 29, 30).

As they do with all other aspects of anxiety, the personality theorists disagree on details. The psychometric art has become so complex that only specialists with knowledge of complex multivariate statistics, and even of computer technology, can hope to understand the basis for most of these continuing disagreements. The debate revolves around whether to use questionnaires, behavioral ratings, or life history data; how many items must be used in each case; whether to use items that are highly or only moderately intercorrelated; whether to use the individual items of the instrument in defining scales, or to use grouped clusters of items; whether to use raw or scaled scores; whether to use intuitive, empirically derived scales, or to use only factor analytically derived scales; whether to achieve simple structure by orthogonal or oblique rotations; how many factors to rotate; whether one has inadvertently mixed primary and second-order factors, and on and on (31, 32, 33, 34).

Most authors agree that this trait has something to do with emotional stability (35), motivation (36, 37), responsiveness to arousal of the ANS (38), self-esteem and ego strength (39). Some have speculated that its antecedents were even broader.

Eysenck (35), in his Pavlovian-oriented dual arousal–activation hypothesis, viewed neuroticism (N) as being related to the functioning of a feedback loop between the visceral brain and the RAS. This loop regulated the autonomic-emotional arousal level. He postulated extraversion (E) as the result of another feedback loop between RAS and cortical areas relevant to the specific input. This latter loop regulated cortical activation and information processing. The two systems interacted, and in conjunction with external drive forces, established the overall level of cortical activation. He argued that both systems were of genotypic origin, and that the behaviors we observe as N and E are respectively the phenotypic expressions of the activities of these two systems.

We (40, 41) obtained results that led us to suggest some modifications of Eysenck's hypothesis. We proposed that N involved the degree and quality of control exercised over the energizing characteristics of behavior rather than merely over the level of arousal. We suggested that neurotics exercised little control over this. We also proposed that E involved not only the establishment of the level of activation and the rate of information processing, but also of the *strategy* used for exploration, acquisition, and analysis of information. Our extraverts used coarse-grained generalized strategies, which had the appearance of impulsive behaviors, while our introverts used fine-grained specific strategies, which appeared as inquisitive behaviors. We suggested that these two interacting systems, N and E, need not have a common link with RAS. We were very near the recent hypothesis of Pribram and McGuinness (42).

State anxiety relates *in some way* to the trait levels—relative intensities, relative thresholds, relative frequencies, relative durations. Certainly the risk of incapacitating anxiety increases with trait N level. The complexity of the relationship was shown by Reeves and May (43) in their learning study: high trait N accompanied high state anxiety, but at the low trait level, the relationship changed from that with a mere low state level to one of high responsiveness. We (44) observed the latter effect with our low N medical students—on anxious pre-examination days they had large increases in the excretion rates of both norepinephrine and epinephrine, relative to calm control days. On the other hand, our high N medical students actually had decreased excretion rates on their anxious days relative to calm control days. This result also agrees with those we obtained with an anxious subject during a 120-day experiment (27).

Cattell (28) has repeatedly pointed out that trait measures are confounded by the state of anxiety at the moment of measurement. Bianchi and Fergusson (45) noted a reduction in trait scores in neurotics after therapy. However, Bartsch (46) failed to alter trait scores either by instructions (i.e., "answer the question as you *generally* feel" versus "as you *presently* feel") or as a result of different situations that actually changed the state scores. A single anxiety factor was isolated in another study (47) even while a stress response was underway.

The difficulties enumerated above pale in the face of a new attack by interactional psychologists (48). These theorists are questioning the entire foundation of traditional personality theory. While traditionalists have long recognized the relevance of the *situation* to behavior, the interactionalists argue that the person-situation is *all-* important.

Without question personal and situational factors do interact to modify behavior. This makes it difficult to predict *exactly* how a particular person will react in a given situation. However, the vast literature of industrial and educational psychology is replete with reports of the high reliability with which we can predict how *most* people of a given personality type will react to *most* situations. A very large proviso must be placed on this assertion: predictability rests squarely upon a large, broad base of variance. The statement is *not* true for single scales of any kind (49), even where they may be second-order ones such as anxiety or N, as I shall discuss below. Even so, we could now predict how our particular anxious subject would react to many situations, knowing his N score (27).

Present personality theory is analogous to present clinical pharmacology theory. Lithium may be prescribed for manic-depressives in comfortable assurance that *most* of them will respond. Yet we also know that *some* patients will *not* respond. These exceptions do not invalidate the treatment any more than responses to specific situations invalidate personality measurements.

WHAT ARE THE LIMITATIONS OF THE CURRENT CONSTRUCTION OF TRAIT NEUROTICISM?

Typical neuroticism (N) scales impose limitations on considering anxiety according to a normal range model. Some of the reasons for this are discussed below.

1. Most current N scales are based on direct questions about feelings and symptoms. Questionnaire constructors generally have found that only straightforward questions about the presence of a given symptom "work." Attempts to disguise questions or to state them in the socially desirable direction usually fail. This exaggerates the influence exerted by the relative willingness of a person to admit his socially undesirable frailties. People with low self-esteem often admit everything, especially if they have been conditioned to do so as a first step toward relief from the anxiety. People with high self-esteem, justified or synthesized, are unlikely to damage their self-esteem by admitting either publicly or privately to neurotic tendencies.

Cattell (28) accepted these tendencies as part of the personality per se. But what of the denials of a truly low ego-strength person who would feel threatened for career or family purposes perhaps, if he admitted publicly—or even worse, privately—to well-guarded secret inner turmoil, as opposed to the case with our anxious subject in the 120-day experiment (27)? What of the highly capable, self-assured, hard-driving workaholic who sees no threat at all in acknowledging the problems with which he copes successfully? These two may have the same N score. What of the admitted alcoholic who is conditioned to acknowledge at every opportunity that "I am an alcoholic," but who all the same may not be highly neurotic? Work such as that of Miller and Magaro (50) provides a means out of this dilemma by suggesting other ways to ask our questions.

2. Most N scales are based largely on symptoms and feelings that hospitalized people experience during anxious states. Most of the wide range of symptoms of anxiety state involve various feelings, moods, bodily concerns, arousal, and feelings of tension that cannot be measured objectively. Thus self-reports about such symptoms are widely used. Because of the effects noted in Section I, the N score becomes mainly the sum of symptoms, "bad" feelings, or facets of "poor" self-esteem a person recognizes *and* is willing to acknowledge. Conversely, the fewer the symptoms admitted or experienced, the less neurotic a person is taken to be. A person who experiences or reports none of the symptoms is simply not neurotic.

The array of "bad" symptoms that presently characterize trait N are really bits and pieces of state anxiety, as we found in the longitudinal study I have mentioned (27). Such a scale is inadequate if the "real" N involves the effectiveness of activities such as *a.* response organization and delivery (including the associated planning, programming, mobilizing, retaining, improving activities); *b.* affect selection, organization, control and expression; and so on.

Because of the failure to provide for positions beyond the mere absence of symptoms on the nonanxious end, there is no way for one non-neurotic person to be more non-neurotic than another. We simply have not viewed as clinical entities a failure to associate *feelings* with *values* and *motives,* a deficiency of tension or drive, as failure to plan, program, review, and profit from past decisions and actions. We do not know how to categorize people who have more ego strength than the scale allows, who have fewer bodily concerns, less drive than any scale of practical length can provide. Are they egomaniacal? Callous? Accident-prone? Unlucky? Irresponsible? Lazy? We do not consider these symptoms as being indicators of maladies. Although the Miller and Magaro (50) approach suffers severely from not having a truly representative sample which included criterion maladjusted people, it still serves as a commendable model for the future.

3. The N scale not only bottoms out when no symptoms are admitted, but it also tops out whenever we stop listing feelings, ego concerns, and bodily symptoms. It simply is not practical to include in a questionnaire every possible symptom of something as vague as anxiety. Possibly all existing questionnaires or inventories measure only a part of the total "anxiety" spectrum, just as visible light is only a segment of the electromagnetic spectrum. Cattell (28), in particular, has attempted to attack this problem with more objective and direct physiological measurements of anxiety-related behaviors.

Different N scales are based on one of two methods of sampling for N— the criterion group approach (e.g., as used by Eysenck), and the representative sample approach (e.g., as used by Cattell). Theoretically, the latter approach has the advantage of pushing the low end of the scale down below a mere absence of symptoms. However, we do not yet know what questions would measure that end of the scale, so most scales still measure only the same upper end. Consequently, the results of different instruments intercorrelate highly, since the rank ordering of people within most systems of scaling anxiety is similar regardless of which part of the full range is sampled. So regardless of how we reify it, we remain locked to a clinical entity rather than to a full-range dimension of individual differences.

4. Related to the above comments, the N scales are treated as independent linear dimensions of individual differences. However, the two ends of this dimension may measure different things, as we (44) and others (43) have found. The admission of many neurotic symptoms is a different behavior from the failure to admit actual symptoms or from the actual absence of symptoms. Table 1 illustrates my point.

Table 1. Differences in discriminability of subjects with high or low neuroticism scores[1]

Categories	Discriminant p Values[2] Neuroticism Groups				Numbers of Subjects Neuroticism Groups	
	Self		Most People			
	Low	High	Low	High	Low	High
Hospitalized Chronically Ill Patients						
Addicts						
vs. Simple Schizophrenics	03	01	05	03	32x20	34x23
vs. Paranoid Schizophrenics	01	01	26	01	32x26	34x26
vs. Alcoholics	01	01	03	01	31x57	34x53
Alcoholics						
vs. Simple Schizophrenics	60	01	68	22	57x20	53x23
vs. Paranoid Schizophrenics	20	01	28	01	57x26	53x26
Schizophrenics:						
Simple vs. Paranoid	91	61[4]	79	73	20x26	23x26
Prisoner Groups[3]						
Group 1						
vs. Group 2	82	36	60	20	48x26	47x26
vs. Group 3	83	01	05	08	48x42	47x50
vs. Group 4	23	19[4]	39	06	48x49	47x50
vs. Group 5	83	67[4]	28	35	48x49	47x49

Group 2						
vs. Group 3	57	06	30	41	26x42	26x50
vs. Group 4	68	36[4]	67	13	26x49	26x50
vs. Group 5	62	26	70	04	26x49	26x49
Group 3						
vs. Group 4	29	01	66	23[4]	42x49	50x50
vs. Group 5	81	02	14	02	42x49	50x49
Group 4						
vs. Group 5	43	09	62	01	49x49	50x49

[1] The neuroticism scale of the Birkman Method (57).

[2] Multiple Discriminant Function Analyses (51) of the ten scales of the Birkman Method first for *Self*, then for *Most People*. Leading decimal omitted.

[3] Group 1 = multiple convictions for violent crimes.
Group 2 = a single savagely violent crime.
Group 3 = single conviction for a violent crime.
Group 4 = threat of violence only.
Group 5 = multiple convictions with no evidence in or out or prison of violence.

[4] Presented merely to show the trend.

The values shown there are the p values of two sets of multiple discriminant function analyses (51) comparing *a*. four clinical groups, including two kinds of chronic schizophrenics and chronic alcoholics, and hard-line long-time addicts receiving methadone, and *b*. five groups of prisoners categorized in terms of manifested violence and "chronicity" of crime. The latter were subsamples selected at random from larger groups so as to make the sizes of their groups about the same as that of the clinical groups. We distributed each group from low to high N scores, and withdrew the central 20 percent of each group so as to establish well-defined low N and High N subgroups. The scores used were from the N scale of the Birkman Method (to be described later). The discriminations were between either the Low N groups or the High N groups of the different categories within each series. Separate discrimination analyses were made on *Self* (personality) and *Most People* (social perception), using only the ten primary scales of the Birkman Method in each case. The important point to note from this table is that with the *Self* variables, half of the 16 high N group comparisons made discriminated at the .05 level, and two others were at the .09 level. Almost all had p values that were smaller than their low N counterparts. Among the low N groups, only the drug addicts discriminated from other groups. The clinical groups had also completed the Eysenck Personality Inventory (EPI) (52), so the analyses were repeated, using that N to separate the groups. The results were essentially identical to those obtained with the Birkman N scale.

With the *Most People* variables (i.e., of social perceptions), seven of the comparisons among the low N groups were significant, and two others had p's of .08. As the *Self* scores, most of the p values were lower than they were among the low N counterparts. Among the latter groups, drug addicts failed to discriminate from paranoid schizophrenics, but the low N habitually violent prisoners now discriminated from the once-only violent prisoners.

Part of the greater discriminatory power of the high end of the N scales lies in the increased opportunity for differences in clusters of neurotic symptoms to operate (e.g., tension versus body concern, apprehension versus high self-consciousness). However, an even greater factor lies in the interaction of N with the E scale. At zero N, a person's score on E is irrelevant vis-a-vis N. This person has no discriminable N characteristics. He simply cannot become less N, and whether he is an introvert or extravert will not influence his zero (or low) N score. However, Eysenck (35) has presented abundant evidence that high N scorers do interact with the E scores— hysterical patients had high E scores, anxiety reaction and depressive patients had lower E scores (ambiverted or introverted) (i.e., high N subjects were separated according to whether or not they had high or low E scores).

Thus the upper end of the scale fans out into the neurotic extravert (NE) and neurotic introvert (NI) territories, rather than lying neatly along a central axis. Cattell's oblique rotation techniques correct for only a part of this problem.

We (40,41,53) and others (e.g., 35,54,55) have stressed the necessity for considering N and E either simultaneously in an analysis or at least by separating the *Es* and *Is* for separate analyses of N-effects. An NE behaves quite differently from an NI. The Miller-Magaro cluster analysis demonstrated this point well—only the character disorder cluster failed to involve an interaction between N and E (50).

5. Another feature of self-inventory questionnaires is the high potential for "faking" the results. This is just as likely to be due to subconscious as volitional reasons. Many people do not "know" themselves, or they have suppressed "bad" or "weak" facets of their behavior, or they are deluding themselves about "good" or "strong" attributes. Most people want to be or to appear to be as compatible with the socially approved value systems of their culture as possible. Exceptions are the relatively rare people who truly don't give a damn and people in groups who have been conditioned to admit their faults (e.g., "I am an alcoholic!").

I agree with Cattell (28) that much of the behavior mentioned above is part and parcel of personality per se. However, if our interest is in how a person *really* feels and thinks, we must peer through an obscuring fog when we utilize an individual's self-reports about himself. Even experienced observers often fail to penetrate this fog.

We are using an indirect quasi-projective way to get at what a person really thinks about himself—an instrument in which people first answer a typical list of personality questions as they believe *most* people would answer them. Then on another page they answer the same questions as they apply to themselves—the Birkman Method (56-61). While this instrument is superficially similar to Leary's Interpersonal Check List (62), it actually is quite different.

Since I am going to describe briefly how we used this technique to explore the anxious-unfriendly relationship revealed in the longitudinal study I mentioned above (27), allow me to pursue the concepts involved a bit further.

Many authors have considered how a person projects his feelings, attitudes, and the like onto others. Few authors have discussed the opposite effect which Schachter (63) noted—"people evaluate their own feelings by comparing themselves with others around them." A person's perceptions may be coarse or fine-grained; superficial or detailed; accurate or grossly inaccurate. These same perceptual habits will apply to one's self as well as to most people. A coarse-grained, superficial, inaccurate perception of most people could operate to place one in either a very "good" or a very "bad" light. The predictive and interpretive power is in the interaction between the *Most People* and the *Self*.

Our hypotheses about how the interaction between *Self* (i.e., personality) and *Most People* (i.e., social perception) may influence behavior relating to N is based on the following speculations. A person who really has none of the neurotic symptoms (or at least who perceives them as being too mild or too rare to mention) has difficulty understanding other people who either do have these symptoms or have low tolerance thresholds for mild symptoms. To this low N person, almost everyone would appear to be neurotic—nervous, insecure, emotional worrywarts with all sorts of ailments which he would strongly suspect were imaginary. The low N person has a secure self-image, and while he enjoys praise, he would tend to take it for granted. His ego does not require constant bolstering. His typically calm, relaxed nature would have several consequences: relative to high N persons, he would tend to be content with routine activities, to exert no more effort than *he* felt necessary on any activity, and to value his time as much or more than material advantages. He would be mystified and perhaps disgusted by the restlessness, the "excessive" effort applied, the willingness to trade time for material benefits of an high N person.

Such social perceptions would tend to lead to attitudes about most people of indifference and impatience of their feelings and egos. Since he does not require praise and reassurance to support his own ego, he would see no need to praise or reassure others. Only "exceptional" behavior, good or bad, would ordinarily induce a low N to comment on another's activities. He would not want others "bothering" him continually about their activities, and accordingly, it would not even occur to him that others might need to be "bothered." However, he would tend to be critical and impatient with behavior he would consider as "wasted" or "useless" effort; with erroneous or "poor" results; with indecisive, compulsive, rigid, moody, irritable, argumentative behavior. He would probably be unconcerned or even contemptuous of the anger or hurt feelings his criticism might incur. Such responses from high N people would continually strengthen his determination not to be or to behave like neurotic people. Prolonged contact with high N people would probably not only change his questionnaire responses, but would increase his intolerance and widen the gap in interpersonal relations with low N people. I would expect him to begin to "look" even less neurotic, at the same time that his *Most People* would "look" more N.

On the other hand, a high N person, who really is nervous, emotionally labile, insecure, and plagued by all sorts of unpleasant problems, lives on the other side of the peak. If he looked carefully, almost everyone else *would* seem more calm, more secure, more self-confident, and less plagued by ailments and problems than he is. He could think that most people blunder through life with little planning or concern about the future. However, a high N person is so involved with himself that he may fail to perceive other people in fine detail. He may never have really analyzed other people at all.

The main things the high N person would tend to notice would be that most people seem unfeeling, cold, even callous about his feelings and needs. His fragile ego needs continual reinforcement. He would become acutely sensitive to criticism, searching for evidences of criticism to the point that mere absence of praise would assume threatening properties. He is likely to expend extra activities and time in searching for recognition and reward. He readily substitutes and justifies effort and time for quantity or quality of his accomplishments. His restlessness facilitates the development of a circularity in his activities such that work for work's sake may replace the quiet periods needed for planning, analysis, correction. His restlessness would also make routine activities distasteful, but at the same time his ambivalence and need for security would make constantly changing situations and activities threatening. His intense self-consciousness would make him so concerned with how he looks to others that he would concentrate so much on himself he would tend to lose empathy with others. Discussions become arguments in which he mainly thinks of his next point to be made rather than in listening and evaluating the points being made by others. His insecurity would encourage him to plan and rehearse for ensuing interpersonal encounters. His restless worrying would tend to drive him toward unrealistically high goals. His low ego strength would make it deadly important to win. Once his plan was launched, he would become so intent on its development that he would not be perceptive of negative reactions to the plan. Furthermore, his insecurity would make him most reluctant to make the rapid on-the-spot adjustments often needed to win. Overall, his moodiness, irritability, ambivalence, restlessness, and self-consciousness, make it difficult to win. Losing would reduce his self-esteem, making it more important than ever to protect his ego against further insults. He may react first to losing with anger-out, then later with chagrin and anger-in. He may find all sorts of objects or situations to blame for his failure, or he may simply become discouraged and move lower on his self-image scale.

The consequences of the high neurotic's often self-defeating behavior could be an increasingly moody, pessimistic, rigid, perseverating personality. Escapes of various kinds may become necessary. These may range from just getting away from things to adopting new facadelike life styles, fads, or hobbies to becoming actively religious, political, or the like. He may become either autocratic or withdrawn. He could become bitter and jealous about "undeserved" rewards others received "after all of his effort." He would build the walls of his ego-fortress higher as he increases his competence at finding everything but himself to blame for his shortcomings. When his fortress is breached, he suffers intensely.

A person who is at the midpoint of N (i.e., of the *Most People* distribution) will be in a position to "see" down both sides of the peak. He will observe some people who seem to worry more and have more problems than he does, but he will also see people who seem to be more self-confident, less careful about the future and less concerned about the past than he is. He may choose to side more with the high ego-strength group, but he is not likely to drift as far afield in self-delusion as will people who are more extreme toward either end of the scale.

The hypothesis was tested that groups with different mean levels of N would not differ in their scores on extraversion related scales. The high and low N groups that were shown in Table 1 were combined with the middle 20% for this comparison. The typical personality scores, *Self,* for the various groups are shown in Table 2 arranged according to their mean N scores. None of the groups can be considered to be "normal representative samples." The laborers were exceptionally low on N, while all the other groups were high on N. The mean educational level for all groups, except the alcoholics and students, was from the seventh (laborers and prisoners) through the ninth (clinical groups) to that of the students. The mean ages of all groups were between 18 and 21 years, except for the schizophrenics and alcoholics (30 and 31 years, respectively).

Three of the Birkman scales that correlate with extraversion are shown— Sociability. Insistence, Energy. The decreasing group means for these three extraversion-related scales is evident. The more "neurotic" a group is, the less sociable it is as a group.

Table 2. Comparison of Self Sociability, Insistence, and Energy of male groups varying on Neuroticism (N) scores

Groups	Birkman Self Scales (Raw Score Means)				
	No. in Group[2]	N Mean[3]	Sociability[4]	Insistence[4]	Energy[4]
Semi-skilled laborers:					
Good	140	6.1	8.9	10.8	7.8
Poor	140	7.8	9.2	10.3	7.3
Prisoners:					
Nonviolent	140	11.0	7.6	9.5	6.4
Violent	140	11.1	7.2	9.4	6.5
Schizophrenics:					
Paranoid	89	12.6	7.4	10.0	5.3
Simple	60	13.0	7.3	9.9	4.9
Alcoholics	154	13.5	7.1	9.0	4.4
Heroin, Addicts	90	14.8	7.0	7.3	4.6
Tenth-Grade Students	140	15.0	6.7	7.0	4.2

[1] Gratitude is expressed to Birkman and Associates, Inc., for the data on these subjects.

[2] Laborers and prisoners were selected at random from larger samples provided by Birkman and Associates; Inc., so as to yield approximately equal sample sizes.

[3] Birkman Self Neuroticism score (raw scores); maximum score = 24.

[4] Maximum scores: Sociability, 13; Insistence, 15; Energy, 11. A given item is used in only one primary scale.

Table 3. Comparison of the difference scores (Most People-Self) for three Birkman scales within nine male groups that varied on group means for Neuroticism (N) scores.[1]

Groups	Sociability		Insistence		Energy	
	High N	Low N	High N	Low N	High N	Low N
Semi-skilled Laborers:						
Good	-1.8	-0.8	-2.3	-1.6	-2.4	-2.4
Poor	-0.9	-0.7	-1.0	-0.8	-2.0	-1.5
Prisoners:						
Nonviolent	0.2	0.0	-0.8	-0.4	0.0	-1.2
Violent	0.5	-0.3	-1.0	-0.6	0.4	-0.9
Schizophrenics:						
Paranoid	1.1	-0.3	0.3	-0.6	0.8	-0.1
Simple	0.9	0.2	-0.4	-0.2	1.2	0.2
Alcoholics	0.6	1.0	0.1	-0.6	0.5	-0.9
Heroin Addicts	-0.7	-1.3	0.1	-0.5	0.5	-1.0
Students Tenth-Grade	-0.6	-0.1	-1.0	-0.4	-0.2	-1.5

[1]See Table 1 for footnotes.

The next question is whether the same applies to within group comparisons. Again, the high N and low N groups shown in Table 1 were used. The comparisons here are the difference between the *Most People* and *Self* scores for the three extraversion-related Birkman scales (Table 3). The laborers and students reported that *Most People* were less sociable, insistent, and energetic than they were. Since the students had scores more than twice those of the laborers, and they accordingly had lower sociability scores, their mean differences were also lower.

The non-normal groups differed from these groups in several predictable respects. The prisoners "saw" *Most People* as being about as sociable as they were, but as being more insistent, and the low N prisoners "saw" *Most People* as being less energetic than they were. The two categories of schizophrenics and the alcoholics were quite similar—*Most People* were more sociable and more energetic but less insistent than they were. All low N drug addicts "saw" *Most People* as less sociable, insistent, and energetic than they were. The high N drug addicts "saw" *Most People* as less sociable but more insistent and energetic than they were.

Thus, not only did groups that differed in mean N scores vary as the anxious man (27) had, but within the "normal" groups, as predicted, the more neurotic the subjects, the more unfriendly and insistent *Most People* were reported. The reports on energy were more independent of N. We cannot expand on the significance of the differences within and between the non-normal groups, but on the whole they were also in the predicted direction.

The power of the interaction between the *Most People* and *Self* reports is evidenced by these very group differences (e.g., in contrast to the schizophrenics and alcoholics, the prisoners "thought" that everyone was just like them on sociability, but *Most People,* naturally, were too insistent). We have found this interaction useful in gaining insight into the interpersonal relations between authority figures and their "clients"—counselor and client (64), and parole officer and parolee (65), and teacher and student (58).

SUMMARY

The concept was stressed that anxiety plays a natural compensatory role that under most conditions and in most people had adaptive advantages. It is the basis for caution, for the pause to reconsider, for the comparison of objectives and capabilities. It has a role in the regulation and application of drive, of motivation, or aspirations. It also plays a central role in the protection of our ego, our "self." Too little anxiety may be as serious as too much anxiety.

Anxiety can also be maladaptive. If the anxiety response pattern is antagonistic to the specific compensatory responses appropriate to various stressors, severe unpleasant physiological and mental effects may occur. If the cautionary, analytical process fails to lead to effective decisions at the appropriate time, or if minor insignificant events or thoughts trigger the process, debilitating churning, worry, tension, and feelings of dread may occur.

The relation of trait and state was discussed, and it was shown that current scales for trait anxiety or neuroticism have severe deficiencies in what they measure, in a lack of bipolarity, and in their lack of linear dimensionality. The consequences of these factors were shown to differences in the ability to discriminate between various clinical and social groups at the high and low ends of the scale. A strong negative relationship between the unhappiness of high anxiety-trait levels and friendliness was shown both within and between groups that varied markedly in mean neuroticism levels.

REFERENCES

1. Tyrer, P. *The Role of Bodily Feelings in Anxiety,* Maudsley Monograph. New York: Oxford University Press, 1976.
2. McReynolds, P. Assimilation and anxiety. In M. Zuckerman and C.D. Spielberger, eds., *Emotions and Anxiety: New Concepts, Methods, and Applications.* Hillsdale, N.J.: Laurence Erlbaum, 1976.
3. Hodges, W.F. The psychophysiology of anxiety. In M. Zuckerman and C.D. Spielberger, eds., *Emotions and Anxiety: New Concepts, Methods, and Applications.* Hillsdale, N.J.: Laurence Erlbaum, 1976.
4. Kierkegaard, S. *The Concept of Dread,* trans. Lowrie. New Jersey: Princeton University Pres,s 1944. (Originally published in Danish, 1884.)
5. May, R. *The Meaning of Anxiety.* New York: Ronald Press, 1950.

6. Grinker, R.R., Sr. The psychosomatic aspects of anxiety. In C.D. Spielberger, ed., *Anxiety and Behavior*. New York: Academic Press, 1966.
7. Costello, C.G. *Anxiety and Depression: The Adaptive Emotions*. Montreal: McGill-Queens University Press, 1976.
8. Izard, C.E., and Tomkins, S.S. Affect and behavior: Anxiety as a negative affect. In C.D. Spielberger, ed., *Anxiety and Behavior*. New York: Academic Press, 1966.
9. Mefferd, R.B., Jr. Catecholamines in high altitude stress—a correlational analysis. *Fed. Proc.* 22:684, 1963.
10. Mefferd, R.B., Jr., and Wieland, B.A. Comparison of responses to anticipated stress and stress. *Psychosom. Med.* 28:795-807, 1966.
11. Mefferd, R.B., Jr. Use of individual differences in personnel selection. In *Prediction and Understanding of Human Behavior*. U.S. Army materiel Concepts Agency, Report AMCA 71-010, 1971.
12. Mefferd, R.B., Jr., Hale, H.B., Shannon, I.L., Prigmore, J.R., and Ellis, J.P., Jr. Stress responses as criteria for personnel selection: baseline study. *Aerospace Med.* 42:42-51, 1971.
13. Hale, H.B., and Mefferd, R.B., Jr. Nitrogen and mineral metabolism at altitude. In W.H. Weihe, ed., *Physiological Effects of High Altitude*. London: Pergamon, 1964. From the Proceedings of International Symposium on the Physiological Effects of High Altitude. Interlaken, Switzerland, September 18-21, 1962.
14. Mefferd, R.B., Jr., and Hale, H.B. Altitude-indiced changes in plasma and urinary nitrogen and electrolyte constituents of rats. In W.H. Weihe, ed., *Physiological Effects of High Altitude*. London: Pergamon, 1964. From the Proceedings of International Symposium on the Physiological Effects of High Altitude. Interlaken, Switzerland, September 18-21, 1962.
15. Weihe, W.H., ed. *The Physiological Effects of High Altitude: A Symposium*. London: Pergamon, 1964.
16. Mitchell, J.H., Sproule, B.J., and Chapman, C.B. The physiological meaning of the maximal oxygen intake test. *J. Clin. Invest.* 37:538, 1958.
17. Bridges, P.K. Recent physiological studies of stress and anxiety in man. *Biol. Psychiat.* 8:95-112, 1974.
18. Teichner, W.H. Interaction of behavioral and physiological stress reactions. *Psychol. Rev.* 75:271-291, 1968.
19. Gellhorn, E. The neurophysiological basis of anxiety: A hypothesis. *Perspect. Biol. Med.* 8:488-496, 1965.
20. Nakao, H., Ballin, H.M., and Gellhorn, E. The role of the sino-aortic receptors in the action of adrenalin, noradrenaline, and acetylcholine on the cerebral cortex. *E.E.G. Clin. Neurophysiol.* 8:413-420, 1956.
21. Titchner, J.L., and Levine, M. *Surgery as a Human Experience*. New York: Oxford University Press, 1960.
22. Levi, L., ed. *Emotions—Their Parameters and Measurement*. New York: Raven Press, 1975.
23. Moran, L.J., and Mefferd, R.B., Jr. Repetitive psychometric measures. *Psychol. Rept.* 5:269-275, 1959.
24. Selye, H. Implications of stress concept. *N.Y. State J. Med.* 75:2139-2145, 1975.
25. Cattell, R.B., and Scheier, I.B. *The Meaning and Measurement of Neuroticism and Anxiety*. New York: Ronald Press, 1961.
26. Spielberger, C.D. Theory and research on anxiety. In C.D. Spielberger, ed., *Anxiety and Behavior*. New York: Academic Press, 1966.
27. Mefferd, R.B., Jr. State anxiety: 120 days in the life of a very anxious man. Unpublished manuscript.
28. Cattell, R.B. *Personality and Mood by Questionnaire*. San Francisco: Jossey-Bass, 1973.

29. Eysenck, H.J. *The Dynamics of Anxiety and Hysteria.* New York: Praeger, 1957.
30. Guilford, J.P. *Personality.* New York: McGraw-Hill, 1959.
31. Cattell, R.B., and Gibbons, B.D. Personality factor structure of the combined Guilford and Cattell personality questionnaires. *J. Personal. Soc. Psychol.* 9:107-120, 1968.
32. Guilford, J.P. Factors and factors of personality. *Psychol. Bull.* 83:802-814, 1975.
33. Guilford, J.P. Will the real factor of extraversion-introversion please stand up? A reply to Eysenck. *Psychol. Bull.* 84:412-416, 1977.
34. Eysenck, H.J. *Biological Basis of Behavior,* 3rd ed. Springfield, Ill.: Charles C Thomas, 1977.
35. Eysenck, H.J. *Biological Basis of Behavior,* 2nd ed. Springfield, Ill.: Charles C Thomas, 1967.
36. Laing, R.D. *The Divided Self: An Existential Study in Sanity and Madness.* Baltimore: Penguin, 1965.
37. Cofer, C.N., and Apley, M.H. *Motivation: Theory and Research.* New York: Wiley, 1964.
38. Lindsley, D.B. Emotion. In S.S. Stevens, ed., *Handbook of Experimental Psychology.* New York: Wiley, 1951.
39. Barron, F. An ego-strength scale which predicts response to psychotherapy. *J. Consult. Psychol.* 17:327-333, 1953.
40. Sadler, T.G., and Mefferd, R.B., Jr. The interaction of extraversion and neuroticism in human operant behavior. *J. Exp. Res. Personal.* 5(4): 278-285, 1971.
41. Sadler, T.G., Mefferd, R.B., Jr., and Houck, R.L. The interaction of extraversion and neuroticism in orienting response habituation. *Psychophysiology* 8(3):312-318, 1971.
42. Pribram, K.H., and McGuinness, D. Arousal, activation, and effort in the control of attention. *Psychol. Rev.* 182:116-149, 1975.
43. Reeves, R.A., and May, W.W. Effects of state-trait anxiety and task difficulty on paired-associate learning. *Psychol. Rept.* 41:179-185, 1977.
44. Roessler, R., Burch, N.R., and Mefferd, R.B., Jr. Personality correlates of catecholamine excretion under stress. *J. Psychosom. Res.* 11:181-185, 1967.
45. Bianchi, G.N., and Fergusson, D.M. The effect of mental state on EPI scores. *Brit. J. Psychiat.* 131:306-309, 1977.
46. Bartsch, I.W. A manipulation study of the effect of instructional set on the convergent and discriminant validity of questionnaire measures of trait-state anxiety: A comparative factor analytic approach. *Educ. Psychol.* 36:885-898, 1976.
47. Wadsworth, A.P., Jr., Barker, H.R., and Barker, B.M. Factor structure of the state-trait anxiety inventory under conditions of variable stress. *J. Clin. Psychol.* 32:576-579, 1976.
48. Magnusson, D., and Endler, N.E., eds. *Personality at the Crossroads: Current Issues in Interactional Psychology.* Hillsdale, N.J.: Laurence Erlbaum, 1977.
49. Mischel, W. *Personality and Assessments.* New York: Wiley, 1968.
50. Miller, I.W., III, and Magaro, P.A. Toward a multivariate theory of personality styles: measurements and reliability. *J. Clin. Psychol.* 33:460-466, 1977.
51. Morrison, D.F. *Multivariate Statistical Methods,* 2nd ed. New York: McGraw-Hill, 1976.,
52. Eysenck, H.J., and Eysenck, S.B.C. *Manual for the Eysenck Personality Inventory.* London: University of London Press, 1964.
53. Mefferd , R.B., Jr., Dickens, Dawson, N.D., and Lennon, J.M. Personality and interpersonal behavior: Effect of teacher-student personality interaction on student performance. Unpublished manuscript.

54. Zuckerman, M. General and situation-specific traits and states: New approaches to assessment of anxiety and other constructs. In M. Zuckerman and C.D. Spielberger, eds., *Emotions and Anxiety: New Concepts Methods, and Aplications.* Hillsdale, N.J.: Laurence Erlbaum, 1976.
55. Eysenck, H.J. Personality and factor analysis: A reply to Guilford. *Psychol. Bull.* 84:405-411, 1977.
56. Birkman, R.W. Development of a Personality Test Using Social and Self-Perception Inventories. Unpublished doctoral dissertation. University of Texas. Austin, Texas, 1961.
57. Birkman and Associates. *The Birkman Method.* Houston, Tex.: Birkman and Associates, 1972.
58. Justice, D.B., and Birkman, R.W. An effort to distinguish the violent from the non-violent. *So. Med. J.* 65:703-708, 1972.
59. Roessler, R., Collins, F., and Mefferd, R.B., Jr. Sex similarities in successful medical school applicants. *J. Am. Med. Women's Assoc.* 30:254-265, 1975.
60. Collins, F., and Roessler, R. Intellectual and attitudinal characteristics of medical students selecting family practice. *J. Family Pract.* 2(6): 431-432, 1975.
61. Dresden, J.H., Collins, F., and Roessler, R. Cognitive and non-cognitive characteristics of minority school applicants. *J. Nat. Med. Assoc. 7:321-323, 1975.*
62. Leary, T.F. *The Interpersonal Check List.* Berkeley, Calif.: Psychological Consultation Service, 1957.
63. Schachter,S. The interaction of cognitive and physiological determinants of emotional state. In C.D. Spielberger, ed., *Anxiety and Behavior.* New York: Academic Press, 1966.
64. Broussard, W.J., Sadler, T.G., and Mefferd, R.B., Jr. The Birkman Method: An industrial psychometric tool applied to vocational counseling and career planning for an ex-offender population. *Sociol. Absts.* 66:2444, December 1976.
65. Eissler, V.C., Sadler, T.G., Kirkpatrick, D.E., and Mefferd,R.B., Jr. Vocational potential: A comparison of inmates and free world workers via the Birkman Method. *Sociol. Absts.* 66:244, December 1976.

NOTES

[1]) *The Birkman Method* (57) is a proprietary instrument owned by Birkman and Associates, Inc., 3637 W. Alabama St., Houston, Texas 77027. I gratefully acknowledge the generous permission of Dr. R.W. Birkman, President, to use *The Birkman Method* in the studies mentioned, and for the access to their on-line data base of more than 38,000 people, as well as to the results from their total base of more than 80,000 people. In our experiments, largely unpublished as yet, we have found that the Birkman N scale has correlated from $r = .85$ to $.96$ with Eysenck's N scale, $.54$ to $.66$ with Cattell's second-order anxiety scale, and $-.55$ to $-.62$ with Barron's (38) ego-strength scale. Some of these correlations among prisoners (58) and medical students have been published (59, 60, 61). Inquiries about *The Birkman Method* should be made directly to Birkman and Associates, Inc.

CHAPTER 6

Suicide and Anxiety

Alex D. Pokorny

I. Introduction

As part of this comprehensive consideration of anxiety, I will review the topic of suicide as related to anxiety. My initial impression was that relatively little had been written on this topic, in spite of the fact that anxiety is probably the most common and central psychiatric symptom, and that suicidal behavior is itself widespread.

There is only a relatively modest literature on the anxiety-suicide relationship. This is particularly true if one restricts the consideration to completed suicide (as I will do), and omits attempted suicide and suicide ideation. However, three distinct areas emerge which are of potential interest:

1. The place of anxiety in the distressing psychopathological states preceding suicide.

2. Follow-up studies of anxiety neurotics for subsequent completed suicide.

3. The possibility that whatever prognostic importance anxiety has is due to its correlation with depression, pain, or psychosis. These three areas will form the outline of this chapter.

One of the common oversimplifications about suicide is that it always springs from depressive mental illness. It is more realistic to acknowledge that completed suicide is not all of one type. Even if we limit our concern to those suicides due to mental illness, there is suicide due to depression, suicide based on paranoid delusions, suicide due to panic, and so forth. Kubie (1) states that "suicide can occur at the end of many different roads." In his thorough review, Kubie lists and describes many formulas or mechanisms leading to suicide; there are two that include an anxiety component: 1. sudden terror of recurrence of psychosis; 2. "initial panics," occurring without warning in a seemingly calm and undisturbed life.

It is of interest to see what several leading psychiatry textbooks have to say about anxiety in relation to suicide. In the new ninth edition of Kolb (2), the section on anxiety disorders contains no mention of suicide; the section on suicide (pp. 131-134) has no mention of anxiety, though there is a reference to Barraclough's study of 100 completed suicides, of whom 3 had experienced a phobic anxiety state.

The *Comprehensive Textbook of Psychiatry,* 2nd ed (3), in the section on anxiety neurosis, makes no specific mention of suicide, although it mentions anxiety reaching "a degree of panic and terror that is far more unbearable... than the worst of physical pains. . . ." The section on suicide (Chap. 29.1) states that suicide "has been related to many emotions: hostility, despair, shame, guilt, dependency, hopelessness, and ennui"; also, "intolerable emotion," "insufferable anguish." There is no mention of anxiety as such.

The *American Handbook of Psychiatry,* 2nd ed (4), has a chapter on anxiety (Chap. 5, Vol. 3) that does not mention suicide. The discussions of suicide in Volume 3 and Volume 5 do not mention anxiety. Chapter 33 in Volume 3 does state that increased suicide risk may occur in any type of psychiatric illness.

Thus it appears that standard textbooks have very little to say about anxiety and suicide in relation to each other. The official view seems to be that they are unrelated.

II. The Place of Anxiety in the Psychopathology of Suicide

When one considers that anxiety is a central concept in psychodynamics and psychopathology and in the consideration of defense mechanisms in general, it is surprising that there is so little mention of anxiety in articles on dynamics of suicide. For example, in Hendin's work on suicide in Scandinavia (5), there is a chapter on the psychodynamics of suicide. This chapter presents many formulas, such as death as self-punishment, death as rebirth, death as retroflexed murder, and so forth, but there is no mention of anxiety as a contributing influence.

In writing about the suicide process, Breed (6) presents data from interviews with families and associates of 264 completed suicides. He deals with the subgroup of "failure suicides," persons who have failed in a major role. He stresses the influence of shame rather than guilt, and talks at length about what might be called self-derogation. There is no mention of anxiety in any of this. Lester (7) reviews the personality correlates of suicidal behavior; in an entire chapter on personality correlates of suicidal inclination, anxiety is mentioned only as part of a dysphoric state, along with depression and hostility. Under the discussion of affect, there is no mention of anxiety.

Farber (8) develops the theme that suicide is more closely related to the concept of hope than to any other construct. He defines hope as the "confident expectation that a desired outcome will occur." He stresses that man is a future-oriented animal, and that much of his world is one of expectations. He also brings in the concept of level of threat. "Suicide occurs when there appears to be no available path that will lead to a tolerable existence." Therefore, suicide is a running away from an unbearable situation. This discussion is of interest because it is future-oriented rather than past-oriented; the threat is from something anticipated. The issue of "future-oriented" versus "past-oriented" will be developed further in Section IV.

Lester (9) discusses the use of demographic versus clinical predictors of suicidal behaviors. He reviews many predictive scales. Prominent among these are: 1. DeVries' Inventory of 13 MMPI items. The only item in this group which taps anxiety is "Sometimes I am really very much afraid." 2. The Tuckman-Youngman and similar scales, none of which has any items suggesting anxiety. 3. The Los Angeles Suicide Prevention Center Scale. This includes one section of eleven symptoms, and one of these eleven is "agitation, tension, anxiety." Lester (7) has a chapter on attempts to predict suicidal risk using psychological tests. Anxiety or anxiety indicators are not mentioned. Poeldinger and coworkers (10) report on a study of suicide risk as related to MMPI scores, particularly on anxiety and depression measures. This was done with 37 depressive patients, 9 of whom had made suicide attempts. It was demonstrated that anxiety and depression were correlated with increased risk (evidently this is a concurrent judgment of risk based on other MMPI features, not a prediction verified by subsequent events). These authors bring out the close relationship of anxiety to depression, to be discussed in Section IV, as follows: "We obtained the following picture: depressive suicidal patients are very anxious, tense, and nervous. . . . Their emotional conflicts appear as somatic symptoms which are typical of anxiety and tension. These patients try to extract secondary gain from their symptoms, usually in the form of avoiding anxiety . . . There is a close connection between anxiety, lack of adjustment, and the risk of suicide." To repeat, this work is based on correlations with a concurrent rating of high suicidal risk.

Dr. Gilliland states in Chapter 16 of this volume that a theory of affects must precede a theory of anxiety. Gilliland describes anxiety as unpleasure associated with the idea that something bad is about to happen. He urges us, however, to think initially of undifferentiated pleasure and unpleasure.

Anxiety does not have a monopoly on mobilization of defensive operations." He urges substitution of the term "unpleasurable affects," for the concept of anxiety as the common target of defense mechanisms. From this point of view, anxiety and depression become more like equals, rather than one being primary to the other.

Dr. Gilliland is also the coauthor of a recent book on defense mechanisms (11). This volume presents in a succinct way the current thinking regarding psychodynamics and defense mechanisms. There are four mentions of suicide in the index. On page 87, completed suicide is interpreted as a turning against the self of hostility. On page 90, attempted suicide is interpreted as a possible attempt to get relief from tension; however, completed suicide is again interpreted as a turning of hostility against oneself. On page 142, it is mentioned that when feelings of hopelessness, worthlessness, and guilt develop and become unbearable, then suicide is common. On page 144, it is mentioned that rage turned against the self to an extreme degree may lead to completed suicide. Therefore, in this entire current summary and restatement of psychopathology and defense mechanisms, the state of anxiety is not linked to completed suicide in any section or statement.

It is often said that anxiety refers to future problems or threats, and that depression is related to past problems or losses (things that have already happened). This seems straightforward when we think of a subject at one point in time. However, it is a little difficult to apply this kind of thinking to longitudinal studies. Let us assume that we will pick up a cohort of subjects at one point in time, and will then follow them to see which individuals complete suicide. We will later try to "predict" suicide from the data available at time of intake. Let us say that at time of intake some patients showed depression (for whom some bad event had presumably already happened), and some showed anxiety (presumably those who are facing a threat of some possible bad event in the future). If both groups of subjects are then followed up for a couple of years, and some do complete suicide, how do we know that some anxiety cases may not have turned into cases of depression, because the feared stresses, losses, or setbacks may already have occurred? In such a case, would we say that this was a suicide occurring in a case of anxiety, or a suicide occurring in a case of depression?

III. Follow-up Studies of Anxiety States and Psychoneuroses in Relation to Subsequent Suicide

If anxiety is viewed not just as a symptom but as a psychiatric syndrome or disease state (anxiety state, anxiety neurosis), then it is of interest to see what the suicide rate of such patients would be on follow-up. It has already been mentioned (4) that the suicide rate appears to be elevated for all psychiatric disorders.

One problem rapidly emerges when one looks into the literature on this topic. Virtually all of the references are in terms of the broader category "psychoneurosis," rather than being limited to anxiety neurosis. It is my impression, from most settings where I have worked, that anxiety neurosis is the most common type of neurosis, and that in fact the majority of cases of psychoneurosis are diagnosed as anxiety neurosis. If this is true generally, then we might properly make some inferences regarding suicide in anxiety neurosis from a review of reported findings for psychoneurosis.

Levy and Southcombe (12), in reviewing suicide in a state hospital for the mentally ill, report a total of 58 suicides occurring during a 60-year span in one state hospital. None of the subjects had a diagnosis of anxiety reaction, but one carried a diagnosis of reactive depression, presumably classified as a psychoneurosis. Sletten and Altman (13) report on suicides within the entire Missouri state hospital system during a 10-year period. They expressed their findings in terms of rates per 10,000, and the highest rate was for "neurotic depression," with 31 per 10,000 per year (310 per 100,000 per year). There is no mention of any rate for anxiety disorders.

One of the best reports in the literature is the study by Temoche and associates (14). These authors identified some 1,500 suicides among residents in Massachusetts during a three-year period, and matched these names against the files of the Department of Mental Health to identify which of these subjects had been in state, private, and VA mental institutions in Massachusetts. From this procedure they derived many findings of interest, including standard mortality ratios for suicide (the standard mortality ratio is a way of comparing a given suicide rate to a standard rate: the rate for the general population is set at 100). Psychoneuroses had a standard mortality ratio of 1840, which was the second highest category, after depressive psychosis, which had a standard mortality ratio of 3610. The psychoneurosis category, however, is not further broken down.

Kerr, Schapira, and Roth (15) report on a follow-up study of "affective disorders in relation to premature death from all causes." They followed up 135 cases and were able to trace 128. They give a breakdown of "affective disorder" patients, which includes 40 subjects with a phobic anxiety depersonalization state, 32 subjects with a simple anxiety state, 25 subjects with an endogenous depression, and 31 subjects with a reactive depression. These subjects were followed up four years later, and there were found to be two suicides, both in male patients with anxiety state diagnoses. If this finding is converted to rates, then male patients with anxiety states would have a suicide rate of 1,786 per 100,000 per year. If the entire anxiety group is used as a basis for computation, then the suicide rate is a still high 694 per 100,000 per year.

Greer and Cawley (16) report on a fourteen-year follow-up of a group of 175 neurotic subjects (56 male, 119 female). Of these 175 subjects, 48 were diagnosed as anxiety reaction and 6 as phobic reaction, whereas 62 were diagnosed as neurotic depressive reaction, 23 as obsessive-compulsive, 17 as hysterical, and 19 as mixed neurotic reaction; therefore, approximately 60 or just under half might be said to be anxiety cases. After a follow-up period of four to six years, there were 4 completed suicides. If we assume that the average follow-up period was five years, this would yield a suicide rate of 457 per 100,000 per year. These authors do not report the neurotic category to which these 4 suicides belonged. These authors also provide an extensive literature review of publications up to 1966. This included these two foreign-language references. Ljungberg (Ljungberg, L. *Acta Psychiatrica Scandinavica,* Supplement 112, 1957) investigated all patients admitted to the University Psychiatric Clinic at Stockholm between 1931 and 1945 with a diagnosis of hysteria. His final figures included 381 patients, 135 males and 246 females. Five years after discharge, 5 of these patients had committed suicide. This yields a rate of 262 per 100,000 per year. Greer and Cauley also cite a study by Ernst (Ernst, K. *Die Prognosen der Neurosen,* Monogr. Neurol. Psychiat. No. 85, 1959). Ernst interviewed a series of 120 psychoneurotic patients who had attended the University Psychiatric Polyclinic in Zurich twenty years previously. Of the starting group of 120 patients, 4 had committed suicide. This yields a suicide rate of 166 per 100,000 per year.

Pitts and Winokur (17) studied 748 consecutive admissions of white patients to the Renard Hospital in St. Louis. These were diagnosed according to the APA standard nomenclature. The authors then identified the cases with a family history of completed suicide. Of the 37 patients with such a history, 25 had been diagnosed as having an affective disorder, and only one had been given a diagnosis of anxiety reaction.

Sims (18) did a twelve-year follow-up of 157 patients with neurosis, focusing on mortality. It was found that 3 of these had died from suicide, and in 5 others the death might have had a suicidal component. The suicide deaths represented 15% of the total deaths. This would translate to a suicide rate of 159 per 100,000 per year. This author states that "suicide occurs with increased frequency in all neuroses—not only in neurotic depression."

In a later report, Sims (19) gives a general discussion of prognosis in the neuroses, and again states that there is an excess death rate for neurosis, and that this is increased in those who are more severely neurotically disturbed. There is also an increased risk of alcoholism and drug dependence.

Moss and Hamilton (20) report on a follow-up of 50 patients of mixed diagnosis who had been hospitalized for serious suicidal attempts. This follow-up ranged from two months to twenty years, and averaged four years; 11 patients had committed suicide. Although actual numbers are not given, the authors state that "each diagnostic category showed about the same percentage of recoveries and of suicides."

Robins and associates (21) did a pioneering and influential study in which they investigated all of the suicides occurring in St. Louis, Missouri, during a one-year period, by interviewing close friends or relatives within a few weeks or months after the suicide. These investigators also interviewed other associates and obtained hospital records, police records, and other sources of data. On the basis of this information, they arrived at a retrospective diagnostic classification. None of these subjects was given a diagnosis of anxiety reaction or neurosis, although a total of 25 subjects were listed as "undiagnosed but psychiatrically ill."

Barraclough and associates (22) reviewed 100 suicides as defined by a coroner at inquests, largely from consecutive samples. They then did an extensive household interview and search of documents. Diagnoses were then given by a panel of three psychiatrists. Under this procedure, 93 of the 100 suicides were diagnosed as mentally ill; 70% were diagnosed as having depressive illness, and 15% as being alcoholics. Three of the 93 diagnosed subjects were given a diagnosis of phobic anxiety state. These authors also listed the frequency with which a list of 58 symptoms had been mentioned by informants as having been present in the subject. Some of the most common ones were: insomnia, 76%; weight change, 66%; looked miserable, 69%. Those symptoms which might be related to anxiety disorders scored as follows: looked anxious, 60%; difficulty in concentration, 35%; restless, 34%; complained of anxiety, 31%; trembling and shaking, 24%. The authors state that the 3 cases of phobic anxiety states were all relatively young married people. They had anxiety symptoms of such a degree that their domestic and social lives had been severely affected. All required daytime sedation, and all had seen psychiatrists. Furthermore, the two women subjects were also dependent on barbiturates, and the male subject drank heavily. Two of the suicides occurred after loss of keenly anticipated jobs, and one after the loss of a boyfriend.

Rennie (23) reported on a follow-up of 240 hospital-treated psychoneurotic patients followed up for a period of twenty years. The sample included 50 cases each of anxiety neurosis, hysteria, hypochondriasis, obsessive-compulsive states, and various fatigue states and motor neuroses. Ten of the 240 psychoneurotic patients committed suicide, which the author reports as being more than 40 times the rate for the general population during the same decade. The suicide group included 3 hypochondriacal patients, 2 neurasthenics, 2 obsessives, 2 hysterics, and 1 anxiety case. By my calculations, the total psychoneurotic group would have had a suicide rate of 208 per 100,000 per year, whereas the anxiety neurosis group would have had a suicide rate of 100 per 100,000 per year.

I have done a number of follow-up studies of psychiatric patients which include information on diagnosis. In one study of 44 former patients who had committed suicide (24), it was found that 9 of the 44 subjects had had a primary diagnosis of neurosis, although some also had associated alcoholism. As part of the same study, I inquired of 17 staff and resident psychiatrists, those who had been the last physicians of the study patients, to list those characteristics of a psychiatric patient that would lead them to consider the patient as suicidal. Twenty-nine separate symptoms were mentioned. The most commonly mentioned, in order, were: moderate or severe depression, talk about possible suicide, previous suicidal attempts, ideas of worthlessness, severe guilt feelings, feelings of hopelessness, withdrawal, and insomnia. There was only one indicator mentioned which suggested anxiety: "overwhelming panic."

In another sample, I (25) studied a list of 117 completed suicides in relation to the psychiatric inpatient group from which these cases had arisen, a total of over 11,000 first admissions. From a calculation of numbers of cases in each diagnostic group and total time at risk, it was possible to derive suicide rates. The suicide rate for the total patient group was 165 per 100,000 per year. The rate for the neurotic group was somewhat lower, 119 per 100,000 per year. The highest rate was for depressive disorders, 566 per 100,000 per year.

In another study, I (26) followed up 618 veteran patients who had initially been seen because of suicide attempts or suicidal ideation. After a follow-up period of 1 month to $14^1/_2$ years, averaging 4.6 years, I found that 21 subjects or 3.4%, all males, had committed suicide. By computation of man-years of risk for each case and summing of these by diagnostic categories, I could derive rates. The suicide rate for neurosis cases was 241 per 100,000 per year, whereas the rate for the total group of suicidal patients was 740 per 100,000 per year.

My associates and I are continuing our major prospective study of 4,800 consecutive psychiatric admissions to the Houston VA Hospital (27). These are still being followed up, for a period now averaging $4^1/_2$ years. To date, 63 completed suicides have occurred in this group, yielding an overall suicide rate of 292 per 100,000 per year. There are 400 subjects in this study with a diagnosis of psychoneurosis (the round number is fortuitous); 3 suicides have occurred in this group, giving a suicide rate of 167 per 100,000 per year (about the same range as other reports for psychoneurosis). We next broke this down by type of neurosis. One of the completed suicides had a diagnosis of anxiety reaction, and two were diagnosed depressive neurosis. The total cohort of 4,800 subjects included 216 subjects with anxiety neurosis and 116 subjects with depressive neurosis. This yields suicide rates of 102 (per 100,000 per year) for anxiety neuroses and 383 for depressive neuroses.

Brill and Beebe (28) reported a massive study in which they followed up 1,475 war veterans who had been diagnosed as having psychoneurosis in the year 1944. The authors mention that the psychoneurosis group included all of the usual diagnoses, presumably in the proportion in which they occurred randomly, but the report does not give exact numbers for subtypes, as for anxiety neurosis, nor does it identify in which subtype the suicides occurred.

By the time of the first attempt to locate the 1,475 subjects (after a lapse of three years), 2 had died by suicide. During the following year, while the study was being organized, there was another suicide. By 1953, or approximately nine years after the intake, there had been 6 suicides, which the authors indicate is 3 times the number expected in the general population. (By my calculations, this would yield a suicide rate of 45 per 100,000 per year.) The authors also tabulate the symptoms found to be present at time of follow-up, and anxiety is the most common (45%), with depression the next most frequent (30%).

This same group of subjects was reported on in terms of mortality after an elapsed period of twenty-four years (30). This report covers the entire initial group of 9,813 psychoneurotics and 9,942 control subjects discharged from military service at the same time. A breakdown by subtype of neurosis lists 3,407 subjects with anxiety type (35%), another 399 with neurasthenia or neurocirculatory asthenia (4%), and 3,570 with "mixed type" psychoneurosis (36%). After twenty-four years there had been 74 suicides in the psychoneurosis group compared to 24 in the control group, a ratio of 3.15 to 1. Unfortunately, the subtype of neurosis is not given for the suicides. The 74 suicides in 9,813 psychoneurotic subjects in twenty-four years yields a rate of 31.4 per 100,000 per year.

Summarizing all of these studies, it appears that the suicide rate in neurosis is definitely elevated as compared to the general population. It appears to run in the range of 100-300 per 100,000 per year. This should be compared to the overall population rate of about 12, and the general rate for adults, which would probably be from 15 to 20. There is only fragmentary information on patients diagnosed as having anxiety reactions. Furthermore, in some of these reports there have been complicating disorders such as alcoholism or drug dependence, both of which are known to have high suicide rates; nevertheless, these fragmentary reports are consistent with the view that suicide rates in anxiety disorders are about the same as in the total group of neuroses.

IV. The Correlation of Anxiety with Depression in Prediction of Suicide

It is well known that there is a strong relationship between suicide and depression. At the same time, anxiety and depression are often present together; therefore, there might be a significant relationship between anxiety and suicide merely because of their common relationship to depression. As already mentioned, some authors prefer to talk of dysphoric affects more broadly. Motto (30), for example, states that "the common denominator of all the factors conducive to suicide is psychic pain." He stresses that no diagnostic category is free of this.

When one speaks of suicide and anxiety disorders, the definition of anxiety becomes all important. If we define anxiety neurosis very narrowly and think of it as a hereditary and lifelong condition, as in the view of Pitts (personal communication), what would be the suicide rate of such a group? To my knowledge, this has never been studied; thus no data are available. The question therefore arises whether the presence of a significant number of completed suicides in the ranks of neuroses may not be simply the result of poor diagnosis. It seems plausible that cases of depressive disorder, schizophrenia, or alcoholism may be misclassified as neurosis. Furthermore, one needs to differentiate between acute states of anxiety, such as might accompany situational upheavals, and the chronic enduring anxiety of anxiety neurosis.

It appears that during the past decade there has been an increasing emphasis on the category of affective disorders. This may be related to the introduction of lithium and the resulting greater sensitivity to affective elements in psychiatric illness. It is also a result of the increasing attention being paid to explicit diagnostic criteria, such as those which are being included in DSM-3 (31). It is my impression that this new system will have the effect of moving into the category of affective disorder a substantial number of patients who would have previously been diagnosed as psychoneurotic. For example, the description of major depressive disorder includes under "onset and predisposing factors" the statement: "In some instances, prodromal symptoms which include generalized anxiety, panic attacks, phobias, or mild depressive symptoms, may occur over a period of several months." Evidently if the person later develops essential features of affective disorder, this would be thought of as a case of depression from the beginning.

In the DSM-3 draft of April 15, 1977 (32), Chapter G, anxiety disorders, there is the statement: "A diagnosis of anxiety disorder is not made if the manifestations of the anxiety are symptomatic of a more pervasive disorder, such as schizophrenia or affective disorder." In line with this, the symptoms listed under generalized anxiety disorder do not include depression. In contrast, the discussion of affective disorders does mention under "associated features" feelings of anxiety, fearfulness, panic attacks, and phobias. It seems clear that this new nomenclature will result in a shift in diagnostic category for many anxious patients.

The correlation between depressive and anxiety syndromes has been stressed in the writings of Overall and coworkers (33). One of his three depressive types, based on factor analytic studies of BPRS ratings, is the category of "anxious depression."

The Zung Depression Scale does not include within its twenty items any one item directly measuring anxiety unless we were to include psychomotor agitation. The Hamilton Depression Scale does include an item, "anxiety, psychic." The Feighner criteria for affective disorders do not include any items suggesting anxiety except for "agitation." The Zung Anxiety Scale, however, does include a list of symptoms which Zung labeled "affective symptoms."

Aside from the issue of changes in diagnostic or classification systems, there remains the real possibility that the clinical picture of a patient may actually change. This has already been alluded to, on a speculative level, in connection with the "feared event" having actually occurred during the follow-up period.

In a follow-up study of 111 non-hospitalized depressed patients for fourteen years, Ziegler and Heersma (34) report 7 patients who died by suicide, and they provide some information on the interval history. They report that one patient committed suicide after he had "become panicky and intensely anxious." Purely from a syndrome standpoint, we might say that this person had shifted from depression to a state of anxiety.

The follow-up of 240 hospital-treated psychoneurotics by Rennie already cited (23) mentions that a number of the anxiety neurosis cases required subsequent hospitalization for conditions other than anxiety. Five of the 50 cases developed subsequent depression. "One patient admitted at the age of 30 with anxiety had a previous history of 4 months depression at 23, and ultimately committed suicide at 50." Another patient, "recovered from her anxiety state, remained well for 19 years, and then developed cancer phobia and an agitated depression." Two other patients were subsequently hospitalized for clear-cut depressions. In addition, 3 of the 50 anxiety cases were later hospitalized for schizophrenic conditions. All of this makes one recognize that diagnostic groupings, at least under our present methods, are not necessarily valid classifications for the indefinite future.

V. SUMMARY

1. Considering the importance, when viewed separately, of anxiety and suicide in psychiatry, there is a surprisingly small amount of literature about their relationship.

2. Anxiety receives minimal emphasis in all writings about the dynamics and mechanisms (of suicide.)

3. In anxiety neurosis (although this is often not separated from the general category of psychoneurosis), it appears that the suicide rates are substantially elevated above those in the general population, but are not as high as rates in affective disorder, alcoholism, and schizophrenia.

4. The whole issue is clouded by the unreliability and lack of systematization of psychiatric diagnosis. It appears that under DSM-3 many cases that would have formerly been diagnosed as anxiety neurosis of psychoneurosis will be diagnosed as affective disorder. It remains to be seen what effect this will have on suicide rates, but it seems likely that suicide rates in the residual psychoneurosis categories would be much lower.

REFERENCES

1. Kubie, L.S. Multiple determinants of suicide, in E. Schneidman, ed., *Essays in Self-Destruction.* New York: Science House, 1967.
2. Kolb, L. *Modern Clinical Psychiatry,* 9th ed. Philadelphia: W.B. Saunders, 1977.
3. Freedman, A., Kaplan, H., and Sadock, B., eds. *Comprehensive Textbook of Psychiatry.* 2nd ed., Vols 1-2. Baltimore: Williams & Wilkins, 1975.
4. Arieti, S., ed. *American Handbook of Psychiatry,* 2nd ed. New York: Basic Books, Vols. 1-3, 1974; Vols. 4-6, 1975.
5. Hendin, H. *Suicide and Scandinavia.* New York: Grune & Stratton, 1964.
6. Breed, W. The suicide process. In N. Farberow, ed., *Proceedings, Fourth International Conference for Suicide Prevention,* Los Angeles: Delmar, 1968.
7. Lester, D. *Why People Kill Themselves.* Springfield, Ill.: Charles C. Thomas, 1972.
8. Farber, M. Suicide and hope: A theoretical analysis. In N. Farberow, ed., *Proceedings, Fourth International Conference for Suicide Prevention.* Los Angeles: Delmar, 1968.
9. Lester, D. Demographic versus clinical prediction of suicidal behaviors. In A. Beck, H. Resnik, and D. Lettieri, eds., *The Prediction of Suicide,* Bowie, Md.: Charles Press, 1974.
10. Poeldinger, W., Gehring, A., and Blaser, P. Suicide risk and MMPI scores, especially as related to anxiety and depression. *Life Threatening Behavior* 3:147-153, 1973.
11. White, R., and Gilliland, R. *Elements of Psychopathology: The Mechanisms of Defense.* New York: Grune & Stratton, 1975.
12. Levy, S., and Southcombe, R. Suicide in a state hospital for the mentally ill. *J. Nerv. Ment. Dis.* 117:504-514, 1953.
13. Sletten, I., and Altman, H. Suicide in mental hospital patients (abstract). *Scientific Proceedings, 124th Annual Meeting of the American Psychiatric Association,* Washington, D.C., 1971.
14. Temoche, A., Pugh, T., and MacMahon, B. Suicide rates among current and former mental institution patients. *J. Nerv. Ment. Dis.* 138:124-130, 1964.
15. Kerr, T., Schapira, K., and Roth, M. The relationship between premature death and affective disorders. *Brit. J. Psychiat.* 115:1277-1282, 1969.
16. Greer, H., and Cawley, R. *Some Observations on the Natural History of Neurotic Illness.* Australian Medical Association Medical Monograph No. 3, Sydney: Australian Medical Publishing, 1966.
17. Pitts, F., and Winokur, G. Affective disorder III. Diagnostic correlates and incidence of suicide, *J. Nerv. Ment. Dis.* 139:176-181, 1964.
18. Sims, A. Mortality in neurosis. *Lancet* ii:1072-1075, 1973.
19. Sims, A. Prognosis in the neuroses. *Am. J. Psychoanal.* 37:155-161, 1977.
20. Moss, L., and Hamilton, D. The psychotherapy of the suicidal patient. *Am. J. Psychiat.* 112:814-820, 1956.
21. Robins, E., Murphy, G., Wilkinson, R., Gassner, S., and Kayes, J. Some clinical considerations in the prevention of suicide based on a study of 134 successful suicides. *Am. J. Public Health* 49:888-899, 1959.
22. Barraclough, B., Bunch, J., Nelson, B., and Sainsbury, P. A hundred cases of suicide: Clinical aspects, *Brit. J. Psychiat.* 125:355-373, 1974.
23. Rennie, T. Prognosis in the psychoneuroses: Benign and malignment developments. In P. Hoch and J. Zubin, eds. *Current Problems in Psychiatric Diagnosis.* New York: Grune & Stratton, 1953.
24. Pokorny, A. Characteristics of forty-four patients who subsequently committed suicide. *Arch. Gen. Psychiat.* 2:314-323, 1960.
25. Pokorny, A. Suicide rates in various psychiatric disorders. *J. Nerv. Ment. Dis.* 139:499-506, 1964.

26. Pokorny, A. A follow-up study of 618 suicidal patients. *Am. J. Psychiat.* 122:1109-1116, 1966.
27. Pokorny, A. Suicide in depression, In W. Fann, I. Karacan, A. Pokorny, and R. Williams, eds., *Phenomenology and Treatment of Depression.* New York: Spectrum Publications, 1977.
28. Brill, N., and Beebe, G. *A Follow-up Study of War Neuroses.* VA Medical Monograph, Washington, D.C., 1955.
29. Keehn, R., Goldberg, I., and Beebe, G. Twenty-four-year mortality follow-up of army veterans with disability separations for psychoneurosis in 1944, *Psychosom. Med.* 36:27-46, 1974.
30. Motto, J. Suicidal Patients in Clinical Practice. Weekly Psychiatric Update Series #18, 1977.
31. Spitzer, R., Endicott, J., Woodruff, R., and Andreasen, N. Classification of mood disorders. In G. Usdin, ed. *Depression: Clinical, Biological, and Psychological Perspectives.* New York: Brunner/Mazel, 1977.
32. Spitzer, R., Cantwell, D., Clayton, P., et al. DSM-3 Draft 4/15/77, American Psychiatric Association, Washington, D.C.
33. Overall, J., Hollister, L., Johnson, M., and Pennington, V. Nosology of depression and differential response to drugs. J.A.M.A. 195:946-948, 1966.
34. Ziegler, L., and Heersema, P. A follow-up study of one hundred and eleven non-hospitalized depressed patients after fourteen years. *Am. J. Psychiat.* 99:813-817, 1942.

CHAPTER 7

Recognition and Treatment of Anxiety in Children and Adolescents

Larry B. Silver

INTRODUCTORY CONCEPTS

A mother calls requesting advice on handling her son. He refuses to leave her, clinging to her when she tries to go. He will scream or have a tantrum if left alone. What advice would a mental health professional offer? Would the answer be different if this son was 1 year old? $2^1/_2$ years old? 8 years old? 14 years old? 26 years old? Whether the described behavior is normal or not would depend on the son's age. One can generalize about adult behavior. The behavior of children and adolescents can only be understood from a developmental view. The uniqueness of the individual from birth to adulthood with the ever-changing physical, physiological, psychological, and social norms must be kept in perspective in assessing what is normal or pathological. For each age the child and adolescent perceives and responds to his or her environment differently and with different resources.

This developmental concept is equally important when using a historic approach to understanding adult behavior. A 32-year-old depressed woman mentions that her parents divorced when she was a child. This information has no meaning unless the therapist asks her age at the time of the divorce. Only then can one suspect how she perceived this event; what effects it might have had on her; the types of defense mechanisms and coping techniques available to her.

Anxiety is usually defined as an unpleasant feeling or affect with an associated sympathetic nervous system response. Anxiety is often distinguished from fear on the basis that anxiety is a response to a subjective, and fear is a response to an objective, danger. With either, the psychological and physiological responses are the same. How children respond to external objects is compounded by their imagination. A boy's father may appear to be pleasant and nonthreatening. Yet a 5-year-old might have fantasies in which Father is threatening and thus anxiety provoking.

Sigmund Freud's modified concept of anxiety regarded it as a reaction of the ego to danger, no matter what the source or kind of danger (1). Anxiety with children and adolescents might occur if: 1. the ego is increasingly flooded with excessive stimulations from internal or external sources; 2. the ego is suddenly and without warning overcome with internal or external stimulation; or 3. the usual defense mechanisms or coping techniques are not available to assist the ego in handling these stimuli.

Before specifically discussing the recognition and treatment of anxiety in children and adolescents, I should briefly review normal development. This developmental model will be necessary to later discuss the sources of anxiety (danger situations), the types of responses a child or adolescent might have to such stress, and the possible therapeutic interventions.

NORMAL PSYCHOSOCIAL DEVELOPMENT

The newborn infant functions primarily as a physiological being, receiving stimuli from his or her body and senses and responding. During these early few months the child is unrelated to anyone and undefined from the environment. As the child perceives the world, there is no differentiation between his or her body and the environment. The baby's stomach hurts; he cries; he is fed, causing the discomfort to go away; and he relaxes and sleeps. I will graphically illustrate this stage of development by letting a small circle represent the child and a larger circle represent the parenting person(s) (objects).

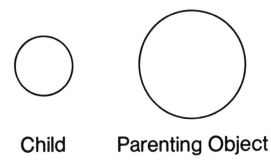

Child   Parenting Object

Gradually the infant begins to discover boundaries. He or she discovers fingers, hands, toes, and feet and finds that these objects belong to the same body that he or she has begun to experience. By three months the infant recognizes pieces or parts of the world and relates to these "part objects" as important. We see the social smile; the child looks at a part of the face and smiles. This social smile is an early psychological landmark of normal development. By 9 months, most children have finalized this process, discovering where they leave off and the world begins. They discover that there are many human objects in the world. By associating pleasurable experiences with certain of these human objects, the child begins to learn that specific ones are very important. He or she establishes *basic trust* in these key people, becoming totally dependent on them. That is, the child establishes "object constancy." With the establishment of basic trust, the infant masters the first major step in psychosocial development. The child now becomes upset if he or she is left alone. He or she has a fear of separation and a fear of strangers. This fear is another psychological landmark, usually appearing at around 9 months. This stage of total dependency can be illustrated:

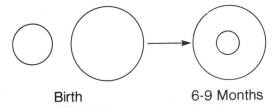

Birth   6-9 Months

The next task in psychosocial development is for the child to learn how to separate from these significant people and still survive. He or she masters this stage of development in steps, starting at 9 to 12 months and usually finishing at 3 to $3^1/_2$ years. This mastery of *separation* leading to autonomy can be illustrated:

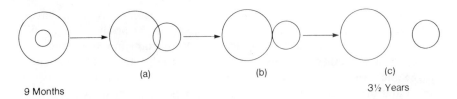

(a)   (b)   (c)

9 Months   3½ Years

Initially, *(a)* the child needs some form of perceptual hook-up with the significant person. The baby cries, then hears a parent's footsteps in the hall and stops. The auditory linkage is enough. A child crawls behind a chair, loses sight of a parent, and cries. As the parent moves into view, he or she stops crying. The visual linkage reestablished contact. A baby cries at night, is picked up in the dark and held, and stops; the touch, smell, and voice provide reassurance of the needed intimate connection.

Slowly, beginning at about 18 to 24 months, the child learns to separate for longer and longer periods of time *(b)*. Yet he or she still must return frequently to the parent for "refueling." A hug or kiss or cookie will do, and he is off again. For some children these early efforts at separation are made easier if something reminding them of a parent can go along. These "transitional objects" are usually selected because they have a familiar smell, a soft touch, or a cuddly feel that they have learned to associate with the parent.

Finally, by about 3 to $3^1/_2$ years the child can separate from his or her parent(s) with no discomfort *(c)*. This full mastery of separation can be seen as another landmark in development.

Two major psychological events take place during this state of mastering separation. Each aids in mastering separation and establishing autonomy; each has a major influence on personality development. The first of these issues is "negativism," which begins at about age 2. Most requests or comments are responded to with "No" or "No, I do myself." The child is beginning to separate and to show that he has a mind of his own.

The other issue occurring at about age 2 is toilet training. In the process of toilet training the child must begin to learn two new concepts. First, the child must shift his or her concept of love and relationships. Until this time the whole world was perceived by the child as being there to take care of him or her. Love and caring were automatic and free. Suddenly the child begins to learn that love is no longer free and available at every request. Now if the child wants love, he or she must do something. Loving relationships are no longer totally centered around the child's wishes and needs but are a give-and-take process. Make in potty and Mommy loves you; make in pants and Mommy frowns or hits or threatens not to love you. To get love requires giving. To be pleased requires pleasing. This is a major shift in the child's concept of the world, of people, and of relationships. This move from primary to secondary narcissism is an essential shift for the child to master.

The second new concept introduced with toilet training is that of having aggressive power. For the first time in a child's life he or she has an active weapon. Prior to this, the child could cry or have a tantrum, but the parents could choose whether to respond or not. Prior to this, the child experienced anger and expressed it. Now the child begins to realize the significance of anger and the influence his or her way of expressing anger has on getting or keeping love. Direct expression of anger does not work; the price to pay might be too great. He or she begins to learn that passive, indirect expressions of anger work as well as hitting or yelling. Now if he is angry with a parent, he can squat right in front of the parent, preferably when company is around, and with a big smile "make" in his pants. If he is pleased with his mother or father he will "make" on the potty. The child begins to learn the importance of controlling anger or of learning more acceptable ways of expressing anger.

These issues—wishing to please and be pleased, loving and being loved, and handling angry feelings—are struggled with individually and together. The two themes can interrelate; at this age it is possible to love and hate the same person at the same time, or to hurt and care for the same person at the same time.

When the child has mastered the first major task of development, establishing basic trust, and the second major task, handling separation, he or she is ready for the third task, *individuation.* This task deals with asking and trying to answer the question "Who am I?" Now that I have learned that I am a separate person and that I can survive without total dependence on important people, what kind of person am I? These questions are usually struggled with between the ages of 3 and 6.

The child is developmentally still at a stage of primary process or non-reality-based thinking. He or she tries out many roles. What is it like to be big, little, active, passive, a boy, a girl? Children play "house" or "school" or "doctor," exploring various roles and differences. One day he or she may be a boy, the next day a girl or a mommy or a daddy or a teacher or a teenage brother. Whenever the child tries to "be" someone in the family, such as his or her mother or father, he or she has to compete with that parent or any sibling who might also want to be this person. He or she also has to become seductive with the opposite parent, trying to get his or her attention. Characteristic of this age period is the child's ability to cause splitting and tension between parents and siblings. One day the child is perceived by a parent as loving; later he or she is annoying.

Since the child's thinking is at the primary process level, he or she has trouble distinguishing between feelings, thoughts, and actions. His thoughts scare him. Nightmares are common. He worries that others, like parents, will know what he is thinking and will retaliate. Thus, the child worries about body integrity and body damage. Any cut or scratch is a disaster; it is the bandaid stage.

For the first time in diagramming it is necessary to identify both parents.

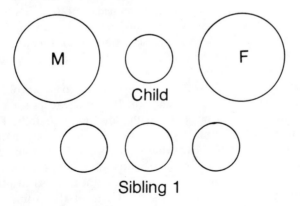

If he or she wants to "be Mother," she has to go as well as any siblings who might compete.

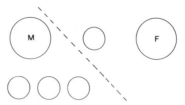

If he or she wants to "be Father," then he has to go as well as any siblings who might complete.

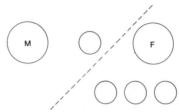

Thus, this stage can be illustrated:

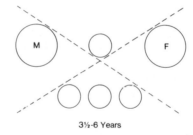

3½-6 Years

By about age 6 most children begin to answer the question "Who am I?" Little boys begin to learn that they are to become "just like Daddy" and enjoy playing this role. They give up wanting Mommy all to themselves and settle for having a girl just like their mother (someday). Little girls begin to learn that they are to become "just like Mommy" and enjoy playing this role. They give up wanting Daddy all to themselves and look forward to some day having someone just like their father. Through the process of identification they become like the parent of the same sex.

It is during this period when the child is from 3 to 6 years old that parents imprint cultural stereotypes of behavior. If a boy reaches for a doll to play with he is often told that boys play with guns, not with dolls. This theme is amazing, since adult men must know how to relate lovingly to their children and not to use guns. Girls learn that they play with dolls and do things in kitchens; they do not use guns or work with tools in shops. Boys learn that it is acceptable to express anger but not love or sadness; girls learn the opposite. Fortunately, the consciousness-raising efforts of the women's liberation movement have helped to free families from these stereotypes. Children should feel free to explore and to learn many roles in becoming a male or female. They should learn that the concept of maleness or femaleness is not based on the kinds of things one does or on how one expresses different emotions but on the kinds of experiences and relationships one has with others.

Two processes occur when the child is about age 6 that help him or her master this stage of individuation. Through maturation of the central nervous system the child moves from primary process (non-reality-based) to secondary process (reality-based) thinking. Opposite feelings and thoughts can no longer be handled. Reality and fantasy are distinguished. The other process is the consolidation of various value judgments into a conscience or superego. This "voice" or conscience remains throughout life and becomes significant. It "tells" the child what thoughts, feelings, or actions are acceptable or not. Initially these concepts are taught by one's parents. In adolescence, these value judgments are reconsidered. The early value systems are usually concrete and possibly harsh. If not reworked in adolescence, such a superego can inhibit or confuse ones identity or one's ability to handle feelings appropriately.

Once the child masters this third task of development, individuation, he or she moves into a period of consolidation. By about the time he or she is age 6, the child is free to move out of the family and into the community. With the major psychological work of childhood done the child's energy is freed to be involved in school, learning, and in expanding relationships.

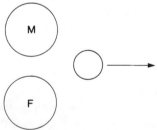

Thus, to summarize development through childhood:

During this latency period, children learn to relate to adults other than their parents and to children other than their siblings.

Children begin to focus on relationships with the same sex and to ignore or move away from heterosexual peer activities. Boys prefer boys and may not like girls. Girls prefer girls and may avoid boys. Very intimate "chum" relationships develop. Unlike the previous stage, the boy will shrug and push his mother away if she wishes to kiss him; the girl will feel comfortable if her father chooses to hold or kiss her. Two girls or two boys may walk down the street arm in arm as the closest of friends. The ability to relate and form friendships with persons of the same sex is explored and learned.

By the age of 12 to 14 this period of consolidation ends. Adolescence arrives. It is useful to distinguish between puberty, the physical processes of change, and adolescence, the psychosocial processes of change. Preferably the two occur simultaneously or close to each other; however, in the cases of some individuals, either may occur much before the other. When one is out of phase with the other, the individual has added stresses to cope with.

During adolescence the individual goes through the same stages of development discussed earlier. He or she usually retreats back to a stage of dependency and has to remaster independence. With this independency comes again the task of establishing one's individuation. Finally the adolescent learns to move out of the family and into the adult world.

The developing physical and physiological changes lead to two conflicting issues and create the first developmental task to be mastered in adolescence, shifting from being a dependent to being an independent person.

The first result of the physical maturation is a loss of self-confidence and a loss of feelings of body mastery. These feelings may lead to withdrawal from peer contacts and retreat into the home. He or she is growing in height and weight. Bodily changes involving menarche, breast development, growth of beard, and the voice occur rapidly. The girl who may have been very graceful and reassured is now clumsy and insecure. The boy who was good at sports and confident is now gawky and uncomfortable. Every day he or she looks into the mirror to see who is there and to readjust.

Although the rapid physical and emotional development may increase one's insecurity and make one wish to retreat into the safety of the home and family, another aspect of this development may force the individual to move out of the home for relationships and interactions.

Unlike the child of 3 to 6, whose feelings and thoughts caused conflicts and anxiety, the adolescent has the additional capacity of actions. When a 6-year-old boy cuddles with his mother he feels pleasant sensations, but when the 14- or 15-year-old boy does so, he may be embarrassed by the development of an erection. A little girl can enjoy the experience of cuddling with her father, but an early adolescent girl may have concomitant physical sensations or secretions that worry her. Wrestling or tickling a sibling of the opposite sex may become equally stimulating and distressing. This new ability to add actions to the feelings and thoughts is upsetting and may force the adolescent to move such relationships and feelings to individuals outside of the family.

The same is true for angry feelings. It is one thing for a little boy to be angry at his mother as he looks up at her. It is another situation when the angry adolescent realizes that he is taller and bigger than his mother and that he really could hurt her.

Thus there is a conflict. The loss of confidence caused by the physical and emotional changes encourages the early adolescent to become more dependent on his home and parents. The maturation of sexual functioning makes it difficult to explore heterosexual relationships again with parents and siblings.

Initially, the early adolescent may attempt to cope by fantasy—i.e., by choosing relationships with individuals who are unavailable and thus safe. He or she might have a mad crush on a movie or record star or on a sports hero. The probability that an early adolescent girl will suddenly find a rock music star at her door and asking for a date is remote enough to allow her safely to fantasize a relationship with him. Gradually relationships with real, potentially available people are explored. Initially these interactions are likely to be found in groups, and then in smaller groups, and then individually. Early individual dating may be narcissistically determined. The adolescent dates someone who makes him or her look good—a cheerleader or a football hero. Often the boy relates to the girl much as he would to boys, by clowning around or hitting. Later, the adolescent will date someone who makes him feel good; this date may resemble the parent of the opposite sex.

As the early adolescent struggles to move from being a dependent to being an independent person, the initial struggles often revolve around the established concepts of sexual roles and identification. Old techniques of mastering separation may be tried again.

Negativism reappears. "No, I can do it myself." "Don't tell me how long my hair can be." "Don't tell me how short my skirt can be." Again, the negativism is an attempt to say that the adolescent has a mind of his own. Again, it can become an active verbal expression of anger.

Clothing and hair style have always been favorite issues by which to prove one's independence. The unisex theme of today resembles the "causes" of other generations, the "racoon coaters," "beep-boppers," zoot suiters," "flappers," and so on.

Other struggles to show that the adolescent has a mind separate form his or her parents may appear. Parents and adolescents may differ on the choice of friends and peer groups, on school plans or courses, on points of philosophy.

All the old struggles with loving and with angry feelings reappear. What do you have to do to be loved or to keep one's love? What do you do with angry feelings? All have to be worked through; in the process, developing concepts of relationships, styles of expressing feelings, and one's personality are shaped.

In the process of separating, the adolescent must reject and reformulate his or her conscience or superego. Unless this is done, the adolescent's parents remain with him or her in the form of the value systems programmed in as a child. Inititally the adolescent may reject the former values, pointing out the contradictions in the parents' values or stating that "one can't trust anyone over 30." For some, this interim "vacuum," when old values are rejected but new ones have not yet been established, is upsetting. The adolescent may temporarily borrow a "packaged"system. Boy Scout or Girl Scout oaths and laws, religious philosophy and ritual, or other value systems may be adhered to vigorously. For some, the peer group may provide this interim system. Close cliques may set rigid rules about how to dress, whom to talk to, who belongs to the in-group or the out-group, or how to behave.

Slowly the adolescent begins to blend many different values from many sources with his or her existing values. By young adulthood a new superego is established. The flexibility and compatibility of this new superego will strengthen or inhibit the individual's ability to handle and express feelings and relationships.

As the adolescent begins to feel independent of his or her family and as the family supports and encourages this emerging maturity, the question of the 3- 6-year-old appears. Now that I am a separate being, "who am I?" He or she can no longer be just like Mommy or Daddy.

Thus, the second developmental task of adolescence, establishing one's *identity*, begins. Becoming a chip off the old block is too restrictive. Unlike the child, the older adolescent will select characteristics from such individuals as religious leaders, scout leaders, teachers, neighbors, relatives, parents and friends, blending these features with himself or herself to become a unique person. This new person, or identity, finalizes one's concepts of self. An individual's identity must be reworked throughout his or her life as his or her life roles changes; for example, one must adjust to becoming a graduate, a spouse, a parent, a grandparent, or a retiree.

Each generation and each culture has different sociological and cultural influences. The child who grew up in the Victorian era would have different external messages influencing his or her identity than one growing up in the first post-Victorian rebellion—i.e., the "flapper stage" of the twenties. In the same way, the adolescent growing up today experiences social and cultural mores and standards different from those his parents experienced. It is important for parents to understand and accept that their adolescent is experiencing a world different from the one experienced as adolescents.

The total developmental process that began at birth culminates in this identity. If all previous tasks were successfully mastered, the individual will have a successful functional identity with healthy and positive feelings about himself or herself. If any tasks were not successfully mastered, the final identity might be restrictive or dysfunctional.

With the developmental task of moving from a dependent to an independent being and establishing one's initial identity complete, the adolescent has one remaining task to master. Until this time, relationships were primarily based on the child-adult model. Now the adolescent or young adult has to learn how to relate to another individual who is an equal. This type of relationship is often referred to as *intimacy.*

When relating in a dependent-independent model, one leans on or depends upon another, and possibly may fuse with that person. In an intimate relationship or an independent-independent relationship, each becomes intra-independent on the other. Although each leans on and needs the other for his or her emotional well-being, neither loses his or her boundaries; at all times each can still stand and function independently.

DEVELOPMENTAL VIEW OF ANXIETY

Anxiety can be a direct and automatic reaction to a trauma—"automatic anxiety." Or it can be an anticipatory reaction to potential trauma—"signal anxiety." Children learn to anticipate the onset of traumatic situations and to react with anxiety before they occur. This response to signal anxiety mobilizes ego forces to meet or to avoid impending danger.

This ability to anticipate potential danger and to respond before one is faced with or overwhelmed by a dangerous situation is essential to healthy development. Anna Freud noted that "the children whose outlook for mental health is better are those who cope with the same danger situations actively by way of ego resources such as intellectual understanding, logical reasoning, changing of external circumstances, aggressive counterattack, i.e., by mastery instead of by retreat." She adds; "Other circumstances being equal, children are more likely to fall victim to later neurotic disturbances if they are unable to tolerate even moderate amounts of anxiety" (2).

What then are these "danger situations," exposure to which causes anxiety or anticipated exposure to which causes signal anxiety? Recall the review of normal development.

From birth until about 6 to 9 months, the child functions much like a physiological being. It is with the establishment of object constancy and the formation of basic trust that the child's ego faces its first potentially dangerous situation, fear of loss of the loved object. By age two this fear generalizes to be more a fear of the loss of the loved object's love ("Billy is naughty . . . Mommy won't love you if you do that.")

With mastery of separation and the establishment of autonomy the child no longer needs to fear these losses. The magical thinking and aggressive fantasies of the 3- to 6-year-old causes the child to worry that others will know what he or she is thinking and will retaliate. As noted earlier, the child becomes concerned with body integrity, body damage, and fear of body damage.

Between the ages of 6 and 7 the child finalizes the development of a superego. This psychic structure, along with the other techniques previously discussed, helps the child repress his 3- to 6-year old oedipal conflicts. From this time on, the child's major fear will be of disapproval by his superego, causing feelings of guilt or shame. It is this fear that is most familiar to adults as a trauamtic situation.

Thus, to summarize childhood:

Age	Developmental Task	Signal Anxiety
Birth to 6 to 9 months	Physiological Development	Physiological distress
6 to 9 months to 2 years	Separation	Fear of loss of loved object
2 to $3^1/_2$ years	Separation-Individuation	Fear of loss of loved object's love
$3^1/_2$ to 6 years	Oedipal	Fear of body damage
6 years -	Latency	Fear of disapproval by superego

During adolescence each of these danger situations may reappear. By adulthood the primary source is disapproval by one's superego. Later in adult life, fear of loss of ego integrity can be perceived of as a danger.

The ego responds to signal or automatic anxiety by mobilizing defense mechanisms (intrapsychic processes) or copii.g techniques (external processes—e.g., running away, changing one's environment). The defense mechanisms available to the ego depend on the child's age.

At birth the child appears to have two primitive defenses, denial and projection. Denial is the process of denying an unpleasant or unwanted piece of external reality either by a wish-fulfilling fantasy or by a behavior (e.g., going to sleep). Projection is the mental process in which an affect or thought is acknowledged but attributed to someone else.

By age 2, with the additional tasks related to mastering separation, new defenses become apparent: identification, introjection, displacement and substitution. Identification is the mental process in which a behavior or person is taken into the ego as a perception; the individual then takes over the attributes and behavior patterns of that object. Introjection is a form of identification in which an object is taken into the ego as a perception but is not imitated; the "introjected object" might be reacted to with hostility or love. With displacement, an affect is acknowledged but attributed to another cause. Substitution is the process of switching one set of unacceptable behaviors for another, more acceptable set of behaviors.

By age 6, with the evolving superego and the shift to reality-based, secondary process thinking, the child develops a final set of defense mechanisms. These are the ones most used by adolescents and adults. Reaction formation is a process one can use if he or she has opposite feelings or thoughts. The acceptable one is exaggerated and the unacceptable one repressed. In undoing, a positive act is done that has the purpose of disproving or undoing an acceptable aciton. Isolation is the psychic process of splitting off feelings from thoughts, the feelings being denied or repressed. With sublimation the energy associated with an unacceptable wish is transformed and directed into socially acceptable behavior. Suppression is the voluntary decision to forget an unacceptable feeling or thought. Rationalization is the process of acting in response to unrecognized motives and then, after the action, offering supposed "reasons" for the conduct. With dissociation an unacceptable portion of an individual's personality is eliminated from the rest when that portion is a source of stress.

In summary:

Primitive Defenses: (birth)	Denial
	Projection
Early Defenses: (age 2)	Identification
	Introjection
	Displacement
	Substitution
Later Defenses: (age 6)	Reaction Formation
	Undoing
	Isolation
	Sublimation
	Suppression
	Rationalization
	Dissociation

RECOGNITION OF ANXIETY

As with adults, if a child or an adolescent has a healthy functioning ego, clinical evidence of anxiety might not be noted. If a child or adolescent is observed to be using one or several defense mechanisms to a greater degree than would be age-appropriate, one might suspect an increased level of conflict and anxiety.

If a child or adolescent cannot tolerate even moderate amounts of anxiety, he or she might have to deny and repress all external and internal dangers that are potential sources of anxiety, developing a neurosis. Or he or she might project internal dangers onto the external world, developing a character disorder. Still others might somatize their anxiety, developing a somatic or psychophysiologic disorder.

When children or adolescents present with established psychopathology, it is not difficult to assume that conflict and anxiety are related to the observed behaviors. However, most commonly a clinician will see a child or adolescent under stress (family dysfunction, illness, hospitalization . . .). How does this individual reflect his or her anxiety? Again, to answer one must use a developmental approach.

From *birth until 6 to 9 months,* anxiety is usually reflected through physiological functioning. The infant may have colic or other eating disorders, may have sleep problems, or may be overly active.

From *6 to 9 months until 3 $^1/_2$ to 4 years,* as noted, the major source of anxiety is inititally fear of loss of the loved object; later it is fear of loss of the loved object's love. At this age, the primitive and early defenses are available. The child might also use fantasy and somatization (i.e., the channeling of anxiety into normal body functions). The anxiety also might be reflected by: fear or anger as the parents depart; somatic responses (urinary frequency, diarrhea, vomiting); depression, with rage, apathy, exploration of environment, and finally, recovery; need for tangible evidence of home and family (shoes, transitional object); feeding difficulties (anorexia, overeating, regression); regression in toilet training; sleep difficulties (insomnia, nightmares, restlessness, regression); motor outlet (restlessness, hyperactivity, irritability); or regression to primitive gratifications (thumb-sucking, rocking, masturbation, head-banging).

For the *3 $^1_2$ to 6-year-old,* the major source of anxiety is fear of body damage. The primitive, early, and later defenses are available. The anxiety might be reflected by any of the behaviors noted above, or by fears—e.g., of a parent being hurt or killed. If a child is at a doctor's office or in the hospital, he or she might be fearful of the needle or a particular doctor. The child might be worried about what he or she will look like after a procedure or operation.

The *6 to 12-year old,* would experience anxiety if he or she feared disapproval by one's superego. This anxiety might be manifested by: any of the previous mentioned ways; excessive verbalization; compulsive behavior; obsessive fears; or conversion reaction.

Adolescents are more likely to reflect their anxiety in ways similar to the 6- to 12-year-old child. The adolescent might also reflect conflicts and anxieties through the types of "negativistic" behaviors described earlier.

DIFFERENTIAL DIAGNOSIS

The most frequent manifestation of anxiety in children and adolescents is increased motor activity. This increased motor activity might be reflective of an endocrine, metabolic, or toxic condition; thus a full medical evaluation is necessary.

There are several clinical pictures in psychiatry that also cause an increase in motor activity and must be differentiated from anxiety.

Children and adolescents with the minimal brain dysfunction (MBD) syndrome show a cluster of behaviors (4). They all have in common one or more types of learning disabilities. In addition, as many as 40% will be hyperactive and/or distractible. Most also develop secondary emotional and social problems. The hyperactivity or distractibility might appear to be anxiety-based but is not.

These children's increased motor activity is physiologically based, probably related to a central nervous system dysfunction of the reticular activity system (5, 6). The history will often help in differentiating anxiety-based from physiologically based hyperactivity. The child who utilizes an increase in motor activity as a means of coping with anxiety usually shows this behavior during specific life-space experiences—for example, only in school, only when parents fight, following a divorce. With physiologically based hyperactivity, there is usually a history of such activity since birth. Parents might report that the child kicked more *in utero*. He or she squirmed in his mother's arms, rolled in his crib, ran before he walked, has been in almost constant motion since birth. The hyperactivity does not relate to any specific time or event. Physiologically based hyperactivity usually improves with the use of the psychostimulants: the anxiety-base hyperactivity will not (7).

Children and adolescents may reflect their anxiety by being unattentive, preoccupied, or distractible. This distractibility might appear clinically like the physiologically based distractibility seen in the minimal brain dysfunction syndrome. Such, MBD children and adolescents are unable to filter out less important sensory inputs. These inputs pass through to the cortex, causing distractibility and a short attention span. As with hyperactivity, the history is helpful. Physiologically based distractibility has been present since earliest childhood; anxiety-based distractibility usually has its onset around specific events and is apparent during specific life-space experiences.

One other clinical picture might be misdiagnosed as anxiety. Some children and adolescents are distractible because of their inability to inhibit their internal stimulations. This "cognitive dysinhibition" looks clinically like the distractibility described above. Clinical observations and assessments will help in recognizing these individuals. In some cases the internal distractibility is a reflection of childhood schizophrenia; however, in other cases it may be a reflection of a central nervous system disorder.

TREATMENT

Anxiety is a symptom; it is not a diagnosis. If a clinician observes that a child or adolescent is experiencing anxiety, he or she must explore the possible cause. Further, with children and adolescents, one must decide if the concerns and anxiety are age-appropriate or not. Treating the symptom is often unsuccessful with this age group.

Because of the dependent and developmental nature of children and adolescents, it is necessary to evaluate the total child in his or her total environment. One must assess the individual's neurophysiological status, intrapsychic functioning, behavioral or learned patterns of functioning, interpersonal style and ability, and pattern of systems functioning (family, school, environment).

In some situations in which the child or adolescent presents with an isolated symptom suggestive of anxiety, symptom-directed therapy using behavioral approaches (relaxation, desensitization) might be appropriate. Because of the increased vulnerability of children and adolescents and the concern that unresolved issues will affect later adult functioning, it is important to do follow-up with children treated symptomatically to be sure that they continue with the developmental process.

The use of minor tranquilizers (anti-anxiety drugs) is less common with children and adolescents than with adults. Again, the issue is treating the symptom rather than the source of the symptom. Such drugs might be used in conjunction with another therapeutic approach if the anxiety level is too high and interfering with functioning. In these cases it is helpful to let the medication be part of the therapeutic process. The individual is told that he or she can take one pill every four hours if nervous, but that each time they take a pill they must write down what it was that probably made them anxious. Such observations can then be used in therapy.

Nightmares are normal during the 3- to 6-year-old reality-based phase of development, if they persist or recur at a later time, one should look for the source of the anxiety being reflected by the nightmares. If necessary, symptomatic relief can often be obtained through the use of thioridazine (Mellaril) at bedtime. This drug blocks REM sleep and may stop the nightmares.

Night terrors, a somnambulant state during which the individual appears to be awake but is still asleep and experiencing a nightmare, occurs in stage IV sleep. Symptomatic relief might be obtained from diazepam (Valium), which inhibits stage IV sleep. If the night terrors persist, the source of the conflicts and anxiety should be sought.

Enuresis can be a reflection of anxiety. Anxiety can also be caused by persistent enuresis. Imipramine (Tofranil) might be used to control the enuresis.

CONCLUSIONS

Unlike adults, children and adolescents cannot be stereotyped. One must use a developmental model to understand their psychosocial as well as physical status. This developmental concept is critical in recognizing and treating anxiety. The possible causes, the resources for coping, and the behavioral manifestations vary with age.

It is essential to assess the total child or adolescent in his or her total environment to understand the source of the anxiety or to design a therapeutic intervention.

REFERENCES

1. Freud, S. *Inhibitions, Symptoms, and Anxiety.* Vol. 10, ed. and trans. J. Strachey. London: Hogarth Press, 1926.
2. Freud, A. *Normality and Pathologyin Childhood.* New York: Interantional Universities Press, 1965.
3. Prugh, D.G. Children's reactions to illness, hospitalization, and surgery. In A.M. Freedman and H.I. Kaplan Eds *Comprehensive Textbook of Psychiatry,* 2nd ed. Baltimore; Williams & Wilkins, 1975.
4. Silver, L.B. Playroom diagnostic evaluation of children with neurologically based learning disabilities. *J. Am. Acad. Child. Psychiat.* 15:240-256, 1976.
5. Silver, L.B. A proposed view on the etiology of the neurological learning disability syndrome. *J. Learning Disabil.* 4:123-133, 1971.
6. Wender, P.H. *Minimal Brain Dysfunction in Children.* New York: Wiley-Interscience, 1971.
7. Silver, L.B. Acceptable and controversial approaches to treating the child with learning disabilities. *Pediatrics* 55:406-415, 1975.

CHAPTER 8

The Developing Biological Concept of Anxiety

Roy B. Mefferd, Jr.

An extremely large body of literature has developed concerning anxiety. This indicates that we are having difficulty with the construct. My intention here is to follow one of the mainstreams of biologically oriented conceptualizations. Of particular interest to me are efforts to integrate the results from authors of diverse disciplines and persuasions. In picking and choosing what specific works to emphasize, I certainly will have underemphasized or overlooked work that may prove in time to have been landmarks. We are still too close to the evolving concepts to make incisive judgments today.

The effectiveness of a growing number of drugs in modifying the level of anxiety either up or down indicates the existence of a site(s) in the brain where anxiety originates, is modified, or culminates. Theories that treat the brain as a black box in this respect do not appear to provide the clinician with a very firm foundation for precise diagnosis and therapy.

The development of a modern theory of emotion and mood has been tortuous. It obviously is not yet resolved. The tremendously influential Wundt (1) formulated the view that one of three feeling dimensions (pleasant-unpleasant, excited-quiet, tense-relaxed) combined with a bodily sensation to produce an emotion. His student Titchner (2), who was equally influential in American thought, modified Wundt's view primarily in that he considered only the pleasant-unpleasant state to be a feeling. The other two states he considered to be primary sensations. The general view of that period was that a change in bodily processes during consciousness yielded sensations which led to emotions.

James (3, 4) and Lange (5) made a complete switch—they classified fear and anger as *instinctive behavior* that led to "felt" emotion. A bear is perceived as dangerous, so you run away, and this activity leads to increased heart rate, etc., and to bodily sensations that in turn lead to identification of the feeling "fear."

Cannon (6) roundly criticized this entire concept, and implicated the thalamus as the seat of emotion—emotion is a feeling resulting from afferent stimulation of the dorsal thalamus. The hypothalamus is also activated, and this mediates the thalamic response. In his view, *both* the feeling and its expression were triggered simultaneously by the thalamus. The proponents of Cannon's point of view stressed a concept of an emergency system (i.e., the sympathetic nervous system—S), and of a balancing or answering system (i.e., the parasympathetic system—PS). They hypothesized that when homeostasis was tipped in either direction, there was a temporary rebound— the answering effects (PS). They speculated that both the S and the PS systems may be activated simultaneously to equilibrate at a higher level. They also emphasized the energy mobilization aspects of emotions as the body prepares for emergency action—strong emotions prepare for vigorous action.

Selye (7, 8) extended the visceral theory by implicating the slower activating, permissive, sustaining endocrine system in the total emotional response. He massively documented the important role placed in alerting and alarming responses by the reciprocal relationship between the anterior pituitary adreno-corticotropic hormone, ACTH, and the hydrocortisone and corticoid steroids produced by cells in the adrenal cortex (and particularly of 17-hydroxycorticosteroids—17-OHCS). Selye recently (9) followed the overall trend toward more holistic concepts by redefining stress as the nonspecific response of the body to any demand made of it—positive or negative. He also incorporated hypothalamic polypeptide hormones into the response system.

Lashley (10), in turn, effectively criticized Cannon. While he agreed that the hypothalamus was the seat of the expressive parts of the emotion, he questioned whether the hyperexcitability of a response was the result of a release from cortical inhibition, and even whether the motor center of the thalamus contributed to the experienced feelings. Lindsley (11) had already implicated the reticular activating system (RAS) in the emotional process. The hypothalamus was viewed as a way-station, producing two simultaneous discharges upon stimulation, one upward through the ascending RAS to produce the subjective feelings (the alertness or excitement typical of emotions), and the other downward through the descending RAS to produce the external aspects of emotion.

The visceral theorists, following Canon, would say that a certain amount of ACTH circulating in the blood is correlated with a specific pattern of peripheral and central neural response in the visceral brain, which in turn corresponds to one or another emotional experience. The activation theorists, following Lindsley, would state merely that a correlation exists between the amount of ACTH, the amount of neural excitation, and the amount of emotional arousal.

Lacey (12) modified the activation concept by implicating afferent autonomic nervous system (ANS) signals as facilitators of either or both the preparation to respond and the execution of the response. Obrist and coworkers (13), however, effectively refuted this hypothesis and showed that the inhibition of an ongoing somatic event is not relevant to either the preparation for or the execution of a behavior response, since both were initiated *directly* by the central nervous system (CNS).

Papez (14) and MacLean (15,16) implicated the visceral brain— and particularly the limbic system—with the long-lasting, intense aspects of the experiences associated with emotion. Duffy (17) wanted to do away with the entire concept of emotion and think only of the feeling experience as resulting from the level of activation. However, Malmo and Smith (18) insisted that the affective aspects of an emotional disturbance must have cognitive aspects to account for the tensional changes.

All this concern about the origin and sequence of "felt" and expressed emotion—which comes first, the chicken or the egg—generated a great deal of steam but little resolution of the problem. Meanwhile, another approach was taking shape—one that would begin to incorporate many exciting new discoveries about consciousness, motivation, memory, selective attention, expectancies, and control mechanisms.

In this stream, Izard and Tomkins (19) presented a persuasive psychologically based concept of anxiety that involved three subsystems— homeostasis, drive, and affect. The product of the interaction of these subsystems was motivation, with the drive system providing for physiological and safety needs, and the affect system providing the "blueprint for cognition and action." They viewed anxiety as a negative affect quite distinct from both fear-terror and from interest-excitement. Anxiety resulted from the unknown, uncertainties, or even from an overabundance of options. An individual oscillates between fear (withdrawing or avoiding) and excitement (exploring, pressing on). The zone between these affects is a state of ambivalence—anxiety. Anxiety was viewed as placing limits on man's trust in the unknown, while interest sustained the exploration needed to reduce the uncertainty.

Now allow me to jump a little ahead of the main force in this development to mention an hypothesis that linked the limbic system and RAS. Routtenberg (20) suggested (with extensive documentation) that these two systems operated in a reciprocal fashion—that they were mutually inhibitory. RAS alerted and maintained the activation to produce the drive necessary for responding to stimuli. The limbic system controlled the responding by means of motives (incentives). It managed the analysis of the reward aspects of the stimulus, consolidated the neural sequences that preceded the reward, reinforced rewards, and retained the response. A dynamic equilibrium as maintained between the two systems—one instant the drive to respond was suppressed so that the limbic system could effect consolidation; the next instant RAS suppressed the motive so that it could mobilize the energy to maintain the attention and response mechanism. The extent to which a precise and effectively dynamic balance was maintained would determine the appropriateness and effectiveness of responding. It is apparent how dysfunction on either side of such a reciprocal system could lead to the perseverating, ineffectual mental turmoil of an anxious person, and to protective strategies, such as not deciding (e.g., hesitating, blocking, stuttering), or deciding to establish a safe, rigid position, right or wrong.

Pribram (21) departed completely from the viscerally based mainstream by discarding the naming approach to emotion and by placing emphasis on memory (i.e., learning). Pribram viewed emotions as a set of processes that reflected the state of relative organization or disorganization of an ordinarily stable configuration of neural systems. Emotions reflected those mechanisms operating to redress any imbalance in this stable configuration. His important distinction was that this redress was not achieved by means of action—fight or flight-but no regulation of afferent input. He identified two such systems: preparatory, in which stability is retained by exclusion of input; and participatory, in which the system is reorganized to include the input.

Pribram's concept differs from those that emphasized the relations between emotion and a viscerally based drive process by linking emotion directly to an amount of neural excitation. The baseline of this system was organized stability and its perturbation, rather than of some arbitrary level of activation. It related emotion and motivation by linking both to ongoing prebehavioral neural organization. This was accomplished by a set of genetic and experiential memory mechanisms he characterized as dispositions, programs, and plans (22). Pribram defined emotion as a process that takes the organism out of action (e-motion). This was done by regulating the input in two ways—reducing redundancy and enhancing it. Effective regulation of these two processes would establish a subtle balance between maximum redundancy (through preparation) and maximum information density (through participation). Emotion was conceived as an essential mechanism for increasing the strength and flexibility of the individual's repertoire of internal alternatives with which new and novel situations were met. Thus, Pribram viewed the nervous system as a stabilizing mechanism as long as the input was irrelevant. The system became responsive when the input was relevant, causing perturbation in the system, but it achieved this responsiveness by regulating the input *through* the drive mechanisms. Motive involved the individual in action, in the execution of the plan.

Motive per se had little control function; rather, the organism depends on emotion for control. Too much emotion leads either to disruption through participation, or to rigidity through preparation. The emotion can become a disequilibrating input itself, introducing additional incongruities that increasingly cannot be acted upon. Note how well this concept explains the churning, purposeless, perseverating worry of neurotic, anxious people in general!

Lacey (12) came close to a part of Pribram's concept, even though the processes hypothesized by the two authors are indeed distant. Lacey postulated that responsiveness depends on whether or not an individual intends to transact with the environment. Simple, passive, non-action-oriented stimuli (e.g., a light, a neutral movie) elicit evidences of decreased activation and of relaxation. In this state, individuals attend their environment more closely. Lacey characterized this PS-dominant state as one with an action-out orientation. On the other hand, action-oriented stimuli (e.g., problem-solving, reaction time measurements) heightened the activation level, and as the individual concentrated upon his task, he rejected the environment with an action-in orientation. Lacey observed a slowing of the heart rate during the concentration in the problem-solving (the narrowed input band width in the Pribram concept). When the problem was solved, Lacey observed that the heart rate increased (the widening of the input and band width of Pribram).

Another major development in the conceptualization of anxiety was Gellhorn's formulation and documentation of the autonomic-cortical-somatic integration that results in nervous system tuning (23, 24, 25). He then related this concept to state anxiety (26). Let me introduce his concept with a preliminary consideration of a related phenomenon—vasovagal syncope. A person who is in autonomic balance and who experiences a strong stimulus that has dangerous aspects (e.g., an apparently imminent car accident) has a prompt increase in S activation. This will be answered more slowly by counterbalancing PS activation. If, however, the stimulus or threat is suddenly removed, the intense S activity may drop below that of the now increased PS activity. The result is a precipitous reversal (switch) from intense S dominance to an equally intense PS dominance. Apnea may occur, and the sudden vasodilation and slowing of the heart (even to the point of cardiac arrest until the heart can "escape" the vagal control) causes a sharp drop in blood pressure. This reduces the blood flow to the brain, and dizziness, wooziness, or even syncope may result (27).

Gellhorn's tuning conept is applicable both to normal and disturbing conditions. An example of a normal process is the autonomic control or cyclic modulation of heart rate. If we step into this process at the point just after systole where the blood pressure is increasing about the PS baroreceptors in the aortic arch, the firing rate of these stretch receptors begins to increase. This change in signal rate stimulates nuclei in the anterior hypothalamus, which increases the PS signal rate both along the descending vagal nerve and directly across to the posterior hypothalamus. The latter signals are inhibitory and cause a reduction of the overall S tone. The combined effect of these changes in firing rates act reflexively to increase the PS and to reduce the S tones. This results in many changes, such as a slowing of the heart and a peripheral vasodilation. As a result, there is a fall in the blood pressure around the baroreceptors, and they decrease their firing rate. This in turn results in a reduction of PS signals and an increased S tone. The result is seen as a vasoconstriction and increased heart rate. The blood pressure again rises and around we go for another cycle. This type of "automatic" relief of the CNS from the necessity of continual involvement in such control processes is what Cannon (28) called the "wisdom of the body."

Autonomic control processes may be modified in several ways: 1. by another cyclic autonomic control process, e.g., the blood pressure control is influenced continuously by the respiratory control cycle seen as sinus arhythmia; 2. by a host of drugs and medications; 3. by volitional control of motor activity, including respiration—to the delight of the relaxation therapists and to the distress of the lie detection specialists; Luria (29) successfully modified verbal behavior by learned muscular control, and vice versa; and Richter (30) noted dire consequences in rats if they were restrained during highly excited states; 4. by the individual's becoming attuned to the results of the control process so that he can perceive changes in it; he then can learn to modify the controls; and 5. by emotion and mood states.

Gellhorn's concept, in part, involves the balance between the S and the PS components of the ANS. Ideas about ANS balance extend to Eppinger and Hess (31) and Cannon (6). Hess (32) introduced the concept of tuning, which Gellhorn (25, 26) developed and documented. Wenger (33) provided support for the concept's foundations by demonstrating factor analytically the existence of two independent factors—muscular activation and neural autonomic activation. The latter bipolar factor demonstrated that there are people who habitually have either an S or a PS dominance.

Hess (32) realized early in his work that the concept of balance within the nervous system involved much more than just the ANS. He recognized that besides the ANS, the activation levels of higher brain centers and of skeletal muscles were involved. His concept of ergotropic (E) and trophotropic (T) balance, therefore, incorporates not only the ANS, but the cortical and the motor systems. In an ergotropic state (E/t), the individual is alert and action-oriented—there is peripheral and GI vasoconstriction that combines with skeletal muscles and brain vasodilation to shift the blood to the "action" organs; the heart rate and respiration rate increases; the efferent skeletal muscle gamma-motor system is activated, leading to increased skeletal muscle tone; and there is a desynchronization of EEG. A significant fact is that in the E/t state, sensitivity to amphetamine increases at the same time that sensitivity to barbiturates decreases.

In the trophotropic state (e/T) the individual is relaxed and non-action-oriented. Both S and muscular tone are reduced, and the EEG becomes synchronized. Sleep is the most common end product of this state. Of course, sleep itself involves the serotonergic system (34). Significantly, the sensitivity to amphetamine and to barbiturates has reversed the e/T state.

Balance in either direction may be partially defined in terms of the degree of sensitivity to compatible stimuli (e.g., in the E/t state, the sensitivity is increased to norepinephrine, cold, pain, and exercise), and of decreased sensitivity to antagonistic stimuli (e.g., mecholyl, warmth, and relaxation). An example of a noncompatible effect is for a fatigued, sleepy person in an e/T balance to be exposed to noncompatible E-activating cold. Rather than reversing the balance, the e/T may simply deepen to e/TT. The person may freeze unless sufficient additional E-activation occurs to prevent this deepening of the e/T balance (e.g., as by volitional movement or by "automatic" shivering).

The significant point to note here is that an observed response depends on the state of activation balance existing at that instant. Gellhorn (23, 25, 35), and Gellhorn and Loofbarrow (36) demonstrated that tuning may be modified by either an increased E tone or a decreased T tone, or vice versa. He could readily manipulate the tuned state by appropriate agonists and/or antagonists. In Gellhorn's concept, whether a change intensified the ongoing state or caused a reversal to the opposite state depends on the intensity of either or both E and T activation. He conceived of the various effects as being straight summations. In a tuned system, the total response to two compatible (e.g., both S-activating) stimuli would be the sum of the contribution of each; to a pair of unlike stimuli, the response would equal their algebraic sum. Large shifts in this balance in either direction would result in quantitative changes in the degree of responsiveness. However, unexpected anomalous changes might also occur (e.g., where a sedative acts as if it were a stimulant). The actual response would depend on the CNS tuning at the time. At a high state of tuning, for example, in a catatonic state, where there is low E(e) and high T(T) activity—e/T, the T state might be intensified by an injection of norepinephrine as the state changes to E/TT and the catatonia deepens. However, at points of extreme imbalance (e.g., e/TTT), the dominant system would become highly unstable and slight stimulations might cause a dramatic reversal or shift to just as unbalanced a state in the opposite direction (e.g., to EEE/t). For example, a narcoleptic who has an arousing experience, such as an orgasm, may reverse abruptly from high arousal to a cataleptic state; a mother awakens from a deep sleep instantly ready for action when her baby cries.

Gellhorn explained abrupt reversals in activation balance that might occur during states of extreme imbalance (e.g., the vasovagal syncope) as being due to spillover of impulses from the E to the T system. His evidence for this is crucial to his hypothesis of anxiety, so let me summarize one of his key examples. In asphyxia, there is first an E/t response, but this quickly rises to EE/t; then it falls back to an E/T. He interpreted this as having been due to some of the intense E stimulation spilling over to the T system. If at this E/T stage, barbiturate was administered (which should have augmented the T activation), there actually was a return of the response to the original E/t level.

Gellhorn viewed anxiety as a special form of fear that occurred when the symmetrical nature of ANS reflexes were disturbed. The disturbance resulted in a change from E/t to EE/t. As the disturbance continued, impulses spilled over and the state became EE/T. This activation and disturbed balance yielded new sensations and enhanced neurotic responses.

The issue of whether various stimuli summate, as Gellhorn assumed, is so crucial to the understanding of anxiety that I must pause and present some of our own efforts to clarify this issue. Although none of the major drive theorists—Hull, Malmo, Spence—actually predicted that increasing increments of the same stimulus would yield summated responses, all implied that this would be the case, when Gallhorn formulated his concept, had he available literature confirmation of such summation for the same stimulus (37,38). It seemed perfectly logical to assume that this would also be the case when two different stimuli were imposed. This assumption was central to Gellhorn's explanation of reversals in tuning.

We (39,40) discovered that Gellhorn's assumption was incorrect. We had given a word association test (WA) to subjects before and during a cold pressor (CP) test (41). Jung (42) reported that cognitive activities, such as WA, caused increases in S activation, and we also observed this. On the other hand, Lewis (43) found that exposure of an extremity to cold caused a generalized S activation, which Hines and Brown (41) later confirmed. Adams and Smith (44), however, reported that emotional stress augmented an ongoing CP-induced S activation with sufficient vasoconstriction to interfere with temperature regulation even in cold-adapted tissue. Therefore, we expected to observe in our experiment an augmentation of the ongoing CP-induced S activation by the imposition of a WA test: E/t to EE/t.

Instead, we observed just the opposite effect—WA imposed during a CP-induced S activation caused a reduction in this S activation. Yet there appeared to be no reversal to e/T, since the reaction times (RT) of the WA responses became significantly faster during the CP phase than during the control phase. This indicated that a state of high E activation persisted.

How were we to explain this effect? Both stimuli above were S stimulators, but together they neither summated nor induced an activation reversal; instead, the S activation simply decreased to e/t!

Goldberg (45) reported that the simultaneous combination of two potent S-stimuli, CP and leg exercise, resulted in a response only as large as that yielded by the more potent CP stimulus alone. Benjamin (46) also reported that pain decreased the perception of nonpainful sensory stimulations. We confirmed the reduction in S activation observed with WA when we combined CP and RT measurements (47). At that time, we were persuaded that the pain of the CP was a major contributor to this effect. It had been known for some time that one pain could be modified by another painful stimulus (48). Gardner (49,50) even used sound to suppress the pain of dental procedures.

Following Gardner's lead, we reasoned that a painful response failed to summate with a nonpainful one because of a mutual distraction—a reduced attending of the pain required by the action-in requirements of the cognitive or exercise task, and a reduced monitoring of the task as a result of the pain. This interpretation was consistent with Lacey's concept.

Neither our WA nor our similar RT results were really consistent with Goldberg's report—we obtained actual reductions in ongoing CP responses. To determine the relative role of the motor activity of this task, we repeated the experiment with CP combined with cognitive tasks in which the subject could remain perfectly still (51,52). We used the subject's comprehension levels of different literary passages as the subject read a passage silently, and as the subject listened to another passage. Once again, an ongoing CP activation was promptly reduced when the subject started reading or listening. However, when we reversed the task, we obtained the same results as Goldberg (45) had reported for exercise—ongoing cognitive activity did nothing to suppress the imposed CP response.

The response patterns to CP and the cognitive activity were markedly different. CP induced and maintained S activation, while cognition alone essentially induced only an orienting response (38). Yet, in spite of this rapid habituation of ANS activities during ongoing cognition, the cognition still caused a reduction in ongoing CP activation.

At that point, we abandoned our preoccupation with the supposed effects of the CP pain and juxtaposed the following stimuli: 1. distracting noise and reading comprehension; 2. continuous flashing light and continuous banging noise; and 3. a single bright flash and a single loud bang (53). In all cases, the responses to the two different stimuli did not summate, whether they were imposed simultaneously or one upon the other ongoing activity. Intense startling stimuli (a bright flash or a loud bang) also failed to summate, whether they were imposed in sequence or simultaneously. However, another significant observation was that such intense stimuli increased the responsiveness level of subjects with high neuroticism scores, as evidenced by faster (i.e., reduced latency), though still smaller electrodermal responses to another succeeding startling stimulus.

With these relatively mild stimuli, habituation effects were marked. It occurred to us that in an habituated person, any different stimulus might elicit a response similar to that of CP noted above. We found that repeated short exposures to a dim spot of light in a darkened room led quickly to the expected decrease in electrodermal responses—habituation. However, a single soft tone instead of the expected light elicited a large orienting response, and the converse order produced the same results (54).

Clearly, hetermodal stimulus responses do not summate for a wide range of complexities and intensities. This, however, does not really damage Gellhorn's basic concept. It only showed that broader provision needed to be made for changes in intensities that do not result in activation reversals. An even greater need, however, was to develop a definitive explanation for reversals at low intensity levels, which Gellhorn had neglected.

Teichner (55) made some of the needed modifications of Gellhorn's concept in his effort to extend the model to include the stressful aspects of information overload (22). First, he categorized stimuli as either physical or symbolic in nature. The latter category included emotional, perceptual, and cognitive stimuli which have meaning via memory mechanisms (i.e., developed as a result of learning). He then implicated the interaction of two basic mechanisms in invoking changes in the strength and direction of ongoing processes—activation and data processing. Teichner pointed out that we must discriminate between *controlled events,* such as body temperature, and the *controlling mechanisms* that maintain the event at a stable level—the many compensatory responses involved in temperature control. The controlled event will remain within normal limits until the controlling mechanism fails; thereafter, the controlled event will fail as well. He argued convincingly that, contrary to Gellhorn's concept, tuning involves only the controlling compensatory mechanisms.

Teichner relied heavily on memory and attention mechanisms, melding the concepts of several divergent theorists neatly into a plausible package. However, some aspects of his concept are subtly distinct. Gellhorn wrote in terms of direct nerve impulses, firing rates, intensities, and other neurophysiological terms. Teichner added dimensions of symbolically stressful stimuli, afferent inputs and outputs from the same subsystem resulting from a single stimulus, and the compensatory changes that in turn result in differences in the rates of change in these two input/output afferent signals. Stress can occur wherever the variation in an output of a controlling mechanism exceeds its normal range. Whether or not stress does occur depends on the state and degree of tuning at the time.

Perhaps Teichner's most useful idea was that reversals occurred due to disparities between the rates of change of an *input* and of an *output* from a subsystem that controlled a compensatory mechanism. As this input/output rate-ratio increases, activation increases and the strength of ongoing compensatory responses also increases. At a critical disparity, the output becomes inhibitory, triggering an overriding control and producing a reversal in the ongoing compensatory reactions. The vigor of the compensatory reaction in the new direction would be dependent on the level of activation.

So long as the input and output rates change uniformly, the intensity would increase or decrease without a reversal. Teichner emphasized the symbolic nature of the afferent inputs as activating events. Thus, he could account for decreases in the apparent intensity of a constant, continuing stimulus, such as occurs with adaptation, boredom, fatigue, reevaluation of the personal significance of emotional stimuli, etc. Such *apparent* decreases in the total activation of a physical and emotional combination could reduce EE/t back to the sole effect of a continuing physical stressor (e.g., cold)—E/t. Since reversals were not the consequence of intensities, but rather were triggered by differences in the rates of change, Teichner's hypothesis can explain the many reversals that occur at low levels of activation—sleep-wakefulness, acquiring-eating food, etc.

Teichner speculated that anxiety might result from information overloads which would cause a decrease in tuning and a broadening of the information processing band width. This would have the effect of admitting irrelevant input (i.e., of distraction) and of reducing the speed of information processing. This overloaded system would result in increased activation (and decreased performance), triggering a protective overriding of various compensatory controlling mechanisms. In turn, a reversal would occur. Depending on the intensity of the activation, various responses typical of anxiety would be observed, even a possible vasovagal reaction. Subsequently, the tuning would increase with a consequent narrowing of the input band width and of reduction in activation. An important feature to note is that Teichner's model involves oscillations about some midpoint (i.e., there are low points as well as high).

Another attractive possibility for involvement in the observed oscillations, one end of which we have reified as anxiety, is to be found in the Pribram and McGuinness (56) concept on the control of attention. Three separate but interacting neural systems were postulated. One of these systems controlled *arousal* (phasic physiological responses to input) centered in the amygdala, while another controlled *activation* (tonic physiological readiness to respond) centered in basal ganglia of the forebrain. The Routtenberg (20) concept was expanded, and the structures relocated by adding a third system centered in the hippocampus that coordinated the arousal and activation systems. This coordination activity required *effort*. They observed that during simple categorization activity, arousal preceded activation, but that this order was reversed during reasoning activities.

This concept would allow for both between and within subject variation in the degree of coordinating control possible, and the amount of effort expended on the control. The behavior we observed as anxiety would be a reflection of a balance in favor of arousal, while that of the "passive" state would be the opposite balance. Highly neurotic people would have a broad and/or loose control system—high "stable" people would have a narrow and/or tight control system.

This review cannot be complete without taking note of the remarkable similarity between the behavioral and physiological symptoms of anxiety and of hypoglycemia (57). Repeated glucose tolerance tests of hypoglycemics probably would even introduce the affective dread of anxiety at the first encounter. It does not strain the imagination to relate the *effort* (56) with blood glucose levels.

The above summary was not intended to be comprehensive, but rather to channel our thoughts into one main current that seems to be relevant to the growing chemotherapeutic armamentarium. Many provocative concepts have not been mentioned, and I apologize to their originators and proponents.

REFERENCES

1. Wundt, W.M. *Outlines of Psychology,* 3rd ed. London: Williams & Norgate, 1907.
2. Titchner, E.B. The psychology of feeling and attention. In *A Textbook of Psychology.* New York: Macmillan, 1901.
3. James, W. What is an emotion? *Mind* 9:188-205, 1884.
4. James, W. *The Principles of Psychology.* New York: Henry Holt, 1890.
5. Lange, C.G. Om Leudoheneegelson. In K. dunlap, ed., *The Emotions.* Baltimore: Williams & Williams, 1922.
6. Cannon, W.B. The James-Lange theory of emotions: A critical examination and an alternative theory. *Am. J. Psychol.* 39:106-124, 1927.
7. Selye, H. *Textbook of Endocrinology.* Montreal: Acta Endocrinologica, 1947.
8. Selye, H. *The Physiology and Pathology of Exposure to Stress.* Montreal: Acta, 1950.
9. Selve, H. Implications of stress concept. *N.Y. State J. Med.* 75:2139-2145, 1975.
10. Lashley, K. The thalamus and emotion. In F.A. Beach, D.O. Hebb, C.T. Morgan, H.W. Nissen, eds., *The Neuropsychology of Lashley.* New York: McGraw-Hill, 1960.
11. Lindsley, D.B. Emotion. In S.S. Stevens, ed., *Handbook of Experimental Psychology.* New York: Wiley, 1951.
12. Lacey, J.I. Somatic response patterning and stress: Some revision of activation theory. In Appley and Turmbull, eds., *Psychological Stress: Issues in Research.* New York: Appleton-Century, 1967.
13. Obrist, P.A., Wood, D.M., and Perez-Reyes, M. Heart rate during conditioning in humans: Effect of UCS intensity vagal blockade and adrenergic block of vasomotor activity. *J. Exp. Psychol.* 70:32-2, 1965.
14. Papez, J.W. A proposed mechanism of emotion. *Arch. Neurol. Psychiat.* 38:725, 1937.
15. MacLean, P.D. The limbic system ("visceral brain") and emotional behavior. *Arch. Neurol. Psychiat.* 73:130-134, 1955.
16. MacLean, P.D. A triune concept of the brain and behavior. In P.J. Boag, ed., *The Clarence M. Hicks Memorial Lectures, 1969.* Toronto: University of Toronto Press, 1973.
17. Duffy, E. The concept of energy mobilization. *Psychol. Rev.* 58:30-40, 1951.
18. Malmo, R.B., and Smith, A.A. Forehead tension and motor irregularities in psychoneurotic patients under stress. *J. Personality* 23:391, 1955.
19. Izard, C.E., and Tomkins, S.S. Affect and behavior: Anxiety as a negative affect. In C.D. Spielberger, ed., *Anxiety and Behavior.* New York: Academic Press, 1966.

20. Routtenberg, A. The two-arousal hypothesis: reticular formation and the limbic system. *Psychol. Rev.* 75:51-80, 1968.
21. Pribram, K.H. Emotion: steps toward a neuropsychological theory. In D.C. Glass, ed., *Neurophysiology and Emotion.* New York: Rockefeller University Press, 1967.
22. Miller, G.A., Galanter, E., and Pribram, K.H. *Plans and Structure of Behavior.* New York: Henry Holt, 1960.
23. Gellhorn, E. *Autonomic Regulations.* New York: Interscience, 1943.
24. Gellhorn, E. *Autonomic Imbalance and the Hypothalamus.* Minneapolis: University of Minnesota Press, 1957.
25. Gellhorn, E. *Principles of Autonomic-Somatic Integrations: Physiological and Clinical Implications.* Minneapolis: University of Minnesota Press, 1967.
26. Gellhorn, E. The neurophysiological basis of anxiety: A hypothesis. *Perspect. Biol. Med.* 8:488, 1965.
27. Graham, D.T., Kabler, J.D., and Lunsford, L., Jr. Vasovagal fainting: A disphasic response. *Psychosom. Med.* 23:493-507, 1961.
28. Canon, W.B. *The Wisdom of the Body,* 2nd ed. New York: Norton, 1939.
29. Luria, A.R. *The Nature of Human Conflict.* New York: Liveright, 1932.
30. Richter, C.P. On the phenomenon of sudden death in animals and man. *Psychosom. Med.* 19:191-198, 1957.
31. Eppinger, H., and Hess, L. *Die Vagotonie.* Berlin, 1910. (Trans. *Vagotonia, Mental and Nervous Disease Monograph,* No. 20. New York: Nervous & Mental Disease Publ. Co., 1915).
32. Hess, W.R. *Das Zwischenhirn: Syndrome, Lokalizationen, Funktionen.* Basel: Schwabe, 1949.
33. Wenger, M.A. Studies of autonomic balance in Army Air Force personnel. *Comp. Psychol. Monogr.* 101:1-111, 1948.
34. Jouvet, M. Paradoxical sleep. In Akert, Balby, and Schade, eds., *Sleep Mechanisms: Progress in Brain Research.* Amsterdam: Elsevier, 1965.
35. Gellhorn, E. Central nervous system tuning and its implications for neuropsychiatry. *J. Nerv. Ment. Dis.* 147:148-162, 1968.
36. Gellhorn, E., and Loofbarrow, G.N. *Emotions and Emotional Disorders.* New York: Hoeber, 1963.
37. Davis, R.C., Buchwald, A.M., and Frankmann, R.W. Autonomic and muscular responses and their relation to simple stimuli. *Psychol. Monogr.* 69 (Whole No. 45): 1-71, 1955.
38. Sokolov, E.N. Higher nervous functions: The orienting reflex. *Ann. Rev. Physiol.* 25:545-580, 1963.
39. Mefferd, R.B., Jr., and Wieland, B.A. The suppression of stress induced sympathetic activation by cognitive activity. *Fed. Proc.* 23:359, 1964.
40. Mefferd, R.B., Jr., and Wieland, B.A. Modification of autonomically mediated physiological responses to cold pressor by word association. *Phychophysiol.* 2:1-19,1965.
41. Hines, E.A., and Brown, G.E. Standard test for measuring variability of blood pressure: Its significance as index of prehypertensive state. *Ann. Intern. Med.* 7:209-217, 1933.
42. Jung, C.G. On psychophysiological relation of the associative experiments. *J. Abnorm. Soc. Psychol.* 1:247-255, 1907.
43. Lewis, T. Observation upon the reaction of the vessels of the human skin to cold. *Heart* 15:177-208, 1930.
44. Adams, T., and Smith, R.E. Effect of chronic local cold exposure on finger temperature responses. *J. Appl. Physiol.* 7:317-322, 1962.
45. Goldberg, D.H. The physiological effects of multiple stressors. *Behav.Sci.* 11:438-443, 196.

46. Benjamin, F.B. Effect of pain on simultaneous perception of non-painful sensory stimulation. *J. Appl. Physiol.* 8:620-634, 1966.
47. McDaniel, C.D., Mefferd, R.B., Jr., Wieland, B.A., Sadler, T.G., and Benton, R.G. Modificaiton of galvanic skin response by reaction time measurements. *Psychophysiol.* 4:340-341, 1968.
48. Duncker, K. Some preliminary experiments on the mutual influence of pains. *Psychologische Forschung* 21:311-326, 1937.
49. Gardner, W.J., and Licklider, J.C.R. Auditory analgesia in dental operations. *J. Am. Dent. Assoc.* 59:1144-1149, 1959.
50. Gardner, W.J., Licklider, J.R.C., and Weisz, A.Z. Suppressing pain by sound. *Science* 132:32-33, 1960.
51. Sadler, T.G., Wieland, B.A., Mefferd, R.B., Jr., Benton, R.G., and McDaniel, C.D. Modification in autonomically mediated physiological responses to cold pressor by cognitive activity: An extension. *Psychophysiol.* 4:229-230, 1967.
52. Sadler, T.G., Mefferd,R.B., Jr., Wieland, B.A., Benton, R.G., and McDaniel, C.D. Physiological effects of combinations of painful and cognitive stimuli. *Psychophysiol.* 5:370-375, 1969.
53. Mefferd, R.B., Jr., Sadler, T.G., and Wieland, B.A. Physiological responses to mild hetermodal sensory stimulation. *Psychophysiol.* 6:186-196, 1969.
54. Houck, R.L., and Mefferd,R.B., Jr. Generalizaiton of GSR habituation to mild intramodal stimuli. *Psychophysiol.* 6:202-206, 1969.
55. Teichner, W.H. Interaction of behavioral and physiological stress reactions. *Psychol. Rev.* 75(4): 271-291, 1968.
56. Pribram, K.H., and McGuinness, D.Arousal, activation, and effort in the control of attention. *Psychol. Rev.* 82:116-149, 1975.
57. Tintera, J.W. Endocrine aspects of schizophrenia: Hypoglycemia of hypoadrenocorticism. *J. Schizophrenia* 1:15-181, 1967.

CHAPTER 9

Biochemical Induction of Anxiety

Ferris N. Pitts, J. and Robert E. Allen

The term "anxiety" denotes an emotion all persons have experienced to some degree. As a result, nearly everyone has personal convictions about anxiety. Nearly everyone is willing to give advice to persons greatly affected by anxiety, and to enter into heated discussion with students of the subject. As with such other universal and emotion-charged topics as religion, politics, and morality, nearly everyone has sufficient personal experience with anxiety to support belief that his view is valid. As with religion and politics, nearly everyone has an *incomplete and biased personal experience* with anxiety. Personal experience, no matter how extreme or complete, does not provide expert knowledge.

Anxiety is not only a universal experience of living but also a *key word* for professionals that denotes an essential intellectual foundation to nearly all the theories and schools of psychology and psychiatry. There are as many different *specific* definitions of anxiety as there are theories and schools. Experts, then, also have a considerable personal *professional* experience with, and conviction about, the emotion-charged topic of anxiety and tend to interpret new data in light of *that* personal experience. Experts are better able to provide open minds in response to new data on a new topic than to new data on an old key topic.

We hope that we can integrate the new data on biochemical inductions of anxiety, and the new data on biochemical inhibitions of pathological anxiety, into psychiatric knowledge without going through the process the experts on Stonehenge are following.

How like the subject of Stonehenge is the topic of anxiety! Ancient; amazing; monumental; mystical; perceived yet not fully grasped; subject of learned discourses for hundreds of years; object of veneration; *still* the subject of scientific speculations about Druids and primitive savage religious rites more than fifteen years after Gerald Hawkins first demonstrated (1,2) that every stone, opening, viewing line, and peripheral picket hole point exactly to a significant celestial circumstance, so that when Stonehenge was intact it served (and thus could *only* serve) as an intricate observatory-calendar-eclipse predictor. If archaeologists and druidologists and Stonehengologists and the British government, which continues to provide special access to the monument to self-styled modern druids, can *simply ignore that kind of evidence*, we fear psychiatrists and psychologists may well ignore the less compelling picture of the pathophysiology of somatic anxiety developed from human experimentation.

We believe enough data are now available to indicate that the mechanism of expression of symptoms of pathologic somatic anxiety in man involve hyperactivity or hypersensitivity somewhere in the complex chain of events triggered by beta-adrenergic agonists. The relationship of conscious apprehensive anxiety to the peripheral somatic symptoms (dependent or independent variable, both, sometimes one or the other), on the other hand, is at present only a matter of opinion resulting in considerable scholastic argumentation (3).

Tompkins, Sturgis, and Wearn reported in 1919 that 5 mg intramuscular adrenaline (mostly epinephrine, some norepinephrine) produced marked exacerbation of anxiety symptoms in neurotic soldiers with the "irritable heart syndrome" (DaCosta's syndrome, neurocirculatory asthenia), but not in normal control soldiers, although both groups manifested physiologic changes with the injection (4). Since that initial report many others have confirmed that epinephrine injection regularly produces anxiety symptoms in neurotics (who generally manifest their specific anxiety symptom pattern with the injection) (5-26). Normal subjects respond less regularly to epinephrine injections with many fewer symptoms. Neither group responded to electrolyte infusions with anxiety symptoms. Much of the later literature consisted of argumentation about the role of the investigator and previously learned associations in evoking anxiety symptoms; a careful reading of these papers reveals that the subjects discussed at such great length varied more in clinical condition than did the role of the investigator in the experiments conducted. Lindemann and Finesinger *were* able to make the critical distinctions and reported that markedly anxious patients with known histories of sympathomimetic symptoms responded to intramuscular adrenaline with anxiety symptoms, but other subjects did not (27,28).

Mendlowitz and coworkers (29) gave intrvenous infusions of norepine-phrine and epinephrine to mild hypertensives under ganglionic blockade. They found no anxiety responses to norepinephrine, but marked anxiety responses to epinephrine infusions *only in patients with histories of anxiety symptoms*. Patients with little or no natural prior anxiety symptoms had little or no anxiety response to epinephrine infusion. An additional correlation of natural prior and experimental-epinephrine-evoked anxiety symptoms was with digital vascular reactivity (DVR) to epinephrine, but not DVR to norepinephrine. Those patients with high DVR to epinephrine were the patients who had histories of anxiety symptoms and developed anxiety with epinephrine infusion (but not with saline or norepinephrine infusion). None of a host of other cardiovascular variables correlated with natural or experimental anxiety. The results of this work tended to demonstrate *increased reactivity to epinephrine in anxious patients.*

Epinephrine has both alpha- and beta-adrenergic actions, although beta predominate. Isoproterenol, on the other hand, is a pure beta-adrenergic agonist with no alpha-adrenergic action used by Frolich (30) in defining the hyperdynamic beta-adrenergic circulatory state. This is a labile hypertensive state with multiple anxiety symptoms, hypersensitivity to isoproterenol infusion, and relief of both hypertension and anxiety symptoms with such beta-adrenergic blocking medications as propranolol. The hypertensive (and nonhypertensive) anxious patients respond to isoproterenol infusion with marked anxiety symptoms and anxiety attacks; normal controls and nonanxious hypertensives develop many fewer and much less severe anxiety symptoms with isoproterenol infusion. A number of others have reported anxiety symptoms and attacks in anxious subjects with isoproterenol infusions (31-33), but to date no psychiatrically sophisticated investigator has systematically infused isoproterenol (and saline control infusions) into anxiety neurotics and normal controls in natural and beta-blocked states with a double-blind design to determine scientifically any individual and group differences in psychologic, psychiatric, and physiologic responses. This shouldn't be as difficult as doing a double-blind drug study of effect of diazepam on anxiety and should yield much more important information.

Gershon and his associates gave separate epinephrine and yohimbine infusions to 7 schizophrenic and 5 nonschizophrenic inpatients and found that both evoked considerable physiological cardiovascular changes of the same sort, epinephrine immediately and yohimbine in a somewhat delayed manner (34). Subjects manifested "anxiety" to some psychologic testing after each drug but not after saline infusion. No anxiety neurotics have been reported to have been given yohimbine, although this alpha-adrenergic blocker might well produce anxiety symptoms in such susceptible persons by producing relative beta-adrenergic accentuations. Thus, systematic admini-stration of yohimbine to anxiety neurotics is another important experiment yet to be performed.

Our own work has been with lactate infusions in anxiety neurosis (35-37). The intellectual stimulus to begin this work was provided by the work of Paul Dudley White, Mandel Cohen, and others at the Army Fatigue Laboratory during World War II (38). These investigators demonstrated that anxiety neurotics, but not matched controls, developed symptoms of anxiety neurosis and significantly greater elevations of blood lactate consequent to a standard exercise test. Would an infusion of lactate to produce the levels obtained in strenuous exercise produce symptoms in anxiety neurotics but not in normal controls? Before proceeding, it is important to review what anxiety neurosis is and some of what is known about it.

Anxiety neurosis is a chronic familial illness characterized by feelings of tenseness and apprehension, breathlessness and shortness of breath, palpitation, nervousness, irritability, chest pain and chest discomfort, easy tiring, dizziness, numbness and tingling of the skin, trembling and faintness — and by acute anxiety attacks. Anxiety attacks are abrupt spells of intense fear of impending doom that come on with or without any apparently appropriate stimulus. The attacks are associated with symptoms of smothering and palpitation and often result in fear of heart attack, cancer, insanity, or some other grave disorder. The condition most often arises when the person is between the ages of 15 and 35 and is found in about 5% of the general population. The symptoms persist with fluctuating intensity for many years without in any way reducing longevity or increasing susceptibility to other diseases. The symptoms are frightening and the fatigue is intense, so the anxiety neurotic seeks medical attention.

Physical examination reveals no abnormality, and laboratory tests are usually normal. The physician is faced with treating an individual who has many subjective physical complaints and great fear of serious illness but who gives no evidence of such illness. The patient is certain that his symptoms signal a distressing condition; he comes to believe his disease is either so serious that the doctor cannot tell him the truth or so early in its course as to be unrecognizable. Naturally, the patient often seeks other medical opinions, and the more active and determined the patient is, the more doctors he sees. Family physicians and internists are consulted about breathlessness and heart palpitations, ophthalmologists about blurred vision, neurologists about dizziness and numbness, otolaryngologists about a "lump in the throat," and psychiatrists about the subjective anxiety and its behavioral consequences. Psychotherapy has little effect on the symptoms of anxiety neurosis, although it may influence the patient to accept his condition (35-38).

Perhaps the best and certainly the most entertaining anecdotal description was by an apparent sufferer, the noted humorist Goodman Ace (39).

Anxiety neurosis has had many names. The first written description was given by Alfred Stille (40), a Civil War military surgeon; he called it palpitation of the heart. Some of the other terms used for this disorder have been muscular exhaustion of the heart (41), nervous exhaustion (42), irritable heart (43), neurasthenia (44), effort syndrome (45), neurocirculatory asthenia (46), vasoregulatory asthenia (47) and hyperdynamic beta-adrenergic circulatory state (30). The term anxiety neurosis was introduced by Sigmund Freud (48).

Early clinical descriptions were sketchy and imprecise, but in 1871 Jacob M. DaCosta listed nearly all the symptoms in a report on more than 300 cases seen in a Union army hospital during the Civil War (43). DaCosta pointed out that the disorder could not be new because he had located complete case reports of the syndrome in British army records from the Crimean War and incomplete descriptions in other military hospital records from campaigns in the preceding two centuries. He emphasized that although the disorder had been recognized and defined by military surgeons evaluating soldiers unable to take the field, it was not caused by military life, since most soldiers had developed the disorder before joining the army and many civilan patients also exhibited it. DaCosta was also the first to demonstrate the familial nature of anxiety neurosis, and described a pair of affected twins. As a result of his report (which was remarkably rigorous in organization and content, even compared with many papers published in medical journals today), the disorder was long known as DaCosta's syndrome. In many ways that is still the best term, since it is the only one that does not imply that the cause is known or implicate any one organ system.

Physicians disagree as to how many distinct conditions are described by the various diagnostic terms and how the terms overlap and interrelate. The fact is that it seems impossible to differentiate DaCosta's syndrome from neurocirculatory asthenia or either of them from anxiety neurosis. The standards for the diagnosis of anxiety neurosis have been the least stringent, but if one does a systematic psychiatric examination of a person labeled an anxiety neurotic (for whatever reason) and is able to rule out the presence of other psychiatric conditions, the patient will usually report enough of the symptoms associated with neurocirculatory asthenia to justify that diagnosis also. In short, although the symptoms of anxiety neurosis are subjective and the disorder may represent a group of symptoms caused by several different specific factors or diseases, we still have no reliable way of subclassifying the group of patients with anxiety neurosis on any clinical grounds. The symptoms characteristic of anxiety neurosis are also seen, in different percentage distributions, in many psychiatric conditions and in the course of many medical conditions. It is important for physicians to learn the complex differential diagnosis of anxiety symptoms if each patient is to be given the best treatment.

Thus, some anxiety symptoms occur briefly in normals in response to stress of examinations (49) or in response to threats of bodily harm (38). Anxiety syndromes occur in the course of depressions of all types (50,51), in the course of hysteria (50,51), in the course of obsessive-compulsive neurosis

(50-52), in the course of sociopathy (53,54), in the course of alcoholism (50,55,56), in the course of schizophrenia of various types (50,57,58). and in the course of many other psychiatric and general medical disorders (59-62). Such anxiety symptoms often differ in types and intensities in the presence of the various accompanying problems (35,49), but the differences often are apparent only in group percentage distributions. In some circumstances, the anxiety symptoms are clearly secondary to the other disorder, but in others the relationship may be one of statistical probability rooted in the relative frequency of the two conditions. Thus, some patients have anxiety symptoms with a brief depressive syndrome but not before its onset or after recovery. Many individuals with hypoparathyroidism find that the most sensitive index to a requirement for increased dosage of calcium and/or vitamin D is the appearance of anxiety symptoms. Although there are many other circumstances of probable causal relationships between other disorders and anxiety syndromes, there are many more in which the relationship is obscure.

The familial nature of anxiety neurosis was demonstrated some years ago in a systematic study by Wheeler, White, Reed, and Cohen (36). They found that the incidence of the disorder in a random control sampling of the general population was 4.7 percent, but that among relatives of patients it was several times higher. With one parent affected, 48.6 percent of the children suffered from anxiety neurosis; with two parents affected, 61.9 percent of the children suffered from the disorder. With neither parent affected but with one child suffering from anxiety neurosis, 27.9 percent of the other children in the family were affected, whereas the incidence in the general population sample was about 4 or 5 percent. These data demonstrated that familial factors operate in the transmission of anxiety neurosis.

Some of the symptoms of anxiety neurosis resemble those produced by physical exertion, and indeed most patients report that physical activity can bring on or intensify their symptoms. These facts led medical investigators to evaluate various physical functions in anxiety neurotics (38,64-69). They found that, compared with normal controls, anxiety neurotics react sooner to increasing levels of noise, light, or heat. They cannot maintain a strong hand grip as long. Their breathing rate increases more in response to discomfort (a tightening blood-pressure cuff, for example). In response to light exercise they show more of an increase in pulse and breathing rates, utilized inspired oxygen less efficiently, and develop a higher level of lactic acid in the blood.

It has been shown by investigations in four countries that the rise in blood lactate with exercise is excessive in anxiety neurotics (38,64-69). The appearance of anxiety symptoms evoked in patients by exercise was concomitant with the extremely rapid rise in lactate; nonpatients serving as controls did not develop anxiety symptoms with exercise and showed only the expected normal increase in lactate. In the anxiety neurotics, the excessive rise in lactate (per unit of work per unit of time) was approximately that seen in patients with such serious medical conditions as arteriosclerotic or rheumatic heart disease.

It occurred to us that perhaps the lactate in itself could produce anxiety attacks in susceptible people. We conducted a pilot study of 9 patients, with 9 nonpatients as controls. In all the patients and in 2 of the controls typical anxiety attacks developed with lactate infusions that were sufficient to raise the venous lactate level to between 10 and 15 millimoles per liter, a range that is normally attained only with maximum muscular exertion or after the administration of adrenalin. Such attacks did not develop in patients or controls with either of two control fusions.

We went on then to perform a double-blind experiment (35). On the basis of rigid criteria we selected a group of 14 patients who could definitely be classified as anxiety neurotics, and we picked a carefully matched group of 10 normal subjects to serve as controls. Each of the subjects received 10 milliliters per kilogram of body weight of each of three experimental solutions by intravenous infusion at three experimental sessions five to ten days apart, with the various solutions administered in carefully randomized order. The physician conducting the procedure was unaware of the contents of each infusion, the medical history of the subjects, or the purpose of the experiment. He gave the infusion, recorded the subject's behavior and comments, and took blood and urine samples. Then the subjects were questioned systematically about their symptoms.

The three infusions were solutions of: 500 m-molar sodium lactate, 500 m-molar sodium lactate with added 20 m-molar calcium chloride, and 555 m-molar glucose and 167 m-molar sodium chloride. The calcium in the control infusion was about enough to saturate the binding capacity of the added lactate, so the lactate would presumably leave the ionized calcium level in the subject's blood and tissue fluids unaltered. The second control solution, glucose in saline, was chosen because its concentration was in the range of the lactate solutions (hypertonic) and its metabolism would not be different from the glucose formed in the liver from the intravenously administered lactate.

After the third session each subject was asked to rate the three infusions in order of the severity of their effects. The blind observer did the same thing for each of the subjects. All 24 subjects were able in effect to "identify" the three solutions by reporting that the sodium lactate had caused the most symptoms, the glucose very few symptoms or none at all, and the sodium lactate with added calcium an intermediate number of symptoms. This result had a high statistical significance. The probability that the 24 subjects would correctly rank all three solutions by chance was one in 10,000. The blind investigator did almost as well. He correctly ranked all three solutions for 11 of the 14 patients and for 7 of the controls, a performance that would be achieved by chance only 5 times in 10,000 trials.

The most striking outcome of the experiment was that the infusion produced anxiety attacks. This was the first time, to our knowledge, that such a result had been systematically achieved with a chemical, physiological, or psychological stimulus. Thirteen of the 14 patients and 2 of the 10 controls had typical acute anxiety attacks during the lactate infusion. None of the subjects in either group had such attacks with either of the control infusions. Thus, the addition of calcium markedly reduced the effect of the lactate on the anxiety neurotics, and the infusion of other hypertonic solutions does not per se cause anxiety attacks in susceptible individuals.

When individual anxiety symptoms are considered, the results again show a strong effect of lactate, a mitigating effect of calcium, and a difference in the response of patients and controls to lactate. It is noteworthy that with the lactate infusion all subjects in both patient and control groups experienced paresthesias. With the lactate-plus-calcium infusion, only a small minority of the subjects reported paresthesia, and none of them did with glucose infusion. Significantly more patients than controls reported experiencing nearly all the other symptoms with lactate, but with the two control infusions there was no significant difference in the extent to which each symptom was reported by the two groups. These observations hold true for the cumulative total of symptoms as well as for the individual reports. Of the 294 possible symptoms (21 symptoms for each of 14 subjects), the anxiety neurosis patients reported experiencing 190, or 64.6 percent, during lactate infusion, 25.5 percent with lactate plus calcium, and 4.4 percent with glucose. Of 210 possible symptoms, the control subjects reported experiencing 34.3 percent during lactate infusion, 17.1 with lactate plus calcium, and 2.9 percent with glucose. Analysis of these figures shows that the anxiety neurotics developed significantly more symptoms than the controls did with lactate but not with the control infusions ($p < 0.99991$). No other symptoms than those listed developed in any of the subjects with any of the infusions.

There were marked after-effects—significant symptoms lasting more than 24 hours—from the lactate infusion in patients but not in controls; there were no marked after-effects for either group from either control infusion. The anxiety-exhaustion after-effects occurred in 10 patients but in none of the controls with lactate infusion.

In summary, a 20-minute infusion of lactate into a patient with anxiety neurosis reliably produced an anxiety attack that began within a minute or two after the infusion was started, decreased rapidly after the infusion, but was often followed by from one to three days of exhaustion and heightened anxiety symptoms. Such patients did not have anxiety attacks and had many fewer individual symptoms when calcium was added to the lactate infusion. Patients had almost no symptoms when they were infused with glucose-in-saline solution. Nonpatient controls had many fewer and less severe symptoms in response to lactate; they had only a few symptoms in response to lactate with calcium and almost none with glucose. The patient group differed from the controls significantly only in the case of the lactate infusion. Clearly the patients were responding to a specific effect of the lactate, not to any psychological effects of intravenous infusion.

A number of other investigators have given these lactate infusions to anxiety neurotics and matched normal controls, and as far as we can determine, all have obtained similar results.

Fink, Taylor, and Volavka (70) reported completing a double-blind replication of the work described above in five patients and four controls. Their results were essentially identical to those we had described. Additionally, "in concurrent scalp-recorded electroencephalograms (EEG), we observed changes with lactate in the patients but not in the controls nor in either group after dextrose-in-saline and lactate-with-calcium solutions. The EEG exhibited increased beta and decreased alpha abundances and a decreased alpha amplitude. These findings are consistent with EEG changes usually seen in anxiety states." Fink and coworkers, then, had found that an objective, independent, measure—the EEG— could determine that an anxiety attack was occurring in the infusion double-blind experiment.

Grosz and Farmer at the University of Indiana Medical School apparently repeated the lactate infusions in some way, for they say "this is not to say that the infusion of sodium lactate into certain susceptible individuals does not induce anxiety symptoms. It certainly does, as we have been able to replicate. But as we have shown, it hardly does so for the reasons, and by means of mechanisms, proposed by Pitts and McClure" (71). Their initial article said nothing more than this about replication and consisted of lengthy scholastic argumentation attacking Pitts and McClure on illogical and *ad hominem* grounds. Especially prominent in Grosz and Farmer's arguments were strong criticisms of Pitts and McClure for *measurements not yet made* and *experiments not yet done,* even though the original report specified that the exact mechanism of the differential production of anxiety symptoms and anxiety attacks in anxiety neurotics as compared to controls by lactate infusion was *not yet established.* The substance of Grosz and Farmer's lengthy disputatious arguments seemed to be that since Pitts and McClure had not paid enough attention to the alkalinizing action of sodium lactate in their original report, the finding of the production of anxiety attacks with lactate infusion in anxiety neurotics but not in normal controls was invalid; this, of course, is an illogical conclusion.

In a second related communication (72), Grosz and Farmer started with the untrue assertion that "Pitts and McClure have recently suggested that all symptoms of anxiety and anxiety neurosis are caused by a raised blood and body fluids lactate level" and again proceeded to destroy that straw man with scholastic argumentation. They reported that the infusion in 30 minutes of 8 milliliter per kilogram of 500 millimolar sodium lactate into 10 normal young men caused 51 of 100 possible anxiety symptoms; of 500 millimolar sodium bicarbonate caused 42 of 100 possible anxiety symptoms, of 555 millimolar glucose in 155 millimolar sodium chloride produced only 3 of 100 possible anxiety symptoms. Both sodium lactate and sodium bicarbonate produced anxiety; both did this with statistically greater potency than glucose in saline; both did this with similar reliability. Grosz and Farmer had shown that the complexation of ionized calcium by the infusion of alkalinizing solutions (bicarbonate and lactate both directly complex ionized calcium and also produce protein-binding of ionized calcium consequent to an alkaline pH shift) into normals is followed by paresthesias and other hypocalcemic symptoms. This is a banal and trivial finding entirely predictable by most medical students and without relevance to anxiety neurosis. Grosz and Farmer *failed* to demonstrate that sodium bicarbonate infusions cause anxiety attacks in anxiety neurotics but not in normals. It is probable that sodium bicarbonate and sodium lactate have similar actions in causing anxiety attacks in susceptible individuals but not in normal controls. After *failing* to make the significant finding that sodium bicarbonate (like sodium lactate) infusions cause anxiety attacks in anxiety neurotics but not in normal controls because it "seemed unnecessary to expose patients with anxiety neurosis to the distressing experience of this experiment," Grosz and Farmer (72) ended their summary by making the entirely illogical and presumptive assertion that because sodium lactate and sodium bicarbonate infusions are roughly equivalent in normals, "neither their study nor their theory is soundly based."

Friedhoff (73) pointed out that Grosz and Farmer's demonstration that anxiety hypocalcemic symptoms could be produced in normals by sodium bicarbonate infusions was an extension of Pitts and McClure's work, not a refutation.

Grosz (74) apparently aroused by Friedhoff's gentle suggestion that "these newer findings should be viewed simply as an extension and refinement of the hypothesis of Pitts and McClure," made several unwarranted, several unproven, and several unprovable assertions. He claimed that the reason his findings were presented as a "refutation of Pitts and McClure's conclusions is first, that the kind of study we did should have been carried out by Pitts and McClure as a necessary control experiment, and secondly, that we do not believe that the results of our study impart any substantially new knowledge. . . ." Grosz then asserted "the common denominator seems to be some deviation from the norm in the patient's internal biophysical environment. This leads us to believe that *anxiety-prone subjects, and perhaps anxiety neurotics, may essentially suffer from an excessive sensitivity or intolerance to disturbances in their internal bio-physical homeostasis*" (italics Grosz's). "*Viewed in this light Pitts and McClure's experiment does little more than illustrate what happens when anxiety-prone subjects are suddenly exposed to major perturbation of homeostasis—in this case to major electrolyte and acid-base disturbances*" (italics Pitts). Not only is this "Grosz theory of anxiety and anxiety neurosis" quoted here a more general and vague restatement of the speculations of Pitts and others, but it is stated to be true without any evidence other than Grosz's unsupported assertions that the same people would manifest anxiety with a wide variety of very different fluid and electrolyte disturbances from very different causes.

There is at present no systematic evidence that anxiety neurotics reliably develop anxiety attacks (and normal controls do not) with anything other than the infusion of beta-adrenergic agonists, sodium lactate, or sodium bicarbonate (74). In fact, the infusion of such more powerful complexing (chelating) agents for ionized calcium as sodium ethylenediamine-tetracetic acid (EDTA) produces profound hypocalcemic symptoms but no anxiety attacks in either anxiety neurotics or controls (75). These facts tend to disprove Grosz's general theories of anxiety being evoked in "nonspecific disequilibrium of internal biophysical homeostasis," and tend, rather, to support a less general theory of somatic anxiety symptoms in anxiety neurotics being due to hyperactivity and/or hypersensitivity somewhere in the complex chain of events triggered by beta-adrenergic agonists. Certainly Mendlowitz and coworkers *(vide supra)* have demonstrated specific psychologic and physiologic *increased reactivity to epinephrine but not to norepinephrine in anxious patients* (29), so the "nonspecific bio-physical disequilibrium of homeostasis" theory of anxiety is disproven unless one would choose to believe that norepinephrine infusions are innocuous to homeostatic equilibrium.

Kelly, Mitchell-Heggs, and Sherman made a most careful and detailed replication of the effects of sodium lactate infusion in anxiety neurotics (76) with added measurements that reflect arousal: forearm blood flow (FBF) and heart rate (HR). Twenty patients were selected who satisfied Pitts and McClure's criteria for anxiety neurosis; they and 10 matched normals were subjected to double-blind experimental infusions after completing numerous psychometric and anxiety ratings. The anxiety neurotics had higher mean Taylor Anxiety scores ($p < 0.001$), Neuroticism scores ($p < 0.001$), Free-Floating Anxiety scores ($p < 0.001$), Phobic scores ($p < 0.001$), Obsessional scores ($p < 0.001$), Somatic scores ($p < 0.001$), Observer Depressive Rating ($p < 0.05$), and Depressive Self Rating ($p < 0.05$). On the Hysteric scale the anxiety neurotics did not differ from controls. Kelly, Mitchell-Heggs, and Sherman made a large number of controlled observations. During pre-injection, cannulation, and saline infusion, several of the anxiety measures and arousal measures were higher in anxiety neurotics than in controls. During the sodium lactate infusions, anxiety neurotics developed anxiety attacks but controls did not; during the sodium lactate infusion, Observer Rating and Self Ratings of Anxiety were significantly greater in anxiety neurotics, as were FBF and HR. The sodium lactate infusions were stopped immediately when an anxiety attack commenced so that the average amount of lactate given was 79 percent for the anxiety neurotics and 99 percent for the controls; nevertheless, the 20 anxiety neurotics reported 249 of 420 possible symptoms ($x2$ 12.5), and the 10 normal controls reported 72 of 210 possible symptoms ($x2$ 7.2, p $<$ 0.001). Neither group of subjects experienced symptoms with saline infusion, so sodium lactate produced significantly more symptoms in anxiety neurotics than in controls and significantly more symptoms than saline in all subjects. Kelly, Mitchell-Heggs, and Sherman treated 8 anxiety neurotics who had experienced anxiety attacks with sodium lactate infusion with monoamine oxidase inhibitor antidepressants for a mean period of 10 weeks (range 5-17 weeks) and then repeated the sodium lactate infusion experiments. The 5 "much improved" patients experienced fewer and less severe symptoms with lactate infusion; the 2 "improved" patients experienced similar symptoms with repeat infusion; and the 1 "unimproved" had an anxiety attack during saline infusion. Kelly, Mitchell-Heggs, and Sherman concluded that they had confirmed Pitts and McClure's observations, that "sodium lactate provides a biochemical means of producing anxiety in the laboratory which may prove useful for testing the anti-anxiety effect of various types of treatment"; and "the Pitts and McClure hypothesis for explaining the relationship between anxiety and sodium lactate may not be correct, but more information about the biochemical changes involved may further our understanding of the aetiology and treatment of anxiety."

In summary, beta-adrenergic agonists (epinephrine, isoproterenol) or metabolic products of their action (lactate) will reliably produce (with dose-response qualification) anxiety symptoms and anxiety attacks in susceptible subjects (anxiety neurotics) but not in matched normal controls. A host of experiments dealing with production of anxiety symptoms await the energetic psychiatrist: systematic use of beta-adrenergic agonists and/or blockers in groups of patients compared to matched normal controls will be the general experimental approach. Anxiety requiring such study occurs secondarily and/or concomitantly to large numbers of patients with unipolar and bipolar affective disorder, with schizophrenia, with obsessive-compulsive disease, with nearly every other psychiatric disorder, with many diseases of the liver, and with many of the infectious and endocrinological diseases. Are all these anxiety states similarly evoked by beta-adrenergic agonists and modulated by beta-adrenergic blockade, or are there many different types of anxiety states? Only further clinical experimentation can provide data allowing reasonable answers to these questions. Other experimental techniques that result in an outpouring of lactate from muscles have produced anxiety symptoms in susceptible individuals in excess over controls: hyperventilation, hypoxia, exercise, and infusion of bicarbonate are measures that can result both in very large increases in lactate production and anxiety symptoms in anxiety neurotics. Clinically and experimentally the infusion of calcium ion or the production of respiratory acidosis or the administration of competitive beta-adrenergic blocking drugs tends to reduce or prevent naturally occurring (or experimentally produced) anxiety symptoms in susceptible individuals. In contrast, alpha-adrenergic agonists such as norepinephrine and phenylephrine and others do *not* produce anxiety symptoms in susceptible individuals. Alpha-adrenergic *blockade* with yohimbine has been shown perhaps to produce some of the symptoms of anxiety.

References

1. Hawkins, G.S. The secret of Stonehenge. *Harper's,* June 1964 pp. 307-313.
2. Hawkins, G.S., and White, J.B. *Stonehenge Decoded.* New York: Doubleday, 1965.
3. Ackerman, S.H., and Sachar, E.J. The lactate theory of anxiety: A review and reevaluation. *Psychosom. Med.* 36:69-81, 1974.
4. Tompkins, E.H., Sturgis, C.C., and Wearn, J.T. Studies in epinephrine. II. *Arch. Int. Med.* 24:247-268, 1919.
5. Basowitz, H., Korchin, S.J., Oken, D., Goldstein, M.S., and Gussack, H. Anxiety and performance changes with minimal doses of epinephrine. *Arch. Neurol. Psychiat.* 76:98-106, 1956.
6. Cameron, D.E. Adrenal in administration in resistant anxiety states. *Am. J. Med. Sci.* 210:281-288, 1945.
7. Cameron, D.E. Behavioral changes produced in patients suffering with chronic tensional anxiety states, by long-continued adrenalin administration. *Psychiat. Quart.* 21:261-273, 1947.
8. Cantril, H., and Hunt, W.A. Emotional effects produced by injection of adrenalin. *Am. J. Psychol.* 44:300-307, 1932.
9. Darrow, C.W., and Gellhorn, E. The effects of adrenaline on reflex excitability of the autonomic nervous system. *Am. J. Physiol.* 127;243-251, 1939.
10. Dynes, J.G., and Tod, J. Emotional and somatic responses of schizophrenic patients and normal controls to adrenaline and doryl. *J. Neurol. Psychiat.* 3:1-9, 1940.
11. Frankenhauser, M., Jarpe, G., and Mattel,G. Effects of intravenous infusions of adrenaline and noradrenaline on certain psychological and physiological functions. *Acta Physiol. Scand.* 51:175-186, 1961.
12. Frankenhauser, M., and Jarpe, G. Psychophysiological reactions to infusions of a mixture of adrenaline and noradrenaline. *Scand. J. Psychol.* 3:21-29, 1962.
13. Frankenhauser, M., and Jarpe, G. Psychological changes during infusions of adrenaline in various doses. *Psychopharmacol.* 4:424-432, 1963.
14. Funkenstien, D.H., and Meade, L.W. Norepinephrine-like and epinephrine-like substances and the elevation of blood pressure during acute stress. *J. Nerv. Ment. Dis.* 119:380-397, 1954.
15. Funkenstein, D.H. The physiology of fear and anger. *Scientific American* 192:74-80, 1955.
16. Gantt, W.H., and Freile, M. The effect of adrenaline and acetylcholine in excitation, inhibition, and neurosis. *Trans. Am. Neurol. Assoc.* 70:180-181, 1944.
17. Hawkins, E.R., Monroe, J.T., Sandifer, M.G., and Vernon, C.R. Psychological and physiological responses to continuous epinephrine infusion. *Psychiat. Res. Rep. Am. Psychiat. Assoc.* 12:40-52, 1960.
18. Jersild, A.T., and Thomas, W. Influence of adrenal extract on behavior and mental efficiency. *Am. J. Physiol.* 43:447-456, 1931.
19. Kraines, S.H., and Sherman, C. Neurotic symptoms and changes in the blood pressure and pulse following injection of epinephrine. *J.A.M.A.* 114:843-845, 1940.
20. Landis, C., and Hunt, W.A. Adrenalin and emotion. *Psychol. Rev.* 39:467-485, 1932.
21. Maranon, G. Emotive action of epinephrine. *Rev. Franc. Endocrinol.* 2:301,1924. Cited by Cannon, 1929, and Cantril and Hunt, 1932.

22. Pollin, W., and Goldin, S. The physiological and psychological effects of intravenously administered epinephrine and its metabolism in normal and schizophrenic men. II: Psychiatric observations. *J. Psychiat. Res.* 1:50-66, 1961.
23. Richter, D. The action of adrenaline in anxiety. *Proc. Roy. Soc. Med.* 33:615-618, 1940.
24. Rothballer, A.B. The effect of catecholamines on the central nervous system. *Pharmacol. Rev.* 11:494-544, 1959
25. Rudolph,G. De M. Unusual results following the injection of epinephrine. *Endocrinology* 23:366-367, 1938.
26. Thorley, A.S. Action of adrenalin in neurotics. *J. Neurol. Psychiat.* 5:14-21, 1942.
27. Lindemann, E., and Finesinger, J.E. The effect of adrenalin and mecholyl in states of anxiety in psychoneurotic patients. *Am. J. Psychiat.* 95:353-370, 1938.
28. Lindemann, E., and Finesinger, J.E. Subjective responses of psychoneurotic patients to adrenalin and mecholyl. *Psychosom. Med.* 2:231-248, 1940.
29. Vlachakis, N.D., DeGuia, D. et al. Hypertension and anxiety. A trial with epinephrine and norepinephrine infusion. *Mt. Sinai J. Med. N.Y.* 41:1615-1625, 1974.
30. Frohlich, E.D., Dustan, H.P., and Page, I.H. Hyperdynamic Beta-adrenergic circulatory state. *Arch. Int. Med.* 117:614-619, 1966.
31. Combs, D.T., and Martin C.M. Evaluation of isoproterenol as a method of stress testing. *Am. Heart J.* 87:711-715, 1974.
32. Easton, J.D., and Sherman, D.G. Somatic anxiety attacks and propranolol. *Arch. Neurol.* (Chicago) 33:689-691, 1969.
33. Frohlich, E.D., Tarazi, R.C., and Dustan, H.P. Hyperdynamic Beta-adrenergic circulatory state: Increased Beta-receptor responsiveness. *Arch. Int. Med.* 123:1-7, 1969.
34. Garfield, S.L., Gershon, S., Sletten, I., et al. Chemically induced anxiety. *Int. J. Neuropsychiat.* 3:426-433, 1967.
35. Pitts, F.N., and McClure, J.N. Lactate metabolism in anxiety neurosis. *New Eng. J Med.* 227:1329-1336, 1967.
36. Pitts, F.N. The biochemistry of anxiety. *Scientific American* 220;69-75, 1969.
37. Pitts, F.N. Biochemical factors in anxiety neurosis. *Behav. Sci.* 16:82-91, 1971.
38. Cohen, M.E., and White, P.D. Life situations, emotions, and neurocirculatory asthenia (anxiety neurosis, neurasthenia, effort syndrome). *Tr. Assoc. Res. Nerv. Ment. Dis.* 29:832-869, 1950.
39. Ace, G. The art of hypochondria. *Saturday Review,* July 11, 1964, p. 12; July 25, 1964, p. 9; August 1, 1964, p.8.
40. Stille, A. On irritable heart, a clinical form of functional cardiac disorder and its consequences. *Am. J. Med. Sci.* 61:17-52, 1871.
41. Hartshorne, H. On heart disease in the army. *Am. J. Med. Sci.* 48:89-92, 1864.
42. Beard, G.M. Neurasthenia or nervous exhaustion. *Boston Med. Surg. J.* 3:217-221, 1869.
43. DaCosta, J.M. On irritable heart, a clinical form of functional cardiac disorder and its consequences. *Am. J. Med. Sci.* 61:17-52, 1871.
44. Hecker, E. Ueber larvite and abortive angstzustande bei neurasthenie. *Centralbl. f. Nervenh.* 4:565-572, 1893.
45. Lewis, T. *The Soldier's Heart and the Effort Syndrome.* London: Shaw, 1919.
46. Oppenheimer, B.S., Levine, S.A., Morison, R.A., et al. Illustrated cases of neurocirculatory asthenia. *Mil. Surg.* 42:711-719, 1918..
47. Holmgren, A., Jonsson, B., Levander-Lindgren, M., et al. Low physical working capacity in suspected heart cases due to the inadequate adjustment of peripheral blood flow (vasoregulatory asthenia). *Acta Med. Scand.* 163:158-184, 1959.
48. Freud, S. Ueber die berechtigung vonder neurasthenic einen bestimmten symptomen complex als "angstneurose" abzutrennen. *Neurol. Centralbl.* 14:50-69, 1895.

49. Pitts, F.N., Winokur, G., and Stewart, M.A. Psychiatric syndromes, anxiety symptoms, and responses to stress in medical students. *Am. J. Psychiat.* 118:333-340, 1961.
50. Woodruff, R.A., Goodwin, D.W., and Guze, S.B. *Psychiatric Diagnosis.* New York: Oxford University Press, 1974.
51. Feighner, J.P., Robins, E., Guze, S.B., et al. Diagnostic criteria for use in psychiatric research. *Arch. Gen. Psychiat.* 26:57-63, 1972.
52. Woodruff, R.A., and Pitts, F.N. Monozygotic twins with obsessional illness. *Am. J. Psychiat.* 120:1075-1080, 1964.
53. Robins, L.N. *Deviant Children Grown Up.* Baltimore: Williams & Wilkins, 1966.
54. Guze, S.B., Goodwin, D.W., and Crane, J.B. Criminality and psychiatric disorders. *Arch. Gen. Psychiat.* 20:583-591, 1969.
55. Pitts, F.N., and Winokur, G. Affective disorder VII: Alcoholism and affective disorder. *J. Psychiat. Res.* 4:37-50, 1966.
56. Amark, C. Study in alcoholism: Clinical, social psychiatric and genetic investigations. *Acta Psychiat. Scand.,* Suppl. 70, 1951.
57. Etinger, L., Laane, C.L., and Langfeldt, G. The prognostic value of the clinical picture and the therapeutic value of physical treatment in schizophrenia and the schizophreniform states. *Acta Psychiat. Neurol. Scand.* 33:33-53, 1958.
58. Astrup, C., and Noreik, K. *Functional Psychoses: Diagnostic and Prognostic Models.* Springfield, Ill.: Charles C. Thomas, 1966.
59. Perrin, G.M., and Altschule, M.D. Psychiatric diagnoses in hospitalized patients with neurocirculatory asthenia. *New Eng. J. Med.* 254:419-420, 1956.
60. Davis, R.H., Fourman, P., and Smith, J.W.G. Prevalence of parathyroid insufficiency after thyroidectomy. *Lancet* 2:1432-1435, 1961.
61. Liss, J., Alpers, D., and Woodruff, R.A. The "irritable colon" syndrome and psychiatric illness. *Dis. Nerv. Syst.* 34:151-157, 1973.
62. Winokur, G., Clayton, P.J., and Reich, T. *Manic Depressive Illness.* St. Louis: C. V. Mosby, 1969.
63. Wheeler, E.D., White, P.D., Reed, E.W., and Cohen, M.E. Familial incidence of neurocirculatory asthenia (anxiety neurosis, effort syndrome). *J. Clin. Invest.* 27:562-573, 1948.
64. Jones, M., and Mellersh, V. Comparison of exercise response in anxiety states and normal controls. *Psychosom. Med.* 8:180-187, 1946.
65. Linko, E. Lactic acid response to muscular exercise in neurocirculatory asthenia. *Ann. Med. Internae Fenniae* 39:161-176, 1950.
66. Tourniare, A., Tartulier, M., Blum, J., et al. Dans les nevroses tachycardiques et chez les sportifs. *Presse Med.* 69:721-723, 1961.
67. Holmgren, A., and Ström, G. Blood lactate concentrations in relation to absolute and relative work load in normal men, and in mitral stenosis, atrial septal defect, and vasoregulatory asthenia. *Acta Med. Scand.* 163:185-193, 1959.
68. Levander-Lindgren, M., and Ek, S. Studies in neurocirculatory asthenia (DaCosta's Syndrome). *Acta Med. Scand.* 172:665-676, 1962.
69. Kelly, D.H.W., and Walter, C.J.S. The relationship between clinical diagnosis and anxiety assessed by forearm blood flow and other measurements. *Brit. J. Psychiat.* 114:611-626, 1968.
70. Fink, M., Taylor, M.A., and Volavka, J. Anxiety precipitated by lactate. *New Eng. J. Med.* 281:1429, 1969.
71. Grosz, H.J., and Farmer, B.B. Blood lactate in the development of anxiety symptoms. A critical examination of Pitts and McClure's hypothesis and experimental study. *Arch. Gen. Psychiat.* 21:611-619, 1969.
72. Grosz, H.J., and Farmer, B.B. Pitts' and McClure's lactate-anxiety study revisited. *Brit. J. Psychiat.* 120:415-418, 1972.

73. Friedhoff, A.J. Pitts' and McClure's lactate-anxiety study revisited. *Brit. J. Psychiat.* 121:338, 1972.
74. Grosz, H.J. Pitts' and McClure's lactate-anxiety study revisited. *Brit. J. Psychiat.* 122:116-117, 1973.
75. Pitts, F.N. Unpublished data.
76. Kelly, D., Mitchell-Heggs, N., and Sherman, D. Anxiety and the effects of sodium lactate assessed clinically and physiologically. *Brit. J. Psychiat.* 119:129-141, 1971.

CHAPTER 10

Animal Models for Human Psychopathology

William T. McKinney, Jr. and Elaine C. Moran

INTRODUCTION

What is an animal model? It could be said that a model is a model: it is not the real thing, and this must be understood at the beginning. It is only possible to engage in successive approximations. Models are created as open systems for research into underlying or associated mechanisms rather than as merely static replicas. As such, their value lies not only in the imitation of the known but in the exploration of the unknown.

Two major misconceptions, which oddly enough occur on opposite ends of the spectrum, surround the usage of animal models. The first of these is that they are often ignored. This disregard also overlooks much valuable information that these models generate. The second is that expectations from animal models are too high. This leads to premature clinical labeling, which creates its own problems and unrealistic research hopes.

Once a consistent and reliable model has been established, which is an arduous task in itself, it can be an invaluable tool for studying those aspects of psychopathology that cannot safely or ethically be studied in humans. However, a thorough understanding of the appropriate and inappropriate uses of animal models is basic to good research regardless of the particular syndrome being examined. In addition to adhering to basic criteria in creating models (discussed later in this chapter), one must also consider the philosophical underpinnings of specific models. This is an area that has, in the past, been all too often ignored and has contributed to the skepticism surrounding the use of some models. For instance, some proposed animal models were created by circumstances totally alien to these seen by clinicians. Symptoms were produced by use of such techniques as electric shock, immobility, etc. These methods not only appeared to have no correlation to the actual events seen in humans but also seemed to have no analogous relationship to any underlying cause or philosophy.

Once these problems have been resolved the use of animal models for research into the problems of psychosis and neurosis offers a number of advantages, not the least of which is simply the opportunity to do any research at all. Along with these advantages, however, come some limitations. Both must be taken into account during explorations of specific syndromes. Starting off on the positive side, some of the advantages in the use of animal models are:

1. Greater experimental control. Studies of human psychiatric problems have historically started at the time of the event and worked backward through the use of diagnosis and recollection. Obviously therapists could not attempt to produce psychological aberrations in their patients. Ethical considerations also hampered the ability to control variables or to analyze most specific factors. The use of animal models brings about a reversal of this situation. It then becomes possible to control environmental boundaries, arrange case histories, produce severe syndromes, and experiment with untested drugs or combinations of drugs.

2. Dissection of underlying mechanisms. The benefit to research from this area cannot be overstated. Biological interrelationships can be directly examined and manipulated through use of various assays, tissue samples, autopsies, etc. Information can be gathered that, whatever its limitations, can be obtained nowhere else. As an example, a current theory suggests an important role for biogenic amines in human depression. However, no direct studies of brain biogenic amine metabolism in humans can be done with present methodology. Animal models, whatever their limitations, do make such direct studies possible.

3. Telescoped life span. The collapsed life cycle of many animal species facilitates longitudinal developmental studies, which are a very important aspect of social and behavioral research. The much shorter lifetime represents a substantial reduction in the amount of time and money needed for this research. Studies can be run in years that otherwise might take decades for completion, or indeed, might not be possible at all.

There are also limitations in the use of animal models that must be recognized and considered in the interpretation of data. Some of these limitations are:

1. Cross-species reasoning. The higher primates hold many behavioral and physical traits in common; however, research has demonstrated that not

all species, even those which are phylogenetically very close, necessarily respond in the same fashion or even in the same intensity to identical events or stimulations. This is exemplified by the research of Kaufman and Rosenblum (1, 2) with pigtail *(Macaca nemestrina)* and bonnet *(Macaca radiata)* monkeys. When the mothers of young pigtails were removed from the established troop, the youngsters went into a decline, evincing signs of being in the state of "despair" or "depression." The infant bonnets in the same situation did not show any of these signs. This difference might be explained by the difference in the social structure between the two species. Adult female bonnets and their infants spend a lot of time in social contact with one another, while adult female pigtails and their infants are very much "dyadic loners." As a result, the infant bonnets had stabilized relationships with both other adults and other infants to draw on when their mothers were removed. This was not the case with the pigtail infants. If, however, the young bonnets lost contact with the supporting members of their troop, they might show the same behavioral traits as the pigtail infants. There would then be a situation in which the primary inducing cause (loss of an important affectional object) was similar, but the actual event was different. With increased study and information, these differences can be accounted for and integrated into the various theories of behavior.

2. Essence of neuroses controversy. Some researchers maintain that since animal models are not human, their "neuroses" are not the "real" thing. This school of thought has been most actively represented by Kubie (3), who states: "Thus, the imitation in animals of the emotional states which attend neuroses in man is not the experimenal production of the essence of neuroses itself." Kubie's contention is that behavior is only the "sign language" of an underlying symbolic disorder that is the real core of psychopathology. He feels that animals do not have symbolic capacities and that therefore it is logically impossible to produce a true neurotic or psychotic state in nonhumans. Several fallacies stand out in this reasoning. The assumption that behavior is important only as an indicator of something more important which is the "real" disorder is a concept disputed by many. Also, the statement that higher order primates do not have symbolic capacities is open to serious question in light of more recent experimental animal research (4,5).

In consideration of this disagreement, these points should be kept in mind, but the final resolution will have to be held in abeyance until more is known about both species.

WAYS IN WHICH THE STUDY OF ANIMAL BEHAVIOR CAN AID IN THE UNDERSTANDING OF HUMAN BEHAVIOR

1. Descriptions and classification of behaviors. Ethologists have contributed to the careful dissection and description of behavior into its component parts. Psychiatrists and comparative psychologists, reawakening

to this vital aspect of social research, have begun directing their attention to this issue again. If this descriptive stage is bypassed or slighted in the study of either human or animal behavior, progress is retarded in both fields.

2. Utilization of limited scope generalizations. Perhaps this concept was best expressed by Hinde (6), who wrote: "The scope of any generalization is inversely related to its precision." As more behaviors are lumped together in broader categories, sensitivity to precise, limited occurrences is lost. Heretofore, animal modeling studies have most often been carried out with groups of animals and have been focused on group behavior. Individual variability has often been neglected or collapsed into group means. This is understandable when the difficulty of experimental control and the many facets of behavior, both social and biological, and their interrelationships are considered. However, it is vital that more specific research be done on particular interactions in order to broaden the understanding of basic underlying mechanisms.

3. Establishment of principles of animal behavior and assessment of their applicability to humans. This is an area where the study of animal behavior can be a special asset. While we are in no way dismissing or discounting the complexity of interactions in animals, suffice it to say that the relative simplicity, as compared to humans, of their "motivations" and interrelationships can help to isolate problems and illuminate theoretical issues. This can be an especially dangerous procedure and has been grossly misused by certain writers who, by selecting facts to fit preconceived theories, neglecting awkward cases, and failing to distinguish fact from flight of fancy, have gone a long way towards reducing people to nothing but naked apes. With caution and concern, this snare can, however, be circumvented and does not negate the value of this principle, properly used, in assessing human behavior.

Humans and their fellow primates are alike in many aspects of social behavior and physical structure. Research into animal behavior that is tempered by an awareness and consideration of not only those traits which are similar but also of those which are unique to either may provide new information and understanding of the model. This in turn may provide a more accurate means by which human behavior can be assessed and interpreted.

CRITERIA FOR EVALUATION OF ANIMAL MODELS

The transition from intuitive parallels to functional animal models has been difficult in part because of the lack of ground rules or criteria. The following standards have been proposed for establishing animal models (7):

1. *Similarity of behavioral states.* There should be a reasonable correspondence between the behavior shown by the animal model and that shown in the human psychopathological state. This is a necessary but not sufficient criteria. For instance, the behaviors seen in two different species may be alike, but may actually occur in response to quite different situations. Hence the difficulty in drawing conclusions strictly on the basis of observable similarities.

2. *Comparability of inducing conditions.* Not only should the behaviors themselves be similar but the conditions that produce them should be comparable. To illustrate this point, separation from an important affectional source is thought to be a significant element in many human depressions. Therefore, in creating an animal model for human depression, separation from such a source would be a logical inducing condition to employ. The disappointing results of the last thirty years of research have been in part due to the neglect of this standard. There has been a preoccupation with producing symptoms that resemble human neurosis without due attention to the precise way in which these behaviors arose. Even when the symptoms were similar, the inducing conditions were often strikingly different and unrelated to the human experience. The very fact that approach/avoidance, motivation conflict, audiogenesis, etc., have historically been lumped together as experimental neurosis reveals the extent to which this measure has been neglected.

3. *Reversal by clinically effective means.* If a valid animal model has been produced, it would be expected that those drugs which are effective in ameliorating or reversing the symptoms in the human instance would also do so in the case of the animal model.

4. *Similarity of underlying neurobiological mechanisms.* When neurobiological traits are known to be associated with a specific human condition, they should also be found in the animal model. This is probably the most difficult standard to fulfill, since so little is actually known about neurobiological alterations which are diagnostically specific to much of human psychopathology. However, it represents a useful guide in studying postulated mechanisms that occur with a specific behavioral pattern.

The above parameters are incompletely understood in most forms of human psychopathology, and in this sense they should be viewed as guidelines for research rather than as immutable validating criteria. No one of the above areas should be viewed in isolation, but rather they should be used as a composite concept instead of simply as a checklist. No model will meet all of these requirements fully, but with intelligent interpretation of data they provide useful guidelines in study with animal models.

HISTORY OF ANIMAL MODELS

Some of the first research on animal psychopathology was conducted by Ivan P. Pavlov of Russia (8). He reported what he termed "experimental neurosis" in dogs. A previously tractable animal, when made unable to distinguish between a circle as a signal for food and an almost circular ellipse as a signal for no food, became quite agitated. Pavlov studied these and other phenomenon in the context of higher nervous system activity. Other researchers such as Gantt (9), Cook (10), Dworkin (11), and Liddell (12) also did some of the earlier work attempting to produce abnormal behaviors in a variety of mammals by using conditioning paradigms. Masserman (13) also attempted to produce behavior aberrations using "motivational conflict situations." Other beginning work on the behavior of animals was done mainly on birds and fowl by Lorenz (14), Tinbergen (15,16), Armstrong

Table 1. Comparison of separation syndromes in rhesus macques with human depression

Criteria for Animal Model	Human Depression	Separation Syndrome in Rhesus Monkeys
Inducing condition	Can be separation	Separation
Behavioral similarities	Activity↓	↓Locomotion
	Intake↓	↓Food and water intake
	Interest in surroundings↓	↓Environmental exploration
	Social activities↓	↓Play; ↓social exploration
	Sleep disturbances↑	↑Probable (Reite, 1974, 1976, personal communication)
	Self-directed behaviors↑	↑Self clasp; ↑huddling; ↑rocking
	Death	Yes
Neurobiological mechanisms	Extensive literature suggest variety of disturbances	Proposed research
Rehabilitation	Social	Yes—needs further study
	Tricyclics	Yes—needs further study
	MAOI	No data
	ECT	No data
	Lithium	No data

(17,18), Iersel (19), and Hinde (20), among others. Specifically, this work on birds studied such things as imprinting, transfer of various behaviors such as courtship displays and preening, and immobility reactions. Interesting as much of this information is, it is difficult to ascertain its comparability to human disorders. Indeed, Kaminskii (21) found it difficult to transfer Pavlov's classic conditioning with the dog to a monkey, an animal much closer than birds to the make-up of humans, and even when conditioning was produced it was very short lived.

Important as these early studies were, many of them suffered from lack of attention to comparable inducing techniques, from premature application of clinical labels, and from neglect of the problems implicit in using nonhumans to study human psychopathology.

USE OF CRITERIA TO VALIDATE ANIMAL MODELS

There are now firm animal models for the study of depression which illustrate the ways in which the discussed criteria can help to establish and validate models. As one example, there is the rhesus monkey separation induced depression model (22-26). In this instance, the inducing condition, separation from an affectional source, produces "depressed" behavior (see Table 1) in the monkey and is also thought to be one of the causal elements in the case of human depression. After the separation experience, decreases in physical movement, food and water intake, interest in surroundings and social behavior, and increases in such inward-directed behaviors as huddling and rocking are seen. These are also the behaviors psychiatrists and psychologists describe as occurring in cases of human depression. Preliminary data suggests that these symptoms of depressive behaviors can be alleviated in both humans and rhesus monkeys by use of social therapy and tricyclics. There is extensive literature that theorizes a variety of disturbances of neurobiological mechanisms as the cause or result of depression in humans. As yet, there is little or no data on underlying mechanisms in rhesus monkeys, but with all the other criteria adequately met, it would seem to be an ideal area for such research and would probably help clarify this aspect in both humans and monkeys.

Another example of a model that has been produced with some success is the model of "learned helplessness" (27-29). In this situation, subjects learned through several trials that no response on their part enabled them to avoid electrical shocks. When subsequently they were placed in a situation where the shocks could be avoided by action on their part, they failed to initiate responses to escape shock or were significantly slower in responding than naive animals. The analogy here is that aspect of human depression characterized by feelings of "helplessness" and "hopelessness." People in this situation often report feeling as if they have no control over the events in their lives. The behavioral pattern shown by both animals and humans is simply not to respond at all. Both animals and people can be rehabilitated—humans by use of therapy to change their perceptions of themselves as having control over their environments, and animals by use of additional experience to learn that they can make controlling responses. The work of Weiss and coworkers (30) provides an interesting adjunct to this model. Their research provides evidence that the behaviors seen with "learned helplessness" may correlate with alteration of neurotransmitters and may be prevented by use of antidepressants.

ANIMAL MODELS OF ANXIETY?

Research into neurotic disorders can be approached in a number of separate stages. The first of these, and perhaps the most widely used, is the study of the immediate response, usually adaptive, to a stressful situation. The second addresses the manner in which these responses become established in the animals' regular behavior patterns—i.e., the underlying mechanisms responsible for a particular manifestation. Very little work has been done which has been specifically designed to address this problem. The third deals with the emergence or carry-over of actions into a context apparently unrelated to the situation in which they were originally located.

The conditioned avoidance response (CAR) paradigm, which deals with the stress arena mentioned in the first of the above approaches, has been used to produce what has been termed a "neurosis" in animal models. In this manipulation, an animal is presented with some stimulus signaling an impending electric shock. The animal learns to emit a response to terminate the signal and thus avoid the shock. Although the subject can be successfully conditioned in this manner, the behavior does not appear to be isomorphic with any human psychopathology, and it is difficult to correlate this behavior with aspects of human disorders. Fear or anxiety has often been invoked to explain the animal's behavior in avoiding the shock. The subject stops the signal and thus eases its feelings of anxiety. This is rather circular reasoning, and to quote Carlton, is not a theory but a tautology (31). Stressful feelings about the impending shock may well be felt by the subject, but the inference of "anxiety" will have to await independent validation. On the other hand, it is interesting to note that the behavior of an animal in a CAR experiment can be altered by those drugs useful in the diagnosis of schizophrenia. Antipsychotic drugs, at doses that do not interfere with the subject's muscular ability to escape from the shock, do seem to interfere in some manner with its ability to emit the appropriate response and thereby avoid the shock.

According to some, the CAR paradigm is an effective screen for some assessment of the pharmacological actions of neuroleptic drugs that correlate with their antipsychotic activity. This does *not* make it a model for schizophrenia. Nor does the fact that it is a screening test mean that it can be assumed that the effects of neuroleptics on CAR are homologous with their therapeutic actions in human patients.

Another approach that is perhaps not as well known to researchers in this country is that used by V. G. Startsev of Russia (32). He suggests that the physiological system most likely to become chronically disturbed when the animal is subjected to nervous stress is the one which is particularly active at the time that the stress is imposed. For example, animals stressed while eating would develop stomach ulcers or gastrointestinal disorders and those stressed during or immediately after exercise would tend to develop cardiovascular problems. Dr. Startsev theorizes that functional motor system disorders are relevant to the psychosomatic ailments which are found in primates.

The creation of an animal model for an anxiety neurosis has not been a success story. There is still a long way to go before a workable model is achieved. To date, the criteria proposed have not been applied with consistency to research in this area. However, future work accompanied by more attention to these standards may well develop a usable model.

SUMMARY

Animal modeling research is acquiring more and more importance in its relationship to human psychopathology in general.This field is moving into new areas of research that are exciting and potentially informative far beyond the hopes generated by the initial work with animal models. As further ventures into this area are made, caution without cynicism must be the byword in developing models. Premature use of clinical labels must be avoided, and due attention to possible underlying mechanisms must be maintained. Also, the problems inherent in extrapolating from one species to another must never be disregarded. This is proving to be a far more complex area than was originally thought, and any attempt to use simplistic reasoning may hinder its development.

There are many different types of models. Models for predicting drug responsiveness (treatment models) are not necessarily the same as mechanism or etiological models. At present, the use of animal models has not attained its first promise. However, by correcting past misuses and misconceptions, this field can open new vistas into previously obsured dimensions of the human psychopathological state.

REFERENCES

1. Kaufman, I.C., and Rosenblum, L.A. Depression in infant monkeys separated from their mothers. *Science* 155:1030-1031, 1967.
2. Kaufman, I.C., and Rosenblum, L.A. The reaction to separation in infant monkeys:

Anaclitic depression and conservation-withdrawal. *Psychosom. Med.* 29:648-675, 1967.

3. Kubie, L.S. The experimental induction of neurotic reactions in man. *Yale J. Biol. Med.* 11:541-545, 1939.
4. Premack, D.A. A functional analysis of language. *J. Exp. Anal. Behav.* 14:107-125, 1970.
5. Gardner, B.T., and Gardner, T.A. *Behavior of Nonhuman Primates.* Edited by A.M. Schrier and F. Stollnitz. F New York: Academic Press, 1971.
6. Hinde, R.A. *Social Behavior and Its Development in Subhuman Primates.* Condom lectures. Eugene: Oregon State System of Higher Education, 1972.
7. McKinney, W.T., and Bunney, W.E. Animal model of depression. I. Review of evidence: Implications for research. *Arch. Gen. Psychiat.* 21:240-248, 1969.
8. Pavlov, I.P. *Lectures on Conditional Reflexes.* New York: International University Press, 1928.
9. Gantt, W.H. Experimental basis for neurotic behavior. In H.D. Kimmel, ed., *Experimental Psychopathology: Recent Research and Theory.* New York: Academic Press, 1971.
10. Cook, S.W. The production of experimental neurosis in the white rat. *Psychosom. Med.* 1:293, 1939.
11. Dworkin, S. Conditioning neurosis in dog and cat. *Psychosom. Med.* 1:388, 1939.
12. Liddell, H.S. *Emotional Hazards in Animals and Man.* Springfield, Ill: Charles C. Thomas, 1956.
13. Masserman, J.H. *Behavior and Neurosis.* Chicago: University of Chicago Press, 1943.
14. Lorenz, K.Z. *King Solomon's Ring.* New York: T.Y. Crowell, 1952.
15. Tinbergen, N. Comparative studies of the behavior of gulls (laridae): A progress report. *Behaviour* 15:1-70, 1959.
16. Tinbergen, N. Derived activities: Their causation, biological significance, orgin and emancipation during evolution. *Rev. Biol.* 27:1-32, 1952.
17. Armstrong, E.A. The nature and function of displacement activities. *Symp. Soc. Exp. Biol.* 4:361-384, 1950.
18. Armstrong, E.A. *Bird Display and Behavior.* London: Drummond, 1947.
19. Iersel, J.A. Van, and Bol, A. Preening of two term species. A study on displacement. *Behaviour* 13:1-89, 1958.
20. Hinde, R.A. A comparative study of the behavior of certain finches. *Anim. Behav.* 97:606-645, 98:1-23, 1955.
21. Kaminskii, S.D. *Biulliten' VIEM* 9-10, 12-13, 1935.
22. Seay, B., Hansen, E., and Harlow, F. Mother infant separation in monkeys. *J. Child Psychol. Psychiat.* 3:123, 1962.
23. Harlow, H.F., Suomi, S.J., and McKinney, W.T. Experimental production of depression in monkeys. *Mainly Monkeys* 1:7-12, 1970.
24. McKinney, W.T., Suomi, S.J., and Harlow, H.F. Depression in primates. *Am. J. Psychiat.* 127:1313-1320, 1971.
25. McKinney, W.T. Animal models in psychiatry. *Perspect. Biol. Med.* 17:529-541, 1974.
26. McKinney, W.T. Animal behavioral/biological models relevant to depressive and affective disorders in humans. In J.G. Schulferbrandt and A. Raskin, eds., *Depression in Childhood: Diagnosis, Treatment and Conceptual Models.* New York: Raven Press, 1977.
27. Seligman, M.E.P., and Maier, S.F. Failure to escape traumatic shock. *J. Exp. Psychol.* 74:1-9, 1967.
28. Seligman, M.E.P. Reversal of performance deficits and perceptual deficits in learned helplessness and depression. *J. Abnorm. Psychol.* 85:11-26, 1976.

29. Seligman, M.E.P. Fall into helplessness. *Psychology Today* 7:43-48, 1973.
30. Weiss, J.M. Effects of coping responses on stress. *J. Comp. Physiol. Psychol.* 65:251-260, 1968.
31. Kornetsky, C. Animal models: Promises and problems. In I. Hanin and E. Usdin, eds., *Animal Models in Psychiatry and Neurology.* New York: Pergamon, 1977.
32. Startsev, V.G. *Primate Models of Human Neurogenic Disorders.* English translation edited by D.M. Bowden. Lawrence Earlbaum, 1976.

CHAPTER 11

New and Old Evidence for the Involvement of a Brain Norepinephrine System in Anxiety

D. E. Redmond, Jr.

INTRODUCTION

The catecholamines were among the first compounds to be linked with emotion, based on the similarities between the physiological effects of "adrenalin" (1) and those occurring during fear and rage (2,3). Since that time the catecholamines dopamine and norepinephrine have been extensively studied in man and animals, producing a huge body of data but few conclusions that could link their activity with specific emotions in humans. In general, the sympathetic nervous system is believed to be involved in a general response to stress or stressors, a kind of general adaptation (4,5) without any specific emotional connections. Selye called the initial phase of this response an "alarm reaction." It is a normal adaptive response in humans and animals of which the more specific emotions fear and anxiety may be a part, may precede, and may precipitate. In this discussion, fear will be defined as the emotion consisting of a distinctive subjective feeling state with physiologic and behavioral manifestations occurring in the presence of stimuli which warn of impending aversive, noxious, painful, or harmful stimuli. The traditional distinction that anxiety is free-floating and nonspecific, whereas the nature of the threat leading to fear is known (6), is not supported by differences in physiologic responses between the two emotions (7) or by common useage (8). Fear and anxiety will therefore be used interchangeably to refer to the same normal human emotion (9,10). Pathological anxiety will be specifically denoted and discussed later.

ANATOMICAL IMPORTANCE OF THE NUCLEUS LOCUS COERULEUS TO NORADRENERGIC FUNCTION

Recent studies have focused on an important and unique brain nucleus, the locus coeruleus, which may supply as much as 70% of the norepinephrine in primate brain. This dark-blue (coeruleus) streak in the dorsolateral tegmentum of the human pons was first described by Reilom 1809 (22), but it was not related to a noradrenergic function until histochemical studies by Dahlstrom and Fuxe in 1964 (23). This small nucleus is now known to have the highest density of norepinephrine-containing neurons in the central nervous system (23,24). Fewer than 19,000 cells in the primate locus coeruleus (Fig. 1) provide the principal noradrenergic innervation to cerebral cortex (25-29), hippocampus (29-35), cingulate gyrus (31,34), and amygdala (34,35).

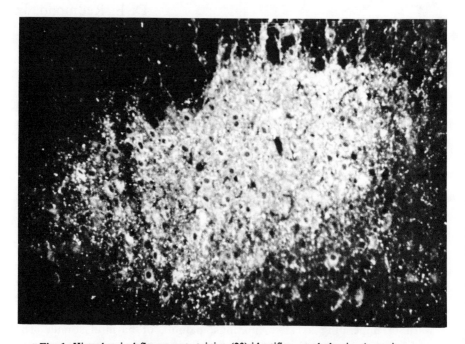

Fig. 1. Histochemical fluorescent staining (23) identifies catecholamine (norepine-phrine) containing cells of the primate nucleus locus coeruleus in the pontine tegmentum. The nucleus is about 1 × 1 × 2mm. in extent in *Macaca arctoides* (photograph courtesy of Dr. John Sladek).

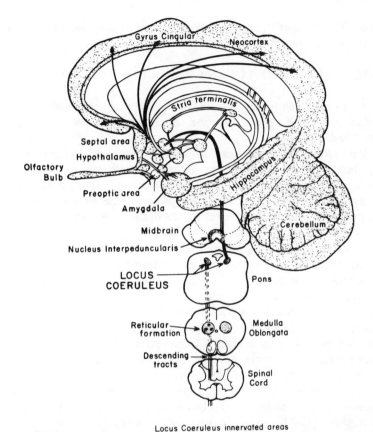

Locus Coeruleus innervated areas

Fig. 2. The extensive complete or partial innervation of norepinephrine-containing brain regions from the locus coeruleus is schematically illustrated in primate brain. The importance of this nucleus in noradrenergic function in the limbic system is apparent. Afferent projections to the locus coeruleus (not shown) come from many of these same areas, as well as from most sensory nuclei and the spinal cord.

These include a major portion of the limbic cortex long associated with emotion (36,37). In addition, axons from the locus coeruleus supply part of the norepinephrine found in the hypothalamus, thalamus, habenula, inferior colliculi, olfactory bulb, spetal nuclei, cerebellum, lower brainstem, and spinal cord (23-26,29-31,34,35,38-44) (Fig. 2). Afferent projections to activate or inhibit the locus coeruleus are similarly widespread, including projections from the reticular formation, the adjacent central gray, the fastigial nucleus, raphe nuclei, substantia nigra, hypothalamus, insular cortex, bed nucleus of the stria terminalis, some preoptic areas, insular and prefrontal cortex, other catecholamine-containing cell groups in the medulla, and large neurons in the dorsal horn of the spinal cord (45-60). This system appears to be essentially similar in the rodent (as generally described above), cat (58,59), monkey (60,61), and human fetal brain (62).

EARLY STUDIES OF LOCUS COERULEUS FUNCTION

One might suspect that such a widely connected neuronal system would have an important general function. Pharmacologic studies of "catecholamines" had suggested effects on nearly every basic physiologic mechanism— cardiac rhythm, blood pressure, respiration, temperature regulation, appetite, thirst, glucose metabolism, smooth muscle and sphincter activity, memory, sexual behavior, sleep, affect, and mood (63). None of these effects appeared to predominate, and although noradrenergic influences on these vital processes could be demonstrated, the brain noradrenergic system did not seem to be absolutely essential to life (63).

It was not surprising, therefore, that early physiologic studies of the function of the locus coeruleus had demonstrated a similar pattern of multiple but generally nonvital effects in rodents. Electrolytic lesions were shown to produce drastic decreases in the concentration of norepinephrine and its metabolite 3-methoxy-4-hydroxy-phenethylene glycol (MHPG) in LC projection areas (24,41,64-67), while electrical stimulation produced increases in MHPG (66). These studies demonstrated the feasibility of studying noradrenergic function via the locus coeruleus; but in spite of large changes in norepinephrine, most animals survived with minor changes in function after destruction of the nucleus. Alterations in the regulation of sleep stages have consistently been found (69-71). But a learning impairment found by some investigators (72-73) was not found by others using slightly different methods (74-75). Such physical effects of lesions as aphagia, urogenital disorders (74), hyperdipsia (75), and deaths of no apparent cause have been reported (74), but these findings have not been consistent across studies (72). Electrical stimulation produced decreases in motor activity (76-77), and increases in eating, grooming, gnawing (78), and blood pressure (79). Self-stimulation of locus coeruleus electrodes has been reported by some investigators (64,76,80-86), evidence cited in favor of "reward" mechanisms dependent on norepinephrine (76,82,86). But the involvement of the locus coeruleus has been questioned by others (77,87-90). Overall, the available data indicated that important rat behaviors may be altered by lesioning or stimulating the locus coeruleus. There were, however, several areas of disagreement, and there was a lack of data dealing with some of the more subtle effects the locus coeruleus may have on behavioral and physiological processes. Although the anatomy of the locus coeruleus suggested that this system probably has a general modulatory function (27), no compelling experimental evidence was available to indicate what this function might be, and data from primates or humans was almost totally lacking.

RECENT STUDIES OF THE LOCUS COERULEUS IN MONKEYS

Changes in fear suggested by electrical stimulation or lesions

Initially, studies of electrical stimulation and lesions of the locus coeruleus were undertaken in monkeys, which were used as experimental subjects because of the possibility that subtle behavioral consequences of brain catecholamine function might be more apparent than in nonprimate species. Stumptailed monkeys *(M. arctoides)* exhibit complex social interactions and a wide variety of individual behaviors that may reflect emotional states. Electrodes were permanently implanted in the locus coeruleus, using specific physiological, histological, and biochemical criteria (91). Very low intensity bipolar, biphasic electrical stimulation (0.5 mA intensity, 0.5 msec. pulse duration) was applied in 10-second trains to monkeys restrained in a chair. Their behavioral responses were different from those following mild electrical shocks, suggesting that the stimulation was not painful. The sequence of behaviors elicited included alerting, head and body turning, yawning, chewing, and scratching of the body. Cessation of stimulation was followed by a specific vocalization and facial gesture (92) called the "grunt-purr" (93) (Table 1). None of the behaviors occurred in exactly the same way each time, with movements to either side and with either hand in spite of unilateral stimulation, suggesting that simple motor system activation was not responsible. Similar responses in each monkey were obtained from stimulation of the dorsal noradrenergic bundle projections (24,25) five mm. from the locus coeruleus, but not by stimulation of nearby areas, suggesting that locus coeruleus activation was necessary for the behavioral effects to occur. These behaviors are all seen routinely in any primate laboratory, are unremarkable, and might have been ignored except

Table 1. Behavioral effects of low intensity stimulation of the locus coeruleus

---

head and body turning
eye scanning
chewing
tongue movement
grasping and clutching chair
scratching
biting fingers or nails
pulling hair or skin
hand wringing
yawning
spasmodic total body jerking

---

for the chance observation that the same exact sequence of behaviors was reproduced by human threats in each animal. Anecdotal reports from field studies mention several of the behaviors produced by electrical stimulation of the locus coeruleus as occurring in situations of impending danger, conflict, or aggression in monkeys (93) and in states of fear and anxiety in humans 94,95). A possible connection with anxiety was noted (92).

Bilateral lesions of the locus coeruleus produced opposite and dramatic changes in seven of eight monkeys studied (96,97). These monkeys showed an absence of emotional responses to threats, although they would eventually withdraw from persistent and vigorous threats and from a mildly painful stimulus. They were without apparent fear in approaching humans or dominant monkeys, maintaining eye contact more than sham-operated monkeys. They were also socially more aggressive and moved about their cage more frequently than prior to the lesions or compared with sham-operated monkeys. Scratching and self-mouthing, seen with electrical stimulation, decreased after lesions (Table 2).

Since it was quite possible that both the effects of locus coeruleus stimulation and lesions were due to some secondary or incidental effect, it was important to determine whether specific pharmacologic alterations in locus coeruleus function were associated with the same behaviors or would block the behavioral effects of locus coeruleus stimulation. In addition, a number of other possibilities might explain the behavioral changes without any specific connection with anxiety or fear mechanisms. A link was needed to elucidate

Table 2. Efects of bilateral locus coeruleus lesions

Loss of emotional aspects of fear
    Slow retreat from threats without pain
    Intact withdrawal from actual pain
    Increased approach and increased eye contact with higher
        ranking monkeys and humans

Increased aggression
    Attacks directed toward higher ranking monkeys and humans
    Quantitative increases in displacements, threats, and
        attacks
    Increased submissive responses by other monkeys
    No impairment of body movement in attack

Hyperactivity
    Increased ambulatory movement
    Increased body movement, shifting posture, fidgeting without ambulation
    Hyperphagia and hyperphagia and hyperdipsia
    Decreases in scratching and self-mouthing from pre-lesion levels

the possible relevance of these effects to human behaviors or to such human emotions as fear or anxiety. The effects of agents known to specifically alter noradrenergic and locus coeruleus function were then studied, with the hypothesis that agents which increased locus coeruleus function would mimic the behavioral effects of locus coeruleus stimulation, and that agents which decreased it would produce lesion-like behavioral effects. Recent pharmacologic studies had demonstrated some unusually specific methods to alter noradrenergic and locus coeruleus function, using specific receptors.

Pharmacologic alterations of specific receptors mimic the effects of electrical stimulation and lesions

α-2Noradrenergic receptors. "Presynaptic" receptors in the vicinity of the cell bodies of the locus coeruleus have been shown to be sensitive to noradrenergic agonists, which inhibit neuronal activity when they are applied directly. Norepinephrine, epinephrine, and the α-adrenergic agonist clonidine all greatly *decrease* locus coeruleus neuronal activity (98,99) with direct iontophoretic administration, with the effect mediated by α-2 type adrenergic receptors (100). Clonidine also has this effect after intravenous administration in low doses, making it possible to study reduced activity of the locus coeruleus in awake behaving animals. The biochemical basis for this strategy has been recently reviewed (101). Mass and coworkers (102) demonstrated decreased brain excretion of MHPG in the awake *M. Arctoides* after 10 μg/kg clonidine, confirming the effectiveness of a specific dose in the monkey.α-adrenergic blockers in low doses have opposite effects (98,103). Piperoxane blocks the effects of iontophoretically applied epinephrine or norepinephrine, and *increases* noradrenergic neuronal firing rates (98,99) and norepinephrine turnover at doses that do not block post synaptic α-adrenergic receptors (104,105) (Fig. 3). Piperoxane also increases brain MHPG excretion in *M. arctoides* (102). Yohimbine probably has identical effects (106), but has not been studied as extensively. Some evidence suggests direct effects of these agents on other α-adrenergically innervated systems (103,107-111) mediating blood pressure, respiration, heart rate, sleep, and spinal reflexes. Effects on other neurotransmitter systems have also been demonstrated (98, 112-114). However, dopamine (98) and serotonin (114) effects appear to be secondary to changes in noradrenergic activity. In spite of these other effects, the behavioral and physiologic effects emanating directly from the locus coeruleus should be produced by piperoxane and reduced by clonidine, although additional effects might be seen due to other systems. A simplified anatomy of a locus coeruleus neuron illustrates where these pharmacologic effects are believed to occur (Fig. 4).

A total of seven monkeys have been studied after piperoxane 1.0 mg/kg and/or clonidine 10 μg/kg. These animals were chair-restrained in a shielded,

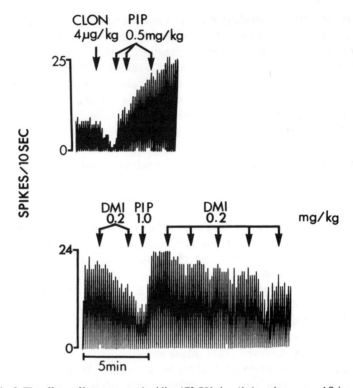

Fig. 3. The effects of intravenous clonidine (CLON, 4 µg/kg) on the neuronal firing of the same locus coeruleus neuron of the rat are illustrated (above). The α-noradrenergic agonist, clonidine, inhibits spontaneous firing; and the α-noradrenergic antagonist, piperoxane, reverses this effect, and increases firing over basal rates. Desmethylimipramine (DMI, 0.2 mg/kg) has a similar effect to clonidine, reversed by piperoxane (below) (courtesy of J.M. Cedarbam and G.K. Aghajanian, from J.M. Cedarbaum, unpublished MD thesis, Yale University School of Medicine, 1978).

sound-dampened chamber after a saphenous intravenous line had been connected for physiological saline or drug administration from outside the chamber. Monkeys were extensively trained for this procedure over a period of weeks prior to the beginning of studies. Baseline videotape recordings were made one hour or more after the chamber was closed, and drug infusions were made so that the monkey could not detect the administration. Videotapes were scored by two raters using objective behavioral definitions for changes occurring each second. These behaviors were summarized and printed by computer into one-minute histograms, grouping behaviors into three categories: those increased by threats, those suggesting a decreased level of conscious awareness or sedation, and neutral behaviors (having no relationship to threats or sedation).

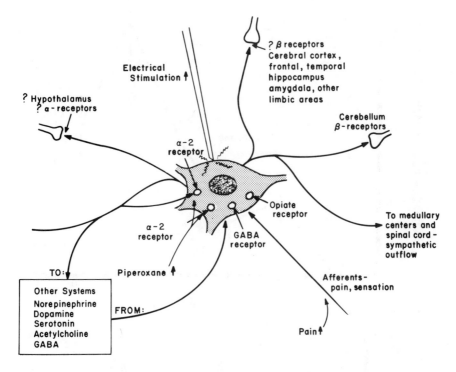

Fig. 4. A simplified schematic diagram of a single locus coeruleus neuron shows receptors in the vicinity of the cell bodies that regulate neuronal firing rates. Intravenous or iontophoretically applied piperoxane *increases* neuronal firing by blockade of recurrent collateral inhibition at α-2 (noradrenergic) receptors. *Activation* may also occur from painful or noxious stimuli, via unknown receptors, or from direct low intensity electrical stimulation. *Decreased neuronal firing* results from clonidine effects at the α-2 receptors, or from effects of other compounds at opiate or GABA receptors. Post-synaptic blocked by β-noradrenergic antagonists, such as propranolol, result also in decreases of β-noradrenergically mediated functional effects.

Piperoxane was found to increase the same behaviors as electrical stimulation of the locus coeruleus (Fig. 5), whereas clonidine reduced these same behaviors and blocked the effects of piperoxane (Fig. 6) or electrical stimulation (115-118). Four raters could not distinguish qualitatively between "spontaneous" threat-associated behaviors, electrical stimulation of the locus coeruleus, and piperoxane administration in randomly edited videotape segments of each condition from the same two monkeys (Table 3). In spite of the probable effects of piperoxane on other noradrenergic nuclei or other cells with α-2 noradrenergic receptors, electrical stimulation of the locus coeruleus alone reproduced all of its behavioral effects. Neither method of activation of

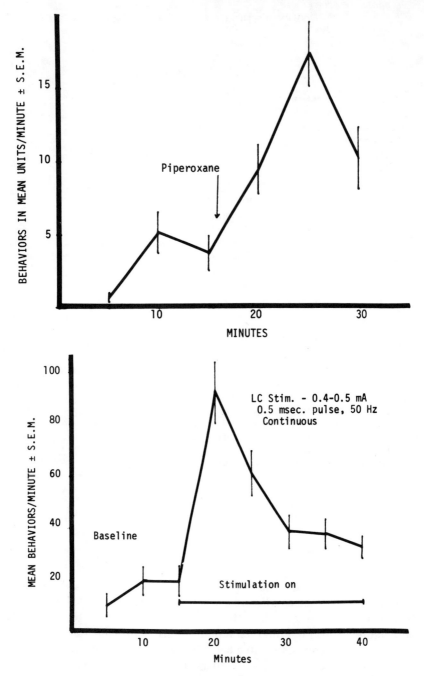

Fig. 5. Piperoxane (intravenous, 1 mg/kg) produced quantitative increases (above) in the same behaviors increased by electrical stimulation of the locus coeruleus (below). "Threat-associated" behaviors of four *Macaca arctoides* are shown, rated per minute by two raters using videotaped records. Sedation and neutral behaviors showed no change. "Threat-associated" behaviors are those listed in Table 1.

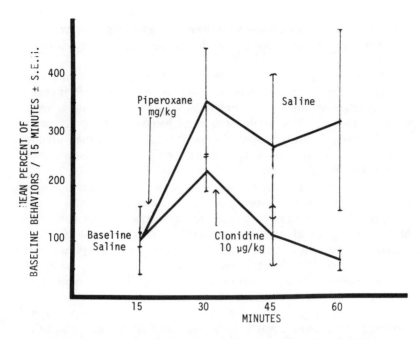

Fig. 6. Effect of clonidine (intravenous, 10 μg/kg) on piperoxane-elicited behaviors in two monkeys is illustrated, compared with piperoxane and saline. The behaviors elicited by piperoxane and reduced by clonidine are the same threat-associated behaviors illustrated in Fig. 5, and were also rated by two raters from videotape recordings. Mean percent of baseline behaviors are shown.

the locus coeruleus produced behaviors that could be distinguished qualitatively from the behaviors seen in response to conditioned or natural threats. These results support the specificity of the electrical stimulation, since adjacent non-noradrenergic systems are not affected by piperoxane or

Table 3. Study of similarities between behaviors elicted by locus coeruleus electrical stimulation, piperoxane, or saline after previous piperoxane administration one week before. Two experienced and two naive raters attempted to identify the eliciting condition from 30 randomly ordered and selected videotape segments illustrating behaviors in monkeys occurring during each condition.

Condition	No. of Episodes Experienced		Naive Raters	Percentage of Correct Identifications	
LC Stim	11	18	9	18	45
Piperoxane	9	44	33	11	67
Saline (Threat)	10	0	30	20	0
Total	30	20	23	16	36

clonidine, and provide evidence for the mediation of piperoxane's behavioral effects by the locus coeruleus, since electrical stimulation produces all of the effects.

Not all monkeys show exactly the same effects during the procedures. Each has different predominant behaviors in response to the stimuli. Some monkeys chew and move their tongues, while some scratch themselves, yawn, or wring their hands, although almost all behaviors are sometimes seen in every monkey. What is consistent is that monkeys show their predominant behavior pattern in response to threats, locus coeruleus stimulation, and piperoxane administration.

β-noradrenergic post-synaptic receptors. Another strategy to determine that the locus coeruleus mediates the observed effects would be to demonstrate that pretreatment with post-synpatic noradrenergic receptor antagonists will block the effects of electrical stimulation of the locus coeruleus. The pharmacologic classification of these receptors as α or β (119) was originally based on adrenergic receptors outside the central nervous system. Recent studies, however, show that both types of receptors exist in mammalian brain (120-123). Specific projections from the locus coeruleus to cells in the cerebellum (125) and the hippocampus (126,127) are blocked by a β-adrenergic antagonist, sotalol (128). Another β-adrenergic antagonist, D,L-propranolol, also acts as an antagonist at brain post-synaptic β-receptors (123,129). But it may also have weak effects on presynaptic receptors (99) in doses greater than 10 mg/kg (130,131). Other projections from the locus coeruleus, particularly to the hypothalamus, may be α-adrenergically mediated (121,122) and not blocked by propranolol.

The behavioral effects of electrical stimulation of the locus coeruleus in monkeys were almost completely blocked by 5 mg/kg of D,L-propranolol (Fig. 7) (117). Some of these effects might have been due to other β-adrenergic receptors besides those receiving projections from the locus coeruleus. However, non-noradrenergically mediated adjacent neurons and axons that might possibly be activated by current spread from locus coeruleus electrodes should not have been affected by β-adrenergic blockade. Profound hypotensive effects of the α-adrenergic post-synaptic antagonists have prevented successful behavioral studies so far. However, propranolol blocks the behavioral effects of locus coeruleus stimulation sufficiently to suggest that most behavioral effects are mediated by β-adrenergic receptors. The neuroendocrine and cardiovascular effects of locus coeruleus stimulation, which are perhaps more likely to be α-adrenergically mediated, have not yet been studied in the monkey. Effects of post-synaptic α-noradrenergic receptors have therefore not been ruled out.

Opiate receptors. Another class of receptors appears to have effects on locus coeruleus function, and there is anatomical and physiological evidence to explain its mechanism. Opiate receptors in the vicinity of the locus coeruleus (132,133) are among the two or three densest concentrations in the rat brain,

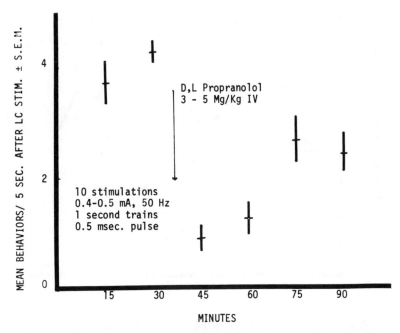

Fig. 7. Propranolol (intravenous, 3-5 mg/kg) decreased threat-associated behaviors occurring during the 5-second period after low intensity electrical stimulation of the locus coeruleus (0.4-0.5 mA, 50 Hz, 0.5 msec. pulse width, bipolar, biphasic stimulation for 1 second train). Each point represents the mean behaviors elicited by 10 episodes of stimulation in each of three monkeys.

and both intravenous (134) and iontophoretically applied morphine (135) have powerful inhibitory effects on locus coeruleus neuronal activity. The administration of morphine is therefore another technique to turn off locus coeruleus activity and to test the hypothesis that such activity is relevant to the behaviors elicited by locus coeruleus stimulation and by piperoxane. Administration of low doses of morphine to monkeys confirmed this hypothesis, blocking the effects of piperoxane in four monkeys (Fig. 8) and the effects of locus coeruleus stimulation in 3 (136). This effect was reproduced by a parenterally active synthetic methionine enkephalin, FK 33-824 (Sandoz) (137). Both the effects of morphine and FK 33-824 are reversed by naloxone, a specific opiate antagonist.

GABA receptors. The effects of inhibitory GABA receptors on the locus coeruleus (99,142) have not been definitively linked with the actions of the benzodiazepines. However, previous evidence suggested that benzodiazepines have effects on dopamine or norepinephrine turnover in the brain (138-140). High doses of diazepam have been shown to attenuate the effects of piperoxane and yohimbine (141), even though locus coeruleus neuronal activity changes after systemic diazepam have not been demonstrated. The

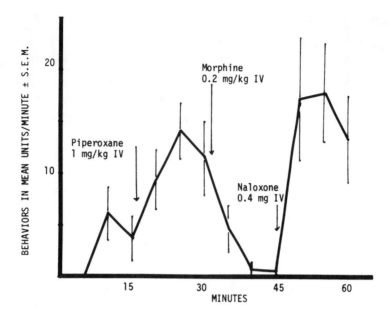

Fig. 8. Morphine (intravenous, 0.2 mg/kg) decreased threat-associated behaviors increased by piperoxane (intravenous, 1 mg/kg) in four monkeys. This effect was reversed by the specific opiate receptor antagonist, naloxone (intravenous, 0.4 mg). The effect of morphine, therefore, was mediated by opiate receptors, and the effects of piperoxane were still present 50-60 minutes after administration.

widespread human use of diazepam, as an anxiolytic, and the biochemical evidence of possible effects on noradrenergic systems, made its effects on locus coeruleus-linked behaviors of particular interest. A single intravenous administration of diazepam, comparable to a human anxiolytic dose (0.15 mg/kg), was found to attenuate the effects of electrical stimulation of the locus coeruleus in monkeys (143).

To summarize the results of studies of locus coeruleus function in monkeys, the same behaviors were associated with specific nonpainful threats and with procedures that increase locus coeruleus activity, and were decreased by procedures that decrease locus coeruleus activity or block its post-synaptic β-adrenergic projections. One might guess that these effects were relevant to human anxiety. However, since so many animal "models" have been assumed at one time or another to be relevant to various human emotions, and later evidence was discovered suggesting otherwise, the human evidence that might support or refute such an interpretation should be carefully reviewed before drawing a conclusion. This review will include studies of catecholamine-related correlates of anxiety, experimental pharmacologic induction of anxiety by α- and β-adrenergic agonists and by specific activation of noradrenergic systems by piperoxane and yohimbine, and finally, noradrenergic involvement in the actions of compounds with anxiolytic activity. The review will selectively focus on evidence implicating noradrenergic function. The reader should consult the original sources or quoted reviews for data suggesting interactions with other neurochemical systems.

EVIDENCE FOR NORADRENERGIC INVOLVEMENT IN ANXIETY IN HUMANS
Physiological and biochemical correlates of anxiety

Darwin's behavioral description of fear merging into terror in humans suggests the many physiological correlates of anxiety and fear (94) that were the basis for implicating the sympathetic nervous system originally (2,3).

"Fear is often preceded by astonishment, and is so far akin to it, that both lead to the senses of sight and hearing being instantly aroused. In both cases the eyes and mouth are widely opened, and the eyebrows raised. The frightened man at first stands like a statue motionless and breathless, or crouches down as if instinctively to escape observation.

The heart beats quickly and violently, so that it palpitates or knocks against the ribs; but it is very doubtful whether it then works more efficiently than usual, so as to send a greater supply of blood to all parts of the body; for the skin instantly becomes pale, as during incipient faintness. This paleness of the surface, however, is probably in large part, or exclusively, due to the vaso-motor centre being affected in such a manner as to cause the contraction of the small arteries of the skin. That the skin is much affected under the sense of great fear, we see in the marvellous and inexplicable manner in which perspiration immediately exudes from it. This exudation is all the more remarkable, as the surface is then cold, and hence the term a cold sweat; whereas, the sudorific glands are properly excited into action when the surface is heated. The hairs also on the skin stand erect; and the superficial muscles shiver. In connection with the disturbed action of the heart, the breathing is hurried. The salivary glands act imperfectly; the mouth becomes dry, and is often opened and shut. I have also noticed that under slight fear there is a strong tendency to yawn. One of the best-marked symptoms is the trembling of all the muscles of the body; and this is often first seen in the lips. From this cause, and from the dryness of the mouth, the voice becomes husky or indistinct, or may altogether fail. . . .

As fear increases into an agony of terror, we behold, as under all violent emotions, diversified results. The heart beats wildly, or may fail to act and faintness ensue; there is a deathlike pallor; the breathing is labored; the wings of the nostrils are widely dilated; 'there is a gasping and convulsive motion of the lips, a tremor on the hollow cheek, a gulping and catching of the throat"; the uncovered and protruding eyeballs are fixed on the object of terror; or they may roll restlessly from side to side. . . . The pupils are said to be enormously dilated. All the muscles of the body may become rigid, or may be thrown into convulsive movements. The hands are alternately clenched and opened, often with a twitching movement. The arms may be protruded, as if to avert some dreadful danger, or may be thrown wildly over the head. . . . In other cases there is a sudden and uncontrollable tendency to headlong flight; and so strong is this, that the boldest soldiers may be seized with a sudden panic."

In subsequent studies of normal and anxious humans, changes have been documented in heart rate, pulse volume, blood pressure, respiration, striated muscle contraction, tremor, eyeblink, startle responses, auditory evoked responses, electroencephalograms, body temperature, skin resistance, skin conductance, palmar sweating, pupillary dilatation, gastric acid secretion, and gastric motility (7, 144-148). The extent and direction of these changes result from complex interactions with the parasympathetic nervous system, which is also involved in regulating the same functions (7). Although these physiological correlates are now generally accepted as a part of anxiety (6), they are not thought to be specific to anxiety or fear, but a part of an arousal response (103) to stresses (4,5).

Biochemical changes supporting the involvement of the sympathetic nervous system in anxiety or fear have been reported for many years. Changes in plasma hydrocortisone (149,150) and cortisol (145) were among the earliest to be measured with accuracy (151). Alterations in norepinephrine, epinephrine, and their metabolites in urine were also reported to be changed in a variety of "stressful" conditions (151-155). Correlations with anxiety were also found in plasma when sufficiently sensitive assays became available to measure norepinephrine and epinephrine in very low concentrations. Wyatt and coworkers (156) reported increased total plasma catecholamine concentrations in a sample of 13 patients with anxiety and depression compared with 47 normal controls. Differential determinations of epine-phrine and norepinephrine on 10 samples from 5 of these patients revealed that epinephrine was threefold and norepinephrine was twofold higher than normal. Total catecholamine concentrations correlated significantly with rated anxiety (r= 0.69, p<0.01), but not at all with depression. Increased levels of plasma epinephrine, but not norepinephrine, were found in 11 patients with dental phobia compared with 11 controls without phobia prior to, during, and after dental surgery (157). There is considerable evidence that the catecholamines measured in these and other similar studies are derived from peripheral sympathetic sources and as such merely confirm the previous physiological data suggesting sympathetic nervous system involvement.

Some urinary metabolites such as MHPG are partially derived from central norepinephrine metabolism (102) and may be of more interest. Sweeney and coworkers recently reported a significant correlation between changes in urinary MHPG and changes in rated anxiety (r= 0.71, p <0.001) in 18 women psychiatric patients off medication (158). Again, these changes probably reflect mostly peripheral adrenergic activity, but they do suggest the possibility of increased noradrenergic activity in brain similar to that reported in animals after a variety of stressful procedures (159-161; see 162 for a review), changes which are directly related to the activity of locus coeruleus neurons (163.)

Recent human studies link peripheral norepinephrine elevations originally reported with increased central noradrenergic activity. Ziegler and coworkers have found that cerebrospinal fluid and plasma norepinephrine are highly correlated (164). Even more directly, Post and coworkers reported positive cerebrospinal fluid norepinephrine correlations with rated anxiety in depressed psychiatric patients (165).

Another biochemical correlate of anxiety has been found consistently, and is of potential significance to psychosomatic medicine. Free fatty acids (FFA) measured in the plasma have been found to be a reliable and specific correlate of anxious states (166-169) and are regulated by β-adrenergic receptors (170). FFA increases can be experimentally induced by a variety of psychological anxiety-provoking suggestions and situations (169-171). These same changes are induced by epinephrine infusion and are blocked by such β-adrenergic blockers as propranolol (170) but not by α-adrenergic blockers (172). Biochemical evidence also links the process of increased free fatty acid production (hyperadipokinesis) and hyperadrenergic function to other processes that may have survival value in "fight or flight" stress, but also have long-term adverse effects on cardiovascular functions. These include increases in blood glucose (119), impaired carbohydrate tolerance (173), hyperβ-lipidemia (174), increased formation of endogenous triglyceride via effects on hepatic triglyceride production and β-lipoprotein release (175), and increased thrombogenicity and blood clotting (176). Specific changes in the function of α-adrenergic receptors on blood platelets may lead to increased thrombogenicity (177) in the presence of increased norepinephrine or epinephrine. These changes, combined with possibly more direct neural mechanisms (178), may link the noradrenergic system with the effects of chronic psychologic stress and anxiety on hypertension (179-181) and on the incidence of arteriosclerotic cardiovascular disease (182).

Another biochemical effect of circulating epinephrine is to produce alterations in lactate production from muscle cell glycogen and glucose (183,184). This metabolic change probably underlies the increases reported in lactate concentrations in anxiety neurotics compared with normals (185-187). Some aspect of these increases may also be responsible for findings by several investigators that lactate infusions precipitate anxiety attacks in "anxietv neurotics," but not usually in normals (18,19,188,189).*

---

*More evidence on this point is presented by Pitts in Chapter 9, and an alternative hypothesis to that of Pitts appears later in this chapter.

Pharmacologic induction of anxiety by noradrenergic system stimulating agents

Correlates can of course be merely coincidental. Hence investigators have also been interested in testing their causal biochemical theories of anxiety by attempts to produce anxiety or fear experimentally.

Mixed α- and β- agonist: Epinephrine. Adrenin or "adrenalin" was infused in humans after its preparation in the early part of the twentieth century because of the evidence for adrenal involvement in the physiology of fear and rage (1,2,3). These early studies demonstrated convincing evidence that physiological correlates of anxiety or fear were reproduced by intravenous administration of epinephrine, with some variation in the doses required to elicit its now well-described physiological effects (190-196). Symptoms included palpitations, arterial throbbing, muscular tremor, tremor of the voice, pallor, sweating, increased respiration, substernal oppression, and headache. Other effects, possibly due to the central nervous system, were quite variable, from restlessness and irritability to depression, anger, fear, and anxiety. Some subjects reported a pleasant feeling, while a larger number reported a "cold" feeling "as if" they were anxious or afraid (193), but denied the presence of emotional feelings at the time of infusion. These results have been interpreted (3) as proving that the peripheral production of the principal physiological symptoms of anxiety is not a sufficient cause for the subjectively perceived emotional feelings. Genuine emotions of anxiety, fear, or grief that occurred in a minority of individuals (197) were attributed to hyperthyroidism (191,193), psychoneurosis, or predisposition (3,193). In support of a predisposition explanation, Basowitz and coworkers (198) noted that 68 physical symptoms of anxiety were reported by 12 normal individuals after low doses of epinephrine. Fifty-three of these were typical of the individual's previous symptoms of anxiety reported prior to the study. Of 71 different anxiety symptoms disclosed, only 18 did not occur after epinephrine. In a study that carefully recorded and rated emotional responses in schizophrenics and normal controls, Pollin and Goldin (199) found that 61% of their subjects showed subjective "anxiety," with no differences between the two groups. In a series of studies, Schacter has elaborated the considerable extent to which the emotional content can be influenced by appropriate environmental and social manipulations (20,201). These studies supported and reinforced the accepted interpretation that the drug alone produced a nonspecific arousal, and led to an intensification of whatever emotion was otherwise present or externally induced.

α-agonist: Norepinephrine. After the identification of norepinephrine as the peripheral sympathetic neurotransmitter (202), it too was studied in humans after intravenous administration. It produced remarkably few symptoms, in spite of substantial elevations in blood pressure (203-206). Some subjects reported merely unfamiliar sensations (207). Efforts to distinguish a particular norepinephrine response as characteristic of pain, fear, or anger (208) were not successful (205). It might seem peculiar that norepinephrine infusion is even less closely associated with anxiety than is epinephrine, especially since evidence reviewed here points to a brain *norepinephrine* system associated with anxiety or fear.

Recent pharmacological data, however, may explain some of these differences, as well as some of the effects of epinephrine. Certain problems and difficulties with the strategy of intravenous infusions in general may limit its usefulness for truly testing a noradrenergic-anxiety hypothesis. Adrenal medullary secretion into the circulation under physiologic conditions is predominantly epinephrine (80%) (119), whereas norepinephrine is the principal synaptic neurotransmitter in the peripheral sympathetic nervous system (119,202). Therefore, with respect to effects on the peripheral sympathetic adrenergic receptors, the injection of epinephrine simulates adrenal secretion. Norepinephrine injection into the circulation may produce conditions that never occur physiologically. The situation in the central nervous system is not so clear, although the extent that either substance crosses the blood-brain barrier becomes a critical question. Neither penetrates the blood-brain barrier well (209), but there is physiological evidence that epinephrine crosses to some extent (119). In that case, an interesting possibility arises in the light of recent studies demonstrating that receptors which inhibit locus coeruleus neuronal firing are sensitive to epinephrine and norepinephrine (99,100). These are the receptors involved in the effects of low doses of clonidine in the monkey studies described previously. These receptors might be activated at lower concentrations, with the paradoxical effect of inhibiting neuronal activity. If epinephrine penetrates the central nervous system in low concentrations, it might *inhibit* some α-2 receptor inhibited noradrenergic systems in the brain at the same concentrations that directly *activated* peripheral receptors. This might explain the majority of subjects having clear peripheral sympathetic symptoms and signs of anxiety or fear while reporting no emotion, cold "as if" feelings, or even pleasurable feelings, if brain noradrenergic systems are in fact involved in anxiety. (A study of single unit activity in the locus coeruleus after intravenous administration of epinephrine might provide confirmation of this hypothesis.) Another difference between epinephrine and norepinephrine may also be relevant to their central nervous system activities. Epinephrine is three times as potent as norepinephrine at brain 2-noradrenergic receptors (210) and about ten times as potent at some peripheral and central β-noradrenergic receptors as well (210). The two are about equipotent at other brain β receptors (210) and at the α-2 receptors (99,100). This would very likely mean that any central nervous system post-synaptic effects of epinephrine would include β-adrenergic projections of the locus coeruleus. If concentrations of norepinephrine were high enough in the CNS for post-synaptic effects, they would be exclusively α-adrenergic, missing many known direct projections of the locus coeruleus. In the periphery the usual physiologic effects of adrenal secretion (due to epinephrine) would include β-adrenergic effects also not reproduced by norepinephrine administration. The greater effectiveness of epinephrine in producing "genuine" anxiety symptoms and signs in some subjects and the predominance of its β-adrenergic effects compared with norepinephrine suggest that other pure β-adrenergic agonists might produce anxiety by activating peripheral and CNS post-synaptic receptors without the possible complication of functional inhibition at CNS α-2 adrenergic presynaptic receptors. For this reason, one might predict that cold, "as if," or pleasurable feelings would be an unlikely subjective effect of β-adrenergic agonist administration and that anxiety would predominate.

β-agonist: Isoproterenol. The "pure" β-adrenergic agonist, isoproterenol (121,210) (Isuprel), has been studied in special populations. A group of patients with increased cardiac awareness, increased heart rate responsiveness to stimuli, and subjective anxiety showed greater heart rate increases than a normal control group during infusion of 1-3 μg/minute of isoproterenol (211,212). Many of these patients had "hysterical outbursts," which suggest similar effects to those reported after epinephrine infusion. These "emotional" outbursts were relieved by the β-adrenergic antagonist, propranolol. No cold "as if" feelings were noted in any subjects, and no psychological effects were mentioned in the control subjects. This finding was replicated in another group of patients in which somatic anxiety predominated over cardiovascular symptoms, with isoproterenol producing typical anxiety attacks in each of 5 patients studied. The attacks were aborted by propranolol, which was subsequently effective in treating their usual symptoms (213). It is not clear, however, whether these effects represent a basic mechanism for the induction of anxiety, or whether these groups have β-adrenergic hyper-responsiveness or other special vulnerabilities to the effects of β-agonists. Normal control subjects apparently do not have anxiety attacks at comparable doses (214), but a systematic study has not been reported. Similar problems also exist with these studies as previously described for epinephrine infusion—unknown degrees of penetration into the CNS to affect post-synaptic receptors, and the nonphysiologic route of administration to those receptors via the blood.

Yohimbine and piperoxane. The problems with intravenous infusion of direct adrenergic agonists suggest that agents known to cross the blood-brain barrier and to produce physiologic neuronal activity in low doses, without directly producing peripheral or post-synaptic effects, would provide a cleaner test of a noradrenergic system hypothesis. As noted in the preceding discussion of the effects of piperoxane in monkeys, both piperoxane and yohimbine activate brain noradrenergic systems such as the locus coeruleus by increasing neuronal firing at doses that do not have peripheral or post-synaptic effects. Piperoxane was used for several years in a test for pheochromocytoma. Reports that severe anxiety, fear, or panic resulted in some patients combined with sympathetic activation largely led to the discontinuation of its clinical use (215,216). Its psychological effects have not been systematically studied. Yohimbine, with apparently similar mechanisms of action, has been studied more carefully. Holmberg and Gershon (217) reported that anxiety states or even panic resulted in 50 mental patients and 9 *normals* who received doses of yohimbine that preferentially activate brain noradrenergic systems. Most physiological symptoms of fear or anxiety were produced, in addition to their subjective effects. Most patients were hesitant to agree to a second dose after their first experience with it, reminiscent of the increases in threat-associated behaviors seen in monkeys after piperoxane. The effects were much more clear than after epinephrine infusions, and correlated with previously rated emotional reactivity. These effects were blocked by the intravenous administration of amobarbital (6.25 mg/kg) and by chlordiazepoxide (1.5 mg/kg).

Noradrenergic system effects of compounds with anxiolytic properties

Investigation of common biochemical properties of pharmacologic agents effective in relieving anxiety might provide further clues to its biochemistry. Many compounds have been used to treat pathological anxiety states and phobias in humans. Alcohol, the opiates, and marijuana are probably the oldest and most widely used by mankind, but the benzodiazepines lead the list of drugs most widely prescribed by physicians (218). Other classes (and examples) include the barbiturates (phenobarbital), propanediols (meprobamate), butyrophenones (haloperidol), phenothiazines (thioridazine), tricyclic antidepressants (imipramine), monoamine oxidase inhibitors (phenelzine), and β-adrenergic antagonists (propranolol) (219,220). These various classes of drugs have been associated with effects on many brain neurochemical systems which may be responsible for anxiolytic, sedative, hypnotic, muscle relaxant, anti-convulsant, and other effects. To what extent can effects on brain noradrenergic function be demonstrated for all anxiolytic and anti-phobic agents?

β-adrenergic antagonists. As noted previously, the β-adrenergic antagonists have anxiolytic activity in special groups of patients (211-213) with β-adrenergic "hypersensitivity." Other early reports also suggested that physical symptoms of anxiety were consistently blocked by propranolol (220-221), but others showed effects on subjective anxiety as well (222-232). The same results have been achieved with other β-adrenergic blockers, such as oxprenolol (228), sotalol (229), and practolol (230). The fact that similar beneficial effects occur with practolol, which does not cross the blood-brain barrier, has been used to support a peripheral mode of action for β-blockers (226), without eliminating the possibility of central effects of other agents that do penetrate the CNS. Some of these studies were double blind against placebo and clearly establish anti-anxiety effects in anxious patients. However, compared with standard agents, such as diazepam, these agents may be inferior (224,232), especially in patients with more exclusively subjective anxiety. The biochemical specificity of these agents for post-synaptic β-adrenergic blockade makes their anxiolytic actions of theoretical interest, even though their role in clinical treatment remains to be defined.

α-adrenergic antagonists. Studies of such "pure" adrenergic blockers as phentolamine and phenoxybenzamine have not reported anxiolytic properties (119). However, as noted, the significant hypotension which they produce limits the doses which can be studied in humans. Some neuroleptic drugs with potent central α-adrenergic blocking effects (233) have anti-anxiety actions in controlled double-blind studies (219). But these effects may be better accounted for by properties other than α-adrenergic receptor blockade.

Benzodiazepines. High doses of the benzodiazepines were first shown by Taylor and Laverty to decrease norepinephrine turnover in rats, and to block the increases in rat brain norepinephrine following electroshock "stress" (139,160). This effect was attributed to the cerulo-cortical norepinephrine pathways by Corrodi et al (140,234). Fuxe and coworkers (141) showed that high doses of diazepam (5mg/kg) will antagonize the effects of piperoxane or yohimbine on cortical norepinephrine turnover in the rat, as well as on "stress-induced" increases. Gray has described similar physiologic effects of chlordiazepoxide (5mg/kg) and decreased norepinephrine function produced by inhibitors of norepinephrine synthesis or lesions of the dorsal norepine-phrine bundle (235). Noradrenergic mechanisms may therefore be involved in the anti-anxiety actions of the benzodiazepines (235,236). The high doses required to produce these effects and the fact that there is tolerance to the changes in norepinephrine turnover during a period when anxiety-reducing activity increases (237) has suggested that alterations in norepinephrine function are not essential (15). But diazepam-induced increases in the threshold for electrical stimulation of the locus coeruleus in monkeys occur at doses that are used clinically in humans (115,116), supporting a functional benzodiazepine-noradrenergic interaction even at low doses. The details of how this effect occurs are unclear. Specific benzodiazepine receptors in mammalian brain have recently been described (238), which are presumably the most direct site of benzodiazepine action. These receptors are not located directly on the locus coeruleus, and the benzodiazepines do not interact directly with the α-2 adrenergic receptors, the GABA receptor, or the opiate receptors located in that vicinity (99,238). Considerable evidence does exist that the benzodiazepines activate GABA pathways (141,239-241) which may activate GABA receptors on locus coeruleus neurons (142) which inhibit locus coeruleus neuronal activity (99).

Opiates. The opiates have long been noted for their anxiolytic and mood-altering properties, which some have suggested are responsible for some of their analgesic effects on pathological pain (119). In people without pain, low doses of opiates are sometimes dysphoric initially, especially if physical symptoms occur. However, a recent study demonstrated that the most consistent effect of heroin is an anxiolytic one (242). There is an extensive and somewhat contradictory literature linking opiate analgesia, tolerance, or withdrawal to dopamine and norepinephrine (recently reviewed by Clouet [243] and Eidelberg [244]). Direct studies of neuronal unit activity in the locus coeruleus have clearly established the inhibitory effects of opiate agonists on the largest noradrenergic nucleus (134,135,245), and have demonstrated their ability to block painful stimulation induced increases in locus coeruleus activity (134). In addition to an effect on pain, it is not clear what the consequences of these findings might be for behavioral, emotional, addictive, or other opiate actions. Low-dose morphine (0.2 mg/kg) induced increases in the threshold for threat-associated behavioral effects elicited by stimulation of the locus coeruleus in monkeys (136). This suggests that, in addition to possible effects on the unpleasant and emotional aspects of pain, behavioral and perhaps anxiety-related effects correlate with the neuronal changes described by Korf and coworkers (134).

Barbiturates. The depressant barbiturate drugs, such as barbital and phenobarbital, also have long been used for their anxiety-reducing properties. Alterations in norepinephrine metabolism have also been noted, along with numerous other biochemical effects (119). Augmentation of inhibitory effects of GABA or the antagonism of excitatory afferents to the locus coeruleus (249) may be responsible for their anxiolytic effects. Definite inhibition of locus coeruleus neuronal activity follows pentobarbital administration in the rat and the monkey (250), although this effect is clearly not specific to the locus coeruleus system (249).

Imipramine-type and monoamine oxidase inhibiting (MAOI) drugs. Both major classes of antidepressant drugs have been reported to be effective in patients with "mixed" anxiety and depression (219, 251, 252), a patient group that also responds to benzodiazepine compounds (218, 219). However, both the tricyclics and MAOIs are effective in treating phobic patients, whereas the benzodiazepines and other "minor tranquilizers" and chlorpromazine are ineffective (253). This effectiveness might seem paradoxical in view of the norepinephrine-potentiating effects of the antidepressants (254-256) and the theory being reviewed in this chapter that increased noradrenergic function may result in fear-anxiety. If phobias were related to normal mechanisms of fear or anxiety, and both were associated with increased noradrenergic function, one might expect both classes of drugs to make them worse. Recent preclinical studies, however, suggest that their actual effect *in vivo* may be to reduce neuronal activity in the locus coeruleus and similar noradrenergic regions. Various tricyclic compounds reduce neuronal activity in the locus coeruleus (257, 258) due either to direct effects at the α-2 adrenergic receptor or to collateral feedback inhibition at that receptor (259). (See Fig. 3) Post-synaptic measures of norepinephrine-sensitive adenylate cyclase activity (260) suggest that this norepinephrine-decreasing effect predominates after chronic treatment. If so, the relevant pharmacologic actions of the imipramine-type drugs in phobic anxiety and panic states would be to prevent or inhibit increases in locus coeruleus neuronal activity. The MAOIs are likely to have a similar mechanism of action. It seems then that the anti-phobic and anti-panic efficacy of these drugs may be due to specific anti-noradrenergic actions.*

Neuroleptics. There is some controversy regarding the anxiolytic actions of the neuroleptic drugs. Some neuroleptic agents have been demonstrated to have anxiolytic activity when compared double blind with placebo (218, 219) or with standard benzodiazepine anxiolytics (218, 219, 269-274). But there is considerable variability in the anxiolytic properties of different compounds, especially in comparison with benzodiazepines in double-blind crossover studies.Chlorpromazine has been consistently less effective than benzodiazepines in anxious nonpsychotic outpatients (218, 219), whereas haloperidol and pimozide are equally effective or superior (274). The potent dopamine receptor blocking properties that these neuroleptics share (275, 276) might suggest that dopamine sytems are responsible for their anxiolytic effects, but this interpretation would be inconsistent with the known effects of other classes of anxiolytics on dopamine activity. All of the anxiolytic neuroleptics also have effects on receptors located on the locus coeruleus which may be relevant to anxiolytic actions. Potent binding of α-adrenergic receptors (233), opiate receptors (277), and muscarinic receptors (278) is reported for all of the major neuroleptics. As noted previously, some anxiolytic effects may occur via post-synaptic α-adrenergic blockade, but similar effects at α-2 adrenergic receptors might cancel these effects or even lead to increased noradrenergic system activity. The relative agonist versus antagonist properties at several of these locus coeruleus receptors would determine a compound's net effect on noradrenergic activity. For example, relatively high potency as opiate agonists and low potency as "presynaptic"α-2 adrenergic receptor antagonists might favor anxiolytic activity. This ratio correlates grossly with the anxiolytic activity of the few compounds whose activity can be determined.

---

*If this is true, clonidine, which is the most potent known inhibitor of locus coeruleus activity, as described previously, should also be effective as an anti-phobic and anti-anxiety agent. Such effects have not been noted in studies of its use as an antihypertensive (261-264) or as a treatment for migraine (265-268). Clonidine's action is so specific that a demonstration of anti-phobic or anxiolytic effects would be supportive of a locus coeruleus anxiety model, or the absence of such effects would be a powerful argument against the validity of the model.

There is no correlation between anxiolytic and sedative effects of these compounds, but sedative effects do correlate with α-adrenergic post-synaptic blockade (233). There is reason to believe on the basis of the present evidence that only the anxiolytic neuroleptics will inhibit locus coeruleus system function, but neuronal single unit activity studies and better clinical data will be required to test the correlation predicted here.

Are there common noradrenergic inhibitory effects of anxiolytic drugs? This review indicates that effects on noradrenergic system function in the direction predicted by a noradrenergic anxiety hypothesis have already been demonstrated for most of the major classes of anxiolytic agents. There are a variety of routes and receptors through which inhibitory effects may occur on the locus coeruleus system—via α-2 adrenergic, GABA, and opiate "cell body" receptors, and post-synaptic α- and β-adrenergic receptors (Fig. 9). Some agents seem to involve each of these. Specific locus coeruleus inhibitory or blocking effects of many other agents have not yet been investigated, but biochemical evidence of their noradrenergic effects already exists (e.g., for

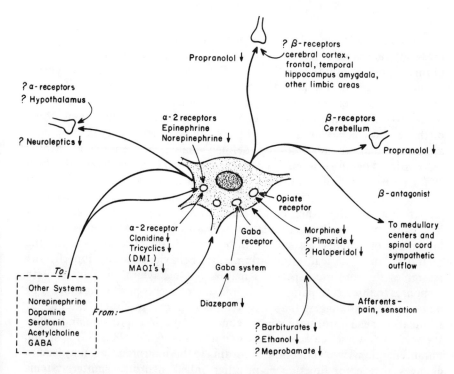

Fig. 9. Effects of anxiolytic compounds on brain noradrenergic function are illustrated schematically on a single locus coeruleus neuron. Various "pre-synaptic" or post-synaptic receptors appear to be involved, with common functionally inhibitory effects on such noradrenergic systems as the locus coeruleus.

ethanol, Δ9-tetrahydrocannabinol, meprobamate, and other "minor tranquilizers" [235, 279, 280]). Many other biochemical changes are also
produced by anxiolytics, and noradrenergic function is no doubt altered in
other nuclei and their projection areas besides the locus coeruleus. Common
noradrenergic effects of anxiolytic drugs, as a single argument, would be
unpersuasive, as others have suggested (15, 16). But these effects are
necessary, if noradrenergic systems are involved in anxiety, and are more
convincing as one component of a much larger body of experimental data.

SOME OPPOSING DATA AND INTERPRETATIONS

Two major bodies of data and hypotheses as to the function of brain
norepinephrine systems appear to be incompatible with a norepinephrine-
locus coeruleus-anxiety interpretation. These hypotheses identify norepinephrine as the most relevant biochemical substrate for the affective disorders
and for "reward."

Catecholamine Hypothesis of the Affective Disorders

The catecholamine hypothesis of the affective disorders states that depression and mania result from relative deficiency and excess of norepinephrine at post-synaptic sites (254, 255). This hypothesis is based on extensive
animal and human data that has been reviewed elsewhere (279, 281). Both the
results of locus coeruleus lesions and stimulation in the monkey seem to be, if
related to this hypothesis at all, in opposite directions to its predictions. None
of the monkey behaviors seen at either extreme of locus coeruleus activity
appear similar to behaviorally defined mania or depression. Motor
retardation, appetite loss, energy conservation, and social withdrawal, which
might be predicted to result from norepinephrine depletion, were not seen
after lesions. In fact, several of these showed opposite changes. Electrical
stimulation, on the other hand, leads to increases in threat-associated
behaviors; but continued stimulation seems to lead to progressively more
inhibition of activity associated with sympathetic hyperarousal. In the
midrange of electrical stimulation, the behavioral state superficially
resembles the motoric aspects of mania, but behavioral similarities with
responses to threats, to pain, and the infusion of agents producing anxiety or
panic in humans suggest that it is without euphoric qualities. The highest
stimulation behavioral state might be more similar to depression and might
support an "inverse" catecholamine hypothesis (156, 279, 282, 283). Chronic
noradrenergic system activation, according to this interpretation, may lead to
changes in receptor function or in other linked neurotransmitter systems
(284-286). This would be compatible with emerging evidence that tricyclic

antidepressants might work by inhibiting noradrenergic activity (257) to produce receptor subsensitivity (260, 287).

The norepinephrine reward hypothesis

The norepinephrine reward hypothesis (288-292,86) is based primarily on intracranial self-stimulation experiments (ICSS) and suggests that norepinephrine is a specific "reward" neurotransmitter. Animals will activate electrical stimulation of a large number of brain regions that contain or are innervated by catecholamines. In addition, pharmacologic agents that affect norepinephrine function alter the rates of ICSS. It might be argued that, if anxiety or fear were noradrenergically related, their unpleasant aspects would be unlikely to be deliberately induced. In other words, they would punish rather than reward locus coeruleus stimulation. Controversy exists over whether self-stimulation of locus coeruleus electrodes is in fact mediated by locus coeruleus neurons, results from effects on adjacent structures, or occurs via other neurotransmitter systems affected by the locus coeruleus (77,87-90,293,294). To side with the position that locus coeruleus neurons were not actually involved would be one way to resolve the conflicting interpretations. However, monkeys will self-stimulate the locus coeruleus (86) at current intensities that produce the precise behaviors associated with threats or with pharmacologic activation of the locus coeruleus (295). Several possible interpretations might still reconcile an anxiety-associated function with self-stimulation of the locus coeruleus: *1.* Low levels of activation may be rewarding due to associated central activation or arousal, possibly via dopamine systems, or to activation of peripheral systems comon to sexual arousal and fear (3). *2.* Low rates of ICSS compared with other areas may be due to mixed reward-punishment effects, with reward perhaps due to an adjacent or secondary system being limited by the induced anxiety-fear state also associated with the locus coeruleus. *3.* Since known pain areas can be made to support self-stimulation in animals (296), the existence of ICSS in an area does not mean that the stimulation is necessarily pleasurable (or not painful). Humans engage in dangerous and fear-provoking behaviors; fear may be the "reward" perpetuating such behaviors as riding roller coasters, sky diving, hang gliding, or mountain climbing. *For some having fun means taking risks* (297).

The most convincing argument against the "reward" hypothesis as being incompatible with anxiety or fear related effects of locus coeruleus activation comes directly from human studies. Electrical stimulation in the region of the locus coeruleus in humans produces a feeling of fear and impending death (298). This appears to confirm an anxiety-fear hypothesis, and leaves the contradictions of ICSS of the locus coeruleus in animals unresolved.

A PROPOSED INTEGRATIVE AND FUNCTIONAL ANATOMY OF ANXIETY

So far this chapter has presented evidence that a brain noradrenergic system in monkeys controls behaviors that are increased by threats and danger. Whether the system was increased by specific low intensity electrical stimulation, or by pharmacologic agents, the behavioral result was the same. These same pharmacologic agents, piperoxane and yohimbine, produce consistent symptoms of anxiety in humans, and electrical stimulation of the same region in humans produces fear. The same monkey behaviors are blocked by lesions of the locus coeruleus, by pharmacologic agents known to decrease locus coeruleus activity or to block post-synaptic projections. With the exception of clonidine, these agents all have potent anxiolytic effects in humans. Pharmacological induction of anxiety in humans suggests the involvement of β-adrenergic receptors, activated by β-adrenergic agonists and blocked by β-adrenergic antagonists. Evidence from the biochemical effects of anxiolytic compounds shows noradrenergic system alterations for every major class. No anxiolytic agents have been found so far which did not have effects on noradrenergic systems.

With this evidence in mind, is the anatomy previously described for the locus coeruleus adequate to subserve the known physiological, behavioral and psychological aspects of anxiety or fear? Are specific functions described for the locus coeruleus consistent with the same phenomena? The following highly speculative schema attempts to integrate these functions with a locus coeruleus-mediated anatomy of anxiety (Fig. 10).

Input pathways

In the normal individual the locus coeruleus is activated by afferent sensory or cortical pathways subserving different types of information with noxious potential for the individual. Activation secondary to pain comes directly from spinal cord afferents (57) from large neurons in the dorsal horns, which are known to be sensitive to noxious stimuli (299), and which give rise to fibers that do not terminate in specific sensory areas of the thalamus (300). This pathway is associated with the noxious rather than the discriminative aspects of pain (300) and may mediate the activation of the locus coeruleus by pain (134,250) via an excitatory neurotransmitter such as acetylcholine or substance P (301). When pain is present simultaneously, this activation of the locus coeruleus is not identified primarily as anxiety or fear, but as the unpleasant "noxious" aspect of pain. This type of activation may underlie the anxiety-fear mechanism itself, laying the basis for *anticipatory* avoidance of pain, with its clear adaptive advantages (9).

Afferent activation might also come via afferents from limbic forebrain areas recently described (57). These would convey interpreted sensory

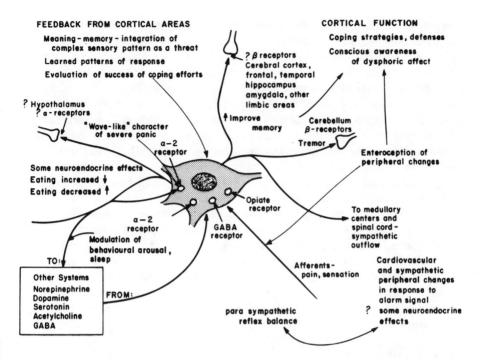

Fig. 10. A locus coeruleus-mediated anatomy of anxiety can be shown to include most of the known phenomenological correlates of anxiety or fear. Physiological, neuroendocrine, and cardiovascular changes are controlled by hypothalamic, medullary, and spinal projections from the locus coeruleus. Effects on memory, "motivation," and feeling tone are due to limbic and neocortical areas. Activation may occur directly from pain pathways, from cortically interpreted "threatening" stimuli, or via enteroception of peripheral anxiety-fear associated effects. At least two feedback loops, to and from cortical regions and to and from medullary and spinal pathways, may increase or decrease locus coeruleus activity, based on the success of coping efforts to decrease locus coeruleus system function. (↑ or ↓ indicates direction of locus coeruleus system activity).

information that warned of possible noxious consequences, but that was not noxious in itself. Even though the teeth and claws alone are noxious, the mere appearance of a tiger is responded to as if it were noxious. This interpretation would depend on learned responses in which dangerous stimuli were correctly identified, or in which innocuous stimuli were associated secondarily with dangerous ones, producing similar activating effects on the locus coeruleus in phobias. More complex threats such as having to speak in public or to perform on an examination would also activate the locus coeruleus by one of these same afferent pathways.

This "cortical" afferent information, in addition to being capable of activating the system alone, may "bias" the sensitivity of locus coeruleus neuronal responses to the next identical stimulus. Cedarbaum and Aghajanian (302) recently demonstrated neurophysiological evidence: locus coeruleus neurons responded in an incremental fashion to repeated noxious stimuli, whereas novel but painless stimuli led to decreased responses. Inhibitory "cortical" afferent information might explain some of the differences in pain tolerance depending on the situation, or explain how some individuals can suppress anxiety (repression, biofeedback, meditation). Other possible ways to decrease locus coeruleus activity might be based on pathways from the central gray to the locus coeruleus (57). These pathways may block pain, anxiety, and fear under circumstances when such blockade might be adaptive (during flight, during fighting, or in shock). Electrical stimulation of these pathways gray in humans, producing pain relief reversed by naloxone (303), would inhibit locus coeruleus activity via opiate receptors (134,135,245,116,136). Considerable evidence also supports collateral inhibition of locus coeruleus neurons (259), which might mean that the system has its own built-in brakes to prevent excessive continuous activity. Physiologically this may underlie the wavelike character of acute anxiety and panic attacks. Wavelike peaks of threat-associated behaviors are also seen in monkeys, with a similar periodicity in all of the conditions eliciting these behaviors.

Output pathways

The efferent aspects of known locus coeruleus function also appear consistent with known anxiety-related phenomena, with the signs, symptoms, and feelings of anxiety or fear coming from these efferent projections. Activation of locus coeruleus cortical or limbic projection areas may have effects on "motivation," memory, and conscious awareness of the emotion. Locus coeruleus activation of these projection areas leads to coordinated efforts to identify and cope with anxiety-fear and/or its cause. These responses might be simple in some cases where the threats were apparent—to flee from danger, or to freeze to avoid detection by a predator. In the case of more psychologic threats, they might be called coping strategies or "defenses" (9). Learning and memory of the associated events, with adaptive significance for future encounters with the same stimuli, would be enhanced (304-306; see 307, 308 for recent reviews). Of the numerous stimuli impinging on the CNS, noxious ones must especially be identified and remembered. The locus coeruleus (72,73) and β-adrenergic receptors (309), known to be innervated by the locus coeruleus, are important for long-term memory formation, but may not be essential for acquisition of new information (310). Limbic and other cortical area projections would register and identify the disagreeable, dysphoric affect of anxiety or fear if the activation were persistent or too strong, although the system might still function at lower levels without this affect (Freud's "unconscious" anxiety as a motivator? [9]).

The locus coeruleus is also clearly related to the physiological aspects of anxiety. Activation of hypothalamic projection areas may lead to neuroendocrine (311), cardiovascular (144,147,312), sympathetic (144,147), and appetitive changes (6) associated with anxiety or fear, although some of these effects are also associated with caudal efferent projections (57) to medullary and spinal centers. The principal endocrine effect of stress, increase in ACTH secretion (151), has been reported in the cat after locus coeruleus electrical stimulation (313). Locus coeruleus stimulation produces increased heart rate and blood pressure (79,314) and secondary parasympathetic alterations that contribute to other visceral manifestations of anxiety (7). Many of the other visceral manifestations, such as bowel and sphincter effects (6), are controlled by spinal and medullary centers with demonstrated locus coeruleus connections (57). Functional effects are supported by decreased bowel motility after bilateral lesions (315). There are also data from primates suggesting that the locus coeruleus system is inhibitory to eating (316,317). Modulation of arousal state and effects on sleep (69,70,318,319) are consistent with anxiety-fear states, and may be interactive with effects in other noradrenergic nuclei (57) or with other neurotransmitter systems in the reticular formation and elsewhere (57,114,320,321). Although arousal is closely related and is sometimes used as a synonym for anxiety, it is not identical. Pharmacologic anxiolytic effects are produced by some agents with minimal sedation, and bilateral locus coeruleus lesions reduce threat-associated behaviors and fearful responses without behavioral sedation (97). On the other side, there are high arousal states—e.g., sexual arousal or anger—that are not necessarily accompanied by anxiety or fear. The characteristic tremor of anxiety (6) may result from cerebellar projections from the locus coeruleus, and like locus coeruleus projections to individual cerebellar cells (125), is blocked by β-adrenergic antagonists (322).

Feedback loops

Anatomical evidence suggests some direct feedback loops that are consistent with and might also explain some previously perplexing and paradoxical data. One pathway is from limbic forebrain areas (57) which also receive innervation from the locus coeruleus (34) and which are connected with other limbic projections from the locus coeruleus. Functionally, cortical evaluation of the success of coping efforts might lead to further increases or decreases in locus coeruleus activity via this pathway, based on the amount of anxiety or fear being perceived. Learned responses to a high level of anxiety might further increase locus coeruleus activity, providing a part of the neuronal pathways by which some individuals might learn to "fear" fear itself. Another feedback loop may be related to the peripheral sympathetic and visceral manifestations of anxiety. Efferent projections to hypothalamic, medullary, and spinal centers produce these effects, and afferent sensory feedback occurs via solitary tract and spinal projections to the locus coeruleus (57). Enteroception of the peripheral physiologic changes of anxiety via these afferents directly, or indirectly via cortical to limbic to locus coeruleus pathways, to sense a pounding heart or an empty feeling in the pit of the stomach, could further activate the system in people who become sensitized to these symptoms. These two feedback loops might provide an anatomical basis for explaining the fact that some anxiety neurotics respond to the induction of peripheral manifestations of anxiety by lactate infusion, without assuming any direct CNS or etiological significance of the lactate itself. Genuine anxiety in response to epinephrine or to isoproterenol infusion might be more complicated, depending not only on previous conditioning, predisposing, or environmentally manipulated factors (200,201) but also on the sensations from peripheral manifestations of an anxiety attack. This could be influenced by other psychologic factors, or by direct inhibitory effects of epinephrine on the locus coeruleus, as previously described. β-adrenergic blockers which acted only on peripheral symptoms might also affect subjective centrally mediated anxiety via this route. According to this schema then, James (11,12) and Lange (13) were correct in pointing out, perhaps too strongly, that awareness of physiologic sensations may lead to the emotion, but Cannon was right that anxiety is a centrally mediated phenomenon (3).

This schema is "at best, a reductionistic oversimplification of a very complex biological state" (254). There may be other receptors on the locus coeruleus that have not been included, and the specific neurotransmitters responsible for inhibitory effects are not known with certainty. There is some evidence for autoregulatory functions mediated by norepinephrine (259) or for inhibition by afferent neurons containing epinephrine (109), opioid peptides (132-136), and GABA (99,142). The excitatory neurotransmitters involved in functional activation are not specifically known, although acetylcholine and substance P are possibilities (301). Although the functional schema proposed centers on the locus coeruleus as an essential "relay center," the phenomenon "anxiety" requires almost every area of the brain, and numerous other transmitter systems as well. As a whole, the evidence also suggests that "anxiety-fear" is not the only, or perhaps even the most important, function of the locus coeruleus system.

Behaviorally, the locus coeruleus appears to have an inhibitory function throughout the entire range of its activity, suggested by experiments from the extreme of locus coeruleus bilateral lesions to extreme continuous activation by electrical stimulation. A possible continuum of cautionary or inhibitory functions encompasses the effects of locus coeruleus lesions, such as fearlessness, through the effects of increasing anxiety or fear to the complete immobilization of terror (Table 4). In a middle or normal range of function, the system would operate without dysphoria, and would have evolutionary advantages, insuring that threats to well-being were respected and, if possible,

Table 4. Effects of locus coeruleus lesions

MAXIMUM LOCUS COERULEUS FUNCTION	Terror	
	Panic	
	Fear	
	Anxiety	Dysphoric
	Dread	
	Alarm	
	Vigilance	
	Wariness	
	Caution	
	Prudence	Euthymic
	Watchfulness	
	Attentiveness	
	Inattentiveness	
	Distractibility	
	Impulsivity	
MINIMUM LOCUS COERULEUS	Carelessness	
FUNCTION	Recklessness	Anhedonic
	Fearlessnecs	

prevented (9). It might be dysphoric and "nonrewarding" at either extreme. Diminished function would produce clear liabilities—the failure to withdraw in the face of lethal danger or the inability to learn from painful experience or to inhibit certain impulsive responses. At the other extreme, continuous excessive activation might lead to the inability to act when necessary.

A brain "alarm" system might be a better name for the overall adaptive functional system. It gets direct and interpreted nociceptive information that it responds to by activation (91) of the structures known to mediate the "fight or flight" response (2,3). It is an automatic system generally, but "rings" a further warning if it is activated too strongly or for too long a time. "Normal" anxiety or fear is our perception of this ringing, along with the accompanying physiologic and behavioral expressions that occur at higher intensities. Pathological anxiety might then be the result of aberrations in the operation of this system at a number of points.

CLINICAL IMPLICATIONS AND DIRECTIONS FOR RE-SEARCH

Much of the preceding discussion has been highly speculative and has assumed that a norepinephrine model of anxiety is at least partly correct. Since it may not be, and since extensive research remains to be done to prove a brain noradrenergic connection with anxiety, is any of this relevant to clinical treatment? The answer, at this point, is probably no. But some directions for further testing of the model and possible implications for clinical psychiatric problems may be of interest.

Further testing of drugs with and without antianxiety activity may provide more evidence for norepinephrine systems as the relevant site of anxiolytic activity in the brain, or may disprove the hypothesis. Screening of new compounds, with carefully tailored receptor profiles to activate or inhibit receptors to produce a net inhibition of locus coeruleus system activity, might uncover more specific and more effective drugs. Multiple targeting of different receptors with similar effects (e.g., α-2 adrenergic and GABA) might increase efficacy of anxiolytic actions and decrease side effects. Similar multiple targeting may improve the control of pain, and to some extent may provide a rationale for current clinical combinations discovered empirically. Careful investigation of the evidence for deleterious effects of chronic treatment with anxiolytics, such as the increases in aggression reported after diazepam (323,324), would be supported by the effects of locus coeruleus lesions and the possible adaptive significance of having an "alarm" system functioning. Research should also look more specifically at what is abnormal and requires treatment, and what is normal and adaptive. Perhaps a substantial percentage of the population (232) should not take tranquilizers.

What then, distinguishes individuals who consult a physician for anxiety-related problems from normals? Research on "trait" differences in anxiety suggests that genetically influenced differences in catecholamine related enzymes (325), receptor function, and neurotransmitter release mechanisms, which are known to be genetically controlled, may be relevant to how active this system is in a given individual. Changes in these same mechanisms due to environmental exposure to chronic anxiety may lead to further increases in function—e.g., induction of synthetic enzyme activity or changes in receptor sensitivity. The effects of learning and experience on the production of anxiety neurosis and phobias outlined by Freud (9) and classical psychological conditioning (326) may also be important for the production of symptoms in some who may or may not have additional biological vulnerabilities. Since anxiety has been thought to be important to the etiology of psychiatric illnesses, studies of the relationship of increased noradrenergic-anxiety systems in depression (156,165,279,283), schizophrenia (327-329), primary autism (330), and anorexia nervosa (317,331,332) may produce new understanding of these conditions. Decreased noradrenergic system function, based on the absence of inhibitory functions, is suggested in minimal brain dysfunction, sociopathy, hysterical and impulsive-aggressive character disorders, and the Research Diagnostic Criteria (RDC) category labile personality. Research in these areas might be directed toward documenting these suspected noradrenergic system deficiencies more clearly.

Improvement in the understanding of the specific connections with anxiety in several psychosomatic conditions may result from the validation of the locus coeruleus-anxiety model reviewed here. Understanding the noradrenergic basis of both chronic anxiety and pathological changes that lead to arteriosclerotic cardiovascular disease may suggest improved methods of blocking these effects and provides a more specific rationale for preventive treatment with anti-noradrenergic agents in these conditions. The same could be said for "functional" bowel diseases such as duodenal ulcer (333), ulcerative colitis, irritable colon syndrome (334), and chronic nonspecific diarrhea (335), which are influenced by psychologic anxiety and stress factors, and which might be studied for possible benefits due to relative adrenergic system blockade.

One final area of possible clinical relevance relates to noradrenergic-opiate receptor interactions in the analgesia, tolerance, anxiolytic effects, and withdrawal syndrome of the opiates. The possibility that the brain's own endogenous morphine system normally acts, like morphine, to inhibit locus coeruleus-mediated effects (anxiety?) in some circumstances should be studied in a variety of experimental conditions. This connection may explain why some individuals begin taking opiate drugs. Noradrenergic system activation that occurs in opiate withdrawal may be an even more powerful motivator of drug-seeking behavior, and in some respects may be a fair model of anxiety-fear in humans. Recent evidence of the complete suppression of opiate withdrawal symptoms in human addicts by low doses of clonidine (336,337) provides further evidence for a noradrenergic system model of anxiety and illustrates the research potential of further studies of the locus coeruleus.

ACKNOWLEDGMENTS

I thank my colleagues who made the primate research possible for allowing me to cite specific data. Dr. Yung H. Huang was a collaborator on all lesion and stimulation studies, Dr. Mark S. Gold collaborated on pharmacologic studies. Dr. James W. Maas, Dr. Keith Levernez, Dr. Daniel R. Snyder, Mr. Jean Baulu, and Mr. Andy Caswell contributed invaluably to specific studies. Dr. George Aghajanian and Dr. Jesse Cedarbaum provided valuable ideas and illustrations, Dr. George Heninger provided helpful criticism, and Mrs. B. G. Erb provided editorial asistance. This research was supported by grants from the National Institute of Mental Health, Nos. MH 24607, MH 25642, and MH 14276, the State of Connecticut, and by a grant from the Harry Frank Guggenheim Foundation.

SUMMARY

This chapter reviews evidence for the involvement of brain norepinephrine systems in the subjective, behavioral, and physiological expression of anxiety. New data from nonhuman primates and humans are presented. Areas reviewed for evidence of noradrenergic involvement in anxiety in humans include biochemical correlates of anxiety or fear, experimental pharmacologic induction of anxiety in normals and psychiatric patients, and biochemical actions of anti-anxiety compounds. This evidence supports the brain noradrenergic system innervated by the nucleus locus coeruleus as an essential relay center involved in an adaptive function which may produce anxiety or fear in normals. A hypothetical neuroanatomical-functional schema centering around the locus coeruleus is outlined which also suggests the importance of other brain areas and neurotransmitters in anxiety-related phenomena. Possible alterations in this system that might lead to pathological anxiety or contribute to other psychiatric illnesses are suggested for future research.

REFERENCES

1. Elliot, T.R. The action of adrenalin. *J. Physiol.* 32:401-467, 1905.
2. Cannon, W.B. *Bodily Changes in Pain, Fear and Rage.* New York: Appleton, 1915.
3. Cannon, W.B. The James-lange theory of emotions: A critical examination and an alternative theory. *Am. J. Psychol.* 39:106, 1927.
4. Selye, H. *The Physiology and Pathology of Exposure to Stress.* Montreal: ACTA, 1950.
5. Selye, H. The evolution of the stress concept. *Am. Scientist* 61:692-699, 1973.
6. Lief, H.I. Psychoneurotic disorders, I: Anxiety, conversion, dissociative, and phobic reactions. In A.M. Freedman and H.I. Kaplan, eds., *Comprehensive Textbook of Psychiatry.* Baltimore; Williams & Wilkins.
7. Gellhorn, E. The neurophysiological basis of anxiety: A hypothesis. *Perspect. Biol. Med.* 8:488, 1965.
8. Epstein, S. The nature of anxiety. In C.D. Spielberger, ed., *Anxiety: Current Trends in Theory and Research.* New York: Pergamon.
9. Freud, S. *The Problem of Anxiety,* trans. H.A. Bunker. New York: Psychoanalytic Quarterly Press and W.W. Norton, 1936.
10. Pavlov, I.P. *Conditioned Reflexes,* trans. G.V. Anrep. London: Oxford University Press, 1927.
11. James, W. What is an emotion? *Mind* 9:188, 1884.
12. James, W. *The Principles of Psychology.* New York: Hold, 1890.
13. Lange, C. *The Emotions. (1885)* Baltimore: Williams & Wilkins, 1922.
14. Stein, L., Wise, C.D., and Berger, B.D. Antianxiety action of benzodiazepines: Decrease in activity of serotonin neurons in the punishment system. In S. Garattini, E. Mussini, and L.O. Randall., eds., *The Benzodiazepines.* New York: Raven Press, 1973.
15. Stein, L., Wise, C.D., and Belluzzi, J.D. Effects of benzodiazepines on central serotonergic mechanisms. In E. Costa and P. Greengard, eds., *Mechanism of Action of Benzodiazepines.* New York: Raven Press, 1975.
16. Snyder, S.H., and Enna, S.J. The role of central glycine receptors in the pharmacologic actions of the benzodiazepines. In E. Costa and P. Greengard, eds., *Mechanism of Action of Benzodiazepines.* New York: Raven Pres,s 1975.
17. Warburton, D.M. Modern biochemical concepts of anxiety. *Int. Pharmacopsychiatry* 9:189-205, 1974.

18. Pitts, F.N., Jr., and McClure, J.N., Jr. Lactate metabolism in anxiety neurosis. *New Eng. J. Med.* 277(25):1329-1336, 1967.
19. Pitts, F.N., Jr. The biochemistry of anxiety. *Scientific American* 220:69-75, 1969.
20. Pitts, F.N., Jr. Biochemical factors in anxiety neurosis. *Behav. Sci.* 16(1):82-91, 1971.
21. Beer, B., Chasin, M., Clody, D.E., et al. Cyclic adenosine monophosphate phosphodiesterase in brain: effect on anxiety. *Science* 176:428-430, 1973.
22. Reil, J.C. Das verlängerte Rückenmark, die hinteren, seitlichen and vörderen Schenkel des kleinen Gehirns und die theils strangförmig, theils als Ganglienkette in der Axe des Rückenmarks and des Gehirns fortlaufende graue Substanz. *Archiv für Physiol.* (Halle) 9:511, 1809.
23. Dahlström, A., and Fuxe, K. Evidence for the existence of monoamine-containing neurons in the central nervous system. I. Demonstration of monoamines in the cell bodies of brain stem neurons. *Acta Physiol. Scand.* 62 (Suppl 232): 1-55, 1964.
24. Loisou, L.A. Projections of the nucleus locus coeruleus in the albino rat. *Brain Res.* 15:563-566, 1969.
25. Fuxe, K., Hökfelt, T., and Ungerstedt, U. Morphological and functional aspects of central monoamine neurons. *Internat. Rev. Neurobiol.* 13:93-126, 1970.
26. Maeda, T., and Shimuzu, N. Projections ascendantes du locus coeruleus et d'autres neurones aminergique pontiques au niveau du prosencephale du rat. *Brain Res.* 36:19-35, 1972.
27. Freedman, R., Foote, S.L., and Bloom, F.E. Histochemical characterization of neocortical projection of the nucleus locus coeruleus in the squirrel monkey. *J. Comp. Neur.* 164:209-232, 1975.
28. Takayama, M., Maeda, T., and Shimizu, N. Detailed noradrenaline pathways of locus coeruleus neurons to the cerebral cortex with use of 6-hydroxydopa. *Brain Res.* 79:139-144, 1974.
29. Ungerstedt, U. Stereotaxic mapping of the monoamine pathways in the rat brain. *Acta. Psysiol. Scand.* (Suppl.) 367:1-48, 1971.
30. Kobayashi, R.M., Palkovitz, M., Kopin, I., et al. Biochemical mapping of noradrenergic nerves arising from the rat locus coeruleus. *Brain Res.* 77:269-280, 1974.
31. Kobayashi, R.M., Palkovits, M., Jacobowitz, D.M., et al. Biochemical mapping of the noradrenergic projection from the locus coeruleus. *Neurology* 25:223-233, 1975.
32. Lindvall, O., Bjorklund, A., Nobin, A., et al.The adrenergic innervation of the rat thalamus as revealed by the glyoxylic acid fluorescence method. *J. Comp. Neurol.* 154:317-348, 1974.
33. Lindvall, O., and Bjorklund, A. The organization of the ascending catecholamine neuron systems in the rat brain as revealed by the glyoxylic acid fluorescence method. *Acta Physiol. Scand.* (Suppl.) 412:1-48, 1974.
34. Pickel, V.M., Segal, M., and Bloom, F.E. A radioautographic study of the efferent pathways of the nucleus locus coeruleus. *J. Comp. Neurol.* 155:15-42, 1974.
35. Segal, M., Pickel, V., and Bloom, F.E. The projections of the nucleus locus coeruleus: an autoradiographic study. *Life Sci.* 13:817-821, 1973.
36. Papez, J.W. A proposed mechanism of emotion. *Arch. Neurol. Psychiat.* (Chicago) 38:725-744, 1937.
37. MacLean, P. Psychosomatic disease and the "visceral brain." *Psychosom. Med.* 11:338-353, 1941.
38. Olsen, L., and Fuxe, K. Further mapping out of the central noradrenaline neuron systems: Projections of the subcoeruleus area. *Brain Res.* 43:289-295, 1972.
39. Sachs, C., Jonsson, G., and Fuxe, K. Mapping of central noradrenaline pathways with 6-hydroxylase. *Brain Res.* 63:249-261, 1973.

40. Ross, R.A., and Reis, D.J. Effects of lesions of locus coeruleus on regional distribution of dopamine-β-hydroxylase activity in rat brain. *Brain. Res.* 73:161-166, 1974.
41. Worth, W.S., Collins, ., Doubravka, K., et al. Serial changes in norepinephrine and dopamine in rat brain after locus coeruleus lesions. *Brain Res.* 106:198-203, 1976.
42. Jacobowitz, D.M., and Broadwell, R.D. Origin of afferent fibers to the olfactory bulb of the rat. *Neurosci. Abst.* 1:677, 1975.
43. Kuypers, H.G.J., and Maisky, V.A. Retrograde axonal transport of horseradish peroxidase from spinal cord to brain stem cell groups in the cat. *Neurosci. Letters* 1:9-14, 1975.
44. Hancock, M.B., and Fougerousse, C.L. Spinal projections from the nucleus locus coeruleus and nucleus subcoeruleus in the cat and monkey as demonstrated by the retrograde transport of horseradish peroxidase. *Brain Res. Bull.* 1:229-234, 1976.
45. Russell,G.V. The nucleus locus coeruleus (dorsolateralis tegmenti) *Tex. Rep. Biol. Med.* 13:939-988, 1955.
46. Shimizu, N., and Imamoto, K. Fine structure of the locus coeruleus in the rat. *Arch. Histol. Jap.* 31:229-246, 1970.
47. Snider, R.S. A cerebellar-coeruleus pathway. *Brain Res.* 88:229-246, 1970.
48. Conrad, L.C.A., Leonard, C.M., and Pfaff, D.W. Connections of the median and dorsal raphe nuclei in the rat: An autoradiographic and degeneration study. *J. Comp. Neurol.* 156:179-206, 1974.
49. Bobillier, P., Segain, S., Pettijean, F., et al. The raphe nuclei of the cat brain stem: a topographic atlas of their efferent projections as revealed by autoradiography. *Brain Res.* 113:449-456, 1976.
50. Conrad, L.C.A., and Pfaff, D.W. Efferents from medial basal forebrain and hypothalamus in the rat. I. An autoradiographic study of the medial preoptic area. *J. Comp. Neurol.* 169:185-220, 1976.
51. Conrad, L.C.A., and Pfaff, D.W. Efferents from medial basal forebrain and hypothalamus in the rat. II. An autoradiographic study of the anterior hypothalamus. *J. Comp. Neurol.* 169:221-262, 1976.
52. Saper, C.B., Swanson, L.W., and Cowan, W.N. The efferent connections of the ventromedial nucleus of the hypothalamus of the rat. *J. Comp. Neurol.* 169:409-442, 1976.
53. Swanson, L.W., and Saper, C.B. Direct neuronal inputs to locus coeruleus from basal forebrain. *Neurosci. Abs.* I:683, 1975.
54. Swanson, L.W. The locus coeruleus: A cytoarchitectonic, golgi, and immunohistochemical study in the albino rat. *Brain Res.* 110:39-56, 1976.
55. Hokfelt, T., Fuxe, K., Goldstein, M., et al. Immunohistochemical evidence for the existence of adrenaline neurons in the rat brain. *Brain Res.* 6:235-251, 1974.
56. Sakai, K., Touret, M., Salvert, D., et al. Afferent projections to the cat locus coeruleus as visualized by the horseradish peroxidase technique. *Brain Res.* 119:21-41, 1977.
57. Cedarbaum, J.M., and Aghajanian, G.K. Afferent projections to the locus coeruleus as determined by a retrograde tracing technique. *J. Comp. Neurol.* 178(1):1-15, 1978.
58. Jones, B.E., and Moore, R.Y. Catecholamine-containng neurons of the nucleus locus coeruleus in the cat. *J. Comp. Neurol.* 157:43-51, 1974.
59. Maeda, T., Pin, C., Salvert, D., et al. Les neurones contenant des catecholamines du tegmentum pontique et leurs voies de projection chez le chat. *Brain Res.* 57:119-152, 1973.
60. Hubbard, J.E., and di Carlo, V. Fluorescence histochemistry of monoamine-containing cell bodies in the brain stem of the squirrel monkey. I. The locus coeruleus. *J. Comp. Neurol.* 147:553-556, 1973.

61. Sladek, J.R., Jr., and Bowman, J.P. The distribution of catecholamines within the inferior olivary complex of the cat and rhesus monkey. *J. Comp. Neurol.* 163:203-214, 1975.
62. Nobin, A., and Björkland, A. Topography of the monoamine neuron systems in the human brain as revealed in fetuses. *Acta Physiol. Scand.* (Suppl) 388:1-40, 1973.
63. Friedhoff, A.J., ed. *Catecholamines and Behavior,* Vol. 2, New York and London: Plenum, 1975.
64. Anlezark, G.M., Walter, D.S., Arbuthnott, G.W., et al. The relationships between noradrenaline turnover in cerebral cortex and electrical self-stimulation through electodes in the region of the locus coeruleus. *J. Neurochem.* 24:677-681, 1975.
65. Arbuthnott, G.W., Christie, J.E., Cow, T.J., et al. Lesions of the locus coeruleus and noradrenaline metabolism in cerebral cortex. *Exper. Neurol.* 41:411-417, 1973.
66. Korf, J., Aghajanian, G.K., and Roth, R.H. Stimulation and destruction of the locus coeruleus: opposite effects on 3-methoxy-4-hydroxyphenylglycol sulfate levels in the rat cerebral cortex. *Eur. J. Pharmacol.* 21:305-310, 1973.
67. Arbuthnott, F.W., Christie, J.E., Crow, T.J., et al. The effect of unilateral and bilateral lesions in the locus coeruleus on the levels of 3-methoxy-4-hydroxyphenyl-glycol (MHPG) in neocortex. *Experientia* 29:52-53, 1973.
68. Chu, N-S., and Bloom, F.E. Activity patterns of catecholamine-containing pontine neurons in the dorsal-lateral tegmentum of unrestrained cats. *J. Neurobiol.* 5:527-544, 1974.
69. Chu, N-S., and Bloom, F.E. Norepinephrine-containing neurons: changes in spontaneous discharge patterns during sleep and waking. *Science* 179:908-910, 1973.
70. Lidbrink, P. The effect of lesions of ascending noradrenaline pathways on sleep and waking in the rat. *Brain Res.* 74:19-40, 1974.
71. Hobson, J.A., McCarley, R.W., and Wyzinski, P.W. Sleep cycle oscillation: reciprocal discharge by two brainstem neuronal groups. *Science* 189:55-58, 1975.
72. Anlezark, G.M., Crow, T.J., and Greenway, A.P. Impaired learning and decreased cortical norepinephrine after bilateral locus coeruleus lesions. *Science*181:682-694, 1973.
73. Zornetzer, S.F., and Gold, M.S. The locus coeruleus: Its possible role in memory consolidation. *Physiol. Behav.* 16:331-336, 1976.
74. Amaral, D.G., and Foss, J.A. Locus coeruleus lesions and learning. *Science* 188:377-38, 1975.
75. Sessions, R.G., Kant, G.J., and Koob, G.E. Locus coeruleus lesions and learning in the rat. *Physiol. Behav.* 17:853-859, 1976.
76. Ritter, W., and Stein, L. Self-stimulation of noradrenergic cell group (A6) in locus coeruleus of rats. *J. Comp. Physiol. Psychol.* 85:443-452, 1973.
77. Amaral, D.G., and Routtenberg, A. Locus coeruleus and intracranial self-stimulation: A cautionary note. *Behav. Biol.* 13:331-338, 1975.
78. Micco, D.J. Jr. Complex behaviors elicited by stimulation of the dorsal pontine tegmentum in rats. *Brain Res.* 75:172-176, 1974.
79. Przuntek, H., and Phillippu, A. Reduced pressor responses to stimulation of the locus coeruleus after lesion of the posterior hypothalamus. *Naunyn-Schmiedeberg-s Arch. Pharmacol.* 276:119-122, 1973.
80. Dresse, A. Importance du systeme mesencephalotelencephalique noradrenergic comme substratum anatomique du comportement d'autostimulation. *Life Sci.* 3:759-762, 1966.
81. Crow, T.J. Map of the rat mesencephalon for electrical self-stimulation. *Brain Res.* 36:265-273, 1972.
82. Crow, T.J. Catecholamine-containing neurons and electrical self-stimulation: 1. A review of some data. *Psycholog. Med.* 2:414-421, 1972.

83. Crow, T.J., Spear, P.J., and Arbuthnott, G.W. Intracranial self-stimulation with electrodes in the region of the locus coeruleus. *Brain Res.* 36:275-287, 1972.

84. Ellman, S.J., Ackerman, R.F., Bodnar, R.J., et al. Comparison of behaviors elicited by electrical brain stimulation in dorsal brain stem and hypothalamus of rats. *J. Comp. Physiol. Psychol.* 88:816-828, 1975.

85. Liebman, J.M., Mayer, D.J., and Liebeskind, J.C. Self-stimulation loci in the midbrain central gray matter of the rat. *Behav. Biol.* 9:299-306, 1973.

86. German, D.C., and Bowden, D.M. Catecholamine systems as the neural substrate for intracranial self-stimulation: An hypothesis. *Brain Res.* 73:381-419, 1974.

87. Clavier, R., and Routtenberg, A. Ascending monoamine-containing fiber pathways related to intracranial self-stimulation. *Brain Res.* 72:25-40, 1974.

88. Clavier, R.M., and Routtenberg, A. Brain stem self-stimulation attenuated by lesions of medial forebrain bundle but not by lesions of locus coeruleus or the caudal ventral norepinephrine bundle. *Brain Res.* 101:251-271, 1976.

89. Clavier, R.M., Fibiger, H.C., and Phillips,A.G. Evidence that self-stimulation of the region of the locus coeruleus in rats does not depend upon noradrenergic projections to telencephalon. *Brain Res.* 113:71-81, 1976.

90. Breese, G.R., and Cooper,B.R. Relationship of dopamine neural systems to the maintenance of self-stimulation. In E.F. Domino and J.M. Davis, eds., *Neurotransmitter Balances Regulating Behavior.* Ann Arbor, Edwards Bros., 1975.

91. Huang, Y.H., Redmond, D.E., Jr., Snyder, D.R., et al. In vivo location and destruction of the locus coeruleus in the stumptail macaque *(Macaca arctoides). Brain Res.* 100:157-162, 1975.

92. Redmond, D.E., Jr., Huang, Y.H., Snyder, D.R., et al. Behavioral effects of stimulation of the locus coeruleus in the stumptail monkey *(Macaca arctoides) Brain Res.* 116:502-510, 1976.

93. Bertrand, M. *The Behavioral Repertoire of the Stump Tail Macaque.* New York: S. Karger, 1969.

94. Darwin, C. *The Expression of Emotions in Man and Animals.* New York: Philosophical Library, reprinted 1955.

95. Ekman, P. Cross-cultural studies of facial expression. In P. Ekman, ed., ed., *Darwin and Facial Expression: A Century of Research in Review.* New York: Academic Press, 1973.

96. Huang, Y.H., Redmond, D.E., Jr., Snyder, D.R., et al. Loss of fear following bilateral lesions of the locus coeruleus in the monkey. *Neurosci. Abst.* 2:573, 1976.

97. Redmond, D.E., Jr., Huang, Y.H., Snyder, D.R., et al. Behavioral changes following lesions of the locus coeruleus in *Macaca arctoides. Neurosci. Abst.* 1:472, 1976.

98. Svensson, T.H., Bunney, B.S., and Aghajanian, G.K. Inhibition of both noradrenergic and serotonergic neurons in brain by the alpha-adrenergic agonist clonidine. *Brain Res.* 92:291-306, 1975.

99. Cedarbaum, J.M., and Aghajanian, G.K. Noradrenergic neurons of the locus coeruleus: Inhibition by epinephrine and activation by the alpha-antagonist piperoxane. *Brain Res.* 112:413-419, 1976.

100. Cedarbaum, J.M., and Aghajanian, G.K. Catecholamine receptors on locus coeruleus neurons: Pharmacological characterization. *Eur. J. Pharmacol.* 44:375-385, 1977.

101. Gold, M.S., Redmond, D.E., Jr., and Donabedian, R.K. Effect of piperoxane on serum prolactin: possible role of epinephrine-mediated synapses in the inhibition of prolactin secretion. *Endocrinology* (102(4):1183-1189, 1978.

102. Maas, J.W., Hattox, S.E., Landis, D.H., et al. The determination of a brain arteriovenous difference for 3-methoxy-4-hydroxyphenethylene glycol (MHPG). *Brain Res.* 118:167-173, 1976.

103. Bolme, P., Fuxe, K., and Lidbrink, P. On the function of central catecholamine neurons—their role in cardiovascular and arousal mechanisms. *Res. Commun. Chem. Pathol. Pharmacol.* 4:657-697, 1972.

104. Starke, K., and Montel, H. Alpha-receptor-mediated modulation of transmitter release from central noradrenergic neurons. *Naunyn-Schmiedeberg's Arch. Pharmacol.* 279:53-60, 1973.

105. Starke, K., and Montel, H. Involvement of α-receptors in clonidine induced inhibition of transmitter release from central monoamine neurons. *Neuropharmacol.* 12:1073-1080, 1973.

106. Starke, K., Borowski, E., and Endon, T. Preferential blockade of presynaptic alpha-adrenoceptors by yohimbine. *Eur. J. Pharmacol.* 34:385-388, 1975.

107. Delbarre, B., and Schmitt, H. Sedative effects of alpha-sympathomimetic drugs and their antagonism by adrenergic and cholinergic blocking drugs. *Eur. J. Pharmacol.* 13:356-363, 1971.

108. Finch, L. The cardiovascular effects of intraventricular clonidine and bay 1470 in conscious hypertensive cats. *Brit. J. Pharmacol.* 52:333-338, 1974.

109. Fuxe, K., Lidbrink, P., Hökfelt, T., et al. Effects of piperoxane on sleep and waking in the rat. Evidence for increased waking by blocking inhibitory adrenaline receptors on the locus coeruleus. *Acta Physiol. Scand.* 91:566-567, 1974.

110. Schmitt, H., Schmitt, H., and Fenard, S. Evidence for an alpha-sympathomimetic component in the effects of catapresan on vascular centers: antagonism by piperoxane. *Eur. J. Pharmacol.* 14:98-100, 1971.

111. Schmitt, H., Schmitt, H., and Fenard, S. Action of alpha-adrenergic blocking drugs on the sympathetic centers and their interactions with the central sympatho-inhibitory effect of clonidine. *Arzyneim Forsch.* 23(1):40-45, 1973.

112. Anden, N-E., Corrodi, H., Fuxe, K., et al. Evidence for a central noradrenaline receptor. Stimulation by clonidine. *Life Sci.* 9:513-523, 1970.

113. Rochette, L., and Bralet, J. Effect of clonidine on the synthesis of cerebral dopamine. *Biochem. Pharmacol.* 24:303-305, 1975.

114. Gallager, D.W., and Aghajanian, G.K. Effect of antipsychotic drugs on the firing of dorsal raphe cells 1. Role of adrenergic system. *Eur. J. Pharmacol.* 39:341-355, 1976.

115. Redmond, D.E., Jr. Alterations in the function of the nucleus locus coeruleus: a possible model for studies of anxiety. In I. Hanin and E. Usdin, eds., *Animal Models in Psychiatry and Neurology*. Oxford and New York: Pergamon Press, 1977.

116. Redmond, D.E., Jr., Huang, Y.H., and Gold, M.S. Anxiety: The locus coeruleus connection. *Neurosci. Abst.* 3:258, 1977.

117. Huang, Y.H., Maas, J.W., and Redmond, D.E., Jr. Evidence for noradrenergic specificity of behavioral effects of electrical stimulation of the nucleus locus coeruleus. *Neurosci. Abst.* 3:251, 1977.

118. Gold, M.S., and Redmond D.E. Jr. Pharmacological activation and inhibition of noradrenergic activity alter specific behaviors in nonhuman primates, *Neurosci. Abst.* 3:250, 1977.

119. Goodman, L.S., and Gilman, A. *The Pharmacological Basis of Therapeutics.* New York: Macmillan, 1965.

120. Davis, J.N., and Lefkowitz, R.J Beta-adrenergic receptor binding: Synaptic localization in rat brain. *Brain Res.* 113:214-218, 1976.

121. Greenberg, D.A., U'Pritchard, D.C., and Snyder, S.H. Alpha-noradrenergic receptor binding in mammalian brain: Differential labeling of agonists and antagonist states. *Life Sci.* 19:69-76, 1976.

122. Wied, D. de, and Jong, W. de. Drug effects and hypothalamic-anterior pituitary function. *Ann. Rev. Pharmacol.* 14:389-412, 1974.

123. U'Pritchard, D.C., Greenberg, D.A., and Snyder, S.H. Binding characteristics of a

radiolabelled agonist and antagonist at central nervous system alpha-noradrenergic receptors. *Mol. Pharmacol.* 13:454-473, 1977.

124. U'Pritchard, D.C., and Snyder, S.H. Differential labelling of α- and β-noradrenergic receptors in calf cerebellum membranes with 3H-adrenalin. *Nature* (London) 270:261-263, 1977.

125. Hoffer, B.J., Siggins, G.R., and Bloom, F.E. Studies on norepinephrine containing afferents to Purkinje cells of rat cerebellum. II. Sensitivity of Purkinje cells to norepinephrine and related substances administered by microinontophoresis. *Brain Res.* 25:523-534, 1971.

126. Segal, M., and Bloom, F.E. The action of norepinephrine in the rat hippocampus, I. Iontophoretic studies. *Brain Res.* 72:79-97, 1974.

127. Segal, M., and Bloom, F.E. The action of norepinephrine in the rat hippocampus, II. Activation of the input pathway. *Brain Res.* 72:99-14, 1974.

128. Lish, P.M., Weikel, J.H., and Dungan, K.W. Pharmacological and toxicological properties of two new beta adrenergic receptor antagonists *J.P.E.T.* 149:161-173, 1965.

129. Wiesel, F.A. Effects of high dose propranolol treatment on dopamine and norepinephrine metabolism in regions of rat brain. *Neurosci. Letters* 2:35-38, 1976.

130. Andén. N.-E., and Strombom, U. Adrenergic receptor blocking agents: Effects on central noradrenaline and dopamine receptors and on motor activity. *Psychopharmacol.* (Berlin) 38:91-103, 1974.

131. Fuxe, K., Bolme, P., Agnati, L., et al. The effect of DL, L- and D-propranolol on central monoamine neurons. Mechanisms. *Neurosci. Letters* 3:45-52, 1976.

132. Pert, C.B., and Snyder, S.H. Opiate receptor: Demonstration in nervous tissue. *Science* 179;111-114, 1973.

133. Pert, C.B., Kuhar, M.J., and Snyder, S.. Autoradiographic localization of the opiate receptor in rat brain. *Life Sci.* 16:1849-1854, 1975.

134. Korf, J., Bunney,B.S., and Aghajanian, G.K. Noradrenergic neurons: morphine inhibition of spontaneous activity. *Eur. J. Pharmacol.* 25:165-169, 1974.

135. Bird, S.J., and Kuhar, M.J. Iontophoretic applications of opiates to the locus coeruleus. *Brain Res.* 122:523-533, 1977.

136. Redmond, D.E., Jr., Gold, M.S., and Huang, Y.H. Opiate effects on noradrenergically mediated behaviors in *M. artoides,* in preparation.

137. Roemer, Buescher, H.H., Hill, R.C., et al. A synthetic enkephalin analogue with prolonged parenteral and oral analgesic activity. *Nature* (London) 268:547-549, 1977.

138. Corrodi, H., Fuxe, K., and Hökfelt, T. The effect of some psychoactive drugs on central monoamine neurons. *Eur. J. Pharmacol.* 1:363-368, 1967.

139. Taylor, K.M., and Laverty, R. The effect of chlordiazepoxide, diazepam and nitrazepam on catecholamine metabolism in regions of the rat brain. *Eur. J. Pharmacol.* 8:296-301, 1969.

140. Corrodi, H., Fuxe, K., Lidbrink, P., et al. Minor tranquilizers, stress, and central catecholamine neurons. *Brain Res.* 29:1-16, 1971.

141. Fuxe, K., Agnati, L.F., Bolme, P., et al. The possible involvement of GABA mechanisms in the action of benzodiazepines on central catecholamine neurons. In E. Costa and P. Greengard, eds., *Mechanism of Action of Benzodiazepines.* New York: Raven Press, 1975.

142. Iversen, L.L., and Schon, F. The use of autoradiographic techniques for the identification and mapping of transmitter-specific neurons in CNS. In A. Mandell and D. Segal, eds., *New Concepts of Transmitter Regulation.* New York: Plenum Press 1973.

143. Redmond, D.E., Jr., Huang, Y.H., and Gold, M.S., in preparation.

144. Lader, M.H., and Wing, L. *Physiological Measures, Sedative Drugs, and Morbid Anxiety.* London: Oxford University Press, 1966.
145. Bridges, P.K., Jones, M.T., and Leak, D. A comparative study of four physiological concomitants of anxiety. *Arch. Gen. Psychiat.* 19(2):141-145, 1968.
146. Lader, M.H. The nature of anxiety. *Brit. J. Psychiat.* 121:481-491, 1972.
147. Lader, M.H. Psychophysiological aspects of anxiety. In M.H. Lader, ed., *Studies of Anxiety.* Ashford, Kent: World Psychiatric Association and Headley Brothers, 1973.
148. Tyrer, P.J., and Lader, M.H. Central and peripheral correlates of anxiety: A comparative study. *J. Nerv. Ment. Dis.* 162(2):99-104, 1976
149. Bliss, E.L., Migeon, C.J., Branch, C.H.H., et al. Reaction of the adrenal cortex to emotional stress. *Psychosom. Med.* 18:56-76, 1956.
150. Persky, H., Grinker, R.R., Hamburg, D.A., et al. Adrenal cortical function in anxious human subjects. *A.M.A. Arch. Neurol. Psychiat.* 76:549-558, 1956.
151. Levi, L. Neuro-endocrinology of anxiety. In M.H. Lader, ed., *Studies of Anxiety.* Ashford, Kent: World Psychiatric Association and Headley Brothers, 1973.
152. Elmadjian, F., Hope, J.M., and Lawson, E.T. Excretion of epinephrine and norepinephrine in various emotional states. *J. Clin. Endocrinol.* 17:608-620, 1957.
153. Elmadjian, F., Hope, J.M., and Lawson, E.T. Excretion of epinephrine and norepinephrine under stress. *Recent Prog. Hor. Res.* 14:513-553, 1958.
154. Levi, L. The urinary output of adrenaline and noradrenaline during experimentally induced emotional stress in clinically different groups. *Acta Psychother.* 11:218-226, 1963.
155. Levi, L. The urinary output of adrenaline and noradrenaline during pleasant and unpleasant emotional states. *Psychosom. Med.* 27:80-85, 1965.
156. Wyatt, R.J., Portnoy, B., Kupfer, D.J., et al. Resting catecholamine concentrations in patients with depression and anxiety. *Arch. Gen. Psychiat.* 24:65-70, 1971.
157. Edmondson, H.D., Roscoe, B., and Vickers, M.D. Biochemical evidence of anxiety in dental patients. *Brit. Med. J.* 4(831):7-9, 1972.
158. Sweeney, D.R., Maas, J.W., and Heninger, G.R. State anxiety and urinary MHPG. *Psychosom. Med.* 39:57, 1977.
159. Barchas, J.D., and Freedman, D.X. Brain amines: response to physiological stress. *Biochem. Pharmacol.* 12:1232-1235, 1963.
160. Bliss, E.L., and Zwanziger, J. Brain amines and emotional stress. *J. Psychiat. Res.* 4:189-198, 1966.
161. Corrodi, H., Fuxe, K., and Hökfelt, T. The effect of immobilization stress on the activity of central monoamine neurons. *Life Sci.* 7:107-112, 1968.
162. Stone, E.A. Stress and catecholamines. In A.J. Friedhof, ed., *Catecholamines and Behavior.* New York: Plenum, 1975.
163. Korf, J., Aghajanian, G.K., and Roth, R.H. Increased turnover of norepinephrine in the rat cerebral cortex during stress: role of the locus coeruleus. *Neuropharmacology* 12:933-938, 1973.
164. Ziegler, M.G., Lake, C.R., Foppen, F.H., et al. Norepinephrine in cerebrospinal fluid. *Brain Res.* 108:436-440, 1976.
165. Post, R.M., Lake, C.R., Jimerson, D.C., et al. CSF norepinephrine in affective illness. New Research Abstracts, American Psychatric Association No. 24, 1977.
166. Post, R.M., Lake, C.R., Jimerson, D.C., et al. CSF norepinephrine in affective illness. *Am. J. Psychiat.,* in press, 1979.
167. Bogdonoff, M.D., Brehm, L., and Back, K. The effect of the experimenter's role upon the subject's response to an unpleasant task. *J. Psychosom. Res.* 8:137-143, 1964.
168. Bogdonoff, M.D., Klein, R.F., Back, K., et al. Effect of group relationship and the role of leadership upon lipid mobilization. *Psychosom. Med.* 26:710-719, 1964.

169. Gottschalk, L.A., Cleghorn, J.M., Gleser, G.C., et al. Studies of relationships of emotions to plasma lipids. *Psychosom. Med.* 27:102-111, 1965.
170. Pinter, E.J., Peterfly, G., Cleghorn J.M., et al. The influence of emotional stress on fat mobilization: the role of endogenous catecholamines and the beta adrenergic receptors. *Am. J. Med. Sci.* 254(5):634-651, 1967.
171. Brown, W.A., and Heninger, G. Cortisol, growth hormone, free fatty acids, and experimentally evoked affective arousal. *Am. J. Psychiat.* 132:1172-1176, 1975.
172. Peterfly, G., Pinter, E.J., and Cleghorn, J.M. The adrenergic receptors and anxiety. *Am. J. Psychiat.* 124:157-158, 1968.
173. Schalch, D.S., and Kipnis, D.M. Abnormalities in carbohydrate tolerance associated with elevated plasma nonesterfied fatty acids. *J. Clin. Invest.* 44:2010-2020, 1965.
174. Feigelson, E.B., Pfaff, W.W., and Karman, A., et al. The role of plasma free atty acids in development of fatty liver *J. Clin. Invest.* 40:2171-2179, 1961.
175. Friedberg, S.J., Klein, R.F., Trout, D.L., et al. The incorporation of plasma free fatty acids into plasma triglycerides in man. *J. Clin. Invest.* 40:1846-1855, 1961.
176. Canon, W.B., and Mendenhall, W.L. The hastening of coagulation by stimulation of the splanchnic nerves. *Am. J. Physiol.* 34:243-250, 1914.
177. Kafka, M.S., Tallman, J.F., and Smith, C.C. Alpha-adrenergic receptors on human platelets. *Life Sci.* 21:1429-1438, 1977.
178. Gutstein, W.H., Harrison, J., Parl, F., et al. Neural factors contribute to atherogenesis. *Science* 199:449-451, 1978.
179. Lamprecht, F., Williams, R.B., and Kopin, I.J. Serum dopamine-beta-hydroxylase during development of immobilization-induced hypertension. *Endocrinology* 92:953-956, 1973.
180. Harris, R.E., Sokolow, M., Carpenter, L.G., et al. Response to psychologic stress in persons who ae potentially hypertensive. *Circulation* 7:874-879, 1953.
181. Friedman, M.J., and Bennet, P.L. Depression and hypertension. *Psychosom. Med.* 39:134-142, 1977.
182. Jenkins, C.D., Rosenman, R.H, and Zyzanski, S.J. Prediction of clinical coronary heart disease by a test for coronary-prone behavior pattern. *New. Eng. J. Med.* 290:1271-1275, 1974.
183. Andres, R., Baltzan, M., Cader, G., et al. Metabolic and circulatory effects of epinephrine in the forearm of man. *J. Clin. Invest.* 40;1022, 1961.
184. Sutherland, E.W., and Robinson, G.A. The role of cyclic 3'5'-AMP in response to catecholamines and other hormones. *Pharmacol. Rev.* 18:145-161, 1966.
185. Jones, M., and Mellersh, V. A comparison of the exercise response in anxiety states and normal controls. *Psychosom. Med.* 8:180-187, 1946.
186. Linko, E. Lactic acid response to muscular exercise in neurocirculatory asthenia. *Ann. Med. Int. Fin.* 36:161-176, 1950.
187. Cohen, M.E., and White, P.D. Life situations, emotions, and neurocirculatory asthenia (anxiety neurosis, neuresthenia, effort syndrome). *Proc. Assoc. Res. Nerv. Ment. Dis.* 29:832-869, 1950.
188. Fink, M., Taylor, M.A., and Valavka, J. Anxiety precipitated by lactate. *New Eng. J. Med.* 281:1429, 1970.
189. Kelly, D., Mitchell-Heggs, N., and Sherman, D. Anxiety and the effects of sodium lactate assessed clinically and physiologically. *Brit. J. Psychiat.* 119:129-141, 1971.
190. Wearn, J.T., and Sturgis, C.C. Studies on epinephrine. *Arch. Int. Med.* 24:247, 1919.
191. Peabody, F.W., Sturgis, C.C., Tompkins, E.M., et al. Epinephrine hypersensitiveness and its relation to hyperthyroidism. *Am. J. Med. Sci.* 161:508-517, 1921.
192. Marañon, G. La reacción emotiva a la adrenalina. *Med. Ibera* 12:353-357, 1920.
193. Marañon, G. Contribution a l'étude de l'action émotive de l'adrénaline. *Rev. Franc. Endocrinol.* 2:301-325, 1924.

194. Koppányi, T. The effect of subcutaneously injected epinephrine in normal human subjects. *Proc. Soc. Exper. Biol. Med.* 25:744-745, 1928.

195. Jersild, A.T., and Thomas, W.S. The influence of adrenal extract on behavior and mental efficiency. *Am. J. Psychol.* 43:447-456, 1931.

196. Cantril, H., and Hunt, W.A. Emotional effects produced by the injection of adrenalin. *Am. J. Psychol.* 44:300-307, 1932.

197. Landis, C., and Hunt, W.A. Adrenalin and emotion. *Psychol. Rev.* 39:467-485, 1932.

198. Basowitz, H., Korchin, S.J., Oken, D., et al. Anxiety and performance changes with a minimal dose of epinephrine. *Arch. Neurol. Psychiat.* (Chicago) 27:98-106, 1956.

199. Pollin, W., and Goldin, S. The physiological and psychological effects of intravenously administered epinephrine and its metabolism in normal and schizophrenic men. *J. Psychiat. Res.* 1:50-67, 1961.

200. Schacter, S., and Singer, J.E. Cognitive, social, and physiological determinants of emotional state. *Psychol. Rev.* 69:379-399, 1962.

201. Schacter, S., Singer, J.E. Cognitive, social, and physiological determinants of emotional state. In C.D. Spielberger, ed., *Anxiety and Behavior.* New York: Academic Press, 1966.

202. Euler, U.S. von. A specific sympathomimetic ergone in adrenergic nerve fibres (sympathin) and its relations to adrenaline and nor-adrenaline. *Acta Physiol. Scand.* 12:73-97, 1946.

203. Goldenberg, M., Aranow, S., Smith, A.A., et al. Pheochroocytoma and essential hypertensive vascular disease. *Arch. Intern. Med.* 86:823-836, 1950.

204. King, B.D., Sokoloff, L., and Wechsler, R.L. The effects of L-epinephrine and L-norepinephrine upon cerebral circulation and metabolism in man. *J. Clin. Invest.* 31:273-279, 1952.

205. Chessick, R.D., Bassan,M., and Shattan,S. A comparison of the effect of infused catecholamines and certain affect states. *Am. J. Psychiat.* 123(2):156-165, 1966.

206. Vlachakis, N.D., De Guia, D., and Mendlowitz, M., et al. Hypertension and anxiety. A trial with epinephrine and noreinephrine infusion. *Mt. Sinai J. Med.* 41(5):615-625, 1974.

207. Swan, H.J.C. Noradrenaline, adrenaline, and the human circulation. *Brit. Med. J.* 1:1003-1006, 1952.

208. Schacter, S. Pain, fear, and anger in hypertensives and normotensives. *Psychosom. Med.* 19:17-29, 1957.

209. Rothballer, A.M. The effects of catecholamines on CNS. *Pharmacol. Rev.* 2:494-547, 1959.

210. Byland, D.B., and Snyder, S.H. Beta-adrenergic receptor binding in membrane preparations from mammalian brain. *Mol. Pharmacol.* 12:568-580, 1976.

211. Frohlich, E.D., Dustan, H.P., and Page, I.H. Hyperdynamic β-adrenergic circulatory state. *Arch. Int. Med.* 117:614-619, 1966.

212. Frohlich, E.D., Taragi, R.C., and Dustan, H.P. Hyperdynamic β-adrenergic circulatory state. *Arch. Int. Med.* 123:1-7, 1969.

213. Easton, J.D., and Sherman, D.G. Somatic anxiety attacks and propranolol. *Arch. Neurol.* 33:689-691, 1976.

214. Cleaveland, C.R., Rangno, R.E., and Shand, D.G. A standardized isoproterenol test. *Arch. Intern. Med.* 130:47-52, 1972.

215. Goldenberg, M., Snyder, C.H., and Aranow, H., Jr. New test for hypertension due to circulating epinephrine. *J.A.M.A.* 135:971-976, 1947.

216. Soffer, A. Reginine and benodaine in the diagnosis of pheochromocytoma. *Med. Clin. N. Amer.* 38:375-384, 1954.

217. Holmberg, G., and Gershon, S. Autonomic and psychic effects of yohimbine hydrochloride. *Psychopharmacol.* 2:93-106, 1961.

218. Greenblatt, D.J., and Shader, R.I. *Benzodiazepines in Clinical Practice.* New York: Raven Press, 1974.
219. Klein, D.F., and Davis, J.M. *Diagnosis and Drug Treatment of Psychiatric Disorders.* Baltimore: Williams & Wilkins Co., 1969.
220. Granville-Grossman, K.L., and Turner, P. The effect of propranolol on anxiety. *Lancet* 1:788-790, 1966.
221. Turner, P., Granville-Grossman, K.L., and Smart, J.V. Effect of adrenergic receptor blockade on the tachycardia of thyrotoxicosis and anxiety states. *Lancet* 2:1316-1318, 1965.
222. Wheatley, D. Comparative effects of propranolol and chlordiazepoxide in anxiety states. *Brit. J. Psychiat.* 115(259):1411-1412, 1969.
223. Stone, W.N., Glesar, G.C., and Gottschalk, L.A. Anxiety and beta-adrenergic blockade. *Arch. Gen. Psych.* 29(5):620-622, 1973.
224. Tyrer, P.J., and Lader, M.H. Response to propranolol and diazepam in somatic and psychic anxiety. *Brit. Med. J.* 2(909):14-16, 1974.
225. Kellner, R., Collins, C., Shulman, R.S., et al. The short-term antianxiety effects of propranolol HCL. *J. Clin. Pharmacol.* 14:301-304, 1974.
226. Gottschalk, L.A., Stone, W.N., and Gleser, G.C. Peripheral versus central mechanisms accounting for antianxiety effects of propranolol. *Psychosom. Med.* 36(1):47-56, 1974.
227. Suzman, M.M. Propranolol in the treatment of anxiety. *Postgrad. Med. J.* 52(Suppl. 4) 168-174, 1976.
228. Gosling, R.H. Clinical experience with oxprenolol in treatment of anxiety in the United Kingdom. In P. Kielholz, ed., *Beta-Blockers and the Central Nervous System,* Baltimoe: University Park Press, 1977.
229. Lader, M.H., and tyrer, P.J. Central and peripheral effects of propranolol and sotalol in normal human subjects. *Brit. J. Pharmacol.* 45:557-50, 1972.
230. Bonn, J.A., Turner, P., and Hicks, D.C. Beta-adrenergic-receptor blockade with practolol in treatment of anxiety. *Lancet* 1:814-815, 1972.
231. Kielholz, P., ed. *Beta-blockers and the Central Nervous System.* Baltimore: University Park Press, 1977.
232. Greenblatt, D.J., and Shader, R.I. Pharmacotherapy of anxiety with benzodiazepines and beta-adrenergic blockers. In M.A. Lipton, A. DiMascio, K.F. Killam, eds., *Psychopharmacology: A Generation of Progress.* New York: Raven Press, 1978.
233. Peroutka, S.J., U'Prichard, D.C., Greenberg, D.A., et al. Neuroleptic drug interactions with norepinephrine alpha receptor binding sites in rat brain. *Neuropharmacol.* 16:549-556, 1977.
234. Lidbrink, P., and Farnebo, L-O. Uptake and release of noradrenaline in rat cerebral cortex *in vitro:* No effect of benzodiazepines and barbiturates. *Neuropharmacol.* 12:1087-1095, 1973.
235. Gray, J.A. The neuropsychology of anxiety. In I.G. Sarason and C.D. Spielberger, eds., *Stress and Anxiety,* Vol. 3. Washington, D.C.: Hemisphere Publishing, 1976.
236. Lader, M. The peripheral and central role of the catecholamines in the mechanisms of anxiety. *Int. Pharmacopsychiat.* 9:125-137, 1974.
237. Margules, D.L., and Stein, L. Increase of "antianxiety" activity and tolerance of behavioral depression during chronic administration of oxazepam. *Psychopharmacol.* 13:74-80, 1968.
238. Squires, R.F., and Braestrup, C. Benzodiazepine receptors in rat brain. *Nature* (London) 266(21):732-734, 1977.
239. Keller, H.H., Schaffner, R., and Haefely, W. Interaction of benzodiazepines with neuroleptics at central dopamine neurons. *Naunyn-Schmiedeberg's Arch. Pharmacol.* 294:1-7, 1976.

240. Dray, A., and Straughan, D.W. Benzodiazepines: GABA and glycine receptors on single neurons in the rat medulla. *J. Pharm. Pharmacol.* 28:314-315, 1976.
241. Haefely, W.E. Behavioral and neuropharmacological aspects of drugs used in anxiety and related states. In M.A. Lipton, A. DiMascio, and K.F. Killam, eds., *Psychopharmacology: A Generation of Progress.* New York: Raven Press, 1978.
242. Mirin, S.M., Meyer, R.E., and McNamee, H.B. Psychopathology and mood during heroin use. *Arch. Gen. Psych.* 33:1503-1508, 1976.
243. Clouet, D.H. Possible roles of catecholamines in the action of narcotic drugs. In A.J. Friedhoff, ed., *Catecholamines and Behavior,* Vol. 2. New York; Plenum, 1975.
244. Eidelberg, E. Possible actions of opiates upon synapses. *Prog. Neurobiol.* 6:81-102, 1976.
245. Kuhar, M.J. Autoradiographic localization of receptor sites in the CNS. In M.A. Lipton, A. Di Mascio, and K.F. Killam, eds., *Psychopharmacology: A Generation of Progress.* New York: Raven Press, 1978.
246. Paalzow, L. Analgesia produced by clonidine in mice and rats. *J. Pharm. Pharmacol.* 26(5):361-363, 1974.
247. Tseng, L.F., Loh, H.H., and Wei, E.T. Effects of clonidine on morphine withdrawal signs in the rat. *Eur. J. Pharmacol.* 30(1):93-99, 1975.
248. Samanin, R., Bendotti, C., Gradnik, R., et al. The effect of localized lesions of central monoaminergic neurons on morphine analgesia and physical dependence in rats. *Proceedings of the thirty-seventh Annual Scientific Meeting Committee on Problems of Drug Dependence,* 1975.
249. Nicoll, R. Selective actions of barbiturates on synaptic transmission. In M.A. Lipton, A.Di Mascio, and K.F. Killam, eds., *Psychopharmacology: A Generation of Progress.* New York: Raven Press, 1978.
250. Huang, Y.H., unpublished observations.
251. Robinson, D.S., dies, A., Ravaris, C.L., et al. The monoamine oxidase inhibitor phenelzine in the treatment of depressive-anxiety states. *Arch. Gen. Psychiat.* 29:407-413, 1973.
252. Ravaris, C.L., Nies, A., Robinson, D.S., et al. A multiple dose, controlled study of phenelzine in depression-anxiety states. *Arch. Gen. Psychiat.* 33:347-350, 1976.
253. Klein, D.F., Zitrin, C.M., and Woerner, M. Antidepressants, anxiety, panic, and phobia.In M.A. Lipton, A. DiMascio, and R.F. Killam, eds., *Psychopharmacology: A Generation of Progress.* New York: Raven Press, 1978.
254. Schildkraut, J.J. The catecholamine hypothesis of affective disorders: A review of supporting evidence. *Am. J. Psychiat.* 122:509, 1965.
255. Bunney, W.E., Jr., and Davis, J.M. Norepinephrine in depressive reactions. *Arch. Gen. Psychiat.* 13:483, 1965.
256. Schildkraut, J.J., and Kety, S.S. Biogenic amines and emotion. *Science* 156:21-30, 1967.
257. Nyback, H., Walters, J.R., Aghajanian, G.K., et al. Tricyclic antidepressants: effects on the firing rate of brain noradrenergic neurons. *Eur. J. Pharmacol.* 32:302-312, 1975.
258. Cedarbaum, J.M. Noradrenergic neurons of the rat locus coeruleus: Anatomical, physiological, and pharmacological studies. MD thesis, Yale University School of Medicine, 1978.
259. Aghajanian, G.K., Cedarbaum, J.M., and Wang, R.Y. Evidence for norepinephrine-mediated collateral inhibition fo locus coeruleus neurons. *Brain Res.* 136:570-577, 1977.
260. Vetulani, J., and Sulser, F. Action of various antidepressant treatments reduces reactivity of noradrenergic cyclic AMP-generating system in limbic forebrain. *Nature* (London) 257:495-496, 1975.

261. Seedat, Y.K., Vawda, E.I., Mitha, S., et al. Clonidine in treatment of hypertension. *Brit. Med. J.* 1(739):47, 1971.

262. Bock, J.U., and Zwieten, P.A. van. The central hyperglycaemic effect of clonidine. *Eur. J. Pharmacol.* 16(3):303-310, 1971.

263. Simpson, F.O. Hypertension and depression and their treatment. *Aust. New Zeal. J. Psychiat.* 7:133-137, 1973.

264. Kellaway, G.S. Adverse drug reactions during treatment of hypertension. *Drugs* 11(Suppl. 1) :91-99, 1976.

265. Shafar, J. Tallett, E.R., and Knowlson, P.A. Evaluation of clonidine in prophylaxis of migraine. Double-blind trial and follow-up. *Lancet* 1(747):403-407, 1972.

266. Anthony, M., Lance, J.W., and Somerville, B. A comparative trial of prindolol, clonidine, and carbamazepine in the interval therapy of migraine. *Med. J. Aust.* 1(26):1343-1346, 1972.

267. Healthfield, K.W., and Raiman, J.D. The long-term management of migraine with clonidine. *Practitioner* 208(247):644-648, 1972.

268. Brogden, R.N., inder, R.M., Sawyer, P.R., et al. Low-dose clonidine: A review of its therapeutic efficacy in migraine prophylaxis. *Drugs* 10(5-6):375-365, 1975.

269. Lord, D.J., and Kidd, C.B. Haloperidol versus diazepam: A double-blind crossover clinical trial. *Med. J. Aust.* 1(12):586-588, 1973.

270. Fyro, B., Beck-Friis, J., and Sjostrand, K.G. A comparison between diazepam and haloperidol in anxiety states. *Acta Psychiat. Scand.* 50(6)586-595, 1974.

271. Stevenson, J., Burrow, G.P., and Chiu, E. Comparison of low doses of haloperidol and diazepam in anxiety states. *Med. J. Aust.* 1(13):451-459, 1976.

272. Abrahams, M., Armistread, R.L., Aspinal, R.J., et al. Pimoxide in anxiety neuroses. *Gen. Practitioner Clin. Trials.* 208:836-838, 1972.

273. Poldinger, W. Application of the neuroleptic pimozide (ORAL-R 6238) for tranquilizer indications in a controlled study. *Int. Pharmacopsychiat.* 11(1):16-24, 1976.

274. Reyntjens, A.M., and Mierlo, F.P. van. A comparative double-blind trial of pimoxide in stress-induced psychic and functional disorders. *Cur. Med. Res. Opinion* 1:116-122, 1972.

275. Carlsson, A. Mechanisms of action of neuroleptic drugs, In M.A. Lipton, A. DiMascio, and K.F. Killam, eds., *Psychopharmacology: A Generation of Progress.* New York: Raven Press, 1978.

276. Burt, D.R., Creese, I., and Snyder, S.H. Properties of ^{3}H-haloperidol and ^{3}H-dopamine binding associated with dopamine receptors in calf brain membranes. *Mol. Pharmacol.* 12:800-812, 1976.

277. Creese, I., Feinberg, A.P., and Snyder, S.H. Butyrophenone influences on the opiate receptor. *Eur. J. Pharmacol.* 36:231-235, 1976.

278. Yamamura, H.I., Manian, A.A., and Snyder, S.H. Muscarinic cholinergic receptor: Influence of pimozide and chlorpromazine metabolites. *Life Sci.* 18:685-692, 1976.

279. Murphy, D.L., and Redmond, D.E., Jr. Catecholamines in affect, mood, and emotional behavior. In A.J. Friedhof, ed., *Catecholamines and Behavior,* Vol. 2. New York: Plenum Press, 1975.

280. Okamoto, M. Barbiturates and alcohol: Comparative overviews on neurophysiology and neurochemistry. In M.A. Lipton, A. DiMascio, and K.F. Killam, eds., *Psychopharmacology: A Generation of Progress.* New York: Raven Press, 1978.

281. Schildkraut, J.J. Current status of the catecholamine hypothesis of affective disorders. In M.A. Lipton, A. DiMascio, and K.F. Killam, eds., *Psychopharmacology: A Generation of Progress.* New York: Raven Press, 1978.

282. Bunney, W.E., Jr., Davis, J.M., Weil-Malherbe, H., et al. Biochemical changes in psychotic depression. *Arch. Gen. Psychiat.* 16:448-460, 1967.

283. Mandell, A.M., Segal, D.S., and Kuczenski, R. Metabolic adaptation to antidepressant drugs: Implications for pathophysiology and treatment in psychiatry.In A.J. Friedhoff, ed., *Catecholamines and Behavior.* New York: Plenum, 1975.

284. Janowsky, D.S., Davis, J.M., El Yousef, M.K., et al. A cholinergic-adrenergic hypothesis of mania and depression. *Lancet* 2:632, 1972.

285. Murphy, D.L., Campbell, I., and Costa, J.L. Current status of the indoleamine hypothesis of the affective disorders. In M.A. Lipton, A. DiMascio, and K.F. Killam, eds., *Psychopharmacology: A Generation of Progress.* New York: Raven Press, 1978.

286. Hughes, J. Isolation of an endogenous compound from the brain with pharmacological properties similar to morphine. *Brain Res.* 88:295-308, 1975.

287. Schultz, J. Psychoactive drug effects on a system which generates cyclic AMP in brain. *Nature* (London) 261:417-418, 1976.

288. Poschel, B.P.H., and Ninteman, F.E. Norepinephrine: A possible excitatory neurohormone of the reward system. *Life Sci.* 1:782-788, 1963.

289. Stein, L., and Seifter, J. Possible mode of antidepressive action of imipramine. *Science* 134:286-287, 1961.

290. Stein, L. Self-stimulation of the brain and the central stimulant action of amphetamine. *Fed. Proc.* 23:836-850, 1964.

291. Stein, L. Reward transmitters: Catecholamines and opioid peptides. In M.A. Lipton, A. DiMascio, and K. F. Killam, eds., *Psychopharmacology: A Generation of Progress.* New York: Raven Press, 1978.

292. Stein, L. Norepinephrine reward pathways: Role in self-stimulation, memory consolidation, and schizophrenia. *Nebraska Symposium on Motivation,* 1974.

293. Clavier, P.M., and Corcoran, M.F. Attenuation of self-stimulation from substantia nigra but not dorsal tegmental noradrenergic bundle by lesions of sulcal prefrontal cortex. *Brain Res.* 113:59-69, 1976.

294. Corbett, D., Skelton, R.W., and Wise, R.A. Dorsal noradrenergic bundle lesions fail to disrupt self-stimulation from the region of the locus coeruleus. *Brain Res.* 133:37-44, 1977.

295. Redmond, D.E., Jr., Huang, Y.H., and Menkes, D., unpublished data.

296. Olds, J. Hypothalamic substrates of reward. *Physical Rev.* 42:554-604, 1962.

297. *The New York Times,* May 1, 1977, p. 1.

298. Nashold, B.S., Jr., Wilson, W.P., and Slaughter, G. *Advances in Neurology,* Vol. 4, New York: Raven Press, 1974.

299. Kimazama, T., Perl, E.R.M., Burgess, P.R., et al. Ascending projections from marginal zone (lamina 1) neurons of the spinal dorsal horn. *J. Comp. Neurol.* 162:1-12, 1973.

300. Kerr, F.W.C. Neuroanatomical substrates of nociception in the spinal cord. *Pain* 1:325-356, 1975.

301. Guyenet, P.G., and Aghajanian, G.K. Excitation of neurons in the nucleus locus coeruleus by substance P and related peptides. *Brain Res.* 136:178-184, 1977.

302. Cedarbaum, J.M., and Aghajanian, G.K. Activation of locus coeruleus noradrenergic neurons by peripheral nerve stimulation. *Neurosci. Abst.* 3:246, 1977.

303. Hosobuchi, Y., Adams, J.E., and Linchitz, R. Pain relief by electrical stimulation of the central gray matter in humans and its reversal by naloxone. *Science* 197:183-186, 1977.

304. Crow, T.J. Cortical synapses and reinforcement: An hypothesis. *Nature* (London) 219:736-737, 1968.

305. Kety, S.S. The biogenic amines in the central nervous system: Their possible roles in arousal, emotion and learning. In *The Neurosciences: Second Study Program.* New York: Rockefeller University Press, 1970.

306. Kety, S.S. The possible role of the adrenergic systems of the cortex in learning. *Res. Publ. Assoc. Res. Nerv. Ment. Dis.* 50:376-389, 1972.
307. Gorelick, D.A., Bozewicz, T.R., and Bridger, W.H. The role of catecholamines in animal learning and memory. In A.J. Friedhoff, ed., *Catecholamines and Behavior.* New York: Plenum 1975.
308. Zornetzer, S.F. Neurotransmitter modulation and memory: a new neuropharmacological phrenology. In M.A. Lipton, A. DiMascio, and K.F. Killam, eds., *Psychopharmacology: A Generation of Progress.* New York: Raven Press, 1978.
309. Gallagher, M., Kapp, B.S., Musty, R.E. et al. Memory formation: evidence of a specific neurochemical system in the amygdala. *Science* 198:423-425, 1977.
310. Mason, S.T., and Iversen, S.D. An investigation of the role of cortical and cerebellar noradrenaline in associative motor learning in the rat. *Brain Res.* 134:513-527, 1977.
311. Persky, H., Grinker, R.R., Hamburg, D.A., et al. Adrenal cortical function in anxious human subjects: plasma level and urinary excretion of hydrocortisone. *Arch. Neurol. Psychiat.* 76:549-558, 1956.
312. Altschule, M.D. *Bodily Physiology in Mental and Emotional Disorders.* New York, Grune & Stratton, 1953.
313. Ward, D.G., Grizzle, W.E., and Gann, D.S. Inhibitory and facilitatory areas of the rostral pons mediating ACTH release in the cat. *Endocrinol.* 99:1220-1228, 1976.
314. Ward, D.G., and Gunn, C.G. Locus coeruleus complex: elicitation of a pressor response and a brain stem region necessary for its occurrence. *Brain Res.* 107:401-406, 1976.
315. Redmond, D.E., Jr., Huang, Y.H., and Maas, J.W., unpublished data.
316. Redmond, D.E., Jr., Huang, Y.H., Synder, D.R., Maas, J.W., and Baulu, J. Hyperphagia and hyperdipsia after locus coeruleus lesions in the stumptailed monkey. *Life Sci.* 20;1619-1628, 1977.
317. Leverenz, K., Redmond, D.E., Jr., and Huang, Y.H. Appetite suppression following discrete and low intensity stimulation of the locus coeruleus. *Neurosci. Abst., No. 543, p. 177, 1978.*
318. Jouvet, M., and Delorme, F. *Locus coeruleus et sommeil paradoxol. Soc. Biol.* 159:895, 1965.
319. Hobson, J.A., McCarley, R.W., and Wyzinski, P.W. Sleep cycle oscillation: reciprocal discharge by two brainstem neuronal groups. *Science* 189:55-58, 1975.
320. Morgane, P.J., and Stern, W.C. Interaction of amine systems in the central nervous system in the regulation of the states of vigilance. In R.D. Myers and R.R. Drucker-Colin, eds., *Neurohumoral Coding of Brain Function.* New York: Plenum, 1973.
321. Morgane, P.J., Stern, W., and Berman, E. Inhibition of unit activity in the anterior raphe by stimulation of the locus coeruleus. *Anat. Rev.* 178:421-426, 1974.
322. Marsden, C.D., Gimlette, T.M.D., McAllister, R.G., et al. Effect of β-adrenergic blockage on finger tremor and Achilles reflex time in anxious and thyrotoxic patients. *Acta Endocrinol.* 57:353-362, 1968.
323. Gardos, G., DiMascio, A., Salzman, C., et al. Differential actions of chlordiazepoxide and oxazepam on hostility. *Arch. Gen. Psychiat.* 18:757-760, 1968.
324. DiMascio, A., Shader, R.I., and Harmatz, J. Psychotropic drugs and induced hostility. *Psychosom.* 10:47-50, 1969.
325. Redmond, D.E., Jr., Murphy, D.L., and Baulu, J. Platelet MAO activity correlates with social affiliative and agonistic behaviors in normal rhesus monkeys, Psychosom. Med., 1979, in press.
326. Pavlov, I.P. *Conditioned Reflexes and Psychiatry, trans.* W.H. Gantt. New York: International Publishers, 1941.
327. Kellner, R., Wilson, R.M., Muldawer, M.D., et al. Anxiety in schizophrenia. *Arch Gen. Psychiat.* 32:1246-1254, 1975.

328. Mednick, S. A learning theory approach to research in schizophrenia. *Psychol. Bull.* 55:316-327, 1958.

329. Lehman, H.E. Clinical features of schizophrenia. In A.M. Freedman and H.I. Caplan, eds., *Comprehensive Textbook of Psychiatry*. Baltimore: Williams & Wilkins, 1967.

330. Lake, C.R., Ziegler, M.G., and Murphy, D.L. Increased norepinephrine levels and decreased dopamine-β-hydroxylase activity in primary autism. *Arch. Gen. Psychiat.* 34:553-556, 1977.

331. Redmond, D.E., Jr., Swann, A., and Heninger, G.R. Phenoxybenzamine in anorexia nervosa. *Lancet* 2:307, 1976.

332. Needleman, H.L., and Waber, D. The use of amitriptyline in anorexia nervosa. In R.A. Vigersky, ed., *Anorexia Nervosa*. New York: Raven Press, 197.

333. Rosenbaum, M. Peptic ulcer. In A.M. Freedman and H.I. Caplan, eds., *Comprehensive Textbook of Psychiatry*. Baltimore: Williams & Wilkins, 1967.

334. Engel, G.L. Intestinal disorders. In A.M. Freedman and H.I. Caplan, eds., *Comprehensive Textbook of Psychiatry*. 1967.

335. Wender, E.H., Palmer, F.B., Herbst, J.J., et al. Behavioral characteristics of children with chronic nonspecific diarrhea. *Am. J. Psychiat.* 133:20-26, 1976.

336. Gold, M.S., Redmond, D.E., Jr., and Kleber, H. Clonidine in opiate withdrawal. *Lancet* 1:929-930, 1978.

337. Gold, M.S., Redmond, D.E., Jr., and Kleber, H. The effects of clonidine in opiate withdrawal: Evidence for a noradrenergic mediation of the opiate withdrawal syndrome. *Proceedings of the Fortieth Annual Scientific Meeting Committee on Problems of Drug Dependence,* Baltimore, 1978, in press.

CHAPTER 12

Medical Illness and Anxiety

Harold Brown

In this age of anxiety the physician in practice is seeing an increasing number of his patients present with the symptoms of anxiety. Anxiety is a normal human phenomenon, and is of concern to the patient or his physician only when it interferes with well-being or efficiency. It is important to recognize this syndrome in order to provide a proper approach to treatment and to save the patient the inconvenience, expense, and hazard of unnecessary diagnostic procedures. At the same time, the physician must be aware that certain well-recognized organic syndromes can present with the symptomatology of anxiety, and of course in these instances treatment should be directed to the underlying disease rather than to the patient's psyche.

The syndrome of anxiety encompasses a wide spectrum of symptoms and signs. Basically it is an unpleasant mood of tension with a feeling of apprehension and fear for some real, imagined, or unknown event. The preoccupation with the fear can result in a disturbance of intellectual function. The disturbance of mood may be accompanied by autonomic, visceral, and endocrine changes resulting in tremor, tachycardia, perspiration, hypertension, voice changes, dilated pupils, reduced salivation and gastric secretion. Patients may have a feeling of suffocation and may respond with deep and sighing respirations even to the point of hyperventilating. A confusing variety of symptoms of a bizarre nature may develop with multiple somatic complaints—headache, anorexia, diarrhea, and weight loss. Patients with the hyperventilation syndrome may also complain of numbness, tingling, lightheadedness, giddiness, blurring of vision, and even loss of consciousness.

With such a panoply of symptomatology attributed to anxiety, it is not strange that certain disease states that may generate many of the anxiety symptoms may be mistaken for the anxiety syndrome. In the following paragraphs I shall review several disease states in which the symptoms and signs of anxiety are prominent presenting manifestations but are attributable to the underlying disordered physiology and will remit with the proper treatment of the disease.

THYROTOXICOSIS

The more frequent symptoms of thyrotoxicosis are given in Table 1. Since many of the manifestations are seen in individuals with anxiety, one might anticipate occasional confusion in the differential diagnosis of the two disorders, although the experienced clinician usually has little difficulty.

The patient with thyrotoxicosis will complain of fatigue, as will the anxious individual, but the former will continue to be hyperactive while the latter tends to be listless with little desire to get things done. Both kinds of patients will perspire, but the patient with anxiety tends to have cold, moist, clammy hands, while the patient with thyrotoxicosis has warm, moist hands because of the markedly increased blood flow to the extremities. The tachycardia of the anxious individual will abate during sleep, in contrast to the thyrotoxic subject, who maintains an elevated pulse rate even during sleep.

Table 1. Incidence of symptoms and signs observed in 247 patients with thyrotoxicosis

SYMPTOM	PERCENT	SYMPTOM	PERCENT
Nervousness	99	Increased appetite	65
Increased sweating	91	Eye complaints	54
Hypersensitivity to heat	89	Swelling of legs	35
Palpitation	89	Hyperdefecation	33
Fatigue	88	(without diarrhea)	
Weight loss	85	Diarrhea	23
Tachycardia	82	Anorexia	9
Dyspnea	75	Constipation	4
Weakness	70	Weight gain	2

Modified from Data of Williams (1)

In the final analysis the diagnosis of thyrotoxicosis is established by the demonstration of abnormal thyroid function, which is always normal in the patient with anxiety. It is of interest that in both disorders treatment with beta-adrenergic blockers such as propanolol will stop the tachycardia and tremor which are caused by epinephrine stimulation even though excessive catecholamine secretion is not demonstrable. It has recently been shown that tissues exposed to thyroid hormone stimulation are more receptive to catecholamine stimulation (2).

PHEOCHROMOCYTOMA

The manifestations of a pheochromocytoma may resemble those of anxiety in that adrenergic overactivity is present in both. In addition to hypertension, these individuals may exhibit sweating, attacks of blanching or flushing, palpitations, tachycardia, tremulousness, hyperventilation, and headache. The significance of the complaint of dizziness or head swimming in association with the postural hypotension seen in pheochromocytoma may also be misinterpreted as a somatic symptom of anxiety. Less common symptoms are visual blurring, tightness in the throat, dyspnea, chest pain, sweating, and attacks of blanching.

This diagnosis should be considered in all hypertensive patients, and particularly in those with a history of the attacks of the symptoms mentioned above. Confirmation of excess catecholamine secretion in blood or excretion in urine should be sought.

HYPOGLYCEMIA

The clinical signs and symptoms of hypoglycemia are the result of a rapid decline in the level of blood glucose and/or low level—less than 50 mg per 100 ml. These changes trigger catecholamine release, and the subject will suffer the effects of epinephrine stimulation—a feeling of nervousness, tremor,palpitations, tachycardia, sweating, weakness, a feeling of hunger. Since the brain is dependent on glucose as a source of energy, the patient may manifest a wide variety of neurological signs and symptoms including headache, confusion, diplopia, incoordination, abnormal behavior, and even seizures, coma, and death. When the glucose level falls gradually, the signs of epinephrine excess may be lacking, and the patient will have predominantly neurological and psychiatric symptoms.

The protean manifestations of hypoglycemia should be considered in a variety of circumstances, and the presence of hypoglycemia verified. The demonstration of hypoglycemia should raise consideration of the following etiologies:

Table 2—Causes of Hypoglycemia

A. Postprandial

1 Reactive hypoglycemia following large glucose load
2 Adult onset diabetes mellitus
3. Alimentary

B. Fasting

1. Insulin secreting tumors
2. Administration of insulin or oral hypoglycemic agents
3. Other tumors secreting insulin-like material
4. Deficiency of growth hormone or cortisol
5. Severe liver disease
6. Alcohol ingestion

For the purposes of this discussion, the principal diagnostic possibilities are the insulin-secreting islet cell tumors and the administration of insulin or oral hypoglycemic agents. These syndromes may evade diagnosis for prolonged periods. I can recall a patient who had numerous hospital admissions (including several to a psychiatric hospital) for bizarre behavior over seven years before his islet cell adenoma was diagnosed.

Transient functional or reactive hypoglycemia is common in individuals who ingest large quantities of sugar, but this is quickly corrected by the usual homeostatic mechanisms of the body. When patients are subjected to an oral glucose tolerance test in which they ingest 100 grams of glucose, their blood sugars at three to five hours after the glucose load may drop to hypoglycemic levels. This is a normal physiological phenomenon and not a disease state to which a wide variety of psychiatric syndromes has been ascribed.

In the early part of this decade it became fashionable to attribute many of the ills of mankind to the diagnosis of hypoglycemia, and this claim was supported by many lay organizations who believed that subtle hypoglycemia was responsible for a wide variety of symptoms frequently associated with anxiety or depression. In 1973 the American Diabetes Association, the Endocrine Society, and the American Medical Association issued a joint statement to the public about the diagnosis and treatment of hypoglycemia. The opening paragraph is particularly apropros.

> Hypoglycemia means low blood sugar. When it occurs it is often attended by symptoms of sweating, shakiness, trembling, anxiety, fast heart action, headache, hunger sensations, brief feelings of weakness and occasionally seizures and coma. However, the majority of people with these kinds of symptoms do not have hypoglycemia; a great many patients with anxiety reactions present with similar symptoms. Furthermore, there is no good evidence that hypoglycemia causes

depression, chronic fatigue, allergies, nervous breakdowns, alcoholism, juvenile delinquency, childhood behavior problems, drug addiction or inadequate sexual performance.

SOME PHYSIOLOGICAL CONCOMITANTS OF ANXIETY

Although certain of the protean manifestations of anxiety can be attributed to excess adrenergic stimulation, we have only a rudimentary understanding of the underlying physiological mechanisms. Pitts and McClure (3) demonstrated production of anxiety symptoms and acute anxiety attacks by the infusion of sodium lactate in 93% of subjects who were diagnosed as having the anxiety syndrome, but in only 20% of individuals who were judged to be normal. Symptoms were largely prevented by the addition of calcium to the infusion. The administration of glucose in saline to normal or anxious subjects did not provoke intensification or production of anxiety symptoms. Both groups metabolized lactate at the same rate.

These observations might be explained by the recent knowledge of receptor mechanisms. Because much of the symptomatology of anxiety results from beta-adrenergic stimulation, it is conceivable that the anxiety-prone individual is more sensitive to each stimulation because he has more such receptors or receptors that have a greater affinity for the adrenergic stimulus. Perhaps the lactate infusions in some manner increase the affinity of the appropriate receptors for the stimulus, and this is inhibited by the simultaneous calcium infusion.

Support for such a hypothesis can be cited in the observations of Frohlich and coworkers (4), who noted that certain patients who had what they called a "hyperdynamic beta-adrenergic circulatory state" had a higher resting cardiac index and heart rate and an increased heart rate response to isoproterenol as compared with a group of normotensive or asymptomatic hypertensive individuals. In 9 of 14 patients, the infusion of isoproterenol produced a hysterical outburst that was promptly reversed by propranolol administration. They ascribed the syndrome to increased receptor reactivity.

Recently Williams and coworkers (2) showed that the administration of thyroid hormone to rats resulted in an increase in the number of myocardial beta-adrenergic binding sites. Thus the beta-adrenergic manifestations seen in patients with hyperthyroidism who do not have any evidence of increased catecholamine secretion can be explained by the increase in the number of beta-adrenergic receptors, resulting in increased sensitivity to the usual level of circulating catecholamines.

In conclusion, I wish to reemphasize that certain organic illnesses may present with the manifestations of anxiety, and the clinician should be ever mindful of the possibility, however remote, of thyrotoxicosis, pheochromocytoma, and hypoglycemia as the underlying cause of the anxiety syndrome.

REFERENCES

1. Williams, R.H. Thiouracil treatment of thyrotoxicosis: I. The results of prolonged treatment. *J. Clin. Endocr.* 6 (1): 1-22, 1946.
2. Williams, L. T., Lefkowitz, R.J., Wantanabe, A.M., Hathaway, D.R., and Desch, H.R., Jr. Thyroid hormone regulation of beta-adrenergic receptor *J. Biol. Chem.* 252:2787-2789, 1977.
3. Pitts, F.N., Jr., and McClure, J.N., Jr. Lactate metabolism in anxiety neurosis, *New Eng. J. Med.* 277:1329-1336, 1967.
4. Frohlich, E.B., Tarazi, R.C., and Dustan, H.P. Hyperdynamic beta adrenergic circulatory state. *Arch. Int. Med.* 123:1-7, 1969.

CHAPTER 13

Disturbed Sleep and Anxiety

Robert L. Williams, J. Catesby Ware, Robert L. Ilaria,
and Ismet Karacan

According to clinical lore, anxiety results in disturbed sleep; sleep latency increases and awakenings during the night are more frequent. The bases for these associations are clinical experience and opinions formed from the descriptive psychiatric literature concerning the symptoms of anxiety states. The complaint of insomnia commonly voiced by anxious patients is almost certainly an important target symptom for which anxiolytics are prescribed. As a corollary to the tenet that anxiety yields poor sleep, the presumption is that a reduction in anxiety will thereby improve sleep. In fact, the opinion of clinicians that the relationship between anxiety and sleep is adverse is so well established, most would question the need to study the issue further.

Aside from his experience and training, the physician's common sense justifies the routine assumption that his anxious patients sleep poorly. A nervous, tense, and apprehensive patient scarcely seems a likely candidate for a normal night's sleep, and our hypothetical clinician assumes that this notion is adequately supported by laboratory sleep research. Unfortunately, a perusal of the pertinent sleep studies yields a conclusion rather more tentative than that which guides clinical practice. This observation constituted an important impetus for this study.

From the standpoint of the central nervous system, anxiety can be considered a variable and complex hyperarousal state reflected psychologically as an unpleasant affect(s), muscularly as a state of increased tonus, and autonomically as increased activity in one or both of its subdivisions. By definition then, anxiety would seem to be directly antagonistic to sleep. This assumption is further supported by the findings of a reasonably convincing body of sleep literature which indicates that a reduction in the activity of the reticular activating system (i.e., decreased CNS arousal) concurrent with the active functioning of hypnagogic center(s) or substances is necessary for sleep.

The clearest way to obtain objective support for an adverse relationship between anxiety and sleep is to induce anxiety in normal subjects, then record their sleep patterns. While it might be argued that the resultant anxiety is not clinically relevant, the method at least allows anxiety to be studied in relative isolation, something difficult to do in naturally occurring anxiety states. A brief look at the few available studies using this approach is worthwhile.

One of the most consistent findings among sleep laboratories is the well-known "first-night effect." On the subject's first night in the laboratory, the percentage of rapid-eye-movement (REM) sleep decreases, the percentage of slow-wave sleep (stages 3 and 4 combined) decreases, sleep latency increases, and generally there are more awakenings noted after sleep commences (1,2,3). Many sleep researchers attribute these effects to anxiety induced by facing an unknown procedure in unfamiliar surroundings, but the basis for this relationship is either subjective or presented as objective, but with unspecified supporting data.

Goodenough and coworkers (4) produced psychometrically determined anxiety in volunteers by showing them a stressful film, a documentary of an Australian aborigine circumcision rite. The effects of this film were assessed before bedtime, and the resulting sleep was compared to that following a nonstressful film viewing. The subjects demonstrated higher test scores on anxiety, hostility, depression, and distrust scales after viewing the stressful film when compared to those obtained after the neutral film was viewed. Sleep obtained after the stress film was characterized by longer sleep latencies. Total sleep time and the number of REM periods per night were similar. The effects on slow-wave sleep (SWS) were not reported. Assuming that anxiety was the dominant affect, this study lends support to the clinical observation that anxiety states produce or are associated with initial insomnia. It also demonstrates the difficulty of producing anxiety in isolation. Both psychometrically and clinically, anxiety is difficult to separate from other affects, especially depression.

The effects on sleep of what was presumed to be more generalized stress were studied by Lester, Burch, and Dossett (5). They studied the response and sleep of medical students in relation to pending examinations and other naturally occurring stress-producing events. When compared to the sleep following nonstressful days, the stress nights evidenced a decrease in SWS, an increase in transient arousals, and an increase in the number of galvanic skin responses (GSRs) per minute occurring during all stages of sleep. The parameters of REM sleep studied were unaffected by stress. Unfortunately, sleep latencies were not recorded, so confirmation of Goodenough's study is not possible.

The relationship reported by Lester and coworkers (5) between the number of GSRs per unit time and reduced SWS after anxiety-inducing stress suggests that perhaps anxiety-associated arousal contributes to sleep disturbance. A recent study of McDonald and associates (6) provides confirmatory data. They found a similar relationship between SWS and GSR activity and demonstrated a positive correlation between anxiety scores as determined by MMPI-derived anxiety measures (Psychasthenia, Welsh's A Factor, and the Taylor Manifest Anxiety Scale) (7) and sleep GSR activity.

The data obtained from relating anxiety to sleep in essentially normal individuals tends to support an adverse effect on sleep latency, a probable adverse effect on the amount of slow-wave sleep obtained, increased frequency of arousals, and little or no significant change in REM sleep. However, the available studies are few in number and differ in methodology; consequently, any conclusion drawn from them on the relationship of anxiety and sleep must be tentative.

Patient studies provide the largest body of information concerning the adverse effects of anxiety on sleep, much of which is derived from the study of insomnia in sleep laboratories. Although there are obvious problems associated with the use of an insomniac population for the purpose of objectifying the relationship of sleep and anxiety, the choice has a certain logic for the sleep researcher, since it reflects a natural area of activity (disordered sleep) and provides a large available supply of patients. Aside from the obvious practical considerations, there is also a clinically relevant basis for this approach. In the standard clinical psychiatric literature, anxiety states are described as usually characterized by some degree of disturbed sleep (8). Cohen and White (9) reported the clinically assessed incidence of "insomnia" in anxiety neurotics to be 53%, as compared to one of only 4% in normal controls. Therefore, in patients whose presenting or primary complaint is insomnia, an important percentage would be expected to exhibit anxiety in some form. This strategy was employed in this study and is supported by the fairly consistent finding that insomniacs (defined broadly enough to include the term 'poor sleeper") are anxious (10,11), but anxiety is not the only psychopathological feature found (12,13).

Monroe (14) has shown that both prior to going to sleep and during sleep insomniacs exhibit increased levels of autonomic arousal which may be a physiological result of anxiety. He demonstrated that their sleep was abnormal in several respects: 1. increased sleep latency; 2. lower percentage of REM; and 3. a decrease in total sleep time. Karacan (15) confirmed the findings of increased sleep latency and reduced total sleep time in insomniacs. While the connection is tenuous, there is some indirect evidence to suggest that anxiety associated with clear-cut autonomic arousal may be reflected as an increased difficulty in falling asleep. While this provides a reasonable explanation for the sleep-onset problem clinically observed in anxiety states, it may remain hypothetical, since in a recent study no significant relationship between levels of presleep autonomic activity and initial sleep onset duration was found in a group of sleep-onset insomniacs (16).

Two recent studies deal rather specifically with anxious patients and attempt to describe their sleep in an objective way. Stonehill, Crisp, and Koval (17), although not recording sleep polysomnographically, did attempt to control and refine the clinical observation and measurement of disordered sleep to an unusually high degree. In addition, considerable attention was paid to obtaining a high degree of intra-observer reliability in ratings and diagnosis through prestudy practice. A total of 376 psychiatric patients admitted for mood disorder to an inpatient unit by consulting psychiatrists were studied. A total of eight parameters of mood were assessed by self-rating, four of which are hallmarks of anxiety: nervousness, tenseness, restlessness, and irritability. Rating psychiatrists assessed each patient relative to 19 common diagnostic categories, made an overall diagnosis as well, and rated patients on four additional scales: anger, anxiety, sadness, and tenseness. As rated by observers, sleep latency was greatest in the anxious group, averaging 73 minutes. Interestingly, sleep latency was lowest in the tense group, in which it averaged 19 minutes, although as a group these subjects went to bed much later than those in all other categories, and approximately 45 minutes later than the anxious group.

Stonehill and his associates found that the sleep of patients diagnosed as exhibiting *primary anxiety states* was characterized by: 1. an increased time to fall asleep, 47 minutes on the average; 2. later awakening time compared to both neurotic and endogenous depressives, 37 minutes later on the average; and 3. time spent asleep averaging $7^1/_2$ hours, virtually no different than that of the depressives. They described the sleep of the anxiety-state patients as being of normal length, but occurring late in the 24-hour cycle.

Foster and coworkers (18) studied 10 patients who met the Research Diagnostic Criteria of Spitzer, Endicott, and Robins for Generalized Anxiety Disorder and recorded their sleep for two consecutive nights, comparing the results to those of patients with primary depression. Their main interest seemed to be in obtaining data relating to the issue of whether or not the two diagnoses represent a continuum or two more or less separate categories. In this regard, none of the sleep variables were statistically significant between groups. Their anxiety patients had sleep latencies of 40.9 ± 7.4 minutes, a clear increase over those of a normal group (19). Other sleep parameters that appear to vary from normals (19) to a degree that may be clinically significant are: 1. decreased total sleep time (330.8 ± 13.2 minutes); 2. decreased sleep efficiency index (83.7 ± 3.0 minutes); and 3. decreased percentage delta sleep (6.6 ± 2.3 minutes).

Based on the studies available, a concise, uniform summary of the relationship of anxiety to sleep cannot be made. There are simply too many variations in methods and patient populations, as well as fundamental problems in regard to diagnostic issues. Most telling, however, is the fact that there are simply too few studies that offer objective assessment of the disordered sleep associated with anxiety. Increased sleep latency offers perhaps the best case that can be made for delineating a fairly consistent reproducible effect of anxiety on sleep. On more tenuous grounds, there is suggestive evidence that total sleep time may be diminished, the percentage of delta sleep lessened, and the efficiency of sleep diminished. This study has been directed toward further clarification of these tentative conclusions.

METHOD

Subjects and Procedures

A group of 25 subjects was selected for this study from a group of 54 patients who had recently been evaluated at the Baylor College of Medicine Sleep Disorders Center for complaints of insomnia (sleep maintenance problems, increased sleep latency, or a combination of these). Patients with insomnia secondary to cerain physical problems (e.g., nocturnal angina, sleep apnea, nocturnal myoclonus, restless legs syndrome) were excluded, as were all patients with obvious psychopathology.

The insomnia subjects were divided into two groups—those who were not taking any medication during the study and had been free of taking any mood or sleep-altering medication for at least 14 days prior to the first night in the sleep laboratory (N = 15; 42.6 years old), and those who were taking medications judged to alter mood or sleep (N = 10; 46.1 years old). These two insomnia groups were compared to a group of 15 normal subjects who had no evidence of disturbed sleep or physical or psychological abnormality. The control subjects were free of any mood or sleep-altering medication and had been so for at least 14 days prior to the first night of laboratory sleep. In the non-drug insomnia group, two patients were taking thyroid replacement medication, one was taking a thyroid medication and chlorothalidone, and one was taking isoxsurpine. In the drug insomnia group, subjects had been using the following sleep agents more than several months: alcohol (two subjects), alcohol and flurazepam (one subject), diazepam and flurazepam (one subject), and flurazepam and meprobamate (one subject).

All patients were assessed for anxiety by means of the t-scale of the Profile of Mood States (POMS-T) (20), the State-Trait Anxiety Index (21), and the MMPI-derived indices (7): Welsh's A Factor, the Taylor Scale, and the Anxiety Index. All assessments of anxiety were done within 48 hours prior to the second night of sleep, from which the sleep data were analyzed.

The data from the insomnia patients were compared to those of a normal control group of subjects who had participated in the same evaluation

procedures as the insomnia patients, both polysomnographical and psycho-
metrical.

Before the study, all participants had been informed of the procedures
and had signed an Informed Consent Form explaining that the data might be
used for research purposes. The data were scored according to standard sleep
EEG procedures, which have been described elsewhere (19).

All of the patients, during their initial evaluation, were given a general
physical examination followed by a three-night polysomnographic evaluation. Recordings included those of respiration, heart rate, leg and muscle
tension, electroencephalographic activity, and eye movement, and were
monitored throughout the night. Each night, following electrode attachment,
patients completed a 22-item presleep questionnaire concerning their daytime
activities and feelings. Prior to the first laboratory night each patient was
allowed to select his preferred retiring and arising times, and these times were
held reasonably constant for each laboratory night. Soon after arising,
patients completed a 31-item postsleep questionnaire concerning the quality
and quantity of their completed night of sleep and their feelings upon
awakening. Patients were instructed not to take naps or drink alcoholic
beverages (except for the insomnia drug group) during the study, and follow-
up indicated that they complied with the request.

Results and Discussion

Sleep and psychometric parameters were tabulated and initially
compared with t-tests. On all measures of anxiety, the insomnia non-drug
group was significantly more anxious than the controls. They were also more
depressed, as determined by the MMPI depression scale and the POMS
depression scale (see Table 1).

The initial analysis of the sleep data indicated that the insomnia non-
drug group differed from controls on measures of percent of stages 0, 1, and 2.
Insomnia non-drug patients spent a greater percentage of total sleep time in
stages 0 and 1 and less in stage 2. Insomnia non-drug patients also had
significantly poorer sleep as indicated by a decrease in sleep efficiency (time of
sleep divided by total time in bed) and increased sleep latency to stage 2 (see
Table 2). The percentage of stage REM sleep, stages 3 and 4 sleep, total sleep
time, and stage REM sleep latency did not differ between the two groups.

Although the difference is not significant, the insomnia non-drug patients
were older (X=42.6±8.8, range 26-56 years) than the control patients (X=39.5±7.8,
range 26-49 years). An analysis of covariance was performed, using age as a co-
variant. This analysis indicated that age accounted for the significant differences
between the insomnia non-drug and the control group on all sleep parameters except for sleep latency and sleep efficiency. In other words, the differ-

Table 1. Anxiety measures for insomnia and control patients

	Insomnia Non-	Control	P<(no drugs vs. control)
State-Trait Anxiety Index (State)	40±9.3	29±6.9	.01
State-Trait Anxiety Index (Trait)	39 ± 8.2	32 ± 8.6	.02
Profile of Mood States (Tension)	11 ± 6.5	6 ± 3.9	.02
MMPI Anxiety (A Factor)	12 ± 6.9	6 ± 4.5	.02
MMPI Taylor Scale (AT)	18 ± 7.8	8 ± 5.5	.01
MMPI Anxiety Index (AI)	62 ± 15.8	44 ± 12.9	.01
Profile of Mood States (Depression)	9 ± 6.2	4 ± 4.6	.03
MMPI (Depression)	24 ± 4.8	16 ± 2.9	.001

Table 2. Sleep parameters of insomnia and control patients

	Insomnia Non-	Control	P<(no drugs vs. control)
Percent 0	11.0 ± 12.3	3.0 ± 5.6	.03
Percent 1	6.5 ± 4.2	3.6 ± 1.7	.02
Percent REM	23.0 ± 7.2	24.0 ± 5.5	NS
Percent Stage 2	53.0 ± 12.0	61.0 ± 8.1	.05
Percent Stage 3	3.1 ± 3.3	3.7 ± 3.4	NS
Percent Stage 4	2.6 .6	4.3 ± 5.8	NS
Total Sleep Time (minutes)	383.8 ± 58.4	390.5 ± 64.9	NS
Sleep Efficiency Index	0.83 ± .13	0.95 ± .01	.004
Sleep Latency (minutes)	22.0 ± 21.0	8.0 ± 9.9	.04
REM Latency (minutes)	79.0 ± 53.8	88.0 ± 37.6	NS

ences in the percent of stages 0, 1, and 2 were associated more with the patient's age than with his study group.

In order to help determine which psychometric variables were more closely associated with the parameters of sleep latency and sleep efficiency index, a second analysis of covariance was performed using age, anxiety, and depression as covariants. The groups were compared on sleep efficiency and sleep latency. Twenty-four separate analyses of covariance were performed (six anxiety measures × two depression measures × two sleep parameters). The results indicated that depression, as assessed by the MMPI, accounted for the significant differences between groups in these sleep parameters. Depression as measured by the POMS, however, did not account for the differences between the control and insomnia non-drug patients. In terms of sleep efficiency or sleep latency, none of the anxiety measures significantly accounted for the differences between groups. Plots of the psychometric and sleep data are included in Figs. 1 to 4, which help illustrate the relationship among age, anxiety, depression, and sleep parameters. There is clearly an age effect for the insomnia non-drug subjects in that the older the subject, the more likely there was to be a disturbance in sleep efficiency. This effect of age on sleep efficiency has been demonstrated with a normal population (19). There is little effect of age on sleep latency. The figures also illustrate the relationship between depression and sleep on both sleep latency and sleep efficiency. The greater the degree of depression, the more likely the subject was to have increased sleep latency or a reduced sleep efficiency index. This relationship between sleep and depression is artificially elevated, since three questions on the MMPI depression scale pertain directly to sleep (e.g., "My sleep is fitful and disturbed"), and several others pertain indirectly to sleep; that is, if a patient merely had a sleep disturbance without any depression, he would very likely answer the questions in the direction that would increase his depression score (e.g., "I find it hard to keep my mind on a task or job"; or "I have had periods of days, weeks, or months when I couldn't take care of things because I couldn't get going").

Of the 24 analyses of covariance examining the relationship between sleep and anxiety, only one indicated that anxiety was significantly related to a sleep disturbance. Increased anxiety, when measured by the MMPI and Taylor Scale, was related to increased sleep latencies when these parameters were covaried with depression as measured on the POMS scale.

We have analyzed the sleep data obtained from the insomnia drug patients separately because their sleep and psychometric data are confounded by their drug status. However, we were interested in seeing if this group would exhibit higher anxiety scores than the insomnia non-drug group. If so, then the more extreme scores would suggest that they were a different group in their predrug state rather than a random selection of insomnia patients whose physicians prescribed medication. As Table 3 indicates, the insomnia drug group are more extreme on all psychometric measures. The sleep parameters

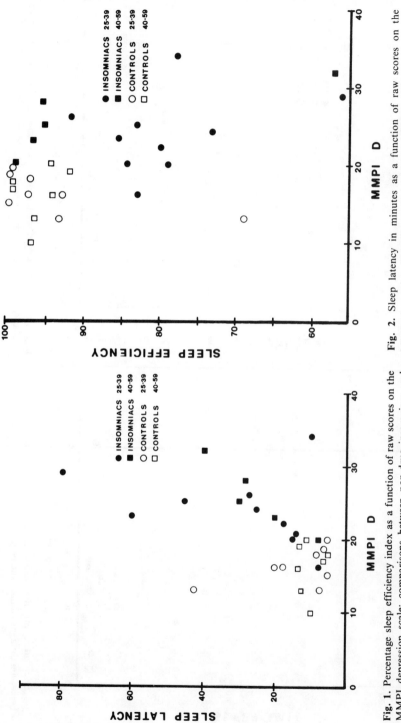

Fig. 1. Percentage sleep efficiency index as a function of raw scores on the MMPI depression scale; comparisons between non-drug insomniacs and controls.

Fig. 2. Sleep latency in minutes as a function of raw scores on the MMPI depression scale; comparisons between non-drug insomniacs and controls.

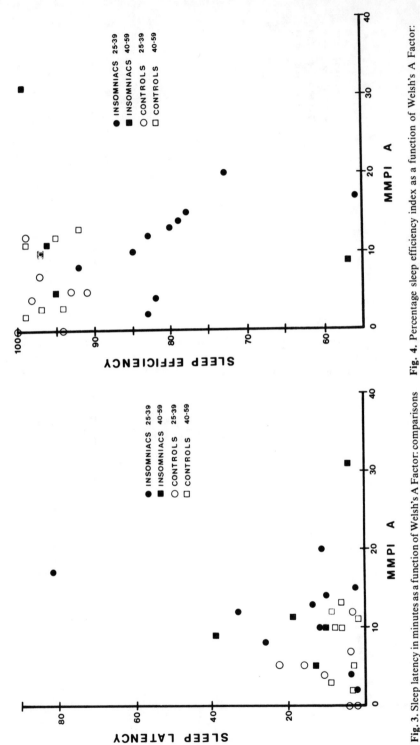

Fig. 4. Percentage sleep efficiency index as a function of Welsh's A Factor: comparisons between non-drug insomniacs and controls.

Fig. 3. Sleep latency in minutes as a function of Welsh's A Factor: comparisons between non-drug insomniacs and controls.

Table 3. Sleep and psychometric parameters of the insomnia drug group

Sleep Parameters:

Percent 0	7.1 ± 6.8
Percent Stage 1	5.0 ± 2.6
Percent REM	19.8 ± 7.8
Percent Stage 2	63.3 ± 8.1
Percent Stage 3	2.5 ± 4.8
Percent Stage 4	2.2 ± 3.8
Total Sleep Time (minutes)	390.0 ± 58.0
Sleep Efficiency Index	.87 ± .13
Sleep Latency (minutes)	29.9 ± 39.0
REM Latency (minutes)	132.0 ± 70.9

Psychometric Parameters:

State-Trait Anxiety Index (State)	49.4 ± 11.9
State-Trait Anxiety Index (Trait)	47.6 ± 10.9
Profile of Mood States (Tension)	18.0 ± 9.1
MMPI Anxiety (A Factor)	19.3 ± 4.8
MMPI Taylor Scale (AT)	22.9 ± 9.3
MMPI Anxiety Index (AI)	83.5 ± 25.5
Profile of Mood States (Depression)	20.8 ± 18.0
MMPI (Depression)	27.8 ± 6.7

(Table 3) are not as different as one might expect from such a heterogeneous drug group. The increased REM latency is one of the differences which is possibly attributable to drug effects. When correlations were computed between the sleep parameters of sleep latency and sleep efficiency and the psychometric parameters, none was significant except for a positive correlation between sleep latency and state anxiety as measured on the State-Trait Anxiety Index (.71, $p < .05$). There was no significant correlation between any of the other five anxiety measures or the two depression measures. This positive correlation may be explained on the assumption that they represent a different population with more extreme anxiety scores.

Overall, the most straightforward interpretation of our findings is that the presence of increased anxiety existing concurrently with depression, as defined by the MMPI, is not reflected in disturbed sleep. As a corollary, it would seem that the disordered sleep of insomniacs is not due to anxiety, with the exception of state anxiety in the drug insomnia group. Within the limits of this design, the conclusions are obvious, but it is quite likely that only a limited aspect of a comprehensive relationship between anxiety and sleep has been explored. Several design characteristics of this study that could have affected the results need to be considered before they are applied to a broader framework.

The insomnia population was obtained from patients complaining not of the usual constellation of symptoms characterizing anxiety states but primarily of patients complaining of only one of these symptoms—disturbed sleep; therefore they cannot be classified as representative of patients primarily anxious. This patient selection factor was heightened by the analysis of the drug-treated insomniacs as a separate group. Psychometrically, members of this group were more anxious than the non-drug group and possibly would have been even more so without the drug(s), since the agents used all exert anxiolytic or sedative activity. Consequently, by removing the 10 patients likely to have the most elevated anxiety scores from the overall analysis, any existing relationship between anxiety and sleep would be much more difficult to detect statistically.

Our method of detecting anxiety, while accomplished in a standard and accepted manner from the standpoint of research psychometrics, is quite different from a clinical assessment technique. One well experienced in clinical assessment of anxiety might pick up a more global anxiety pattern to which psychometric testing is not sensitive. An additional issue is that the separation of anxiety and depressive states is not entirely possible. There is an important body of clinical and research findings that questions the ease or reliability with which anxiety and depression can be distinguished. There is a considerable halo effect in the traditional diagnostic categories of reactive (neurotic) depression and anxiety neurosis. Seldom does a reactive depressive fail to exhibit clinically important, if not preeminent, anxiety, at least during certain phases of the condition.

Within any phase of anxiety neurosis, and especially so with increasing patient age, depressive symptomatology may be dominant. While a comparatively clear bimodal distribution has been put forth for these conditions, subsequent work has questioned this. Indeed, the sleep study of Foster and coworkers (18) suggests a rethinking of these issues, certainly as they are related to sleep.

Traditionally, insomniacs have been described clinically as exhibiting mild hypochondriacal concerns, mild anxiety and depression, and excessive worry (13). This constellation could as easily constitute the complaints of syndromal anxiety or depressive states, depending upon patient, interviewer, or psychometric emphasis and bias. Clearer and more objective markers of mood disorders are going to be required before the relationship of anxiety and sleep can be unequivocally discerned.

Finally, besides the advances that are possible in classifying patients, it now appears feasible to refine the method of examining polysomnographic data. By examining only total sleep time for each of our three groups, no differences would have been detected among them. However, other measures did uncover clear differences among the groups. The refinement of EEG-sleep data can now be taken even a step further. Computer technology allows us to examine phasic events such as the frequency and morphology of sleep spindles. These and other measures will perhaps aid in detecting and understanding the relationship between psychological states and sleep.

REFERENCES

1. Agnew, H.W., Webb, W.B., and Williams, R.L. The first night effect: An EEG study of sleep. *Psychophysiology* 2:263-266, 1966.
2. Antrobus, J.S. Patterns of dreaming and dream recall. Unpublished doctoral dissertation, Columbia University, New York, New York, 1962.
3. Rechtschaffen, A., and Verdone, P. Amount of dreaming: Effect of incentive, adaptation to laboratory, and individual differences. *Percept. Mot. Skills* 19:947-958, 1964.
4. Goodenough, D.R., Witkin, H.A., Koulack, O., and Cohen, H. The effects of stress films on dream affect and on respiration and eye-movement activity during rapid-eye-movement sleep. *Psychophysiology* 12(3):313-320, 1975.
5. Lester, B.K., Burch, N.R., and Dossett, R.C. Nocturnal EEG-GSR profiles: The influence of presleep states. *Psychophysiology* 3:238-248, 1967.
6. McDonald, D.G., Shallenberger, H.D., Koresko, R.L., and Kinzy, B.G. Studies of spontaneous electrodermal responses in sleep. *Psychophysiology* 13:128-134, 1976.
7. Dahlstrom, W.G., and Welsh, G.S. *An MMPI Handbook.* Minneapolis: University of Minnesota Press, 1960.
8. Mayer-Gross,W., Salter, E., and Roth, M. *Clinical Psychiatry,* 3rd ed. Baltimore: Williams & Wilkins, 1969.
9. Cohen, M., and White, P. Life situations, emotions, and neurocirculatory asthenia (anxiety neurosis, neurasthenia effort syndrome). *Ass. Res. Nerv. Dis. Proc.* 29:832-869, 1950.
10. Kales, A., Caldwell, A.G., Preston, T.A., et al. Personality patterns in insomnia. *Arch. Gen. Psychiat.* 33:1128, 1976.
11. Kales, A. Psychophysiologic studies of insomnia. *Ann. Intern. Med.* 71:625, 1969.
12. Rechtschaffen, A., and Monroe, L.J. Laboratory studies of insomnia. In A. Kales, ed., *Sleep Physiology and Pathology.* Philadelphia: Lippincott, 1969.
13. Coursey, R., Buchsbaum, M., and Frankel, B. Personality measures and evoked responses in chronic insomniacs. *J. Abnorm. Psychol.* 84(3):239-249, 1975.
14. Monroe, L.J. Psychological and physiological differences between good and poor sleepers. *J. Abnorm. Psychol.* 72:255, 1967.
15. Karacan, I., Williams, R.L., Salis, P.J., and Hursch, C.J. New approaches to the evaluation and treatment of insomnia (preliminary results). *Psychosom.* 12:81-88, 1971.
16. Freedman, R., and Papsdorf, J.D. Biofeedback and progressive relaxation treatment of sleep-onset insomnia. *Biofeedback Self Regul.* 1:253, 1976.
17. Stonehill, E., Crisp, A.H., and Koval, J. The relationship of reported sleep characteristics to psychiatric diagnosis and mood. *Brit. J. Med. Psychol.* 49:381, 1976.
18. Foster, G., Grau, T., Spiker, D.G., et al. EEG sleep in generalized anxiety disorder (abstract). *Sleep Res. Abst.* 6:145, 1977.
19. Williams, R.L., Karacan, I., and Hursch, C.J. *Electroencephalography (EEG) of Human Sleep: Clinical Applications.* New York: Wiley, 1974.
20. McNair, D., Lorr, M., and Droppleman, L. *EITS Manual Profile of Mood States.* San Diego: Educational and Industrial Testing Service, 1971.
21. Speilberger, C., Gorsuch, R., and Lushene, R. *STAI Manual for the State-Trait Anxiety Inventory.* Palo Alto: Consulting Psychologists Press, 1970.

CHAPTER 14

Vocal Patterns in Anxiety

Robert Roessler and Jerry W. Lester

We use many types of information to identify and quantify anxiety in di-agnosing and treating our patients. One type of information is change in the voice. Our clinical assessment of voice changes is currently subjective, however. It is therefore relatively inaccurate compared to the accuracy that might be achieved by more objective methods of measurement.

PREVIOUS RESEARCH

Research on the relationship between the physical characteristics of the voice and emotion began in the 1930s (1,2). The early studies employed cumbersome and relatively inexact methods; the results were therefore largely inconclusive. When the clinical spectrogram became available, there was a considerable increase in research relating changes in frequency and power to emotions. This type of spectrogram is currently used by speech pathologists. An example is shown in Figure 1. The Y axis shows the frequency range in cycles per second, or Hertz (Hz), and the X axis is elapsed time. The relative degree of darkness in the trace indicates the amount of power (volume) in each frequency range. Note that both the frequency contour and the distribution of power varies with the particular words and speech components. These facts emphasize the limitations of this instrument in

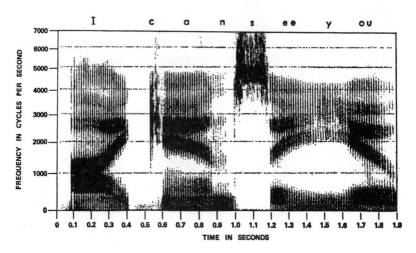

Fig. 1. Clinical spectrogram of the sentence "I can see you." (From P.B. Denes and E.N. Pinson, **The Speech Chain**. Garden City, N.Y.: Anchor, 1973)

attempts to study the relationship between emotions and the frequency and power characteristics of the voice. This effect of speech components on frequency and power must be controlled if we are to succeed in studying the effects of emotion. Control was achieved in most earlier research by using the same phrases expressed with different simulated emotions. The results of such studies must be interpreted cautiously, therefore, because there is no evidence that simulated emotion is similar in its physical characteristics to spontaneous emotion. In addition, the amount of power represented by the darkness of the trace in the various frequency ranges was difficult to quantify with any appreciable degree of accuracy.

In the early 1960s, with the wider use of the general-purpose computer, Starkweather developed computer programs that generated averaged voice spectra (3). This signal-averaging, which averaged the effects of specific speech components by using longer speech segments, made it possible to use spontaneous speech. Although this was an important methodological improvement, and Hargreaves, Starkweather, and Blacker subsequently showed that averaged voice spectrum variables were predictive of the degree of depression in patients' speech (4), its use was prohibitively expensive.

AVERAGED VOICE SPECTRA (AVS)

Since the 1960s, computer technology has not only advanced further but has become relatively inexpensive. A number of special-purpose instruments have been developed that are capable of computing averaged spectra on relatively long segments of speech at relatively low cost. Since 1974 we have been utilizing such a special-purpose spectrum analyzer to study the relationship of emotions to averaged frequency and power in samples of spontaneous speech in psychiatric patients. This instrument computes averaged power spectra by performing Fast-Fourier transformations on each voice sample, resolving the component frequencies in each sample into 5 Hz band widths within the 0-1,000 Hz range, and averages each voice sample either 32 times (6.4 second samples) or 64 times (12.8 second samples). We selected the 0-1,000 Hz frequency range after the results of pilot work suggested that this range contained most of the change related to emotion. The output of this analyzer is plotted on logarithm paper on an X-Y plotter.

Two examples of such averaged spectra are shown in Figure 2. The ordinate values on this graph are volts^2/Hz, a measure of averaged power. In interpretations of these spectra, it is important to emphasize that an apparent doubling of power is in fact a tenfold increase on this logarithm scale. The abscissa is the frequency range from 0-1,000 Hz. Direct your attention first to the lower trace. Note that the first and largest power peak in this speech sample occurs at approximately 150 Hz. In this female with a low voice, this is the approximate frequency of the fundamental frequency, the frequency at which the vocal chords vibrate. The second highest power peak is at approximately 350 Hz. This is the approximate frequency of the first harmonic of the fundamental frequency. These frequencies are only approximate because they have been modified by all the structures in the vocal tract above the vocal chords. Note also that the amount of power above 500 Hz falls off rapidly in this voice sample, a sample judged reliably by three raters to be one of low affect intensity. Contrast this to the envelope of the higher spectrum. This plot was reliably judged as a high affect intensity speech segment. Note that the fundamental frequency is also greater than the

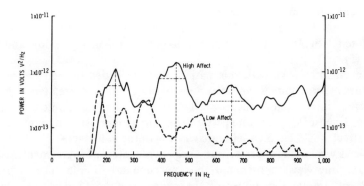

Fig. 2. Averaged spectra of high and low affect segments of spontaneous speech.

corresponding one in the low affect plot. Note also that the first formant (the modified first harmonic) is at approximately 450 Hz. In addition, the amount of power above 500 Hz is appreciably greater than that in the corresponding segment of the low affect spectrograph.

After further pilot work, we selected nine scores to characterize the spectral envelopes: the fundamental frequency (FF), the first formant frequency (2F), and the frequency with the highest power above 500 Hz (+500F); the amount of power in each of the foregoing three frequency peaks (FP, 2FP, +500FP); and the width of each of the foregoing peaks measured half of the distance from the power peaks in logarithm scores (FFD, 2FD, +500FD). These latter three parameters are a measure of the variability of the power over time in each speech sample. All nine scores are shown in Figure 2. We have related these scores to the intensity of emotion in two experiments. The first experiment was designed to study changes in fear, anger, depression, and total affect *states* within individual patients, and the second experiment was designed to examine group differences in subjects scoring high and subjects scoring low on a measure of *trait* anxiety. We will summarize the results of those experiments presently. Before doing so, however, an additional fact requires emphasis. There are large individual differences in voices. The most obvious of these is the sex difference, male voices having generally lower fundamental frequencies. In addition, the frequency and power characteristics of individual voices are so distinctive that it is possible to identify many people from their voice quality alone.

RESEARCH ON AFFECTIVE STATES
IN INDIVIDUAL PATIENTS

Because of these individual differences and because results of earlier research suggested that voice changes with emotions were also subject to wide individual differences, we focused first on a single patient in psychotherapy. We attempted to define changes in averaged voice spectra that were associated with rapid changes in the levels of fear, anger, depression, and total affect (5).

Seven interviews with this patient were recorded in their entirety on videotape. Three judges whose ratings of state affects correlated well with each other rated each of these seven interviews every 20 seconds on a nine-point ordinal scale for the intensity of fear, anger, depression, and total affect. Each affect was rated on a separate viewing of the videotapes. The first three interviews were used for practice and improving interrater agreement, and the last four interviews constituted the experimental sample. The degree of agreement among the judges of the experimental interviews was highly significant (p<.001) for every affect. Those 20-second epochs in which there was sufficient continuous speech were subsequently subjected to averaged spectrum analysis. The spectra were then scored for the nine frequency, power, and variability parameters previously described. These values were then used to develop multiple regression equations (6) based on the data from two interviews (4 and 5), with the mean values for each affect as the dependent variables. These equations yield multiple correlations (Rs), which can be interpreted as simple correlations (r). For example, an R of .90 indicates a strong covariation between a combination of variables (e.g., voice spectrum variables) and a dependent variable (e.g., affect scores). Highly significant multiple correlations between combinations of voice spectrum parameters and the ratings of each affect were demonstrated in those interviews. The constants and beta weights from each of these equations were used subsequently along with the appropriate values of the spectrum parameters entering each equation to predict the level of affect for each emotion in two separate interviews (6 and 7). Table 1 shows the results of this *predictive* cross-validation. The correlation between the predicted and actual values is significant for all four affects in interview 6 and for three affects in interview 7. The one nonsignificant correlation was positive and approached statistical significance. The combination of voice spectrum predictor variables and their weights differed for each affect, indicating that the nature of the affect as well as its intensity could be discriminated in this patient.

Table 1. Correlations of predicted affects and rated affects

	Interview 6 (98)	Interview 7 (74)
Fear	43[B]	20[D]
Anger	39[B]16	
Depression	29[C]	37[B]
Total Affect	33[B]	38[B]

Theoretically, anxiety is the product of conflict in emotions. In some circumstances anger is experienced, for example, but fear of experiencing and expressing this anger is also present. Similarly, depression is present, but simultaneously there is anger directed toward the source of this feeling, again producing conflict and therefore anxiety. To examine the vocal characteristics of anxiety, we then selected 36 20-second segments from these interviews that were relatively "pure" in the affect present (defined as the upper third of intensity range for one affect and in the lower third for the remaining affects) and compared them with 53 segments in which two or more affects were in the upper third of the intensity range. We then subjected the nine spectrum parameters from these two sets of mixed and pure epochs to a discriminant

Table 2. Voice variables differentiating mixed from pure affect epochs

	Mixed (N = 53)		Pure (N = 36)	
	X & S.D.		X & S.D.	
FF	229.85	(25.47)	214.92	(24.87)
FFP	9.22	(8.02)	7.09	(5.29)
2F	456.87	(80.95)	453.08	(120.8)
+500FD	229.42	(304.63)	108.14	(170.05)

function analysis (6). This statistical procedure identifies those parameters that discriminate between the two classes of epochs at statistically significant levels. The result is shown in Table 2. In this patient a combination of fundamental frequency, fundamental frequency power, second frequency, and the amount of variability in the frequency peak above 500 Hz entered into the discriminant function. The values of all of the foregoing voice spectrum parameters were larger in the mixed affect segments. Using the weights associated with each of these variables, a classification was then generated for mixed and pure affect segments. The result is shown in Table 3. Forty-two of 53 mixed affect (conflict) segments were correctly identified, and 22 of 36 pure affect segments were correctly identified. However, the accuracy of classification, although statistically significant (p [3]), is considerably less than perfect.

The foregoing results on one patient suggested that it was possible to develop equations from voice spectrum parameters predictive of the intensity of fear, anger, depression, and total affect in single patients. At best, however, these results established feasibility; they did not tell us whether it would be possible to develop predictive equations for additional patients and nonpatients. We therefore followed the identical procedure on four additional patients. Since anxiety is the focus of this discussion, we will confine the presentation of the results on these four patients to the equations for fear, the affect most closely related conceptually to anxiety. Although significant multiple regression equations were developed on all four patients,

Table 3. Classification of mixed and pure epochs

Predicted Affect	Mixed	Pure	Total (Rated Affect)
Mixed	42	11	53
Pure	14	22	36
Total			89

Table 4. Multiple regression equations and cross-validation coefficients for fear

		Test 1		Test 2
Subject 1	2.1962	C* + .0063 FF†(3) + .1653 FFP(9)††- .08172 FP(1) - .2882 (+500P) (5) = .43	.43	.20
Subject 2	2.8964	C + .1406 FFP(14) + .0045 FFD(1)+ .1228(+500P)(2) - .0008(+500F) (1) = .41	.68	++
Subject 3	5.4669	C - .0163 FFP(2) - .0020 (2F)(1) - .0096 (2FD)(3) + .049 (+500FD)(1) + .35	.06	.56

*	C=Y intercept constant.
†	See text for abbreviation key.
††	Percent of variance related to criterion variance.
++	No second test interview available on this subject.

on only two patients did they cross-validate predictively. The fear equations for these two patients and that for the patient already described are shown in Table 4, along with the correlations between predicted and actual values for fear levels in test interviews. Note the dissimilarity between the variables that enter the predictive equations for each of the three patients.

Although we have established that it is possible to develop predictive equations for fear for three persons, we failed with two others. Both of the patients with whom we failed were hysterical patients, and although the histrionic ("as-if") character of their emotions may have contributed to our failure, this result does highlight the limitations of the method. In addition, even with those patients with whom we were successful, the evidence of individual differences, along with the time-consuming nature of the procedure and its expense, led us to seek evidence of similarities between averaged voice spectrum parameters and emotion in groups of persons. If we could demonstrate such differences, we might be closer to a practical application of averaged voice spectra to the identification and quantification of anxiety in clinical contexts.

RESEARCH ON TRAIT ANXIETY AND SIMILARITIES AMONG SUBJECTS

Voice samples were recorded on each of six high ego strength males and six high ego strength females and six low ego strength males and six low ego strength females during the course of a prisoner's dilemma experiment. The high ego strength males were defined by scores above 47 and the low ego strength subjects by scores below 41 on the Barron Ego Strength Scale from the MMPI (7). Scores on this scale correlate at approximately the .70 level with measures of trait anxiety, such as the Taylor manifest anxiety scale, and they correlate with measures of neuroticism such as the Neuroticism Scale of the Eysenck Personality Inventory at similar levels. As might be expected, psychiatric patient samples usually score below 41 on ego strength.

Subjects participated in the experiment in pairs. Each of the two members of the pair was isolated in separate rooms. Each subject faced a console on which there were four feedback lights, each light designating a monetary reward or loss. Subjects were told that they would be paid a bonus based upon the sum of the rewards and penalties they and their partner incurred by their joint choices. This procedure is a familiar one to social psychologists. The details of this game are not relevant here except that the outcome, in terms of monetary reward for each subject, was dependent on his partner's responses. It was possible to play competitively—i.e., maximize one's winnings relative to one's opponent, or cooperatively maximize the joint or total winnings of the pair. In the first 30 trials they were told that they were competing against a "random signal generator." Following this block of trials, they were permitted to speak over an intercom between the two rooms with their partner, but discussion of strategy on the game was prohibited. Following the second block of 30 trials, the subjects were again permitted to communicate with each other by intercom, and they were also permitted to discuss a joint strategy. A third block of 30 trials then followed, but after 22 trials the agreed-upon strategy was frustrated by modifying the circuitry and making success impossible. Following this third block of trials, the subjects again communicated via the intercom regarding the outcome. It was hypothesized that the communications following the first trial would be relatively low in anxiety, that communications following the second trial during which strategy was discussed would be relatively high in anxiety, and that the communications following the third trial would also be relatively high because of the frustration of any agreed-upon strategy. Twelve and eight-tenths seconds of voice data for each subject following each block of trials were subjected to spectrum analysis and scored for the same nine voice parameters previously described.

It was hypothesized that the two ego strength groups would differ on combinations of one or more of these parameters. They did not differ on any of the frequency or variability measures. There were differences on the power parameters. The three power measures were therefore summed, and a repeated measures analysis of variance was conducted for differences between ego strength groups, sex, and trial blocks and for the ego strength by sex, ego strength by trials, and ego strength by sex by trials interactions. The ego strength group difference was significant ($p < .05$, $F = 5.72$, $df = 1/20$), as was the trials effect ($p < .05$, $F = 5.14$, $df = 2/40$). The ego strength group difference was entirely attributable to differences between high and low ego strength females, as shown in Figure 3. High and low ego strength males did not differ significantly in the mean power of their voices. This difference between sexes

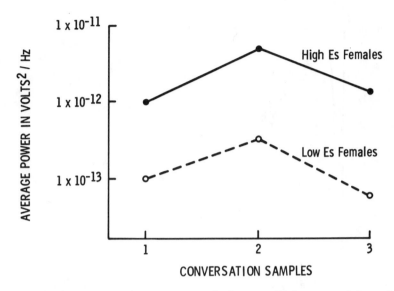

Fig. 3. Average power in the spontaneous speech of a group of high ego strength-low trait anxiety subjects and a group of low ego strength-high trait anxiety subjects under three experimental conditions.

was reflected by a significant ego strength by sex interaction ($p < .025$, $F = 7.41$, df $=1/20$). The significance of the trials effect was related to the greater amount of power in both male and female subjects associated with the conversations following the second block of trials during which the subjects discussed strategy. The hypothesis that the voice samples following the third block of trials would also reveal higher power was not confirmed.

Figure 3 shows that it is the high ego strength females (the low trait anxiety females) who are characterized by greater power under all three conditions. Low ego strength-high trait anxiety females speak more softly. This direction of difference related to ego strength parallels other physiological differences between high and low ego strength subjects that have been defined previously in our laboratory (7). These results also underscore the importance of differentiating between the effects of state and trait anxiety on physiological measures, including those related to the voice.

In summary, there is evidence that averaged voice spectra derived from spontaneous speech during psychotherapy and in experimentally manipulated laboratory circumstances are related to the levels of both state and trait anxiety. There is also evidence in female subjects that low ego strength-high trait anxiety is associated with lesser averaged power in the voice. These facts bring us closer to the clinical use of averaged voice spectra to quantify degree of state and trait anxiety and other emotions. However, it is also clear that we

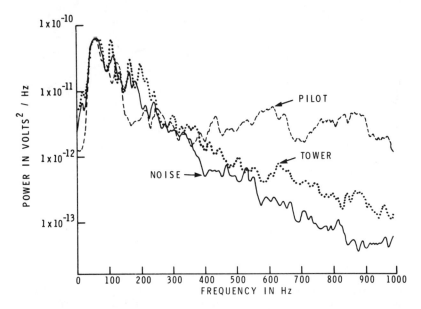

Fig. 4. Averaged power of background noise, the speech of a pilot, and the speech of an air controller just prior to a crash.

have not yet defined relationships of such consistency and universality that they lend themselves to immediate clinical application.

Nevertheless, these results are sufficiently encouraging to stimulate further research. We are currently designing an experiment in which the level of state anxiety is experimentally manipulated to produce a greater range of state anxiety than was observed in either of the two studies reported here. The potential of this strategy is illustrated by the results of a dramatic experiment in nature.

Figure 4 shows three spectrograms generated from a tape recording of the radio communications between the pilot of a small airplane and an air traffic controller just prior to a crash (8). There was considerable background noise on this tape. This noise was intermingled with the voices of the pilot and controller in the frequencies below 400 Hz, and the contours of the spectrograms are therefore atypical below this frequency. Above 400 Hz, however, the power of the extraneous noise dropped below the power in the voices of the pilot and the controller. You can see the sharp difference in the amount of power in the voice of the pilot compared to that in the voice of the air traffic controller. Compare these differences to the high and low affect segments shown in Figure 2. The results of this experiment in nature suggest that comparison of greater extremes of state anxiety may highlight differences common to all subjects and thereby bring us closer to the clinical application of averaged voice spectra for quantifying anxiety and other emotions in psychopathology.

REFERENCES

1. Lynch, G.E. A phorophotographic study of trained and untrained voices reading factual and dramatic material. *Arch. Speech* 1:9-25, 1934.
2. Fairbanks, G., and Pronovost, W. Vocal pitch during simulated emotion. *Science* 88:382-383, 1938.
3. Starkweather, J.A. Variations in vocal behavior. In D. Rioch and E. Weinstein, eds., *Disorders of Comunication*. Res. Pb. Assoc. for Res. in Nerv. Ment. Dis., vol. 42, pp. 424-449. Baltimore: Williams & Wilkins, 1964.
4. Hargreaves, W.A., Starkweather, J.A., and Blacker, K.H. Voice quality in depression. *J. Abnorm. Psychol.* 70:218-220, 1965.
5. Roessler, R., and Lester, J.W. Voice predicts affect during psychotherapy. *J. Nerv. Ment. Dis.* 163:166-176, 1976.
6. Overall, J.E., and Klett, J.C. *Applied Multivariate Analysis.* New York: McGraw-Hill, 1972.
7. Roessler, R. Personality, psychophysiology, and performance. *Psychophysiology* 10:315-327, 1973. Presidential Address, Society for Psychophysiological Research, November 9-12, 1972, Boston, Massachusetts.
8. The audiotape recording of the voices of the pilot and controller was provided by Richard I. Thackray, Ph. D., Chief, Stress Behavior Research Unit, AAC-118 Aviation Psychology Laboratory, Civil Aeromedical Institute, Oklahoma City, Oklahoma 73125. The use of the tape is gratefully acknowledged.

CHAPTER 15

Anxiety, Anxiolytics, and the Human EEG

Max Fink

Anxiety is an unpleasurable affect with somatic and psychologic components. Altered respiration, increased heart rate, pallor, dryness of the mouth, cold skin, increased sweating, weakness, and trembling are common somatic components; apprehension, tension, feelings of impending danger, awareness of pounding in the chest, and shortness of breath are frequent psychological events.

Anxiety is distinctly disagreeable, and depending on one's frame of reference, the syndrome is *normal*—when associated with a defined danger and equated with 'fear'—or *pathologic*—when a danger is not defined, or when the reaction is inappropriate to the stress either in intensity or duration, or both (1). Anxiety is usually defined by behavioral phenomena, by subjective response (usually using symptom rating scales), or by measures of somatic components (e.g., heart rate, blood pressure, salivary flow, galvanic skin response, respiratory rate, or skin temperature). Unfortunately, descriptions vary widely, so that no single syndrome with a commonality of symptoms and measures has emerged; nor does any single measure adequately define the variety and intensity of the states described as anxiety.

While anxiety is usually described in psychodynamic terms, some authors have examined physiologic models. A neurophysiologic thread may be seen, beginning with the studies of excitation and inhibition of the nervous system by the Russian physiologists of the Pavlovian school. They suggested that temperament reflected an innate state of CNS excitability, with irritability and high temperament associated with an excess of central inhibitory processes. Eysenck (?) proposed that individuals differed in the rate at which central inhibition developed, suggesting that extroverted individuals developed cortical inhibition more easily than introverted individuals. In individuals with psychoneuroses, similar processes were active, with cortical inhibition developing more rapidly in subjects with neurotic hysteria than in those with anxiety (3). These studies laid the basis for a personality view of anxiety.

"Arousal" is another concept used to describe anxiety. It is a term usually used to describe the continuum of behavior from sleep to increasing vigilance and alertness to emotional excitement and panic (3,4). Behavioral arousal has been related to the structure and functions of the reticular activating system, and psychiatric patients have been described to differ from normal subjects in "arousal" (4). Arousal is also an element of pharmacologic theories of the autonomic nervous system. Some patients with neuroses are said to suffer from an imbalance of sympathomimetic and parasympathomimetic activities. This imbalance is particularly severe in patients with anxiety (5).

Arousal is often equated with anxiety, and neurophysiologic measures of arousal are used to describe the affect "anxiety." The degree of arousal may be defined by a symptom of anxiety (e.g., salivary rate for dryness of the mouth), by autonomic measures (e.g., blood pressure response to methacholine [Mecholyl]) or by CNS activity (e.g., the EEG and the sedation threshold). Recently, Claridge (6) and Lader (7) described the findings in anxiety states for skin conductance and GSR (8), heart rate, respiratory rate, visual after-imagery, and electromyogram.

Other students have assessed the contingent negative variation (CNV) (9,10,11) and the averaged evoked response to sensory stimuli (12) as additional indices of arousal. If "anxiety" is a reflection of central processes, we would anticipate that the EEG would show systematic changes in relation to the severity of the dysfunction. The remainder of this discussion examines EEG measures as indices of anxiety.

A number of questions are posed: Are there characteristic EEG patterns related to the symptom "anxiety" or to clinical diagnoses in which anxiety is prominent, as "anxiety reaction," "acute schizophrenia," and "neurotic depression"?

Do EEG measures relate to the changes in anxiety that may be induced experimentally?

Do EEG measures relate to the activity of anxiolytic drugs?

1. EEG AND THE DIAGNOSIS OF ANXIETY

The same problems that make it difficult to provide a psychopathological definition of anxiety also interfere with the successful definition of the central components of anxiety. Clinical diagnosis is usually so imprecise that populations remain heterogeneous, so that any physiologic-diagnostic relationship would have to be remarkably strong to be found. However, a relationship between EEG pattern and personality typology was sought. Saul, Davis, and Davis (13) reported that patients in psychoanalysis who had active (extroverted) personality tendencies showed little or no EEG alpha activity, while passive-receptive (introverted) subjects exhibited high alpha indices. The findings were confirmed by some observers (14,15) but not by others (16,17).

Low voltage fast activity has been described as a feature of the EEG records of anxious and tense patients (18). In an experimental study of situational anxiety in normal subjects, Williams (19)reported that low voltage fast and delta activities increased as anxiety increased. Finley (20) found a similar EEG pattern in patients with psychoneurotic reactions, and in patients with psychoses. In a comparison of psychoneurotic and normal adults, Brazier, Finesinger, and Cobb (21) described well-modulated alpha dominant records in the normal subjects, while the psychoneurotic group showed multiple peaks in the frequency distribution with more activity in the beta band of 13.5 to 17.5 Hz. They suggested that the incidence of beta activity increased with the level of anxiety.

The findings were elaborated by EEG activation studies. The continuity of alpha activity was less in neurotic subjects, and with hyperventilation, the amount of alpha activity decreased further (22). Ulett, Gleser, Winokur, and Lawlor (23) compared the EEG frequency patterns at rest and in response to photic stimulation of 40 patients with anxiety neurosis and 150 normal volunteers who were classified into anxiety-prone and non-anxiety-prone groups by psychiatric examination and psychological tests. The alpha index was lowest both at rest and with stimulation in the patients with anxiety, more in the anxiety-prone controls, and highest in the non-anxiety-prone controls. Shagass (24) found that EEG driving response to photic stimulation was higher for female anxious patients than for controls.

The increase in fast EEG activity after intravenous amobarbital injected at a rate of 0.5 mg/kg/40 seconds was described as the "sedation threshold," and was proposed as another test of cerebral activation by Shagass (25,26). In psychiatric populations, the sedation threshold was higher in patients with the greater amount of manifest anxiety. The sedation threshold also bore a relation to the treatment response, with patients with the lower thresholds (more depressed, less anxious) improving more with ECT than patients with higher sedation thresholds. Despite difficulties with the interpretation of the inflection and end points, others confirmed these findings (3,6,27,28,29). Others have used the EEG response (30) or the induction of sleep (31) after pentothal for similar purposes.

Similar findings are cited in the principal reviews of the diagnostic use of the EEG (17,18,32), and the conclusion remains that the resting EEG does not identify patients with anxiety any better than psychopathologic means. Activation procedures, however, show some promise.

2. EEG and Experimental Anxiety

In studies of the effect of drugs on the human EEG, Wikler (33) observed that ". . . shifts in the pattern of the electroencephalogram in the direction of desynchronization* occurred in association with anxiety, hallucinations, fantasies, illusions or tremors, and in the direction of synchronization with euphoria, relaxation, and drowsiness." The EEG/behavior relationships were not related to specific drugs, occurring with drugs of different classes (34,35).

Wikler's findings were confirmed in studies with hallucinogens and anticholinergic deliriants, drugs that characteristically desynchronized EEG frequencies and increased EEG fast activity. The findings were clearly elaborated in drug interaction studies (36). Itil and Fink (36) found that the fear, anxiety, excitement, and psychomotor activity after atropine or Ditran were directly related to increases in EEG fast beta activity. In patients with a behavioral delirium after these drugs, they found that the administration of chlorpromazine increased the severity of the confusional state, often leading to stupor and coma. At such times, the EEG exhibited increases in the amount of slow delta EEG activity and a sharp reduction in the amount of fast beta activity. The administration of yohimbine or dextroamphetamine after these anticholinergic drugs, however, increased the amount of low voltage, irregular fast frequencies, and the degree of desynchronization of the records. At these times, the patients became increasingly anxious, restless, and irritable, and they remained so until the desynchronized activity waned or was replaced by the slow waves following an antipsychotic drug. In parallel studies, the symptoms of anxiety which were stimulated by carefully monitored infusions of yohimbine (0.5 mg/kg/6 minutes) or epinephrine (0.2 micrograms/kg/20 minutes) were accompanied by increases in heart rate and systolic blood pressure (37).

Another test of the EEG activity to anxiety is seen when anxiety is experimentally induced by verbal stress. Words or films are usually used, although the relation between anxiety and the EEG has received little attention. Hanley (38) summarized the findings of some authors, and found that with verbal stress, increases in the autonomic measures of heart rate and pulse volume were accompanied by a 70% increase in the fronto-temporal beta activity as well as changes in the distribution of theta and alpha activities.

A more interesting association is found in the experimental studies of anxiety precipitated by an infusion of sodium lactate. In 1967, Pitts and McClure (39) reported that infusions of sodium lactate elicited severe attacks of anxiety in 93% of subjects diagnosed as anxiety neurotic but in only 20% of

---

*"Desynchronization" is the change in EEG patterns characterized by a loss of a dominant frequency, a decrease in the amplitude of the record, and an increase in variability of amplitudes and frequencies.

the normal controls. As symptoms resembled those of patients with pretetanic hypocalcemia, they were able to minimize the effects of the infusion by intravenous calcium.

In a replication study, Fink, Taylor, and Volavka (40) examined the effects of similar infusions and confirmed their observations. Five patients with anxiety neurosis and four normal controls were subjected to three experimental sessions each in random order at weekly intervals. They received infusions of 500 mM sodium lactate, sodium lactate with 20mM calcium chloride, or glucose in saline. Infusions were given in 20 minutes with a maximum total dose of 10mg/kg sodium lactate. The difference in response to the three solutions between the patients and the controls was dramatic. With the lactate, each patient developed acute symptoms of anxiety. The symptoms appeared first between the 8th and 12th minutes of the infusion, peaked at 15 minutes, and remained severe for 15 to 30 minutes. The patients reported that the symptoms were similar to those they usually experienced.

Each patient experienced an "aftereffect" for two to seven days. The aftereffects were characterized by irritability, tension, dysphoria, fatigue, weakness, and headaches.

In response to the lactate/calcium combination, the patients experienced some of the symptoms of anxiety, but these were less in intensity and duration, and were not associated with aftereffects. The patients had no observable effect of the dextrose/saline solution, and both the observers and the patients could distinguish among the active and saline solutions.

The response of three of the four control subjects to the lactate solution was insignificant. Eight to twelve minutes after the infusion started, the pulse and respiratory rates increased, often associated with sighing. There was an increase in restlessness, without anxiety symptoms or aftereffects. Some anxiety symptoms developed in one control, but without aftereffect. The controls became drowsy with both the lactate/calcium and the dextrose/saline solutions.

The analysis of variance of the rating scale scores yielded significant F scores between the groups (F=25.2, p < .01), the drug conditions (F=75.8, p < .01) and for the interaction of drug condition and groups (F=16.9, p < .01) (Fig. 1).

In EEG, the dextrose/saline infusions failed to elicit any systematic changes in either group, and the lactate solution had no clear effect in three of the four control subjects. In the one control subject who did develop anxiety symptoms, and in four of five anxiety patients, the EEG exhibited a decrease in percent time alpha, an increase in percent time fast beta (18.5-24.5 Hz) activity, and a decrease in the mean amplitude of alpha activity (Figs. 2,3). Heart rates also increased in the subjects who showed the EEG changes and behavioral effects of the infusions.

The EEG effects of the lactate/calcium combination were similar in type but less in degree than the lactate solutions alone. A comparison of the effects

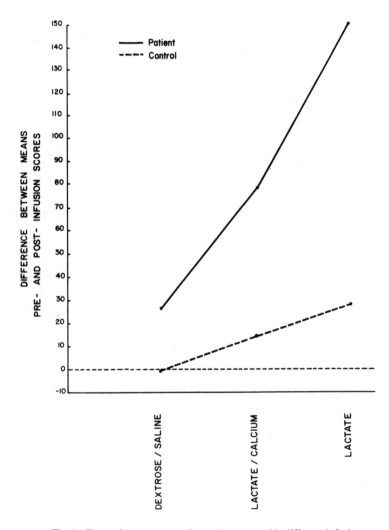

Fig. 1. Change in symptom rating scale scores with different infusions.

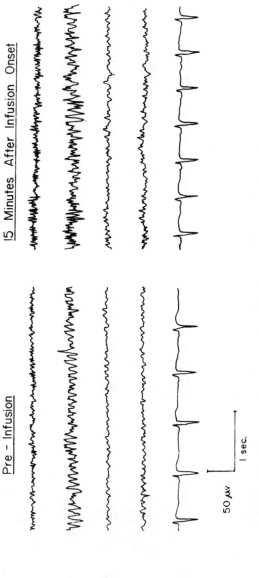

EEG EFFECTS OF SODIUM LACTATE INFUSION

(500 mM/20 minutes ; vol = 10 ml/kg)

Pre - Infusion

15 Minutes After Infusion Onset

F₃-F₄

F₃-O₁

O₁-C₂

O₁-O₂

EKG

50 μv

1 sec.

Fig. 2. EEG effects of sodium lactate infusion of 500 mM in 20 minutes. The volume of solution was 10 ml/kg.

243

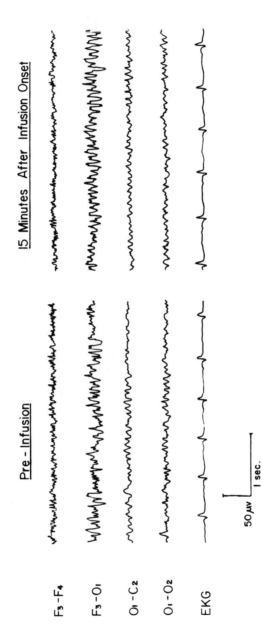

EEG EFFECTS OF SODIUM LACTATE WITH CALCIUM

(500 mM/20 minutes, +20 mM CaCl₃ ; vol = 10 ml/kg)

Pre - Infusion

15 Minutes After Infusion Onset

F₃ –F₄

F₃ –O₁

O₁ –C₂

O₁ –O₂

EKG

50 μv

1 sec.

Fig. 3 EEG effects of sodium lactate infusion of 500mM in 20 minutes plus 20 mM Calcium chloride. Volume as on Fig. 2.

of the three solutions on the 18.5-24.5 Hz activity in one subject with anxiety is presented in Figure 4.

Thus, regardless of how anxiety is induced, there is an associated change in the EEG that accompanies the behavioral and autonomic effects. The EEG is characterized by desynchronization of frequencies, an increase in the percent time of fast beta activity (15 to 25 Hz), and a decrease in the percent time and amplitude of alpha activity (8.0 to 12.5 Hz). It is probable that EEG desynchronization is the neurophysiologic index of anxiety and increased arousal.

3. CLINICAL PSYCHOPHARMACOLOGY OF ANXIOLYTIC DRUGS

While the clinical concept of anxiety does not relate to a single psychopathologic entity, it seems to be accompanied by desynchronization of electrical (EEG) activity as a neurophysiologic index. In operational terms, we would anticipate that procedures which reduce the behavioral, symptomatic, and physiologic signs of anxiety should also block EEG desynchronization. Many psychoactive compounds and such therapeutic maneuvers as psychotherapy, EEG alpha biofeedback, and transcendental meditation which reduce symptoms of anxiety also increase the synchronization of brain electrical activity. The syndrome of anxiety did not materialize when lactate and calcium were given simultaneously, nor did the EEG exhibit desynchronization after this combination. After the lactate infusions, we gave three patients and one control subject infusions of diazepam (0.2 mg/kg/2 minutes) when they exhibited the symptoms of anxiety. Diazepam reduced both the symptom rating scale scores and the EEG desynchronization as effectively as calcium (Fig. 4.)

In clinical practice, compounds other than the conventional "anxiolytics"—benzodiazepines, barbiturates, and carbamates—reduce the symptoms of anxiety (41). Antipsychotic agents (phenothiazines, butyrophenones, and thioxanthines), alcohol, opioids, cannabis, and the monoamine oxidase inhibitors are among the compounds exhibiting this property. When psychoactive compounds were classified by quantitative EEG methods, the principal axes of the classification were synchronization-desynchronization (often equated with amplitude) and changes in frequency bands (35). In a drug classification based on EEG criteria, the antipsychotic drugs, alcohol, and the MAOI were classified as EEG synchronizing agents (35). In more recent studies, the opioids (particularly diacetylmorphine and methadone), marijuana, and THC-delta-9 were also found to be EEG synchronizing agents (42,43). While these agents are not routinely used to treat neurotic patients, they do reduce anxiety in patients with schizophrenia and mania, and occasionally depressive psychosis (41). The conventional use of the term

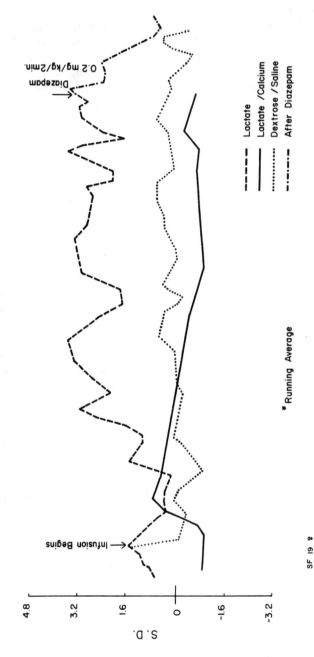

CHANGE IN EEG (18.5 - 24.5 cps) FOLLOWING LACTATE INFUSIONS *

*Running Average

SF 19 ♀
Anxiety Neurosis

- - - - - Lactate
———— Lactate /Calcium
············ Dextrose / Saline
—··—··— After Diazepam

Fig. 4. Change in EEG beta activity (18.5 to 24.5 Hz) with sodium lactate, sodium lactate and calcium, and glucose in saline. EEG values change in standard scores from pre-infusion mean, using variance of pre-mean. For details see reference 44. Abscissa is time with 30 minutes between infusion onset and diazepam. Note the effect of intravenous diazepam (0.2 mg/kg/ 2 minutes) after 30 minutes.

"anxiolytic" primarily for the barbiturate-benzodiazepine compounds is too restrictive and deserves reexamination.

The sedation threshold is a singularly useful index of the degree of anxiety. The end point used by Shagass (25,26) was the inflection point in the increase in the amplitude of EEG beta activity. The greater the anxiety scores, the more barbiturate was needed to develop well-synchronized EEG activity. From the available EEG studies, it is probable that the greater the anxiety, the greater the degree of EEG desynchronization, making the sedation threshold a measurable index of the neurophysiologic basis of anxiety.

The EEG is also an index of the intensity and duration of the anxiolytic activity of proposed therapeutic agents (44). We found that diazepam blocked the anxiety-producing effects of lactate as effectively as calcium in our experiments. Perhaps the lactate infusion model could be used as an assay for the anxiolytic activity of other drugs and treatments.

Quantitative EEG measures have enjoyed another application in the study of anxiolytic drugs. Modern pharmacokinetic analysis focuses on the blood levels of drugs. For drugs that may be CNS active, blood levels may or may not be linearly related to the effective levels of compounds in the CNS (44). In such instances, a measure of the direct influence of a compound in the brain would be more useful, and the EEG is one such "pharmacodynamic" index. We have examined the relationships between the EEG changes after three benzodiazepines (45,46). For diazepam and bromazepam, we found that the CNS activity of bromazepam was greater than diazepam in the first two hours after ingestion, suggesting that bromazepam may be directly active in the brain or have a greater transfer across the blood-brain barrier than diazepam. In another study, we found that the experimental compound triflubazam (ORF-8063) was slowly active, exhibiting CNS activity only after considerable delay, suggesting that it was transformed to an active metabolite slowly metabolized or slowly transferred to the CNS (46). In another pharmacodynamic analysis, the tetracyclic compound mianserin (GB-94) was found to be as rapidly active in the CNS after oral administration as the benzodiazepines (47).

Much of the interest in the lactate precipitation of anxiety is related to issues of whether lactate precipitation for anxiety is a biochemical peripheral stimulation, a central event, or a conditional response to peripheral events. In their review, Ackerman and Sacher (48) take the position that the anxiety response to lactate is a conditional response to the peripheral stimulation of the alkalosis produced by the infusion. The EEG findings suggest that central events accompany the changes in symptoms and the peripheral events, but the EEG measures do not clarify the ambiguity. But if the issue is to be studied further, it may be important to assess central measures of brain change to determine the temporal sequence between the central and peripheral measures, the symptoms of the subjects, and the pH measures.

CONCLUSION

This essay surveys the relations between the clinical syndrome of anxiety and a single physiologic measure, that of the alert EEG, both at rest and after activation. The syndrome of anxiety—the psychopathological state of discomfort accompanied by defined visceral components—is accompanied by EEG desynchronization, a reduction in alpha abundance, and an increase in irregular fast frequencies. In the experimental induction of anxiety, EEG desynchronization accompanies the behavioral discomfort, and when drugs or other remedies are applied, synchronization of the EEG characterizes the treatment response. The quantitative EEG has been used to classify psychoactive drugs, and provides a model to broaden the term "anxiolytic" to drugs and procedures outside the usual restricted range of the barbiturates and benzodiazepines. It has also been useful in the pharmacodynamic analysis of anxiolytic drugs.

This review of the relation of the symptoms of anxiety with EEG patterns provides further evidence for the EEG-behavioral association hypothesis—a hypothesis that has been useful in identifying and classifying new drugs. The EEG studies also provide operational means to check the validity and the homogeneity of populations provided by psychopathological descriptors customarily used in clinical psychiatry (49,50).

ACKNOWLEDGMENTS

I am indebted to Michael A. Taylor, M.D., of the Chicago Medical School, and Jan Volavka, M.D., of the Missouri Institute of Psychiatry, for their collaboration in the studies of sodium lactate and anxiety reported here. This study was aided in part by USPHS MH-13358 to the New York Medical College.

REFERENCES

1. Lief, H.I. Anxiety reaction. In A.M. Freedman and H.I. Kaplan, eds., *Comprehensive Textbook of Psychiatry*. Baltimore: Williams & Wilkins, 1967.
2. Eysenck, H.J. *Experiments with Drugs*. Oxford: Pergamon, 1963.
3. Claridge, G.S. *Personality and Arousal*. Oxford; Pergamon, 1967.
4. Duffy, E. *Activation and Behavior*. Wiley: New York, 1962.
5. Gellhorn, E. *Physiological Foundations of Neurology and Psychiatry*. Minneapolis: University of Minnesota Press, 1953.
6. Claridge, G.S. Psychophysiologic indicators of neurosis and early psychosis. In M. Kietzman, S. Sutton, and J. Zubin, *Experimental Approaches in Psychopathology*. New York: Academic Press, 1975.
7. Lader, M.H. Arousal measures and the classification of affective disorders. In M.L. Kietzman, Sutton, and J. Zubin, eds., *Experimental Approaches in Psychopathology*. New York: Academic Press, 1975.

8. Perez-Reyes, M., and Cochrane, C. Differences in sodium thiopental susceptibility of depressed patients as evidenced by the galvanic skin reflex inhibition threshold. *J. Psychiat. Res.* 5:335-347, 1967.
9. McCallum, W.C., and Walter, W.G. The effects of attention and distraction on the contingent negative variation in normal and neurotic subjects. *Electroenceph. Clin. Neurophysiol.* 25:319-329, 1968.
10. Knott, J., and McCallum, C. Event-related slow potentials of the brain. *Electroenceph. Clin. Neurophysiol.,* Suppl. 33; 1973.
11. Tecce, J., Savignano-Bowman, J., and Cole, J.O. Drugs and event-related slow brain potentials. In M. Lipton, A. DiMascio, and K.F. Killam, eds., *Psychopharmacology: A Generation of Progress.* New York: Raven Press, 745-758, 1978.
12. Shagass, C. *Evoked Brain Potentials in Psychiatry.* New York: Plenum, 1972.
13. Saul, L.J., Davis, H., and Davis, P.A. Psychologic correlations with the EEG. *Psychosom. Med.* 11:361-376, 1949.
14. McAdam, and Orme, J.E. Personality traits and the normal EEG. *J. Ment. Sci.* 100:913-921, 1954.
15. Mundy-Castle, A.C. The electroencephalogram and mental activity. *Electroenceph. Clin. Neurophysiol.* 9:643-655, 1957.
16. Henry, C.E., and Knott, J. A note on the relationship between "personality" and the alpha rhythm of the electroencephalogram. *J. Exp. Psychol.* 28:362-36, 1941.
17. Ellingson, R.J. The incidence of EEG abnormality among patients with mental disorders of apparently non-organic origin: A critical review. *Am. J. Psychiat* 111:263-275, 1954.
18. Wilson, W.P., and Short, M.J. The neuroses and EEG. In W.P. Wilson, ed., *Applications of Electroencephalography in Psychiatry.* Durham, Duke University Press, 1965.
19. Williams, A.C. Some psychological correlates of the electroencephalogram. *Arch. Psychol.* 34:240, 1939.
20. Finley, K.H. On the occurrence of rapid frequency potential changes in the human electroencephalogram. *Am. J. Psychiat* 101:194-200, 1944.
21. Brazier, M.A.B., Finesinger, J.E., and Cobb, S. A contrast between the electroencephalograms of 100 psychoneurotic patients and those of 500 normal adults. *Am. J. Psychiat* 101:443-448, 1945.
22. Strauss, H. Clinical and electroencephalographic studies: The electroencephalogram in psychoneurotics. *J. Nerv. Ment. Dis.* 101:19-27, 1945.
23. Ulett, G., Gleser, G., Winokur, G., and Lawlor, A. The EEG and reaction to photic stimulation as an index of anxiety-proneness. *Electroenceph. Clin. Neurophysiol.* 5:23-32, 1953.
24. Shagass, C. Clinical significance of the photomyoclonic response in psychiatric patients. *Electroenceph. Clin. Neurophysiol.* 6:445-453, 1954.
25. Shagass, C. The sedation threshold. A method for estimating tension in psychiatric patients. *Electroenceph. Clin. Neurophysiol.* 6:221-233, 1954.
26. Shagass, C. A measurable neurophysiological factor of psychiatric significance. *Electroenceph. Clin. Neurophysiol.* 9:101-108, 1957.
27. Perez-Reyes, M. Differences in sedative susceptibility between types of depression: Clinical and neurophysiologic significance. In T.A. Williams, M. Katz, and J.A. Shields, eds., *Recent Advances in the Psychobiology of the Depressive Illnesses.* Washington, D.C.: U.S. Government Printing Office, 1972.
28. Nymgaard, K. Studies on the sedation threshold. *Arch. Gen Psychiat.* 1:530-536, 1959.
29. Boudreau, D. Evaluation of the sedation threshold test. *Arch. Neurol. Psychiat.* 80:771-775, 1958.
30. Itil, T. Pentothal induced changes in EEG as prognostic index in drug therapy of psychotic patients. *Am. J. Psychiat.* 121:996-1002, 1965.

31. Goldman, D. Differential response to drugs useful in treatment of psychoses revealed by Pentothal-activated EEG. In J. Wortis, ed., *Recent Advances in Biological Psychiatry.* New York: Grune & Stratton, 1960.

32. Hill, D. and Parr, G., eds., *Electroencephalography.* New York: Macmillan, 1963.

33. Wikler, A. Clinical and electroencephalographic studies on the effect of mescaline, N-allylnormorphine and morphine in man. *J. Nerv. Ment. Dis.* 120:157-175, 1954.

34. Fink, M. Effect of anticholinergic compounds of post-convulsive electroencephalogram and behavior of psychiatric patients. *Electroenceph. Clin. Neurophysiol.* 12:359-369, 1960.

35. Fink, M. EEG and human psychopharmacology. *Ann. Rev. Pharmacol.* 9:241-258, 1969.

36. Itil, T., and Fink, M. EEG and behavioral aspects of the interaction of anticholinergic hallucinogens with centrally active compounds. In P. Bradley and M. Fink, eds., *Anticholinergic Drugs and Brain Functions in Animals and Man.* Amsterdam: Elsevier, 1968.

37. Garfield, S., Gershon, S., Sletten, I., Sundland, D.M., and Ballou, S. Chemically induced anxiety. *Int. J. Neuropsychiat.* 3:426-433, 1967.

38. Hanley, J. Electroencephalographic correlates of verbally induced stress in man. *Int. J. Psychiat. in Med.* 6:3-13, 1975.

39. Pitts, F.N., and McClure, J.N. Lactate metabolism in anxiety neurosis. *New Eng. J. Med.* 227:1329-1336, 1967.

40. Fink, M., Taylor, M., and Volavka, J. Anxiety precipitated by lactate. *New Eng. J. Med.* 281:1429, 1969.

41. Klein, D.F., and Davis, J.M. *Diagnosis and Drug Treatment of Psychiatric Disorders.* Baltimore: Williams & Wilkins, 1969.

42. Fink, M. EEG effects of drugs of dependence. In S.J. Mule and H. Brill, eds., *Clinical and Biological Aspects of Drug Dependence.* Cleveland, Ohio: Chemical Rubber Co., 1972.

43. Fink, M., Volavka, J., Panayioutopolis, C.P., and Stefanis, C. Quantitative EEG studies of marijuana, delta-nine-tetrahydrocannabinol, and hashish in man. In M.C. Braude and S. Szara, eds., *The Pharmacology of Marijuana.* New York: Raven Press, 1976.

44. Fink, M. EEG profiles and bioavailability measures of psychoactive drugs. In T. Itil, ed., *Psychotropic Drugs and the Human EEG. Modern Problems in Pharmacopsychiatry.* Basel: S. Karger, 1974.

45. Fink, M., Irwin, P., Schwartz, M., and Conney, A. Blood levels and EEG effects of diazepam and bromazepam. *Clin. Pharm. Therap.* 20:184-191, 1976.

46. Fink, M., and Irwin, P. Relation of EEG to blood levels of psychoactive drugs. In L. Gottschalk and S. Merlis, eds., *Pharmacokinetics, Blood Levels, and Clinical Response.* New York: Spectrum Publications, 1976.

47. Fink, M., Irwin, P., Gastpar, M., and deRidder, H. EEG blood level, and behavioral effects of the antidepressant mianserin (Org. GB94). *Psychopharmacology* 54:249-254, 1977.

48. Ackerman, S.H., and Sacher, E.J. The lactate theory of anxiety: A review and re-evaluation. *Psychosom. Med.* 36:69-81, 1974.

49. Fink, M. Neurophysiological response strategies in the classification of mental illness. In M.M., Katz, J.O. Cole, and W.E. Barton, eds., *The Role of Methodology of Classification in Psychiatry and Psychopathology.* Washington, D.C.: U.S. Government Printing Office, 1968.

50. Fink, M. EEG response strategies in psychiatric diagnosis. In R. Spitzer and D.F. Klein, *Critical Issues in Psychiatric Diagnosis.* New York: Raven Press, 1968.

CHAPTER 16

Anxiety: A Psychoanalytic View

Robert M. Gilliland

The unpleasant experience known as anxiety had been an object of interest to philosophers long before Freud addressed himself to the phenomenon. Natural-scientific psychologists and philosophers such as Nietzsche, Schopenhauer, and Kierkegaard had anticipated Freud in appreciating the significance of the irrational, dynamic, unconscious elements in personality, but Freud was the first in the scientific tradition to insist that these elements were as worthy of serious investigation as any other, thus opening the way to an entirely new dimension in the understanding of affects, beginning historically with anxiety. Freud was the first major articulator of the basic significance of anxiety in human behavior. He repeatedly modified his theory of anxiety and at one point (1926) even made a major revision, but he never wavered from the view that anxiety occupied a central position in the neuroses, both as causative agent and as key to successful treatment. Although I take minor exception to this latter position, in my opinion there has been no significant contribution to or noteworthy modification of the psychoanalytic theory of anxiety since Freud's major revision in 1926. I shall not attempt to describe, or even enumerate, the better-known publications addressed to this topic. Many of them deal with some specialized aspect of anxiety, and hence are presented from an idiosyncratic point of view without engaging the problem in a general sense; but for those who may be interested in pursuing some of these publications, I call to your attention the bibliography of an excellent review paper by Allan Compton in the *Journal of the American Psychoanalytic Association,* Vol. 20, No. 2, April 1972. (1).

Before the turn of the century, Freud's clinical work centered upon hysteria and the now uncertain clinical entity known as neurasthenia. To explain his observations, he invoked the notions of trauma and affect, or excitation. An experience that evoked a distressing affect was a trauma, which resulted from an increase in excitation in the nervous system without discharge. Since discharge of excitation was seen as curative, the therapeutic modality of this period was abreaction. The pathological condition was flooding with excitation. The only affect mentioned in connection with hysteria was anxiety, which even then Freud regarded as capable of being detached from one idea and attached to another idea or function. Anxiety as such received little attention for a while, and even in 1900 in "The Interpretation of Dreams," anxiety was relatively neglected, while affects were treated at some length, although they were still regarded as processes of discharge.

Growing out of the work on dreams, the systems Unconscious, Preconscious, and Conscious were postulated. Anxiety was related to ideas or wishes belonging to the Unconscious, while at the same time being objectionable to the Preconscious. In this so-called Topographic Model, the concept *signal unpleasure* (which was mentioned earlier in the Project of 1895) again surfaced as part of the mechanism of the relations among the various systems. Freud used the term "signal" to refer to the early phase in the evocation of unpleasurable affect, before a "traumatic state" or feeling of being overwhelmed and helpless had supervened. This concept comes to occupy a central position in Freud's theory of anxiety in his major revisions of 1926.

From the turn of the century to 1914, Freud made no significant changes in his theory of anxiety. He continued to view it as something that was "generated," was partially somatic, and resulted from the transformation of warded off (subsequently repressed) libido. This anxiety could remain free, become "bound," or "find an object." The "sources" of anxiety at this period were multiple, and, as enumerated in the Compton review, included 1) perception of external danger, 2) transformation of warded-off libido, 3) other somatic sources (cardiorespiratory problems), 4) automatic response to erupting repressed wishes, 5) transformation of any distressing affect, 6) perception of the danger of drive or of omnipotence of wishes, and 7) force of conscience.

By 1919, Freud acknowledged realistic anxiety and ascribed it to the self-preservative instincts of the ego. He questioned the adaptive value of realistic anxiety, since only a signal is expedient. In the instance of anxiety arising from internal sources, defense is instituted and symptoms are formed to prevent feelings of "unpleasure or anxiety." He invoked birth trauma as the specific precipitate of significant experience of human prehistory which gives the coloration to the affect anxiety, (2) and greatly simplified the "sources" of anxiety: 1) perception of external danger, and 2) any affect (excitation) may be trafisformed into anxiety and discharged.

Perhaps a brief restatement of the 1919 theory is in order: repressed or warded-off libido is transformed into anxiety. The individual experiences libidinal impulses that he interprets as dangerous, the impulses are repressed, and they become "automatically" converted into anxiety, finding their expression in either a free-floating form or as symptoms that are "anxiety equivalents." These symptoms were presumed to arise as a result of the free anxiety attaching itself to "the common phobias of man," or to sexually related functions such as urination and defecation. Objective or realistic anxiety had been recognized and was defined as a flight reaction to external danger. In response to the question of what the individual fears in neurotic anxiety, Freud answered in the Introductory Lectures of 1914 that it represented "a flight from the demands of one's own libido, treating this internal danger as if it were an external one."(3)

Freud attributed the particular quality of the anxiety experience to the trauma of birth, and subsequently to the related fear of castration. The relationship was viewed thusly: the affect of anxiety was a reproduction of the birth experience: "An experience which involves just such a concatenation of painful feelings of discharges and excitation, and of bodily sensations, as to have become a prototype for all occasions on which life is endangered, ever after to be reproduced again in us as the dread of anxiety condition." (4) Noting that this prototypical anxiety arose on the occasion of the separation from the mother, he attributes subsequent stranger anxiety, fears of darkness and loneliness, and other unpleasurable experiences of alienation and isolation to the child's dread that he will be separated from his mother. Castration is related to the loss of mother, since the loss of the genital deprives the individual of the potential means of later reunion with the mother substitute. In anticipation of his later theory, Freud stated in 1914 "the preparation for anxiety seems to me to be the expedient element in what we call anxiety and the generation of anxiety the inexpedient one." This remains a succinct statement of the distinction between anxiety as an adaptive response and anxiety as part of a neurotic process. The energy source for all anxiety—infantile, neurotic and possibly realistic as well—is seen as unitary and always the same: transformation of libido.

This brings us to the point, historically, that I regard as the end of the first phase in Freud's theory of anxiety. In 1920, with the publication of "Beyond the Pleasure Principle," some new steps are taken that demand a revision in the theory as it then stood. Freud concluded that the intensity of a given affect was independent of the quantity of excitation, thereby requiring a differentiation in the theory of affects and the theory of energy. It is now unnecessary to view anxiety as, inevitably, transformed libido, although the possibility of its being such is not removed. However, the door has been opened to viewing anxiety in Structural Theory (id, ego, superego) terms, and ascribing the anxiety response to the ego. This was accomplished in 1923 with the publication of *The Ego and the Id.*

Freud always viewed the capacity for anxiety as innate and phylogenetically inherited in the human being. In 1926 (Inhibition, Symptom and Anxiety), he reaffirmed this position: "A certain *predisposition* to anxiety on the part of the infant is indubitable. It is not at its maximum immediately after birth, to diminish gradually thereafter, but first makes its appearance later on with the progress of psychic development, and persists over a certain period of childhood." His second theory of anxiety in no way required a modification of this view.

The "new" (1926) theory describes anxiety in terms that would probably not offend any of us. As described by Compton, "It has three components: 1) a feeling with a particular unpleasant character, different from other unpleasant feelings; 2) certain physiological accompaniments—'processes of discharge'; 3) perception of these processes. Anxiety has a relation of expectation, a quality of indefiniteness, and (when distinguished as a term from "fear") a lack of object." (1).

Two concepts dating back to Freud's early writings assume important roles: first, *a danger situation.* This danger situation represents a psychological viewpoint, which may or may not coincide with an objective viewpoint, and is one in which the subject anticipates helplessness—physical helplessness if the threat is external, psychic helplessness if the threat is instinctual or internal. A second new element is the *traumatic situation,* which is the occurrence or experience of helplessness.

The new theory makes use of the concepts danger situation and traumatic situation in the following way: States of helplessness are present from birth, but the capacity of the ego to give the anxiety signal does not come into being until later. Therefore, traumatic situations in early life are integral to the experience of all of us. These early experiences of helplessness resulting from accumulated excitation from either external or internal origin cannot be dealt with apart from outside assistance. Through experience, "the percept of the mother is associated with repeated satisfactions, and absence of the mother in a situation of 'growing tension due to need, against which it (the infant) is helpless' threatens to repeat" (2) the earlier traumatic situations, which in turn are prototypical of the birth trauma. But note that the danger has now changed from the internal disturbance itself to the "loss of object or nonperception of the mother. This is simultaneously a change from an experience of trauma to a signal of anxiety. Early in this phase, however, if the mother's absence coincides with need, a traumatic situation rather than a danger situation results."(2)

This newly postulated *signal of anxiety* has major implications for the theory as it stood before this time. Recall that anxiety was *always* the transformation product of repressed libido. Now, the situation is reversed: the anxiety signal calls into play defensive operations of the ego, notably repression, which are directed against the wishes or impulses that are experienced as threatening and potentially dangerous. In "The New Introductory Lectures" of 1938, Freud made a retrospective reassessment of the case of Little Hans (1909). He stated that "it was not the repression that created the anxiety; the anxiety was there earlier and created the repression." This may be regarded as a succinct, if oversimplified, statement of the second theory of anxiety.

Even with this reversal in the reciprocal roles of repression and anxiety, however, there was nothing in the revised theory that *required* that affect and energy always be distinguished, or that anxiety is *never* transformed libidinal energy. Quoting Compton, "Generally, in fact, this remains precisely the root of the anxiety theory: under certain circumstances anxiety is a discharge of excessive excitation. Among these conditions are the traumatic moment and the unpleasure states of birth and early infancy. The sense of helplessness which accompanies such states is remembered. And it is the memory which triggers the ego signal-anxiety reaction." This awakens echoes of 1911 when, in the paper titled "A Special Type of Object Choice Made by Men," Freud stated: "Birth is both the first of all dangers to life and the prototype of all later ones that cause us to feel anxiety, and the experience of birth has probably left behind in us the expression of affect which we call anxiety."

Nevertheless, we have arrived at the point at which "the danger situation-signal anxiety concept applies to the great majority of anxiety phenomena: to hysteria, phobias, conversions, obsessional neurosis; to all developmental phases after the establishment of permanent object cathexis; and to normative adult psychic function. The traumatic situation-energic discharge concept is based on: actual neurosis, traumatic neurosis; certain traumatic moments in adult life; on birth and early infancy prior to permanent object cathexis; and on infantile (childhood) neuroses." But we cannot escape the fact that even at this time Freud had not repudiated the idea of anxiety as transformed libido. The single most important distinction between the first and second anxiety theories involves the difference in seeing anxiety as a largely exclusive intrapsychic process in the first theory, and the view that anxiety arises out of the individual's endeavor to relate himself to his world in the second theory. Perhaps the most familiar theoretical proposition which derives from the second theory is the emphasis on loss and the developmental loss hierarchy. Freud's view that anxiety has its source, as far as a primal source is reactivated in later neurotic anxiety, in the fear of premature loss of or separation from the mother is reflected by a fear of some loss in each developmental stage. The form which the fear of loss takes in succeeding developmental phases is usually listed successively as 1) loss of object, 2) loss of object's love, 3) loss of penis (castration), 4) loss of approval of the superego.

Since 1926, many analysts have addressed the theory of anxiety from a variety of perspectives, but for the most part these approaches have been concerned with some individual aspect of Freud's theory. The more ambitious revisionists tend to lean heavily on speculation at the expense of clinical observation, and the astute clinical observers tend to approach the problem from a particular idiosyncratic point of view, such as work with exclusively psychotic patients. They suggest the presence of factors in the anxiety response that, if not unique, are at least differentially weighted in some of the clinical situations Freud had not investigated extensively. While they suggest areas for exploration and highlight Freud's neglect of the factor of aggression in anxiety, they hardly constitute major challenges to Freud's fairly tight, though admittedly not flawless, reasoning.

Among the many obstacles to the understanding of anxiety, terminologic confusion ranks high on the list. Not only is the term used to designate an affect or affective state, but it is also used to designate a syndrome or a psychopathological entity. Even within these two general categories further confusion exists. "Anxiety" as affect, for example, is often used interchangeably with "tension," a state that may have a pleasurable component, while anxiety by definition never has. The frequent use of such other terms as apprehension, dread, terror, panic adds to the confusion, since they all imply a major anxiety component but lack precision. "Anxiety" as disease compounds the problem, since the affect anxiety is a common ingredient in so many clinical syndromes. I should stress that in this paper I confine myself to affects, whether anxiety, depression, or other.

Beginning with the most parsimonious definition possible—that anxiety is unpleasure associated with the idea (conscious, unconscious, or both) that something bad is about to happen—I would like to illustrate briefly some of the obstacles, as I see them, to understanding anxiety and to developing a coherent and inclusive theory. To this end, I enlist your participation in thinking about these notions in relation to your own experiences, both personal and clinical. Over the years, I have seen many patients who sought help because of anxiety, though to be sure, they seem to present with the complaint much less often now than formerly. First, I realized early that "I am anxious" was often a less than accurate, less than precise communication. Secondly, individual response to the affect designated, whatever its composition, shows a wide variation ranging from constructive motivation in the highest degree to almost total paralysis in all of life's activities.

To illustrate the first point: I recently saw a middle-aged businessman in consultation. He complained of anxiety, but when encouraged to describe the feeling, he indicated that he could not visualize himself in the future, had serious misgivings about this business (which was prospering), and worried endlessly during the early morning hours about his declining sexual powers. I might feel more comfortable about describing such an experience in terms of depressive affect, but I also know that so-called anxiety and depression are often companions.

To illustrate the second point: many years ago I treated a young attorney who complained of severe anxiety, and indeed his demeanor and facial expression were in total consonance with his complaint. He described a driven life style that was evident at least as early as his high school years, and had probably increased gradually in tempo since that time. Nonetheless, his activities were highly productive in several different ways: he had achieved national recognition in a special field of law; he was a prominent member of the bar association of the state in which he lived; he was active and recognized for a variety of civic and philanthropic activities; and he had made a great deal of money by applying his specialized legal knowledge to certain business situations in a wholly ethical and honest manner. Despite his considerable subjective suffering, his efforts to cope with his anxiety were instrumental in his highly productive life.

My thesis here is that clinical anxiety provides us little reason to treat it as a monolithic condition; on the contrary, it is fairly protean in its manifestations and effects, and is much more readily circumscribed by definition than by phenomenology. Even if we can agree on some definition of anxiety, the opportunity for observing it in "pure culture" in the clinical setting is minimal. "Pure culture" affects are probably rare, if they can be said to exist at all. Anxiety attacks may approach the concept, but even so, their "pure culture" state is usually transient. They tend to become attached to physical symptoms and merge into hypochondriasis, or to external objects, events, or ideas and merge into phobias; they are compounded by an overlay of shame and guilt, or become complicated by paranoid projections and delusion formation. Their vicissitudes are many, and their purity, questionable to begin with, is fleeting.

Since it is so much easier, both as subject and as observer, to discriminate between pleasurable affects and unpleasurable affects, I submit that this is where the theory of anxiety rests today. A theory of affects, of which class anxiety is one, must precede a theory of anxiety. Even if we accord anxiety a preeminent place among affects, the rationale for proceeding in this order can still be defended. You will recall that it was not possible to have a usable, consistent theory of repression until there was a more encompassing theory of defense, even though repression is certainly central to all defensive operations. With the publication of *The Ego and the Id* in 1923, the ego was accorded the role as "the seat of anxiety," and it continues to claim this distinction in present-day theory. I would like to extend this function to being "the seat of affect," of which anxiety is one example. The Ego is the psychological agency that perceives and attaches meaning to inner and outer stimuli, and it organizes, directs, and coordinates behavior prompted by such stimuli so that it is most advantageous to the person. Early in infancy, affects or feeling states are the automatic experiences that arise in the infant when needs which are strong enough to enter awareness are frustrated. Still helpless to take action to alleviate needs when they become intense, the small child experiences them as unpleasant feeling states and endures them until they are met by the mother. Pleasurable feelings automatically occur when needs are met by her. Unpleasant feeling states can only be signaled to her by his motor agitation and wailing. As his own Ego functions develop and he becomes increasingly able to take effective action on his own, feeling states associated with the build up of strong needs gradually become useful as signals that prompt him to take action. Hunger, a feeling state originally passively endured by the child until the mother fed him, now prompts him to seek her out and ask for food, or in later childhood, to find food for himself.

The affect of *anxiety* is assumed to be the original feeling state experienced when intense needs become so urgent that a state of painful, helpless tension develops. Gradually, fear, signaling a threat from an external danger, becomes distinguished from anxiety, which signals a threat from an internal danger. Although anxiety is conceptualized as the primary motive for defense, and the one which calls into play the unconscious defense mechanisms of the Ego, there are other familiar unpleasant feeling states against which the person attempts to defend himself by any means available. For the most part, these other feeling states (which are also experienced by the Ego) are mostly determined by the Superego. They include depression, shame, and guilt, unpleasant feelings with which we are all familiar.

Depression becomes the affect that signals actual or fantasied loss of love and approval. Around age 3 to 6 years, when the Superego is becoming a dependable inner psychological agency, the affects of guilt and shame become established. Guilt signals the threat of self-disapproval for acting or intending to act in ways at odds with the moral standards of the Superego—of being deemed bad and unworthy by one's own moral standards. *Shame,* closely related to guilt, signals the danger of being judged as foolish or inadequate in the eyes of others and of being ridiculed by them—or of appearing foolish in the eyes of oneself as when one feels "ashamed of himself." Thus, when the sensing functions of the Ego signal an impending loss of control over unconscious impulses, anxiety is experienced. When fantasied or real loss of love and approval is sensed as a consequence of such loss of control of unconscious impulses, depression is the signal. When the threat of humiliation and ridicule is sensed, shame is the signal.

The Ego may sense such impending threats before the dangerous impulse or urge is translated into action or even before it enters awareness. When that occurs, signal affects evoke Ego defenses to lessen the threat. In response to such signals, the mechanisms of defense are silently instituted. The person concerned is unaware that defenses are being called into play and has no knowledge of their purpose (5).

Infant observation and developmental studies suggest that undifferentiated pleasure-unpleasure affects precede the appearance of discrete affects with individual coloration. As psychic structure develops, shading of undifferentiated affect becomes possible through the association of ideational content. In the traditional scheme, anxiety calls forth defensive operations to protect against danger. Why should anxiety enjoy exclusive right to this role? I would like to suggest, in close parallel with Brenner (6), that anxiety does not in fact have a monopoly on the mobilization of defensive operations and hence the precipitation of conflict. It seems to me that all unpleasurable affects can, and sometimes do, function in this capacity, and that this is particularly true for depressive affects on an equal or nearly equal basis with anxiety. It is much more common nowadays to see patients with complaints of discontent, dissatisfaction with life, lack of fulfillment, emptiness, and disappointment, than it is to see patients who complain of some form of anxiety. A stripped-down definition of depressive affect would be unpleasure associated with the idea (conscious, unconscious, or both) that something bad has happened. Again, this is not to suggest that the depressive affects are unmixed any more than are the anxiety affects, but simply that they are of comparable importance in psychic life. The significance of this view in working with patients is that the therapist must be as much concerned with the patient's fantasies and experiences with bad things that have already happened as he is with bad things which the patient fears will happen. To illustrate this aspect of the clinical implications, in closing I shall present a brief vignette.

A young woman sought treatment for feelings of inadequacy that dated back to childhood. These feelings had waxed and waned over the years, but were unaccountably intensified following her marriage, and became severe shortly after the birth of her first child. For the preceding year, she had employed a scheme in which she plotted each day's activities carefully in advance, and wrote out on a sheet of paper designated times at which she would take a 5mg Dexedrine tablet. Each tablet was taken about 30 minutes before some duty or function she was expected to perform, and on some days she had taken as many as sixteen. Without her Dexedrine fuel she was inert, and even with it was unable to derive satisfaction from any of her activities.

In the course of her analysis, the patient achieved recognition of the fact that she had reacted to her miserable feelings of inadequacy as if they were her proper due, and that she had since childhood felt herself in a state of perpetual punishment. Further analytic work revealed that the patient had experienced an intense rivalry with her mother for the attention and love of the patient's father, and there was considerable evidence to suggest that the mother herself experienced equally intense rivalrous feelings toward the patient. When the patient was six years of age, her father developed a peritonitis from a ruptured appendix and died a few days later. Her grief was profound, and a sense of alienation, apparently mutual, developed between her and her mother. After the eventual passing of the grief reaction, the patient was left with feelings of inadequacy and worthlessness and an inability to derive much pleasure from anything. We were eventually able to get to her feelings of personal responsibility for her father's death, whom she felt had been taken away from her as a punishment because of her intense feelings of greed in wanting him for herself, along with her angry, hostile, and destructive feelings toward her mother. The fact that the mother played some role in the development and perpetuation of this fantasy was in part supported by the information that no intimacy ever again existed between mother and daughter following the father's death, and that the mother had remained cool, aloof, polite, and distant throughout all of the patient's growing-up and adult years.

While this is admittedly a sketchy comment on a long analysis, it serves to suggest that the patient was not troubled by what might happen, but rather was struggling with the punishment that had been levied many years earlier for her imagined crime.

Especially since 1926, but even before, anxiety has been regarded as the central problem in neurosis. I would simply recommend for your consideration the substitution of the term "unpleasurable affects" for the term "anxiety." We attempt to protect ourselves from unpleasurable affect of whatever kind, and I stress depressive affect in particular because of its universality. If we bear this in mind in our work with patients, there are dividends to be derived.

REFERENCES

1. Compton, A.: A study of the psychoanalytic theory of anxiety. II. Development in the theory of anxiety since 1926. *J. Am. Psychoanal. Assn.* 20:341-394, 1972.
2. Compton, A.: A study of the psychoanalytic theory of anxiety. I. The development of Freud's theory of anxiety. *J.Am. Psychoanal. Assn.* 20:3-44, 1972.
3. Freud, S.: Introductory lectures on psychoanalysis. SE 15,16 London, The Hogarth Press, 1963.
4. May, R.: *The Meaning of Anxiety.* New York, W.W. Norton & Co., Inc., 1977.
5. White, R., Gilliland, R.: *Elements of Psychopathology.* New York, Grune & Stratton, 1975.
6. Brenner, C.: *Psychoanalytic Technique and Psychic Conflict.* New York, International Universities Press, Inc. 1976.

CHAPTER 17

The Sullivanian Concept of Anxiety

Hilde Bruch

Anxiety is to Sullivan what libido is to Freud: the dynamic force that molds personality and determines whether we grow up mentally healthy or sick. Freud did not neglect the importance of anxiety. In his earliest formulations he conceived of it in quasi-physiological terms, as resulting from the damming up of the libido due to faulty sexual practices. Anxiety was subsequently related to internalized sexual conflicts. In contrast, Sullivan's definition of anxiety is entirely psychological; he conceives of it as resulting from the drop in well-being and self-esteem due to disturbances in the interaction with the human environment. Sullivan felt that an individual could not be conceived of as existing at any time in isolation. He emphasized that the human condition, by its very nature, was at all times a communal existence, and that all psychological development took place in interaction with others. He defined psychiatry as the study of interpersonal relations. He conceived of "immutable private" intrapsychic experiences as not accessible to observation by someone else. Even a person reporting about his inner life, including dreams and fantasies, transforms them by the process of communication from the absolutely private into something public. Only processes that take place in the interpersonal field are considered legitimate psychiatric observations.

Sullivan's contributions should be examined against the background of psychiatric and psychoanalytic thinking at the time when he formulated his most substantial innovations, the late 1920's and early 1930's. He was one of the early American psychoanalysts who was greatly appreciative of Freud's contributions, for having drawn attention to the fact that abnormal mental phenomena are capable of being understood, for having focused our interest on the individual person suffering from a mental disorder, and for having developed a therapeutic method. His own work with schizophrenics led him to disagree with certain of Freud's theoretical elaborations, but he retained most fundamental psychoanalytical concepts: that personality develops in stages from infancy to maturity, that mental processes take place within and outside of awareness, and that the specific patterns of an individual's style of experience are reenacted in the treatment situation.

Sullivan's essential innovation does not rest in his agreeing or disagreeing with one or the other aspects of psychoanalytic theory but in his knowingly employing a conceptual framework derived from development in modern physics according to which phenomena could no longer be explained as occurring in an isolated organism, according to deterministic, one cause/one effect mechanisms of old fashioned physics. This deterministic conceptual frame underlies classical psychoanalytical thinking. Sullivan stressed that the changes in scientific thinking which at that time had been formulated as field theory demanded changes in theoretical orientation, that human behavior could not be studied in terms of isolated events but had to be approached in terms of processes resulting from the interaction of multiple forces within the prevailing field. He dropped the whole psychoanalytic vocabulary and made great efforts to formulate his own observations in strictly defined scientific language.

The difference in the concept of anxiety is probably the clearest example of these changes. Just as Freud remained dissatisfied with all his efforts to formulate a fixed theory of instincts, so Sullivan remained critical of his efforts to define anxiety and how to integrate it into a theory. In a late paper (1948), he wrote: "Do not assume from this statement that you are about to hear 'the last word,' the solution of everything. I am bringing you nothing but a theory; a theory which, like every other theory, will doubtless undergo much improvement as the years pass" (1). There are countless statements and efforts at definition. It must be remembered that the books published under Sullivan's name are compilations of previously published papers or of lectures given over the course of many years. He felt it was important to differentiate anxiety from fear. "As felt experience, marked fear and uncomplicated anxiety are identical, that is, there is nothing in one's awareness of the discomfort which distinguishes the one from the other. Fear, as a significant factor in any situation, is often unequivocal. Anxiety, on the other hand, in anything like the accustomed circumstances of one's life, is seldom clearly represented as such in awareness." He goes on to explain that fear is related to some definable situation and is roughly the same for all people. "The significant pattern of situations which arouse anxiety is generally obscure; it can be almost infinitely varied among people; it shows much less, and very much less obvious, effects of habituation." Whereas with other tension states appropriate action can be taken to relieve them, this is not the case in anxiety. "The tension of anxiety and its congeries does not ensue in energy transformation directed to its relief by the removal of the situational factors obviously concerned in its provocation. Actions toward avoiding or minimizing anxiety certainly occur, but anxiety combines with other tensions only in opposition" (1).

I have quoted these few sentences to illustrate Sullivan's efforts to differentiate between anxiety and fear, and also the difficulties a student might encounter in grasping his exact meaning from various formulations. Yet in his basic thinking he was consistent and clear, that anxiety is a sign that one's self-esteem and self-regard is endangered and that all kinds of security operations are developed to avoid this unpleasant sensation.

THE INTERPERSONAL THEORY OF PERSONALITY DEVELOPMENT

Sullivan conceived of "personality" not as a static or stable entity but as an abstraction, referring to "the relatively enduring patterns of recurrent interpersonal situations which characterize the human life" (2). If these patterns change in significant ways, what is apparent as personality also changes. The organization and integration of such patterns begin practically at the moment of birth and signify the transformation of the newborn, the purely physiological human organism whom Sullivan calls "man the animal," into a person.

He considered the human neonate to be endowed with a viable physiological organization, which though immature has the full potential for mature adaptive development. The organization is, however, remarkably labile and therefore continuously subject to changes by experience. Individual biological differences were rated as relatively less important, and as becoming less and less clear-cut the further away from birth, in comparison to the paramount significance of interpersonal influences for the development of the personality.

In view of his immaturity and nearly total helplessness, the infant's survival depends on the administration of the "mothering one," to use Sullivan's expression. The fulfillment of the needs of the infant from birth on has two components. One is concerned with achievement of *satisfaction,* the relief of bodily tension, experienced as need for food, drink, warmth, sleep, and physical closeness. The other is the experience of a *sense of security,* which has to do with the need to feel accepted and approved by the person providing this relief. Without this sense of security, anxiety is experienced, a highly unpleasant, disruptive sensation that interferes with other pursuits and may stand in direct opposition to the satisfaction of concurrent needs. Avoidance of anxiety, or pursuit of security, is the important factor that shapes the personality, is involved with the development of the human potential in a cultural setting, and also in the development of self-esteem and the feeling that one enjoys the respect of the other person in a situation, and the assurance of competence in pursuing one's goals.

Sullivan considered anxiety in mild doses as "functionally effective" and a necessary part of normal human development, a prerequisite for acquiring control over one's biological needs and for acquiring the habits of social living. Sullivan was critical of permissive schools for "nicely cheating their charges of the experiences in social accommodation absolutely necessary for untroubled opportunity to amount to something socially useful in later years" (3). Excessive anxiety, caused by harshness and contradictory stimulation, makes for disturbed development that becomes manifest in the various forms of mental illness. In its extreme state it calls into being what is called "uncanny emotions," chilly crawling sensations, periods of horror and dread. This type of severe anxiety is entirely disruptive of functioning, making the individual unable to learn or even to stay in rapport. There are various degrees of seriousness; quite early in life anxiety becomes labeled "to be avoided," but often it cannot be escaped, since interpersonal entanglements usually persist. The need to maintain security is so important that only those patterns of behavior develop that succeed in avoiding anxiety. Only those processes that have this effect become integrated inso the symbolic organization and make up the mental processes which are in awareness.

Sullivan postulated that this integration of experiences occurs in different modes, depending on the state of maturity and the quality of the interpersonal relatedness, whereby severe anxiety and also fatigue may be interfering factors. The earliest mode of experience, the least elaborate form, with the infant not yet feeling differentiated from others, and without any verbal representation, was called the *prototaxic* mode. Later in life, this mode is found only during marked disturbances, the uncanny component of terror states.

Experiences from about three or four months on, persisting until the third year of life and beyond, are made in the *parataxic* mode. This is also the time of earliest language learning, which is still to a large extent autistic and magical in its application. Though with increasing maturity this mode is superseded, parataxic components can be recognized in many and various manifestations later in life, particularly during mental disturbances.

The next level is represented by what Sullivan called the *syntaxic* mode of experience which is capable of "consensual validation," whereby events and meanings are checked with others, so that what one observes and experiences is brought in agreement with that of others. Thus mutually understandable communication is established. Mature and rational assessments of events and interactions with others occur in this mode. A large part of therapy is taken up with recognizing and correcting parataxic distortions that interfere with realistic self-appraisal of events and of oneself in relation to others.

The earliest experiences are not susceptible to later recall, and knowledge about the inner experiences of infants rests at best on inferences, though these earliest experiences leave a lasting impact on the developing personality. Practically from birth on, the infant, in an unknown way for which Sullivan used the term "empathy," perceives the feeling tone of the mother, and becomes anxious when she is tense and upset; and the way the mother performs her tasks thereby has an effect on shaping his personality. Her ways of handling him are an expression of her own personality, but also of socially and culturally patterned attitudes. The mother herself does not live in isolation, and persons other than the mother exert an influence on the infant long before they enter into direct interpersonal relation to him.

If satisfaction is attained through relaxed warm tenderness, it is associated with a feeling of well-being and security, and the child will grow up relatively free from the restricting effects of anxiety. But if the mother is tense and anxious when handling the child, anxiety is induced in him and this may interfere with his needs for satisfaction, and conflictual situations develop. The inner conceptualization of when things are relaxed and peaceful will become that of "good mother," whereas when contact arouses anxiety and discomfort, the personification will be that of "bad mother." The "mother" about which a patient reports will reflect these early integrations and may bear little resemblance to the real mother.

Only those expressions of a person's actions, motivations, thoughts, desires and drives that meet with approval from significant people and thus do not provoke the disintegration experience of anxiety develop within range of awareness, mature, and become capable of rational usage. This part of the personality experienced as "I" or "myself" represents the *self*. Sullivan referred to it as the "self system" or "self dynamism," since it has a functional existence—that of screening the permissible and approved from the forbidden and disapproved. Everybody develops a sort of tubular vision early in life, surrounded by an aura of anxiety that excludes and distorts: what is outside its field is noticed only in a vague and foggy way, or not at all. In the inner integration of one's self-concept, that which is associated with a sense of security becomes personified as "good me"; those aspects that are still within awareness but are labeled as disapproved become "bad me," to be held in check or concealed. Those impulses, feelings, and needs that arouse severe anxiety remain completely outside of awareness, and are disassociated and experienced as "not me." However, they are not nonexistent but are expressed in many unwitting acts and unconscious motivations that interfere with the rational and mature conduct of one's life.

The self, then, is not an inborn tendency or a static trait that comes suddenly into existence. It is the dynamic functional capacity to view and deal with others that has developed out of the interaction with significant people. In a way, it is not original with the individual but is "reflective appraisal" by others. Sullivan described the self as "the content of consciousness at all times when one is thoroughly comfortable about one's self respect, the prestige that one enjoys among one's fellows, and the respect and deference which they pay one. Under these estimable circumstances there is no anxiety" (1).

This is what happens under fortunate circumstances, when the self has developed with a wide range of possibilities and only few aspects of the personality are disassociated. If, however, a child has been exposed from earliest infancy on to the influences of harsh and mechanical training, without consistent attention to his needs, the self dynamism will develop into a harsh and rigid instrument, hemmed in by anxiety at every step, excluding from awareness corrective and broadening experiences essential for healthy progress of personality growth.

Under certain unfortunate conditions, a development Sullivan called the "malevolent transformation of personality" takes place. If expressions of need for tenderness have frequently been rebuffed or ridiculed, then manifestations of the need for tenderness come to be associated with anticipation of pain and anxiety. Instead of showing his need for tenderness, such a child will manifest behavior characteristic of his "bad me" component, something that provokes unpleasantness. The most common manifestation will be a tendency to tear everybody down and then to become anxious. Such a person will always feel surrounded by enemies, and show paranoid traits as time progresses.

Sullivan elaborated in great detail the significance and possible vicissitudes of interpersonal experiences during infancy and early childhood. He also recognized the importance of the entire childhood development, the long-continued influence of perplexing and contradictory interpersonal relationships, and also the absence or presence of corrective experiences. Sullivan stressed the great importance of the interpersonal experiences during the juvenile era. If conditions are favorable, the growing child may have the experience of intimacy and closeness with one particular friend. This experience of intimacy in preadolescence, before sexual urgency and pressing realities of life begin to complicate the picture, is of crucial significance for emerging from the family bonds and developing a more realistic and competent self-concept. The quality of these experiences determines to a large extent the way an individual will be able to meet the tasks of adolescence. Under favorable circumstances, old and restrictive patterns and their association with anxiety will be reevaluated. If at this stage the adolescent's insight and awareness are broadened, the danger of the personality solidifying into permanent patterns of maladjustment may be prevented.

Psychotherapeutic Implications

Applied to treatment, the term "interpersonal" has often been misinterpreted as implying treatment by environmental or behavioristic manipulations, or even by getting personally involved with patients, and as neglecting the investigation of inner psychological processes. This formulation is incorrect. Sullivan's emphasis throughout his work is on the *inner* component of any event or experience. Anxiety, though "interpersonally induced," is so important because it affects the way experiences are internalized and conceptualized.

Sullivan conceived of the therapeutic interaction as a particular kind of interpersonal relationship that differed from other intimate relationships by its purpose—namely, that "something useful" should be accomplished for the patient. The role of the therapist is defined as that of a *participant observer* who possesses particular skills in the evaluation of the interpersonal processes (4).

Sullivan's emphasis was on how to achieve clarification of the underlying disturbances; he was quite specific in describing how to go about this business, how to look and where to look, but without emphasis on what one would find, which he expected to differ from one individual to the other. The main guide during the therapeutic inquiry is recognition of signs and indications of anxiety; the first signs may be mild, in anticipation of more severe anxiety. What the psychiatrist observes is that the patient is doing something that disorders the situation. He might become angry because most people who are even faintly anxious are apt to get angry. Next to anger, the most frequent move to avoid anxiety is to develop some misunderstanding through what Sullivan called "selective inattention." Other minor manifestations of anxiety are changes in the quality of the voice, change of topic, or just stopping. If these moves fail, a person may experience severe anxiety and then becomes incapable of any constructive or useful communication. Therefore the therapist must be alert to the minor forms of anxiety and focus with the patient on the situations that arouse it. In this way the underlying problems become susceptible to clarification. The therapist's skillful attention to what is going on gives the patient some hint of what psychiatry is able to do.

By definition a patient is insecure and will be concerned with his prestige in the eyes of the therapist. Often he will not be able to be simply frank and to describe what he feels. The chief handicap to communication is anxiety. The psychiatrist's expertise is his ability to avoid unnecessary anxiety by not arousing it, as for example through premature confrontation with painful issues or by actions to restrain its development. Even when one proceeds carefully, situations develop in which a patient will feel tense and uncertain. Anxiety is always a handicap to adjustment and a block to communication. Its appearance in the psychiatric session is not necessarily a reflection on the psychiatrist's lack of skill. Usually the patient's background has ingrained him with the necessity to avoid particular topics. Evasions too are part of established patterns of reaction. It is important that the psychiatrist does not consider them to be offensive or deliberately misleading, but to be something that a patient's background has deeply ingrained in him. The psychiatrist's irritation with a patient's evasiveness reduces the possibility of clarifying the situation.

Even a composed-appearing, polite, and cooperative patient may be quite anxious and therefore unable to follow complex explanations during the early part of treatment. Something that appears clear to the therapist may be completely misunderstood and immediately disassociated by the patient. If one has made an important observation, it should be conveyed with a minimum of words. Sullivan thought little of explicit reassurance, which he felt often does not amount to more than reassuring verbalisms, attempts by the therapist to do magic with language; usually it is a matter of the therapist reassuring himself rather than the patient.

In many ways the therapist presents a new point of view or a different opinion on many things that have troubled the patient throughout life. The more sensitive the psychiatrist is to situations that arouse anxiety and that he then can clarify, the smoother the interview will progress. Much more useful than direct questions, which often produce severe anxiety or blocking, are indirect questions composed of running comments, additions, or corrections, implying what he wants to know, or suggesting the information desired. It is necessary to proceed by steps within the grasp of the patient so that he feels that he knows what the therapist is driving at and talking about. In this way information can be obtained without arousing too much anxiety.

If a patient becomes acutely anxious, then he needs help out of this particular situation and it becomes necessary to postpone discussion of the particular topic and make an abrupt transition. Sullivan stressed in particular that one should not let a patient get into severe anxiety toward the end of a session.

The therapeutic investigation is primarily concerned with clarification of the context of the established patterns. Patient and therapist begin with mutually unknown assumptions and proceed to reach mutually validated conclusions. The patient brings into the therapeutic situation his habitual patterns of living, preconceptions, and fantasies, and the therapeutic investigation is primarily concerned with clarification of the context of the established patterns. Sullivan considered it advisable to study some current situation, outside of treatment, to find out the precise patterns of the ongoing difficulties. Only then should one attempt to clarify whether and how the same patterns manifest themselves in relation to more significant people, and in particular in relation to the therapist.

A precondition for the therapist to function effectively as a participant observer is that he be aware of his own actions, reactions, and feelings. He should be alert to any situation or process that arouses uneasiness in him, or to impulses that interfere with his objectivity. Such sensitive attention to one's own feelings is a helpful guide to further inquiry and thus to successful resolution of a patient's problems.

A common manifestation of anxiety is a patient's talking about everything but the problem that most concerns him. To find out what the problem is, the therapist needs to become alerted at the point at which anxiety makes its appearance. One will observe that a patient veers away from certain topics and thus strongly suggests the general area of the problem. A remark such as "it is obviously difficult for you to discuss this topic" markedly reduces the anxiety. If the patient agrees with this comment, the next question will be what is so difficult about it. The main goal of treatment is to work toward uncovering those factors that are concerned in a person's recurrent mistakes, and that lead to his taking ineffective and inappropriate action. As Sullivan expressed it, there is no necessity to do more (3).

An expression of this alert attention to anxiety is continuous consideration for a patient's particular sensitivities and low self-esteem. Sullivan was meticulous about being respectful to the individuality of each patient, and warned against calling behavior "immature" or "childish." In particular, tact was needed to discourage a patient from showing himself as overconforming when agreeing with the therapist. Annoying, irritating, and "hostile" expressions need to be respected as signaling severe underlying anxiety or a conviction of inner worthlessness. Sullivan's basic humanistic approach was probably best revealed by his speaking of people whose whole development had been distorted by their conviction of their inner badness as "we are all more human than otherwise."

REFERENCES

1. Sullivan, H.S. *The Fusion of Psychiatry and Social Science* (reprints of papers from 1934-1949). Introduction and commentaries by H.S. Perry. New York: Norton, 1964.
2. Bruch, H. Interpersonal theory: Harry Stack Sullivan. In A. Burton, ed., *Operational Theories of Personality*. Brunner/Mazel, 1974.
3. Sullivan, H.S. *The Psychiatric Interview*, H.S. Perry and M.L. Gawel, eds New York: Norton, 1953.
4. Bruch, H. Participant observation. *Contemp. Psychoanal.* 13:347-350, 1977.

ADDITIONAL READING:

1. *Schizophrenia as a Human Process* (reprints of papers from 1924-1935). Introduction and commentaries by H.S. Perry. New York: Norton, 1962.
2. *Personal Psychopathology: Early Formulations* (ca. 1932). New York: Norton, 1972.

3. *Conceptions of Modern Psychiatry.* The First William Alanson White Memorial Lectures, *Psychiatry* 3:1-117, 1940. Republished New York: Norton, 1953.
4. *The Interpersonal Theory of Psychiatry.* H.S. Perry and M.L. Gawel, eds. New York: Norton, 1953.
5. *Clinical Studies in Psychiatry.* H.S. Perry, M.L. Gawel, and M. Gibbon, eds. New York: Norton, 1956.

CHAPTER 18

Anxiety as It Relates to "Success Phobia": Developmental Considerations

David W. Krueger

INTRODUCTION

"So much the more surprising, indeed bewildering, must it appear when as a physician one makes the discovery that people occasionally fall ill precisely because a deeply rooted and long cherished wish has come to fulfillment" (1). This observation by Freud that the unconscious forces that induce illness when success is obtained is integrally connected with the Oedipus complex has been substantiated and illustrated by other analytic authors since Freud (2-4). Psychopathology as it relates to performance and "success"—specifically the work inhibition created by anxiety which takes the form of a "success phobia"—is examined in this paper. Attention has been given in the literature to Oedipal-level pathology as the etiologic foundation of inhibition of a final step of success or completion. This paper will consider the developmental aspects of anxiety as they relate to performance and success, will expand the consideration of dynamic and genetic material which results in the manifestation of a "success phobia" from primarily Oedipal to those cases in which the pathology is at the level of separation-individuation issues, and will offer differentiating aspects based on clinical examples. The importance of the role of ego development in the evolution of the anxiety affect with specific manifestations in success phobia and the importance of a developmental diagnosis in analytic psychotherapy will be primary themes.

DEVELOPMENTAL ASPECTS OF ANXIETY

Anxiety has been defined as "the response of the ego to a traumatic situation or danger, present or anticipated" (5). A danger situation is one in which helplessness is anticipated; a traumatic situation is one in which helplessness occurs or is experienced (6). Real (normal or objective) anxiety is a reaction to an external danger that is proportionate to the objective threat and does not involve intrapsychic conflict or regression, thus not requiring neurotic defense mechanisms for its management. Neurotic anxiety is a reaction disproportionate to the objective danger, involving intrapsychic conflict and regression, and therefore requiring neurotic defense mechanisms that eventuate in the development of symptoms so that the neurotic anxiety may be managed (7).

Brenner (8) states that "anxiety occupies a special position in mental life, as it is the motive for defense"; Brenner functionally defines anxiety as "the unpleasure associated with a particular set of ideas, namely that something bad is going to happen." The "something bad" may have different meanings for each patient, and the ideational content and developmental history of this affect are crucial in diagnostic and therapeutic work. Affective life is an integral part of the developmental process, and particular components of affective life, especially those of adaptation, significantly influence ego development. Anxiety must be scrutinized as any other mental event would be, especially in those cases in which symptomatology relating to anxiety plays a major role developmentally.

A phobia, a specific form of anxiety in which the ego defends itself by an inhibition of function or the avoidance of a dangerious situation (4), is a symbolic projection and displacement of unacceptable sexual or aggressive urges that have been repressed, usually due to unconscious fear of castration. The phobic idea or thought is basically a mental representation of intimidation (9). The phobic thought consists of an image, the origin of which is usually external, or violence toward one's self (as in Little Hans [10]).

Anxiety proceeds from primitive to higher levels as the ego develops; fear of annihilation progresses to fear of loss of the object, to fear of loss of love, to castration anxiety and finally to fear of the superego. The assessment of success phobia must be considered in the overall picture of the degree of ego integration and strength, including both developmental and descriptive diagnoses. The therapeutic function of psychodynamic reconstruction and working through is predicated on the differentiation and developmental understanding of the psychodynamic picture manifesting as success phobia. The content, origin, and functional role of each of the mental events of affect, behavior, and cognition must be determined in an analytic way from a patient's associations, behavior, and history. The developmental diagnosis of the anxiety component of success phobia as being either at the Superego-castration anxiety developmental level or at the earlier loss of love or object

level, with separation anxiety and separation-individuation being paramount, is an extremely important task of differentiation for appropriate
diagnosis and effective treatment.

SUCCESS PHOBIA: OEDIPAL ISSUES

The vicissitudes of the Oedipal situation, involving in boys the fear of
castration by the father and in girls the fear of angry abandonment by the
mother, serve as an important impetus in the inhibition or avoidance of
success with the opposite-sexed parent. The determinant of the formation of
this conflict in boys into manifest symptomatology, and specifically into
inhibition of success in vocation or work performance, is the inability to
tolerate surpassing the father. The unconscious equation of this with
patricide, and its associated sense of guilt and fear of retaliation, culminate in
a protective self-imposed defeat. To succeed would be perceived unconsciously as murderous retaliation or violence, linked developmentally with earlier
rivalries between a child and a parent. A situation that intensifies Oedipal
fears involves alienation between parents such that the child can win the
parent of the opposite sex away from the other parent. This may occur when
one or both parents is narcissistic, when attempts at individuation are stifled
by a parent, or when a parent is psychologically or physically absent.

Ovesey (11) demonstrates the specificity of the manifestation of
Oedipally based success phobia and the presence of physical intimidation. In
those cases where there is physical intimidation either from a parent, usually
the father, or from a sibling, there is reinforcement of the unconscious
equation between success on one side and aggression and violence on the
other. The desire, usually unconscious, for the destruction of a powerful rival
or intimidator generates both guilt and fear of equally violent retaliation,
resulting in the inhibition or the withholding of aggression. This inhibition of
aggression and violence is then extended in application to assertion in
general. The phobic extension of the conflict is an inhibition of assertion. Any
subsequent competition is identified unconsciously with the original rivalries
of childhood and is extended to vocational success, which is unconsciously
perceived as retaliatory murder of the competitors, invoking guilt and,
ultimately, the inhibition of aggression. The view by Freud and succeeding
analysts that success phobia, conceptualized in terms of psychic energy and
instinct, as derived from Oedipal sexual success and ensuing guilt is extended
by Ovesey's considerations of adaptational dynamics in which physical
intimidation by parent or sibling adds to the inhibition of aggression. An
atmosphere of physical violence or hostile competition results in the
anticipation of attack or retaliation by others.

This inhibition of aggression undermines self-confidence and esteem and
results in a chronic feeling of inadequacy. If abusive or violent behavior by the
parent becomes a reality in the sense of *actual* retaliation, that reality assumes

the characteristics of a traumatic neurosis when the reality for the child of weakness and helplessness is inescapable.

Assertion, through its unconscious equation with success, is defended by a passivity in which the objective of success-striving is abandoned, substituted, or distorted in some way. It is not the wish or preference to fail, yet failing before the final step of success is equated unconsciously with the position of passivity and safety, thus sparing one the danger of the possible consequences of retribution and retaliation in asserting one's self. The central conflict is the fear to be and act as a full-fledged man because the powerful father is seen as a prohibitive and threatening force who does not approve of erotic feelings because of their incestuous aim and who would punish their expression (3). The later derivatives of anxiety on "exposing" one's self in business and social situations result in the expectation of catastrophe as a product of these efforts. The final step or passageway into successful completion of a task (promotion, graduation, etc.) causes manifestation of anxiety by strong unconscious forces, and the fear of retaliation ultimately is given ascendancy.

While anxiety about homosexuality may reflect true homosexual panic (homosexual object arousal), it may in some cases reflect a nonsexual issue such as a fear of success. Acute anxiety accompanying the idea or thought that one is homosexual may occur in those who never have had an experience of homosexual arousal. This phenomenon, referred to as pseudohomosexuality (12), involves conflict around issues of dependency or power, with the homosexual act or thought being the confession of masculine failure resulting from the concretization of the need to stop short of success and thus fail, based on neurotic needs. In work-related matters, the anxiety reaction that may be precipitated by a promotion involving money, status, or some other particular success may be equated with an Oedipal conflict with an unconscious expectation of retaliation manifesting as a fear of attack for successful performance (13). To ensure safety from this retaliation, the desired goal may be relinquished, and accompanying that surrender, the self-image of masculinity is given up as well. The threatened loss of heterosexual aspirations and of masculinity manifests as a homosexual fear.

The characterological resolution of the success phobia may be the belief that staying in the background guarantees safety and will not reveal weaknesses or inadequacies. The fear of being discovered to be an impostor is a common element in success phobia; therefore, with the greater success comes the potentially harder fall. Being viewed from without as highly competent is often coupled with the internal feeling of being incompetent, inadequate, or an impostor. The rationalized lowering of one's ambition is the stepping back from the anxiety-provoking success situation. With this step backward, a depression usually develops, the reaction to a loss reverberating with the past loss of an important object (mother), and the concomitant revisiting of self-esteem issues.

Case I

S.L. is a 34-year-old man who presented with chronic anxiety punctuated by marital stress in which his wife threatened to leave him should he not complete the Ph.D. thesis on which he had been working for four years. The patient observed that he had been on the brink of completing this thesis, involving a specialty area of mathematics, for the last two and a half years but had not yet finished. He consciously desired to do the work and to succeed, but he experienced an underlying feeling of incompetence as if "programmed so that I shouldn't succeed." He had psychotherapy twice during the past three years, and both times he prematurely terminated. S.L. elaborated on the struggles he had had with his thesis supervisor, seeing him as an authority figure who capriciously and arbitrarily decided what should and should not be done regarding the thesis. The patient consequently felt insecure and incompetent, believing that he would never be the equal of the supervisor, and he would not risk exposure of his incompetence by completion of the thesis.

Early transferential perceptions of the therapist as a controlling authority are illustrated by the patient's request to be given tasks to do, to be "reprogrammed," and to have a more active "behavior modification" therapy, one in which we would "actively grapple" with the issues at hand.

S.L. felt much bitterness about his father's authoritarianism and his need to control, exemplified by the memory of the father never allowing the patient to express any views or facts that would contradict him. The patient viewed his not succeeding in school as a way of expressing anger and getting back at his father. In scrutinizing more closely the failure to succeed, he noted that he would get to the point of success, become scared, and pull back, wanting commiseration or sympathy with his plight. His association to this sequence was that if he were to get in an argument with his father now, as he now had much more education, he would "destroy" the father in an argument, which would be unacceptable because of his love for the father.

The father had often helped with the patient's homework, insisting that it be done perfectly. If the homework was not done perfectly, the father would become angry and vindictive, accusing the patient of not trying, but forcing him to continue. When he asked the father questions about other tasks, the patient felt that he never asked the right things, that he was not supposed to ask questions of the father since he would either get mad or not answer. This aspect was re-created vividly by transference phenomenon around direct questioning of the therapist's "technique," evaluation of the patient, and demands to know who was in control of his treatment.

S.L. had begun to consider leaving his academic position as well as permanently scrapping plans for his thesis completion, and as an alternative, amassing wealth, consciously equated with power. The underlying equation that gradually became more apparent in treatment was the unconscious connection of success in completing the thesis with aggression and the concomitant guilt with the retreat to depression and sympathy elicitation as a protection. The angry and murderous fantasies S.L. as a little boy had toward his father became conscious; the necessity of stopping short of completion of the final action came to seem obviously adaptive. The loss of self-esteem and depression followed from the concluding belief that stopping short of success or of completion meant inadequacy and ineptness. A success was seen as "getting away with something," which created feelings of vulnerability and fear (i.e., guilt). S.L.'s protection from retaliation was to avoid the outcome of success (aggression). This therapeutic work can be illustrated by an acting-out episode:

The patient had begun an affair at a point midway in treatment. He chose a married woman whose husband was out of town for two months; she was essentially unattainable for marriage, so that ultimate success was safely eluded. This affair resulted in impotence accompanied by an intense feeling of inadequacy, combined with the fear that if his wife were to find out, "all hell would break loose." The affair with this woman occurred at a time when her husband was out of town but would be returning, ending the affair. This was associated by the patient with the giving up of freedom and closeness with his mother upon his father's return from hunting trips. The hunting trips were anticipated eagerly by the patient, since he felt a special warmth in having all his mother's attention at these times. His feelings were projected onto the mother, whom he perceived as "having more freedom" at these times. The common ending of "it doesn't matter any more" upon his father's return was the attitude that prevailed just before a task was left undone when success or completion was imminent.

The father, seen as an awesome and threatening force, was viewed as someone who would punish the expression of erotic feelings for their incestuous intent; these were inhibited. The fear of succeeding—rationalized by S.L. as a fear of failing, as it was associated with physical and emotional intimidation—resulted in a retreat to safety and passivity. The later expectation of catastrophe as a result of academic success resulted in assurance of safety and passivity by stopping short of "exposure," thereby precluding success.

The focus extended at this point in treatment to depression caused by his feelings of incompetency and to broader issues of dissatisfaction with his life. His feeling of inadequacy was exemplified by his inability to urinate when other people were present. The feeling of "not wanting to be exposed" permeated not only his professional but his personal life as well. His performance in schoolwork, athletics, and relationships was seen as involvement only to a degree, never complete. One solution to his struggle was to plan more than he possibly could accomplish, certain to forestall completion, yet just as certain to perpetuate his sense of inadequacy. S.L. fantasized about having fights with his father in which he would "smash him" or argue with him and win; these fantasies were associated with the expectation of some disaster or failure that would reveal his incompetence. The father would vigorously compete with the patient to establish his superiority and to express his desire that the patient do things better. This intimidation resulted in the patient's feeling helpless in the face of overwhelming anger toward his father. Expression of his feelings was associated with being overwhelmed and out of control, or alternatively, with being "trampled on."

The obsessive behavior and the fear of success were traced to childhood struggles for power with the father, with the ensuing rage being unconsciously projected as a fantasied threat of violent retaliation combined with the realistic violence and threat of more violence in often-repeated intimidation of the patient by the father. The development of affects and their expression was thwarted by the patient's authoritarian family, who created the expectation of danger.

S.L. had the pervading wish to acquire money and material possessions, which he equated with independence and power, unconsciously warding off the revisitation of the helpless, traumatized state in childhood when he was the object of aggression and felt powerless to do anything about it, unconsciously associated as well with murderous retaliation from the father. Any of these successes were thus associated with the prohibition against acquiring something that was not deserved, (the guilt of) an Oedipal victory.

The expectation of angry retaliation by the father, either physically or verbally, and its unconscious extension to success in academic pursuits and accomplishments were in a working-through phase when the patient was able to complete the thesis. The patient was able also to complete some scientific papers he had abandoned just before their completion.

SUCCESS PHOBIA: SEPARATION-INDIVIDUATION ISSUES

The mental mechanism of symbolic displacement terminating in phobic avoidance is a theme that may vary markedly in developmental history and psychodynamic pattern. The anxiety derived indirectly from the repressed sexual wish is not the exclusive underlying dynamic of the manifestation of success phobia, as the following cases will demonstrate. This does not mean that there is an absence of sexual motivation or of Oedipal features, which are ubiquitously present at some degree and level in all patients, but that Oedipal issues are not the motivating psychopathological force in all success phobias.

The developmental impediments to individual maturation based on separation-individuation issues may present as "success phobia," with descriptive aspects similar initially to Oedipal impediments but with very different dynamic and genetic material. The following cases will illustrate the differentiation of adaptational and intrapsychic organization which expand the view of success phobia to considerations of the developmental line of separation-individuation.

Case 2

N.D. is a 25-year-old medical student whose onset of anxiety occurred prior to a planned graduation from medical school. He had postponed his completion by deciding to take an extra year of electives at the point when he entered therapy. He experienced marked anxiety about success both in relationships with women and in professional functioning. He defended himself against this anxiety by stopping short, never fully completing a task, then taking an extended vacation, after which he would gradually and with much anxiety begin again to engage in the previously avoided task. This anxiety took an obsessional quality in that he questioned himself about whether he really wanted to be a doctor and whether he really loved the female currently in his life. His goal at the beginning of therapy was to "feel more complete as an individual" and to "find the one thing missing in my life . . . something I can commit myself to."

He previously had less pervasive anxiety episodes at the beginning of college and with the initiation of his first clinical rotation in medical school. He experienced both anxiety and depression at the termination of three relationships with women over the previous six years. The relationships were of marked similarity and importance; his wish for an ideal woman was captured by numerous long extemporations on the qualities of an ideal woman. With each of the relationships, he was unable to get involved completely, as he would compare the current relationship to the past and find the current woman falling short in some particular way of the last woman, who was idealized.

Transference phenomena re-created the wish that the therapist, as well as the current woman in his life and his attending resident on a clerkship, would direct and supportively gratify him in the same way his mother had done. Mother was presented as a woman who was overprotective of the patient to the degree that she sheltered him from any concerns and day-to-day worries by taking care of any problems herself so that the patient would not be troubled by them. The patient was a student of unusual promise and brilliance throughout high school, but when deprived of his mother's direction and supportive gratification while away from home, he desperately sought substitution for this narcissistic functioning by her in women whom the patient idealized, yet later denigrated as they were seen at some unconscious level as not quite as good as his mother. He felt he was not able to get completely involved with any (other) woman. This lack of commitment lest he fail and reveal weakness, inadequacy, and deficits pervaded the patient's relationships as well as his work.

The panic at the approaching graduation was associated with being alone, frightened, not in control, and wishing to have someone with him both for companionship and for support in clinical situations. He expended great energy in being sure he was "covered" by an intern or resident, and the anxiety about functioning independently was exacerbated secondarily by difficulty with memory and with concentration, confirming his view that he did not have the capacity to function independently. His association to his mother's anticipating his needs and his reliance on her functioning for years eventuated in the belief that he was not capable of self-reliance and that the answer to his problems always resided in another person. Envy of idealized attending physicians or fellow students regarding their competence and dedication was heightened at times of stress. His reliance on others for direction and his own lack of initiative and direction were rationalized as laziness.

The fantasy of being the only physician in charge of an emergency and the feelings of panic and helplessness associated with his perceived ability to know how to begin effective treatment and his need to anxiously call for help served as a retardant to more independent pursuits. The anxiety that he would be alone and without support seemed an awesome abandonment to N.D.

The transference expectation that the therapist would do things for him—e.g., make interpretations to the exclusion of the patient's putting together even obvious connections in deference to his waiting for the therapist to do it—was scrutinized as a part of this same process. His rationalization for the wish to be "given" insight and interpretation, thus effectively having the work done for him, was that the therapist was more capable, had more training, and was able to do it better.

The mourning for this past position of gratification is illustrated by the sadness experienced as N.D. became involved in treating a resident's wife who had a terminal illness. The recognition that "there is only so much someone else can do" captured his frustrated wish for gratification from others. As he was able to mourn the past position of narcissistic gratification, the current wish for those "supplies," N.D. increasingly was able to experience and to differentiate regressive security and security based on mastery and accomplishment. Accomplishment by his own efforts, previously meticulously avoided, could now be accepted and be effectively dealt with as a fear of success based on the equation of success and autonomy.

Case 3

K.V. is a 30-year-old married man with a Ph.D. in a science field. He presented for therapy with anxiety and depression after being offered a position at a university as head of the division in his science specialty. He reported his anxiety as beginning the day he was offered the new position. He began to experience increasing anxiety, becoming more and more uncertain that he could do the job, although wanting the position very much and having consciously striven for this success for many years. His thoughts included: "Am I as good as I think I am?" His ruminations included a lack of confidence about being able to handle a division on his own and an uncertainty of his ability to carry out independent research. He noted that he felt safe and secure in his present position, which he saw as being unpressured and in which he was comfortably dependent on a senior faculty investigator. He reported that since the new job offer, he had had difficulty concentrating and was losing motivation and interest in his current work, as well as feeling anxious and depressed. He began to think about giving up his work completely, wondering if he was "cut out to do work like this at all." He noted that he was not a competitive person and that "if you can't compete, you might as well pack up your bags and leave." He reported thoughts such as these when he was most anxious about the potential move and responsibility.

As he reflected on similar difficulties in the past, K.V. noted that he had never taken anything to completion, had always stopped just short of success. His backing away as success was imminent subserved the anxiety, which heightened as a completion neared. His first major anxiety episode came when he finished graduate school and began his first position of postgraduate work. At that time he experienced similar symptoms of inability to concentrate, feelings of inadequacy and "dumbness," and a general concern that he could not function well. K.V. had a brief psychiatric hospitalization at that time and then returned to live with his wife's parents for a few months, relinquishing his post-doctoral fellowship. Upon his decision to forgo the post-doctoral fellowship, his symptoms abated. As he took another position, anxiety again became manifest, but he was able to overcome the anxiety as he viewed the position as "sheltered" and directly under someone's supervision. K.V. functioned in this situation for several years until the job offer which crystallized his current symptomatology occurred.

He immediately began preparing his wife for his declining the new offer, resulting in marked protest by her. K.V. and his wife previously had been in marital therapy in which the patient was observed to have developed, according to his therapist, a transference of a "symbiotic relationship with a parent" with his wife and had subsequent difficulties in the marriage with making decisions. K.V.'s rationalization for declining the new position, evolving from his unconscious belief that any major success would be concomitant with disaster, was the anticipation of his wife's leaving him were he to accept the new position.

Dr. V.'s childhood memories reconstructed an idealized and overprotective mother who "did everything for me." He recalled instances in which she did things he could have easily done for himself. He noted one instance in which she even wrote a paper for him for a school assignment. He remarked that he seldom had to do any work and that he did not have to do anything he did not want to do, resulting in a lack of initiative in many areas except studying.

Dr. V. noted the difficulty, especially in times of crisis, in differentiating his own feelings from those he perceived to be of his wife, particularly regarding the wish to, and simultaneous fear of, moving to assume the new position. He had additional doubts about his ability to function should his wife leave him. His dependence on her for many aspects of decision-making, as well as his anxiety about functioning well if separated from his wife, were manifest in both past history and present concern.

The focus of K.V.'s concern about the new job centered around doubts of his ability to initiate ideas and carry them to completion, since having his own department and laboratory was associated with independence rather than with working under direct supervision. Anxiety and waning confidence, concomitant with this step toward autonomy, ushered in critical self-scrutiny, with the feeling that proper evaluation would have precluded the offer of the more responsible position: K.V. saw himself as a fake or as an impostor. The neurotic conclusion established by K.V. was that he remain in his current position. This conclusion introduced associations of doing things in childhood in which he would "just get by" and of other times in which his mother would assume responsibilities and functions; this was illustrated by an association to a paper route his mother would handle for him if the patient did not wish to deliver papers on a particular day.

K.V. reported a dream that further illustrates this issue: he was both driving a car and standing beside a bridge observing traffic. He observed that the bridge was incomplete and that each passing car would fall off, toppling into oblivion. Just as he observed himself driving the car and approaching the bridge, he became tired and allowed the female passenger to drive. Upon the switch of drivers, the woman noted the condition of the bridge and remarked on having narrowly escaped disaster. K.V.'s association to this dream was of his mother's taking over many functions and tasks for him. He associated stopping on the bridge just prior to disaster with stopping short of completion in order to avoid imminent catastrophe.

As the patient began to examine and work through more characterologic dependency positions and his underlying wish to have things done for him, which resulted in his avoidance of a task, defending the fear that he was not adequate to accomplish the task, he was increasingly able to scrutinize his use of other people as need-meeting objects. The perception of not wanting to be assertive and self-reliant, unconsciously equated with aggressively antagonizing the mother who fostered his reliance on her and lack of individuation for her own narcissistic purposes, was seen to belie his current expectation of antagonizing someone with his own independent self-assertion, as well as introducing intolerable anxiety on himself.

The issue of individuation and autonomy arose in a specific way upon termination in the patient's request to "check in once in a while" to look at issues that might present occasionally. In examining this request, the patient was rather quickly able to discern and work through this final derivative of individuation and autonomy from the therapist, relating it to his initial complaints of inability to effect completion or success in his endeavors.

DISCUSSION

Mahler (14) has demonstrated that when the symbiotic phase of develop-ment is unpredictable and painfully frustrated rather than need-satisfying, or alternatively, marked by too much exclusiveness when the mother cannot accept the child's separation, the result in either case may be separation panic, dread of dissolution of the self, and fear of loss of identity. The step of separation-individuation is then experienced as a catastrophic threat. The awareness of separateness with its concomitant need for more individuated coping with expanding outside reality occurs in the midst of the phase-specific psychosexual conflict with its own developmental line and issues of separation-individuation.

Several steps of separation-individuation are to be attained in the progression from infancy to adulthood: the increasing psychological and physical separation from primary level objects, the associated internal representation of these objects, and the intrapsychic reorganization in the relationship to these objects. The term separation refers not to physical separation but to the psychic phenomenon of experiencing one's self as separate from the maternal object. Separation anxiety can therefore persist even when the mother is present if the pathologically intense symbiotic tie results in accumulation of aggression that cannot be neutralized for use in separation and individuation (14).

Individuation is an intrapsychic process, with the attainment of self-regulation and individual autonomy reverberating through the course of life (15). The auxiliary ego-functioning of the mother initially, and subsequently of both parents, provides a homeostatic constancy. The goal of individuation is the achievement of a secondary autonomy of these ego functions in a gradual and step-wise manner. The separation-individuation process is a continuing one that is reworked incrementally at each successive stage of development. The corresponding intrapsychic restructuralization is increas-ing autonomy from the external parental ego, superego, and narcissistic regulatory functions.

Individuation is an adaptive aspect of development that includes the giving up of more infantile ideals with the dependence on external objects for narcissistic supplies and the acquisition of ever-increasing mastery over experiences, opening new vistas of potentialities that allow the previously ideal state to be relinquished. Individuation is a line of development continuing throughout life in which early developmental failures make later individuation and development of autonomous ego functions a specific struggle (16). The adaptive process of individuation requires the renunciation of earlier ideals and ideal self-object relationships in order that pleasure in mastery may be exercised in constantly evolving achievements through independent activity. The freedom to discover and pursue novel solutions without disrupting a stable sense of well-being or safety and the ability to independently and comfortably depart from stereotyped and automatic responses to drive and reality demands, as well as ability to give up reliance on a structured environment, are a part of this process of autonomy.

Halpern (17) has demonstrated that work inhibition in children is due to a developmental disturbance in ego individuation. Earlier, Menaker (18) noted that the success of work life, and alternatively, of work inhibitions, correlates with the "separateness of the ego from the personality of the parents." Menaker associates this particular type of ego maldevelopment in children with two patterns of family interaction: narcissistic, controlling parents who create anger in a child and force his taking an extreme position in order to attain individuation; and parents who have intensified the Oedipal conflict, which requires extreme efforts toward individuation to be expressed in a negativistic, self-defeating, and passive way rather than with an appropriate degree of positive assertion. Pittman et al. (19) describe a syndrome of work phobia, a type of separation anxiety precipitated by leaving home to go to work, which they view as an adult's version of school phobia. An adequate differentiation based on dynamic and developmental principles is not made, however.

Developmentally, anxiety is provoked when the infant and young child anticipate the possibility of the mother's not relieving his discomforts. Experiences of frustration foster the separation of self and object images and self-representation. The failure of an adequate, or optimal, sense of frustration—i.e., the continuation of need-meeting when it is no longer appropriate or necessary—inhibits this differentiation of self and object, and ultimately the sabotage of the separation and individuation process is effected, creating the *inhibition of independent assertion.* Since independence assertion is usually concomitant in this society with the cessation of the psychosocial moratorium of adolescence allowing education and training, one of the crystallizations of this issue as it reverberates through adulthood may be seen as a phobic avoidance of success. Although seen as a fear of success, or of successful completion, this actually is a fear of final individuation and autonomy. When the mother spares the child the pains of ordinary experiences of trial and error, the ensuing emotional component in the child is the belief that he cannot do those things which have been done for him by his mother, that he *needs* an object functioning for him—in short, that he is inadequate.

The threat of abandonment by a parent or primary figure provides enforcement of phobias. That phobias are compatible with character structure and regressive functioning in pre-Oedipal relationships has previously received attention (20). Success phobia based on the threat of absence or separation from a primary figure or the equivalent symbolic and functioning surrogate of that figure is in essence a fear based on the fear of abandonment, with phobic ideation and consequent avoidance of the phobic objects sparing the adult, by his self-imposed constraint of behavior, from the threat of abandonment.

SUMMARY

The understanding and utilization of ego-psychological principles to differentiate and more sharply to classify the clinical picture in which success phobia is prominent are presented to provide a more accurate distinction of psychodynamic issues important for analytic therapy. A review of the Oedipal conflicts creating success neurosis is presented and illustrated by case 1, and an extension to the consideration of developmental issues of separation-individuation that create similar initial clinical manifestations of success phobia is demonstrated with cases 2 and 3 to illustrate the developmental, genetic, and adaptational issues involved.

The view of anxiety as relates to work or success inhibition is an intrapsychic one that provides the basis for differentiation from a psychoanalytic psychological point of view the considerations of adaptation and drives in Oedipal success phobia and for expansion of this view to those considerations in the developmental line of individuation, focusing on those aspects of ego organization necessary to integration and to independent functioning. This differentiation of success phobia is presented in the hope of facilitating psychodynamic reconstruction and the clinical management of psychotherapy.

REFERENCES

1. Freud, S. Some character types met with in psychoanalytic work (1915). In *Collected Papers,* Vol. IV. New York: Basic Books, 1959.
2. Fenichel, O. *The Psychoanalytic Theory of Neurosis.* New York: Norton, 1945.
3. Schuster, D. On the fear of success. *Psychiat. Quart.* 29:412-420, 1955.
4. Kardiner, A., Karush, A., and Oversey, L. A methodological study of Freudian theory: IV. The structural hypothesis, the problem of anxiety, and post-Freudian ego psychology. *J. Nerv. Ment. Dis.* 129:341-356, 1959.
5. Schur, M. The ego in anxiety. In R.M. Lowenstein, ed., *Drives, Affects, Behavior.* New York: International Universities Press, 1953.
6. Freud, S. Inhibitions, symptoms, and anxiety (1926). *Standard Edition,* Vol. 20, London: Hogarth Press, 1959.
7. Crosby, J. Theories of anxiety: a theoretical perspective. *Am. J. Psychiat.* 36:237-248, 1976.
8. Brenner, C. On the nature and development of affects: A unified theory. *Psychiat. Quart.* 43:533-546, 1974.
9. Galdston, R. Some functions of intimidation in growth and development. *Curr. Concepts Psych.* 3:2-7, 1977.

10. Freud, S. Analysis of a phobia in a five-year boy (1908). *Standard Edition,* Vol. 10. London: Hogarth Press, 1955.
11. Ovesey, L. Fear of vocational success. *Arch. Gen. Psych.* 7:82-92, 1962.
12. Ovesey, L. *Homosexuality and Pseudohomosexuality.* New York: Science House, 1969.
13. Bieber, I., and Bieber, T. Heterosexuals who are preoccupied with homosexual thoughts. *Med. Asp. Human Sexuality* 9:152-168, 1975.
14. Mahler, M. On the significance of the normal separation-individuation phase (with reference to research in symbiotic child psychosis). In M. Schur, ed., *Drives, Affects, Behavior,* Vol. 2. New York: International Universities Press, 1965.
15. Winestine, M. (reporter) The experience of separation-individuation in infancy and its reverberations through the course of life: I. Infancy and childhood. *J. Am. Psychiat. Assoc.* 21:135-154, 1973.
16. Joffe, W., and Sandler, J. Comments on the psychoanalytic psychology of adaptation, with special reference to the role of affects and the representational world. *Int. J. Psychiat.* 49:445-454, 1968.
17. Halpern, H. Psychodynamic and cultural determinants of work inhibition in children and adolescents. *Psychoanal. Rev.* 51:173-189, 1964-65.
18. Menaker, E. Clinical aspects of work inhibition. Paper presented at the meeting of the New York Society of Clinical Psychologists, May 23, 1959.
19. Pittman, F., Langsley, D., and Deyoung, C. Work and school phobias: A family approach to treatment. *Am. J. Psychiat.* 124:1535-1541, 1968.
20. Ross, N. (reporter) An examination of nosology according to psychoanalytic concepts. *J. Am. Psychiat. Assoc.* 8:535-551, 1960.

CHAPTER 19

Anxiety in the General Hospital

Norman Decker

INTRODUCTION

To say that anxiety is ubiquitous in a general hospital is an observation so self-evident as to appear superfluous. Nevertheless, we in the healing arts, desensitized by constant contact, lose sight of this obvious reality so often that its restatement is a necessity. If we can emotionally touch and intellectually understand some of the many presentations of anxiety, both we and our patients will be better served. My emphasis will be on anxiety suffered by patients, but I will also touch on that experienced by staff. In this, I will draw on my observations as a psychiatrist working and supervising the work of others in a general hospital. I will also draw on my self-observation as both physician and patient. I will focus predominantly on medical and surgical wards, but I will also touch briefly on the psychiatric ward. I will conclude with a few suggestions.

Three Important Distinctions

The following three clarifications will permeate the remainder of this work. It is well to keep them in mind as you read further.

1. Anxiety versus Fear

Anxiety and fear look alike but should be distinguished, at least conceptually. Both are characterized by a sense of fright and impending doom as well as the physiological sequelae of these emotions (i.e., fast pulse, shortness of breath, etc.) detailed elsewhere in this volume. Fear follows perception of a realistic danger situation—i.e., a tiger escaping from its cage. Anxiety follows perception of an imaginary danger—i.e., the fantasy that a tiger might have escaped from its cage.* The former is a reaction to external reality, the latter to internal fantasy. We often see combinations; distinctions are not always easy. Hospital wards are populated by both real and imaginary tigers.

2. Bad Experience versus Trauma

It is essential to distinguish a bad experience from a traumatic one. The former is a period of unpleasantness, remembered as such, but with a relatively benign recovery. The individual always feels that he is in control of his fate and able to cope with whatever pain and suffering he has to face. A trauma is a period of severe unpleasantness that exhausts coping resources. The individual feels stretched beyond his limits and unable to bear the suffering and terror. Such experiences leave psychic wounds which are slow to heal. An individual so afflicted repeatedly probes the wound much as we all probe the cavity left by a dental extraction with our tongues. The probing of a traumatic psychic wound takes the form of a fantasized reoccurrence of the traumatic experience (either asleep or awake), with repeated reexperiencing of the original terror. Such a sequence is known as a traumatic neurosis and is discussed more extensively elsewhere in this volume. In the general hospital, bad experiences are the rule, but traumatic experiences are unfortunately not unusual. I will say a word on prophylaxis in this area later.

3. Overt versus Covert Anxiety

Anxiety can be either overt or covert. In one or the other form it is nearly universal in hospitalized patients. Overt anxiety is easy to recognize. Covert anxiety may be either consciously suppressed or unconscious to the patient. Its presence is indicated by restlessness, inappropriate defensive maneuvers (i.e. excessive denial, helpless passivity, markedly regressive postures, etc.), insomnia, and the physiological sequelae of anxiety. People suppress or repress their awareness or communication of anxiety for a variety of reasons.

---

*From a strict psychoanalytic point of view, both of these would be classified as anxiety, a mental signal generated by a perceived danger, either external or internal. The function of the signal is to set defensive and protective maneuvers into motion.

These include excessive masculinity ("A man is not afraid"), excessive religiosity ("It would be sacriligious to question God's will") denial, fear of offending the medical staff, as well as other reasons. Patient empathic listening and questioning on the part of the doctor allows many patients to communicate anxiety they would otherwise not dare face or voice.

Fear of the Institution

Aside from those lost souls who frequent public institutions as a haven from the rigors of life,* most people approach hospitalization with dread. Separation from home, loved ones, and comforting routine leads to the same restless uneasiness that many of us feel while away alone in strange, unfamiliar places. This is aggravated by the hospital routine, which is designed primarily for efficiency, not comfort. The universality of hospital anxiety is tacitly acknowledged by physicians, who routinely write sedation orders for all incoming patients. The strangeness of hospital odors and foods heightens this separation anxiety.

Separation fears are of particular importance in the hospitalization of children. Many facets of adult neuroses can be traced to *traumatic* childhood separation experiences during hospitalizations. Extensive preparation and 24-hour visiting privileges are mandatory to make this separation a bad experience, not a traumatic one (1).

Sometimes hospitals acquire a reputation.

Case 1. A large municipal county hospital was widely described in the community as "the place where you go to die." There was some truth to this allegation, due not to poor care but instead to patient selection. Only the most desperately ill were admitted, and the death rate was accordingly high. Many avoided hospitalization at all costs, imperiling their health. Others were admitted terrified, fearing the end had come.

Sometimes hospitals are feared because of a highly personal experience, memory, or association. Disabling or fatal illness to parents or other loved ones may lead a patient, through identification, to fear the worst for himself. Problems of excessive unconscious guilt or masochism will accentuate this tendency markedly.

Case 2. A woman in her mid-forties persistently refused hospitalization for surgical correction of an increasingly disabling megaesophagus. She feared surgery of any kind, feeling that its result was inevitably death ("You always die under the knife"). She had a significantly ambivalent relationship with her own mother, who died many years earlier as an immediate complication of surgery for a different condition.

---

*These people develop what has come to be called a positive institutional transference. They unconsciously equate the hospital with a nurturant parental image.

Fear of Diagnosis and Diagnostic Procedures

It is relatively safe to assume that virtually all patients with an undiagnosed condition, however inconsequential it may seem to the physician, fear that the diagnosis will be ultimately fatal. Although many patients will not readily admit it, the fantasy of cancer is ubiquitous. Many patients will avoid diagnostic procedures so as to avoid finding out the diagnosis.

Case 3. A physician in his thirties rather casually avoided a new skin lesion for over three months. When he finally "got around" to having it investigated, he was able to face his own fear of finding out what the diagnosis was.

As noted above, guilt, masochism, and frightening identifications will greatly amplify diagnostic fears.

Case 4. A man in his thirties was admitted to a general medical ward for evaluation of abdominal pain characteristic of peptic ulcer disease. Upper G.I. series confirmed this diagnosis, following which the patient became greatly agitated, particularly when surgery was considered. His agitation was so severe that a psychiatrist was consulted, and it was then learned that his father, many years before, had also had surgery for presumptive peptic ulcer disease. During the operation, it was discovered that the father's disease was instead gastric cancer, which eventually proved fatal. Open discussion of this issue greatly relieved the son's anxiety and allowed him to proceed with his treatment.

Sometimes diagnostic procedures are indeed frightening and even hazardous (e.g., bronchoscopy or gastroscopy with a rigid instrument, cerebral arteriography, etc.). When these procedures are fully described to patients, alarm and apprehension are quite justified. Even relatively innocuous procedures such as the barium enema may be greeted with extreme apprehension from patients because of the severe discomfort from the preparation and the procedure itself. If a patient is either paranoid or extremely obsessional, this latter procedure may be virtually terrifying.

For some patients extremely fearful of physical injury (excessive castration anxiety), any physically intrusive diagnostic procedure may be seen as an overwhelming threat in and of itself.

Case 5. A man in his mid-twenties was found to have persistently abnormal liver function studies. A liver biopsy was suggested. Many aspects of the man's life denoted extreme concern about his masculinity and fear of injury or damage. He persistently refused the liver biopsy, stating that he was terrified of needles and could not tolerate a needle being pushed into his abdomen. Although fear of diagnosis was clearly a factor, it seemed apparent that excessive fear of injury or mutilation was the prime source of his anxiety and secondary refusal to allow the diagnostic procedure.

FEAR OF SURGERY

It is self-evident that surgery, oftentimes carrying significant risk, invariably engenders real fear in patients. According to the patient's predilection, this fear may revolve around the diagnostic implications of surgery, the fear of death or mutilation, fear of pain, fear of disability, and fear of dependency and helplessness. It is not at all uncomon for surgical fear to progress to excessive anxiety reactions. In a classic paper (2), Helene Deutsch elucidated the major dynamics behind this anxiety. She distinguished an inordinate fear of dying from an inordinate fear of mutilation. The former, which she termed "narcosis anxiety," was related to anesthesia; the latter, or castration anxiety, was related to the surgical procedure itself. Deutsch attributed narcosis anxiety to a revival of early conflicts revolving around fears of separation and fusion. Put otherwise, being put to sleep revived earlier fears revolving around sleep from childhood. The anxiety relating to the surgical procedure itself had to do with the revival of earlier fears of bodily injury revolving around conflicts from the Oedipal period of development.

If these above-mentioned anxieties are so severe as to prevent adequate treatment, psychiatric intervention may be indicated. On the other hand, in the vast majority of cases, adequate ventilation of fears followed by factual reassurance will generally allay most severe anxiety. It is important that reassurance follows expression of anxiety rather than precede it. When the patient has not been given the opportunity to ventilate, reassurance often misses the mark and has little therapeutic value. Premature reassurance may serve to block open expression of anxious concerns.

Postoperatively, the patient is faced with pain, extreme weakness, immobilization. and a variety of artificial devices protruding from various orifices, natural and otherwise. This combination is often terrifying, so much so as to constitute a trauma as described above. On top of this, viewing the surgical wound is often a horrifying experience of fantasied severe mutilation realized.

Case 6. After a laparotomy, a middle-aged man was visited by his surgeon and a retinue of students. The surgeon undid the dressing for the first time since the operation. The patient looked down at the incision and saw an angry red, swollen line extending the length of his abdomen, with circular wires crossing this line at regular intervals. The areas around the wires also looked red and swollen, and the entire sight looked, to the patient, horrifying and unreal. The surgeon looked down and said, "beautiful incision."

The extent to which all of these strange and frightening experiences can remain bad experiences insteadof traumata depends largely upon preoperative preparation by the surgical staff. Once an individual has been told the difficulties he must face, he has an opportunity to gather his strength, fortify his defenses, and when the time comes, better handle the experience. Without preparation, the experience can be overwhelming. These considerations are particularly relevant to the question of pain.

Immobilization and helplessness during the postoperative state bring forth an automatic regression. This is not to say that none the other frightening, embarrassing, and anxiety-provoking experiences that occur during one's hospitalization do not also bring forth regression. It is a truism that regression is an automatic response to the stresses of hospitalization and surgery, and this has been much discussed in the literature (3). My focus here will be on the regression secondary to immobilization. All patients facing this experience will reexperience feelings from childhood involving helplessness and being cared for. For many, this is no problem because their early life experiences were generally favorable. For others, however, frightening fears of neglect, desertion, and lack of help while in distress will be terrifyingly revived. For others, independence won through hard struggle and a none-too-solid sense of masculinity will be imperiled. Patients reliving these frightening emotions will become excessively demanding, filled with "too much pain" or resistant to accepting their immobilized state (4). Unaware of the reasons for these emotions, physicians become first confused and then irritated at their patients, thus increasing stress and anxiety and further regression.

FEAR OF PAIN

Much has been written in recent years about pain (5). It is now widely recognized that pain is a subjective experience multiply determined by physiological, psychological, and social forces. Fear of pain (associated with a diagnostic procedure, surgery or secondary to the pathological process itself) may be related to a variety of psychological phenomena. These include a long-standing proclivity toward being pain-sensitive, a masochistic need to suffer with consequent fantasies of unbearable pain, and experience with significant others who have had severe pain, particularly when "pain behavior" has been rewarded.

Case 7. A man in his thirties delayed for two years diagnostic evaluation of chronic diarrhea. He had been evaluated some years before for similar complaints with proctoscopy and barium enema. The former had been performed by an inexperienced surgical resident and had been prolonged and painful. The barium enema was similarly painful, particularly the air contrast study. The delay of the current workup was largely due to the patient's unwillingness to face these painful procedures again.

The painful experience itself, as has been noted elsewhere, is markedly augmented by anxiety or depression. It is important to note here that pain can be a symptom of conversion hysteria. Pain, with large components of anxiety and depression, can enormously exceed demonstrable physiological etiologies. In an interesting study by Hackett and his coworkers (6), it was noted that patients emotionally prepared for postoperative pain required one-third the analgesia of patients without such preparation. The clear significance of this finding is that reduction of anxiety related to preparation for postoperative sensations also led to reduction of pain experienced.

FEAR OF DEATH

Hospital patients fear death for many reasons. Some are afraid without any actual knowledge that death is forthcoming. This fear may be realistic, based on the actual imminence of death, or neurotic, based on largely internal concerns. Most patients know when death is approaching. In the broad field of thanatology (7,8,9), I will focus on one major facet of the fear and anxiety experienced by the terminal patient.

In this author's opinion, it is hard to know what fear of death means in any individual case. The following dynamic explanation is frequently true. All dying patients face ubiquitous separations on many fronts. They face losses of husbands, wives, parents, children, friends, coworkers, future pleasures, future ambitions, and so forth. There is an invariable regression, once again, under the stress of all of these forthcoming losses and separations. It revives early childhood fears of separation and loss. The pervasive feeling is one of loneliness, alienation, and fear of being alone and uncared for. This is, for many patients, the essence of what fear of death is. This fear is augmented by poor communication between patient and physician and patient and family and loved ones. The desire on all sides to spare the other the pain of excessive knowledge leads to increasing distance and a further sense of alienation and loss in the patient. It is incumbent on all caretakers of the terminally ill to address themselves to this very basic problem and to make some attempt to solve the problem of alienation, loneliness, and feelings of loss in the terminally ill. Again, I will not here go into the other multiple facets of fear in the dying patient except to note that many of them are implicit in my prior discussions of fear of pain, fear of diagnosis, fear of surgery, etc.

FEAR ON THE PSYCHIATRIC WARD

Within the field of hospital psychiatry, my comments will be limited to a few common anxiety situations in psychiatric inpatients.

1. Acute Anxiety upon Being Hospitalized

Freud, long ago, described a sequence of events in psychotic processes (10). This included an initial withdrawal or decathexis from objects in the external world. This was followed by a reconstitution process that incorporated most of the features of what we currently regard as overt psychosis. This process (presented here in a highly simplistic version) has been much debated over the years. Nevertheless, it is instructive in understanding the severe anxiety some patients have upon first entering the hospital. At a time when a patient is grappling with an increasing sense of loss of contact with the people and things of his world (often experienced as a world destruction fantasy), it is vitally important for him to maintain some sense of connection. Coming into the hospital, for many patients, augments their sense of decreasing contact with the world. We are perhaps more familiar with those frequent cases wherein coming into a psychiatric hospital with its structure, security, compassion, and separation from the stresses of the external world all lead to a rapid amelioration of anxiety and decrease of symptomatology. Nevertheless, the cases I am describing wherein anxiety becomes worse are not infrequent. In such cases being forced into hospital clothes, strange routines, unfamiliar food, and loss of contact with people and things in the outside world may be all that is required to thrust someone from incipient to overt state of psychosis. We are accustomed to rely heavily on the phenothiazines for the control of this anxiety. It is well, however, to also pay attention to the strangeness, loss and separation from familiar objects associated with most psychiatric hospitalizations. When this coincides with the internal detachment of incipient psychosis, the net result can be devastating. Several environmental manipulations can be helpful here. These may include frequent visitation, retention of familiar objects and clothing, and *gradual* rather than sudden immersion in hospital routine.

2. Anxiety about Loved Ones

Many patients entering the hospital find it to be an inordinately painful experience because of severe unremitting fear about the well-being of loved ones. This can be understood as a variation of the process just described. It is also complicated by severe ambivalence conflicts revolving around these loved ones. If a patient is struggling with unconscious hostile, murderous wishes toward those closest to him, the only reassurance possible may be keeping them in constant surveillance in order to reassure himself of their well-being. With this in mind, frequent early visitation can often be extraordinarily comforting in the initial stages of hospitalization. This sometimes runs counter to hospital routine, and it is unfortuante when routine prevails over patient benefit.

3. Claustrophobic Panic

Acute claustrophobic anxiety may occur at any stage during a psychiatric hospitalization. There are several possible etiologies, but most frequently it has to do with regression to an early infantile mental set involving wishes for and fears of fusion with important figures in the current environment. Perception of these figures is massively distorted through confusion with figures from the past. These panic attacks are often brought about by experiences of feared loss and separation and a regression to a wish-fear of fusion. The patient reports the experience as one of feeling trapped, closed in, suffocated, or unable to breathe. Frequently at these times he will leave the hospital against medical advice. Pharmacologic intervention is important here, but a judicious admixture of reassurance against potential separation and temporary increases in freedom and mobility will markedly relieve the anxiety.

FEAR AMONGST THE HOSPITAL STAFF

I will focus here on reactions that are common to all hospital personnel. Although potentially extremely gratifying, the job of the medical caretaker in the general hospital can be extraordinarily anxiety-provoking as well. The sources of this anxiety are manifold.

1. Frightening Identifications

The patient's age, sex, disease type, or profession may lead to ease of identification on the part of the medical caretaker. This in turn can lead to extreme fears that physician, nurse, or student might one day come down with dread illness too. The patient may also be unconsciously identified with a loved one, family member, or close friend.

Case 8. A 35-year old biochemist was admitted to a university hospital with recent and sudden onset of ascites. He had just completed his academic training and moved into a lucrative job with a drug company. He had two small children and a young wife and had recently purchased a new home. His ascites was found to be secondary to a highly malignant reticulum cell sarcoma, and he died within a few weeks of admission. The anxiety among house staff and medical students during his admission was so severe as to be virtually palpable. It was extraordinarily difficult for most of those involved to attend his autopsy.

This fear of illness and its complications is well known to be a frequent motivating factor in the career choice of health professionals. The counterphobic aspects of this choice have been discussed elsewhere.

Case 9. A 25-year-old intern fell into a severe, incapacitating agitated depression on her first emergency room rotation. In psychotherapy it was discovered that she witnessed the sudden hemorrhagic death of a beloved grandparent during her early childhood. The emergency room rotation revived this memory and the fear of reexperiencing the same unbearably painful childhood affects.

2. Attachment and Loss

The normal human tendency to form close emotional relationships is not absent in the health care professions. There is an inevitable tendency to become attached to one's patients. When these patients deteriorate and die, it is a painful experience. The sense of loss is often hard to bear, particularly if the health worker has experienced early prior experiences of significant loss. After going through one or several such experiences, anxiety over potential loss becomes a major factor in one's relationships with patients. These two factors then—fear of identification and fear of loss—account for the ubiquitous defensive maneuver that many hospital workers invariably employ—namely, emotional distance and isolation from patients.

3. Fear of Failure

In any individual's career, success or failure are causes for strong emotion. To varying extents, neurotic components may accentuate the need for success and the pain of failure. Fear of failure is a relatively normal emotion in any professional situation. The hospital situation tends to accentuate this fear, however, for a variety of reasons. First and foremost, the stakes are very high. The well-being and very lives of patients are involved in the success-failure equation. This is particularly true for those in training, who feel particularly vulnerable to the danger of causing the possible disfiguration or death of patients. It is well known that most physicians pass through their internship year believing that on at least one occasion they caused the death of a patient, largely through inexperience or ignorance. This fear is compounded by the belief, sometimes accentuated by the training institution, that anything short of success may lead to termination of career training.

Case 10. An intern in a busy county hospital encountered a young boy whose lip had been badly split open through trauma. Under the tutelage of a surgeon, he carefully constructed a plastic repair of the young boy's lip. A number of days later, on the advice of his superiors, he saw the young boy in a follow-up visit and began to remove the sutures. To his horror, the lip split open once again and although he deferred removal of the remaining stitches, he remained with the belief that the boy would have a permanently scarred lip. It is of note that the intern's father had a badly scarred lip from his own childhood. The intern approached all future plastic surgical experiences during his internship year with apprehension and anxiety.

Case. 11. A medical student on a sub-internship in a busy municipal hospital admitted a patient with spinal meningitis. He did a spinal tap on the patient at night, looked at the spinal fluid under the microscope, and cultured it. He then went to sleep for the remainder of the night without initiating antibacterial therapy. The next morning he was severely chastised by his superiors and ultimately suspended from the class. This anecdote was well known by his colleagues in the medical school class, and most approached sub-internships with considerable apprehension.

Fear of failure can be markedly enhanced by stern teachers who teach by fear, making the educational experience into a kind of initiation rite. The medical and surgical rounds of many attending physicians in teaching hospitals are well known and feared for this reason.

A FEW THERAPEUTIC STRATEGIES

The control and alleviation of anxiety in the general hospital may be divided into strategies of therapy. In the hospital staff, much can be done to prevent painful experiences from becoming traumatic through careful advance preparation. An adequate forum for description and discussion of the stresses the health care worker will encounter in the hospital setting prior to going into that setting will go a long way towards preventing anxiety levels and their unfortunate sequelae from getting out of hand. Diminishing extreme emphases on competition and success and failure will also alleviate much of the anxiety in a general hospital. Finally, in a therapeutic vein, episodic scheduled discussion groups among hospital workers, during which stresses and reactions to stresses are aired, can be enormously helpful in alleviating anxiety. Weekly meetings covering psychological issues are now an important component of many oncology unit programs.

In dealing with anxiety in patients, several general principles are applicable. As has already been noted several times in this paper, careful preparation of patients for future stresses will make those stresses less anxiety-provoking and therefore not traumatic when they occur. Painful though it may be for the hospital worker, an attempt to empathetically identify with the patient's plight during hospitalization will highlight simple aspects of the hospital experience that can be changed in small ways, thus alleviating potential anxiety. In this regard, it is particularly important to occasionally sacrifice efficiency for comfort.

With respect to the patient who is already anxious, opportunities to ventilate the sources of anxiety are vitally important. Reassurance and education can then profitably be employed to alleviate distorted beliefs and their consequent fears. Once again, this kind of intervention is only minimally effective if the opportunity to ventilate is not offered first.

This discussion is not intended to diminish the importance of pharmacotherapeutic agents in the alleviation of hospital anxiety. It is beyond question that these agents have an important role to play in hospital life. This area is discussed extensively elsewhere in this volume. It is this author's belief, however, that many physicians employ pharmacotherapeutic agents (most notably diazepam in recent years) in place of taking the time to become skilled in psychologically informed and humane hospital care. Empathic understanding of fear and anxiety in the hospital will invariably lead to anxiety relieving practices

REFERENCES

1. Branstetter, E. The young child's response to hospitalization: Separation anxiety or lack of mothering care. *Am. J. Public Health* 59:92-97, 1969.
2. Deutsch, H. Some psychoanalytic observations in surgery. *Psychosom. Med.* 4:105-115, 1942.
3. Janus, I.L. *Psychological Stress.* New York: Wiley, 1958.
4. Bibring, G.L., and Kahana, R.J. *Lectures in Medical Psychology.* New York: International Universities Press, 1968.
5. Melzack, R. *The Puzzle of Pain.* New York: Basic Books, 1973.
6. Hackett, T.P., and Cassem, N.H. The psychology of intensive care: Problems and their management. In *Psychiatric Medicine.* New York: Brunner/Mazel, 1977.
7. Kübler-Ross, E. *On Death and Dying.* New York: Macmillan, 1969.
8. Roose, L.J. The dying patient. *Int. J. Psychoanal.* 50:385-395, 1969.
9. Weisman, A.D. *On Dying and Denying: A Psychiatric Study of Terminality.* New York: Behavioral Publications, 1972.
10. Freud, S. On narcissism: An introduction. In *Collected Papers,* Vol. 4. New York: Basic Books, 1924.

CHAPTER 20

Anxiety, Self-Derogation, and Deviant Behavior

Howard B. Kaplan

The following serves to test proposed relationships between anxiety, self-rejecting attitudes, and deviant behavior against a recently stated general theory of deviant behavior (1). Anxiety (reflected in the subjective experience of vulnerability to circumstances having self-devaluing implications) is said to influence the subsequent development of characteristically self-rejecting attitudes (self-derogation, in its extreme form). Unable to defend against the subjective belief that he possesses disvalued attributes and performs disvalued behaviors, lacks valued attributes and behaviors, and is the object of solely negative attitudes expressed by significant others, the individual experiences feelings of worthlessness and self-reproach. The experience of self-rejecting attitudes in turn exacerbates anxiety. Continued frustration of the need for self-acceptance within the very environment that engendered self-rejection intensifies the felt vulnerability to the self-devaluing implications of life events and further increases the need for positive self feelings. The frustrated self-esteem motive and consequent exacerbation of anxiety in turn influence the adoption of deviant response patterns. When past experiences in his membership groups become consistently associated with distressful feelings of self-rejection and anxiety, the individual begins to perceive such membership group experiences as intrinsically distressing. He consequently loses motivation to conform to, and becomes motivated to deviate from, the normative patterns associated with the membership groups. Likewise, the continuing frustration of the self-esteem motive and consequent experience of anxiety influence the person to seek alternative response patterns that might serve self-enhancing/anxiety-reducing functions. These alternative responses, insofar as they fail to conform to the normative expectations of membership groups, constitute, by definition, deviant responses. Whether or not these alternative responses successfully reduce anxiety and enhance self-image depends upon the extent to which they result in avoidance or destruction of sources of self-rejection and anxiety, or themselves become sources of adverse consequences by virtue of their deviation from normative behavior.

RELATED LITERATURE

Numerous reports have observed an association between anxiety and low self-esteem (1,2,3,4). However, the generally cross-sectional research designs have not permitted the investigator to establish the temporal priority of one or the other factor. On the one hand, as Rosenberg (4) notes, the observed relationship is consistent with a position similar to Horney's (5), that self-rejecting attitudes are consequences of anxiety. It is argued that a basic anxiety in the child develops as a result of a variety of adverse familial circumstances. In an attempt to cope with the anxiety the child creates in his imagination an idealized image which provides him with a sense of strength and confidence. However, when this idealized self is compared with the actual self, the real self seems so inferior by comparison that the person feels hatred for it.

On the other hand, the frequently observed association between indices of anxiety and self-attitudes are congruent with the argument that low self-esteem, by virtue of certain specifiable factors associated with it, influences the genesis of anxiety. Rosenberg (4) observed that low self-esteem was related to each of four factors which in turn were associated with secondary physiological manifestations of anxiety, and that, when these factors were controlled on, the observed relationship between self-esteem and anxiety decreased. The four factors said to be associated with low self-esteem relate to unstable self-images, presenting a false front to the world, vulnerability, and feelings of isolation. These factors influence anxiety by depriving the person of a major anchorage point to which new stimuli are related (instability of self-attitudes), by the strain and fear of letting one's guise slip (associated with the presenting self), by inordinate sensitivity to experiences that are interpretable as testimony to the person's worthlessness, and by the absence of social supports in the face of threat (feelings of isolation).

Of course, the observed association between low self-esteem and anxiety may reflect the mutual influence of these factors as well. Indeed, such a mutual influence is postulated in the model presented above. However, a reciprocal relationship can be demonstrated only in the context of a longitudinal research design.

For each of several modes of deviant behavior, numerous sources could be cited which assert that deviant patterns are consequences of self-devaluing and anxiety-inducing antecedents, and are intended by the subject, and so function, to enhance self-attitudes and reduce levels of anxiety. Other sources report positive or negative relationships between low self-esteem and/or anxiety-related states on the one hand and deviant responses on the other, variously interpreted as ineffective or effective attempts to assuage self-rejecting or anxiety-filled states. With regard to *drug abuse* it has been noted that numerous psychoanalytic theories of drug dependence have in common "that some form of early childhood deprivation results in inadequate development of ego mechanisms of defense and coping, and this lack of effective coping capacities is reflected later in life in maladaptive behavior. Drug abuse is viewed as a regressive response to the pain and anxiety evoked by inadequate role performance"(6).

Jessor and his associates (7) have argued that problem behavior, such as marijuana use, may function as attempts to achieve otherwise unavailable goals, a way of coping with frustrations and anticipated failure, an expression of rejection of conventional society,a claim upon status transformation, and an expression of peer solidarity or subcultural membership. Empirically, Mellinger and associates (8) reported that among those individuals making the transition from nonuse to use of marijuana only, or from marijuana use to use of other drugs, a pattern of restlessness and discontent emerged. Other studies reported associations between drug use and such related variables as indices of insecurity, dissatisfaction with self, a desire to change oneself, defensiveness, low self-esteem, and low self-confidence (9,10).

Alcoholism has been related to a broad range of personal meanings and motives depending upon the sex and personality type of the subject (11). For example, Pearlin and Radabaugh (12) concluded that "intense anxiety is especially likely to result in the use of alcohol as a tranquilizer if a sense of personal efficacy is lacking and self-esteem is low." Self-enhancing functions of alcohol abuse are suggested by the occasional reports of favorable influences of experimentally induced intoxication upon the self-concepts of alcoholics and by observations of an inverse relationship between interval of sobriety and favorability of self-concept among alcoholics (1).

Much of the literature dealing with causes of middle-class *delinquency* has been summarized in terms of such etiological dimensions as anxiety regarding sex role identification, ambiguity about the adolescent role, feelings of status deprivation, and ineffective role performance (13). It has been argued (14) that "delinquent behavior is a mechanism whereby a derogated self-image may be reclaimed for more positive conscious apperception." The delinquent role is a clearly defined role, consists (although it is negatively regarded) of such positively valued features as potency and daring, and is available as an alternative role on the occasion of self-devaluation due to failure to fulfill other salient roles. "In the process of refurbishing the self-image by adopting the delinquent role, the adolescent anesthetizes himself from the anxiety generated by realization of an ineffective and unworthy self." It has also been argued, however, that delinquency is an ineffective means of assuaging anxiety about self. Members of delinquent groups experience continuing anxiety both about their status in the group and about their masculinity. These anxieties are symptomatic of more profound anxiety about the self. The intensity of such anxieties is reflected in the *pattern* of *sounding*, or challenging the status and masculinity of other group members. "Sounding others reflects one's own anxieties, and, though it may temporarily relieve such anxieties, in the end it is intensified. He who challenges is also challenged, and thus the derogation of others does nothing to improve self esteem" (15). In any case, the relationship between low self-esteem and delinquency has been observed frequently (16).

With regard to *psychiatric disorders,* both their association with self-rejecting attitudes and their presumed self-protective/anxiety-reducing functions have been noted (1). Wylie (17) has cited several studies in which neurotic subjects and/or mixed psychiatric patient groups displayed significantly lower levels of self-acceptance than the normal controls. Arieti (18) has provided several examples of the self-protective functions of psychiatric disorders: "The detached or schizoid person decreases his emotional or actual participation in life in order not to feel inadequate and injure his self-image. The hypochondrical person protects his self by blaming only his body for his difficulties. A woman leads a promiscuous life; she feels she is unacceptable as a person, but as a sexual partner she feels appreciated . . ." With regard to paranoid patterns, Becker (19) states: "By holding others responsible for one's fate and accusing them of plotting and hatred, the paranoiac salvages a sense of self-value. He is at least *worth hating,* and his life takes on a positive meaning, if only in relation to the malevolence of others." Of the psychopath, La Barbara (20) argues that, by focusing during the clinical interview upon affectively neutral and externalized aspects of behavior, and by admitting to and describing his socially undesirable behavior, the psychopath is allowed to maintain his distorted sense of superiority and keep any felt anxiety covert. Obsessions and phobias have been interpreted as avoidance methods that arise by way of defending against threats to self-esteem (21). Observations by Field (22) were interpretable as indicating that pre-schizophrenic and pre-character disorder children manifested alternative ways of dealing with anxiety, with the former trying to withdraw from threatening experiences and the latter tending to assuage anxiety through action.

Social protest activities in like manner have been associated with self-rejecting activities and have been considered with regard to their psychodynamic functions. For example, a study of psychological variables in student activism (23), using projective test data, differentiated between radicals and moderates on the basis of such variables as "negative identity" and "masochistic surrender." Usdin (24) has considered civil disorder or urban revolt (as well as hippiedom, civil rights actions, and fanatical patriotism) as forms of acting out behavior that frequently constitute ways of maintaining psychological equilibrium. Those who engage in civil disorder in the name of moral causes are said to do so in order to satisfy any number of psychodynamic needs: "Their needs may be to destroy, to rebel, to get caught and punished, to be one of the group, to secure attention, or to be martyred by injury or imprisonment."

Similar literature could be cited with regard to violence against self and others (1,25).

Unfortunately, the observations made above are deficient in a number of ways. Frequently they were not based on systematically collected data. Where data were available, the research designs tended to be cross-sectional, thus precluding conclusions regarding antecedent-consequent relationships. Where longitudinal designs were employed, the samples tended to be small and nonrepresentative, and in any case, the studies did not consider all of the variables encompassed by the model described above. In short, while there is a good deal of evidence that is *compatible* with hypotheses regarding the reciprocal relationship between anxiety and self-derogation, and between these factors and deviant behavior, empirical investigations that have permitted tests of the *temporal* relationships between these factors within the context of the *same* research design for a *broadly based* sample have heretofore been lacking. However, a number of analyses carried out in the course of a longitudinal study of the relationship between self-attitudes and deviant behaviors (some of which have been described in earlier reports) are relevant as tests of certain of the hypotheses comprising the theoretical model described above. The presentation and discussion of these hypotheses make up the substance of this report.

HYPOTHESES

The following hypotheses in large measure describe the theoretical model under consideration.

1. Antecedent high level of anxiety is related to subsequent increases in self-derogation.

2. Antecedent high level of self-derogation is related to subsequent increases in anxiety.

3. Antecedent high level of anxiety is related to the subsequent adoption of deviant response patterns.

4. Antecedent high level of self-derogation is related to the subsequent adoption of deviant response patterns.

While other hypotheses could be derived as further tests of the theoretical model, those hypotheses stated immediately above are believed to constitute a strategic test of the theoretical model.

METHOD

The four hypotheses were tested using data collected in the course of a longitudinal survey of junior high school students. Since the method has already been described in a series of reports (26-33), only a brief overview will be presented here.

Sample and Data Collection

The target sample was all of the seventh-grade students in 18 (randomly selected) of the 36 junior high schools in the Houston Independent School District as of March 1971. The students who were to take the test at a particular school generally were convened during the morning of a school day at one or two common locations (lunch room or auditorium) in each school, where they responded to a 209-item structured self-administered questionnaire. The test was administered three times, at annual intervals, during March or April 1971, 1972, and 1973.

Of the 9,459 seventh grade students in the selected schools 7,618 (80%) returned questionnaires that were usable in the longitudinal analysis. Of these 7,618 students, 3,148 (41.3%) responded to all three tests, 1,546 (20.3%) responded to the first two tests only, 640 (8.4%) responded to the first and third tests only, and 2,284 (30%) responded to the first test only. Subject characteristics associated with sample attrition have been considered elsewhere (29,300).

Operational Definitions

The relevant operational definitions for present purposes refer to anxiety, self-derogation, and deviant behavior.

Anxiety, conceptualized as the subjective experience of defenselessness against or vulnerability to circumstances having self-threatening implications, was measured by the number of affirmative responses to the following factorially derived items.

Are you often bothered by nervousness?

Do you often get angry, annoyed, or upset?

Do you often feel downcast and dejected?
Do you often have difficulty keeping your mind on things?
Do you have a lot of accidents?
Do you often have trouble sitting still for a long time?
Do you become deeply disturbed when someone laughs at you or blames
     you for something you have done wrong?
When my parents dislike something I do, it bothers me very much.
When the kids at school dislike something I do, it bothers me very much.
I get nervous when things aren't just right.
I spend a lot of time daydreaming.
When my teachers dislike something I do it bothers me very much.

These items may be thought of as falling into two subsets—those indicative of subjective distress, and those suggesting extreme sensitivity to negative attitudes expressed by others. Thus, a high score on this variable is understood to be indicative of anxiety in the sense that the individual is apparently unable to reduce the subjective distress associated with sensitivity to negative attitudes toward him expressed by others.

It may be noted that this factorially derived index appears to reflect such manifestations of anxiety suggested by Fromm-Reichmann (34) as interference with thinking processes and concentration, objectless feelings of uncertainty and helplessness, and intellectual and emotional preoccupation.

Self-derogation is here defined as the extreme negative pole of a self-attitude continuum conceptualized as the affective component of self-responses—that is, as the person's emotional responses to his perceptions and evaluations of his own traits and behaviors. Self-derogation was measured by scores on the following seven-item scale; the parenthetical entries indicate self-derogating responses:

I wish I could have more respect for myself. (true)
On the whole, I am satisfied with myself. (false)
I feel I do not have much to be proud of. (true)
I'm inclined to feel I'm a failure. (true)
I take a positive attitude toward myself. (false)
At times I think I'm no good at all. (true)
I certainly feel useless at times. (true)

The derivation of the scale, the scoring procedure, and reliability and validity issues are considered in earlier publications (26,29,30).

Although a much broader range of deviant responses was considered in the more inclusive study, for present purposes *deviant behavior* was defined in terms of a factorially derived delinquency scale consisting of self-reports of the following five behaviors: taking things worth $50 or more that didn't belong to you; taking a car for a ride without the owner's knowledge; selling narcotic drugs; breaking into and entering a home, store, or building; and using force to get money or valuables from another person. Issues relating to the validity of the self-report measure were considered in an earlier publication (30.

ANALYSIS

The analysis relating to each of the four hypotheses will be considered in turn.

HYPOTHESIS 1

The first hypothesis was tested by comparing subjects who were low and high respectively on anxiety at the first test administration with regard to the mean residual gain in self-derogation between the first and second test administrations. Significance of difference between means was determined by t-test (one-tail) assuming unequal variances (35).

For purposes of the analysis, the person was considered to be high anxiety if he responded affirmatively to six or more of the items, and low if he responded affirmatively to only five or fewer items.

With regard to measuring change in terms of residual gain scores, a gain is said to be residualized by expressing the post-test score as a deviation from the post-test-on-pre-test regression line. The effect of residualizing is to remove "from the post-test score, and hence from the gain, the portion that could have been predicted linearly from pre-test status . . . The residualized score is primarily a way of singling out individuals who changed more or less than expected" (36).

As hypothesized, subjects with initially (test 1) higher anxiety levels showed significantly ($p < .001$) greater subsequent increases in (or lower than expected decreases in) self-derogation between the first and second testings than initially lower anxiety subjects (29). The high anxiety subjects had a mean residual gain score of 2.5 (standard deviation = .001) greater subsequent increases in (or lower than expected decreases in) self-derogation between the first and second testings than initially lower anxiety subjects (29). The high anxiety subjects had a mean residual gain score of 2.5 (standard deviation = 26.4, n = 2201), while the low anxiety subjects showed a mean residual gain of –2.4 (standard deviation = 22.8, n = 2249).

Since residual (rather than raw) gain scores were used, it was possible to establish a temporal relationship between antecedent anxiety and subsequent increases in self-derogation. If raw gain scores were used, it might have been argued that the change in self-derogation was a function of initial level of self-derogation, which in turn was correlated with initial anxiety level, thus precluding demonstration of an antecedent-consequence relationship.

Hypothesis 2

The second hypothesis was tested by comparing three initial (test 1) self-derogation groupings with each other with regard to subsequent (between test 1 and test 2) change in anxiety score. The initial level of self-derogation was determined by arbitrary division of the distribution of self-derogation scores at the time of the first test administration into three score intervals. As in the preceding analysis, change was expressed in terms of residual gain scores.

As hypothesized, the initially high self-derogation subjects manifested significantly ($p < .001$) greater subsequent increases (or lower subsequent decreases) in anxiety than the initially medium or low self-derogation subjects (28). The low and medium self-derogation subjects were not significantly different with regard to subsequent changes in anxiety. The initially high self-derogation subjects manifested a mean increase of 0.31 (standard deviation = 2.42, n = 1317), compared to a mean residual gain score of −0.16 (standard deviation=2.30, n=1710) for the initially low self-derogation subjects. Again, the use of residual gain scores, uncorrelated with observed initial scores, precludes arguments that change in anxiety level was a function of initial level of anxiety correlated with initial level of self-derogation. If this was true, a temporal relationship between antecedent self-derogation and subsequent change in anxiety could not be established. Rather, the use of residual gain scores to test the first two hypotheses permitted establishment of temporal sequences between anxiety and self-derogation. These sequences were necessary for causal arguments of reciprocal increasing influence between anxiety and self-derogation.

Hypothesis 3

The third hypothesis was tested by comparing subjects who were initially high and low on anxiety at test 1 with regard to reports at test 2 of having performed one or more of the acts comprising the delinquency index during the year between the two tests. Chi-square analysis was used to test the hypothesis of no relationship. Only subjects who denied performing all of the delinquent acts during the month prior to the first testing were considered in the analysis. This precluded interpretation of any observed relationship between antecedent anxiety and subsequent adoption of delinquent responses in terms of their common relationship with delinquent acts prior to the first testing. This interpretation would of course have precluded establishing a temporal relationship between antecedent anxiety and subsequent adoption of delinquent responses.

As hypothesized, antecedent anxiety was significantly related to the subsequent adoption of delinquent responses. Among subjects who had denied performing any of the delinquent responses during the month prior to the first testing, 14.3% of the subjects who were relatively high in anxiety at the first testing (n=1907) compared with 11.8% of the subjects who were relatively low in anxiety at the first testing (n = 2012), reported subsequent adoption of one or more of the delinquent responses (x^2 = 5.3, p< .05).

Hypothesis 4

In order to test the fourth hypothesis, students who were high, medium, and low respectively in self-derogation at the time of the first administration were compared with regard to the relative frequency with which they reported (at the time of the second administration) performing any of the deviant behaviors under consideration between the first and second test administrations. Chi-square analysis was used to test the hypothesis of no relationship, as in the immediately preceding analysis. As in the test of the third hypothesis, and for the same reason, only those students who denied performance of all of the delinquent acts comprising the index during the month preceding the first testing were considered in the analysis. Among these students, 16.8% of the initially high self-derogation subjects (n = 1195), compared with 14.3% of the medium self-derogation subjects (n = 1385) and 98% of the low self-derogation subjects (n = 1622), reported subsequent adoption of one or more of the delinquent responses (x^2 = 31.3, 2 degrees of freedom, p< .001).

Each of the four hypotheses derived from the theoretical model presented above have been supported by data from a longitudinal study of a broadly based sample of adolescents. The subjective experience of defenselessness against or vulnerability to life circumstances having self-threatening implications (that is, anxiety) increases the likelihood of subsequent elevation in feelings of self-rejection. Feelings of self-rejection in turn influence subsequently experienced increases in anxiety. What has been suspected appears empirically to be the case. Rather than one exclusively influencing the other, anxiety and self-derogation appear to be mutually influential, so that defenselessness against the self-devaluing implication of life events in fact breeds self-rejecting attitudes, and self-rejecting attitudes increase the subject's sensitivity to the self-threatening implications of life events.

The mutually influenced higher levels of anxiety and self-derogation in turn are related to an increased probability of subsequent adoption of deviant responses. This observation is consistent with the theoretical position that deviant responses are more or less effective self-enhancing/tension-reducing alternatives to normative patterns previously associated with the genesis of anxiety and self-rejecting attitudes and now disvalued.

Although the observed relationships were statistically significant, the degrees of association between the variables were not in any sense appreciable in terms of portions of variance explained. This should not be too surprising, in light of the act that the conditions under which these relationships are said to hold (implicit in the theoretical model) are not uniformly present throughout the subject population. Analyses are currently in process in which the same relationships are examined for those segments of the population in which these conditions are met. Other current analyses concern the conditions under which the adoption of deviant response patterns will have self-enhancing/anxiety-reducing consequences. The former analyses should increase the amount of variance accounted for by relationships already tested without specification of conditions. The latter analyses will examine yet-untested relationships derived from the theoretical model. In any case, the group of hypotheses that have already received limited support confirms the explanatory relevance and stimulus value of the general theory of deviant behavior articulated here.

REFERENCES

1. Kaplan, H.B. *Self-Attitudes and Deviant Behavior.* Pacific Palisades, Calif.: Goodyear Publishing Co., 1975.
2. Kaplan, H.B., and Pokorny, A.D. Self-derogation and psychosocial adjustment. *J. Nerv. Ment. Dis.* 149:421-434, 1969.
3. Rosenberg, M., and Simmons, R.G. *Black and White Self-Esteem: The Urban School Child.* Washington, D.C.: American Sociological Association, 1971.
4. Rosenberg, M. *Society and the Adolescent Self-Image.* Princeton: Princeton University Press, 1965.
5. Horney, K. *Neurosis and Human Growth.* New York: Norton, 1950.
6. Naditch, M.P. Ego mechanisms and marijuana usage. In D.J. Lettieri, ed., *Predicting Adolescent Drug Abuse: A Review of Issues, Methods and Correlates.* Washington, D.C.: U.S. Government Printing Office, 1975.
7. Jessor, R., Jessor, S.L., and Finney, J. A social psychology of marijuana use; Longitudinal studies of high school and college youth. *J. Pers. Soc. Psychol.* 26:1-15, 1973.
8. Mellinger, G.D., Somers, R.H., and Manheimer, D.I. Drug use research items pertaining to personality and interpersonal relations: A working paper for research investigators. In D.J. Lettieri, ed., *Predicting Adolescent Drug Abuse: A Review of Issues, Methods and Correlates.* Washington, D.C.: U.S. Government Printing Office, 1975.
9. Stokes, J.P. Personality traits and attitudes and their relationship to student drug using behavior. *Int. J. Addict.* 9:267-287, 1974.
10. Segal, B., Rhenberg, G., and Sterling, S. Self-concept and drug and alcohol use in female college students. *J. Alcoh. Drug Educ.* 20:17-22, 1975.
11. Mogar, R.E., Wilson, W.M., and Helm, S.T. Personality subtypes of male and female alcoholic patients. *Int. J. Addict.* 5:99-113, 1970.
12. Pearlin, L.I., and Radabaugh, C.W. Economic strains and the coping functions of alcohol. *Am. J. Sociol.* 82:652-663, 1976.
13. Shanley, F.J. Middle-class delinquency as a social problem. *Sociol. Soc. Res.* 51:185-198, 1967.

14. Gold, M., and Mann, D. Delinquency as defense. *Am. J. Orthopsychiat.*, 42(3):463-479, 1972.
15. Hewitt, J.P. *Social Stratification and Deviant Behavior.* New York: Random House, 1970.
16. Fitts, W.H., and Hamner, W.T. *The Self-Concept and Delinquency.* Nashville, Tenn.: Counselor Recordings and Tests, 1969.
17. Wylie, R.C. *The Self Concept.* Lincoln: University of Nebraska Press, 1961.
18. Arieti, S. Some elements of cognitive psychiatry. *Am. J. Psychother.* 124:723-736, 1967.
19. Becker, E. *The Birth and Death of Meaning: A Perspective in Psychiatry and Anthropology.* New York: Free Press, 1962.
20. LaBarbara, R.C. The psychopath and anxiety: A reformulation. *J. Individ. Psychol.* 21:167-170, 1965.
21. Salzman, L. Obsessions and phobias. *Contemp. Psychoanal.* 2:1-25, 1965.
22. Field, H. Early symptoms and behavior of male schizophrenics, delinquent character-disorder individuals and socially adequate subjects. *J. Nerv. Ment. Dis.* 148:134-146, 1969.
23. Isenberg, P., Schnitzer, R., and Rothman, S. Psychological variables in student activism: The radical triad and some religious differences. *J. Youth Adolesc.* 6:11-24, 1977.
24. Usdin, G.L. Civil disobedience and urban revolt. *Am. J. Psychiat.* 125:91-97, 1969.
25. Kaplan, H.B. Toward a general theory of psychosocial deviance: The case of aggressive behavior. *Soc. Sci. Med.* 6:593-617, 1972.
26. Kaplan, H.B. The self-esteem motive and change in self-attitudes. *J. Nerv. Ment. Dis.* 161:265-275, 1975.
27. Kaplan, H.B. Increase in self-rejection as an antecedent of deviant responses. *J. Youth Adolesc.* 4:281-292, 1975.
28. Kaplan, H.B. Sequelae of self-derogation: Predicting from a general theory of deviant behavior. *Youth and Society* 7:171-197, 1976.
29. Kaplan, H.B. Antecedents of negative self-attitudes: membership group devaluation and defenselessness. *Soc. Psychiat.* 11:15-25, 1976.
30. Kaplan, H.B. Self-attitudes and deviant response. *Soc. Forces* 54:788-801, 1976.
31. Kaplan, H.B. Self-attitude change and deviant behavior. *Soc. Psychiat.* 11:59-67, 1976.
32. Kaplan, H.B. Antecedents of deviant responses: predicting from a general theory of deviant behavior. *J. Youth Adolesc.* 6:89-101, 1977.
33. Kaplan, H.B. Increase in self-rejection and continuing/discontinued deviant response. *J. Youth Adolesc.* 6:77-87, 1977.
34. Fromm-Reichmann, F. Psychiatric aspects of anxiety. In M.R. Stein, A.J. Vidich, and D.M. White, eds., *Identity and Anxiety.* Glencoe, Ill.: Free Press, 1960.
35. Welch, B.L. The generalization of 'students' problem when several different population variances are involved. *Biometrika* 34:28-35, 1947.
36. Cronback, L.J., and Furby, L. How we should measure "change"—or should we? *Psychol. Bull.* 74:68-80, 1970.

CHAPTER 21

Anxiety, Sexual Dysfunctions, and Therapy

Harold I. Lief

The two themes of anxiety and sexuality have been in the forefront of analytic psychodynamics since Freud postulated that anxiety is the consequence of repressed or dammed-up libido. A quarter of a century later Freud recognized that in his first formulation he had put the cart before the horse. In *The Problem of Anxiety* (1) he stated that anxiety was the cause, rather than the consequence, of repression. It is now accepted as a truism that anxiety is a psychobiological alerting signal, warning the organism of a real or potential threat.

The usual distinction between fear and anxiety, wherein the unpleasant alerting response to a known external danger is called *fear,* and the vague, ill-defined tension in a situation that should not realistically elicit this reaction is called *anxiety,* breaks down upon psychodynamic examination (2). Often enough the external object feared (e.g., the horse in the case of Little Hans) is an externalization or projection of an internalized object such as one's father or mother, while the vague tension we usually call anxiety may in fact be related to a repressed real person or other object. A more meaningful distinction between fear and anxiety, a distinction that has both developmental and functional meaning, is possible. In this view, fear is the alerting signal that may cause repression, as the individual defensively struggles to remove from awareness some or all of his dangerous thoughts. Anxiety, on the other hand, is the unpleasant affect that is a consequence of unresolved internal conflict between motivational and counter-motivational impulses. The conflict may be wholly, in part, or not at all outside awareness.

Psychoanalysts are familiar with the unpleasant affect generated by a patient's struggle to master a wholly or partially repressed conflict. This affect is known also to experimental psychologists who create a hypnotically induced conflict in their subjects. This type of anxiety has to be differentiated from a chronic state of tension, in the absence of internal conflict, that can occur more simply from feelings of inadequacy generated by the anticipation of failure in various life situations. Both types of anxiety, those with and those without internal conflict, are present in instances of sexual dysfunction. Anxiety is a *consequence* as well as a *cause* of sexual inadequacy (3,4,5,6).

The main psychological difference between fear and anxiety lies in their acuteness or chronicity. Darwin mentioned that the word "fear" is derived from what is sudden and dangerous. Duration also seems to be vital in the neurophysiological distinction between fear and anxiety. Acute fear is associated with a preponderance of parasympathetic or cholinergic activity, whereas chronic anxiety is associated with a dominance of sympathetic or adrenergic activity (7,8). Although sexual function involves a complex interaction of both autonomic systems, it seems reasonable to hypothesize that excessive adrenergic activity is responsible for both the apparent excessive discharge of the sympathetic system in premature ejaculation and the inhibition of the parasympathetic in impotence. What creates the inhibition of the sympathetic system in the presence of normal parasympathetic activity as in retarded orgasm in both men and women is unclear. The specificity of symptom formation in a particular individual is likewise unclear. Paradoxical reactions to stressful situations, however, are fairly common, so that while most persons will show an increased heart rate or adrenergic response to a given situation, others may actually show a fall in heart rate or cholinergic response. Sometimes these are dissociative reactions, so that one body system—such as the cardiovascular system—goes in one direction and others—e.g., respiratory rate and pupillary dilation—go in the other. To compound the complexity, while a majority of persons show a fairly equal balance between sympathetic and parasympathetic responses, a few demonstrate a dominance of either sympathetic or parasympathetic activity. Clinically, the effects of antihypertensive medication (especially the adrenergic blocking agents), principally impotence and retrograde ejaculation, demonstrate aspects of the differential effects of the autonomic nervous system. It may be that these phenomena, in addition to CNS processes (inhibition of specific brain sites, alterations of neurotransmitters, and of tropic hormones [9,10,11,12]) account for the specificity of sexual symptom formation. While most men, for example, respond with a decrease in testosterone production in the face of stress, others show no evidence of such inhibition (13). These potential relationships in sexual dysfunctions remain to be studied.

A certain amount of anxiety ("nervous tension") appears to be optimal in a variety of life situations—e.g., sports (it is common to hear a physician-tennis player say, "I am much better when I get the adrenalin flowing"), speaking or performing in public, or even during psychotherapy. Too little or too much anxiety is counterproductive. Perhaps some anxiety is needed as a stimulus to the reticular activating or facilitating system (rostral septal, and limbic areas of the brain), whereas too much anxiety is inhibitory. There is experimental evidence demonstrating that this is true of sexual arousal. Subjects had the greatest degree of sexual response to erotic videotapes after having been first presented with anxiety-producing stimuli (14). This presumably accounts for the high degree of sexual excitement most people report with new partners or with familiar partners in unfamiliar settings or during unfamiliar experiences. The psychophysiologic similarities and differences between "excitement" (pleasant tension) and "anxiety" (unpleasant tension) are largely unknown.

Anxiety is an abstraction that must be dereified and pluralized. To aid our understanding of anxiety and sexual functioning, we have to talk about anxiety in its contextual sense. Such basic and ubiquitous anxieties as fear of separation or the loss of love from one on whom one is dependent, fear of bodily damage or loss of bodily integrity, fear of punishment for disapproved behavior, fear of losing control, fear of becoming excessively dependent on a partner, fears of closeness because of the upsurge of hostile feelings, and fears of humiliation play their roles in sexual dysfunctions as they do in other aspects of life.

Many sexual dysfunctions are the consequences of simple inhibition of function. In order to avoid carrying out an act which may eventuate in one of the fears mentioned above, the function is not at all or only partially executed. Impotence is an inhibition of function that may be defensively used to avoid something even more dangerous. However, this is an incomplete and perhaps misleading statement about the etiology of many and probably most cases of impotence. As indicated earlier, the inhibition of function may be the consequence of anxiety *associated* with the attempt to perform sexually and is simply an unpleasant anticipation of failure. Thus, we have to differentiate between the *long-range psychodynamic* causes of impotence and the *immediate operant* causes of impotence, or anxiety as a cause and anxiety as a consequence *and* a cause of sexual failure.

The experience of sexual failure and the injury to self-esteem (usually more pronounced in the male) lead to a fear of failure in sexual performance. Other immediate causes of sexual dysfunctions are: excessive monitoring of one's performance (Masters and Johnson termed it "spectatoring"), which in turn decreases the capacity to register pleasurable erotic sensations during sexual activity; avoidance of sex itself; and the avoidance of talking about it with one's partner. Coping with the sexual dysfunction becomes even more difficult if the partners avoid sex and avoid talking about their mutual concern. Performance anxiety is often augmented by another form of anxiety—namely, an extreme sensitivity to the feelings and reactions of the partner. If the anxiety associated with anticipated sexual failure is added to anxiety over the anticipated negative response from the partner, the result is often a massive inhibition of function.

One of the characteristic ways in which sexual function is impaired is through a decrease in sexual desire. If the interest in sex is lost, it takes a great deal of persistence and persuasion by the partner to engage the interest of the affected spouse or other partner in sexual relations, and even then, sex is often entered into in a reluctant or grudging fashion. Eventually the partner who is still desirous of sex gives up. It is not uncommon to be consulted by marital partners who for many years have had no sex or who have attempted sexual relations only once or twice a year.

Freud's summation of the effects of anxiety on sexual functioning are valid today. Inhibition due to anxiety can cause "a turning aside of the libido . . . impairment of the execution of the function . . . rendering it difficult through the imposition of special conditions . . . its prevention by means of precautionary measures . . . its discontinuance by the development of anxiety, when the initiation of the function can no longer be prevented" (1).

All of these impairments can occur in the absence of any of the long-range psychodynamic conflict-related anxieties, the impairments having been caused by the operant factors associated with failure in performance. If the sexual dysfunction is created entirely or almost entirely by the immediate causes of anxiety and the avoidance mechanisms described above, the couple (it is almost always better to treat the couple than to treat only the "patient" with the symptom) may be cured in most instances by the behavioral techniques pioneered by Masters and Johnson, which they labeled "sensate focus" exercises. The exercises are designed to increase communication between partners in an atmosphere of decreased anxiety created by the reduction, if not the absence, of the demand (from self, partner, or therapist) for performance. The decrease in demand for performance allows a natural reflex response to follow. Instead of sex being linked with the failure (e.g., the man with erectile problems who loses his erection at the point of penetration), it becomes linked with success; the increased pleasure and communication become reinforcing and the couple has started on the road to the extinction of the symptom. (In the eighteenth century John Hunter's prescription for impotent males was "avoid coitus in six consecutive amatory experiences.")

An interesting case illustrates that such reinforcement may occur in unexpected and unplanned contexts. It is a startling and in some ways a puzzling case. A man of 43, referred by a psychoanalyst, told me the following story. About four years previously he had developed impotence. For various reasons he did not wish to involve his wife in the treatment of his sexual dysfunction. He went to a therapist, who first tried systematic desensitization, which did not help. The therapist then tried to use sensate focus by having the patient transmit the recommended methods to his wife. That also failed. The therapist then referred the patient to a partner-surrogate. That did not work. Finally, the therapist, apparently out of desperation, sent the patient to an endocrinologist, who inserted 18 pellets of testosterone. That did nothing for the patient, who eventually ended up with a psychoanalyst. After approximately two years of analysis, when no change in the symptom occurred, the analyst sent the patient to me. The patient reported very infrequent and inadequate morning erections; he also said that he was unable to get erections with masturbation. Hearing this, I made arrangements for him to go into a sleep-dream laboratory, where he was examined and tested by Drs. Charles Fisher and Raoul Schiavi (15,16). During the first night at the laboratory, while being tested for nocturnal penile tumescence, the patient awoke and discovered that he had a very good erection. This happened several more times during the course of that evening. He went home the next day and for the first time in four years had successful intercourse with his wife. A week later he returned to the laboratory for additional testing, with the same result. During REM sleep he awoke and noticed that he had a very firm erection. He returned home the next day and again had successful intercourse. An additional reinforcement of this occurred a week later, during his third visit to the laboratory. Almost a year later he reports complete success in sexual performance. A diagnostic procedure had proved to be therapeutic, whereas the variety of therapies previously employed had failed completely. Follow-up has been by telephone alone; the patient, now functioning well, saw no need to return for additional therapy, and I did not encourage him to do so. Clearly the simple reinforcement was effective, but why had the other procedures not succeeded?

Reducing the demands for performance is the core of all behavioral methods of therapy and by itself may be curative. The following case illustrates this point. A prominent political figure called me on the phone to say that he had been troubled by impotence for the past several months. Because he was a well-known person, he was reluctant to be seen in our waiting room. I suggested that he try the method prescribed by Dr. John Hunter, previously mentioned. He followed my suggestion, refraining from intercourse for six consecutive sexual encounters. I had heard nothing more from him for over five years, when the patient decided to see me because he was having a marital problem. When he appeared he told me that our telephone conversation had been all that had been necessary for a cure of his impotence.

INHIBITION AND SYMPTOM

The differentiation between inhibition and symptom formation is not always clear. Are impotence and premature ejaculation inhibitions or symptoms? Most clinicians would probably regard them as both inhibition and symptom. Yet if the function of a symptom is to decrease anxiety or to substitute a less anxiety-provoking behavior for one that is more so—e.g., the fetishistic object instead of a human one—premature ejaculation and impotence are more inhibition than symptom.

Freud differentiated the two on the basis of morbidity: "Inhibition relates specifically to function and does not necessarily denote something pathological; a normal restriction or reduction of a function may also be termed an inhibition of it. To speak of a symptom, on the other hand, is tantamount to indicating a morbid process. Thus an inhibition may also be a symptom" (1).

With regard to premature ejaculation and impotence, one can say that developmentally they begin as inhibitions and usually end as symptoms.

The differentiation between inhibition and symptom might be of only theoretical interest were it not for the issue of coital orgasm in women. A large number of women do not regularly experience coital orgasm. Most sex therapists believe that this approximates 70%. If only 30% of women regularly experience coital orgasm, does its absence in 70% represent an inhibition, symptom, or normal variation? I believe that it can be any of these. If a woman has neither intrapsychic nor interpersonal conflict and regularly receives sufficient sexual stimulation but does not reach an orgasm during coitus, this probably represents a normal variation. If, however, she is not sufficiently turned on by that particular partner, the failure to achieve coital orgasm with that partner represents an inhibition. This woman may readily achieve orgasm with another partner. A third woman, for example, may be fearful of losing her sense of independence, even a spurious independence, believing (usually unconsciously) that she will become excessively dependent if she responds with extreme pleasure to a male partner. The failure to completely respond in such a situation does represent a symptom. Inhibitions are usually situational, whereas symptoms and normal variations are generalized.

LONG-RANGE CAUSES OF SEXUAL DYSFUNCTION

Previously I have differentiated the immediate causes of sexual dysfunction from the long-range ones. One must also differentiate between intrapsychic and interpersonal causes. Interpersonal conflict requires couple therapy, while intrapsychic conflict should receive individual psychotherapy. Since almost all sexual dysfunctions are either caused by interpersonal conflict or become a source of them, couple sexual therapy is the treatment of choice in the great majority of cases. (In any case, therapy is greatly enhanced by engaging the patient's partner's cooperation; indeed, he or she becomes a sort of co-therapist.) The minority, however, are created by internal conflict. Combinations of both intrapsychic and interpersonal conflicts are also seen often. Because of these diagnostic complexities, a "cookbook approach" to sex therapy, in which the same regimen is followed with every patient, will fail in many cases.

The following is a case vignette demonstrating a type of interpersonal conflict. A 38-year-old woman bitterly complained about her lack of orgasm with her husband. She took every opportunity to derogate him. She sabotaged early attempts at sensate-focus exercises by a variety of excuses, mostly in terms of her husband's ineptness, passivity, or irritability. In an individual session with the female co-therapist, the woman confessed to an extremely gratifying extramarital relationship. Only by demeaning her husband, causing in him enough anger and anxiety to maintain his impotence and her frustration, could she justify to herself her extramarital relationship.

Some of the long-range causes of sexual dysfunction have already been described. Although Freud made the Oedipal conflict with castration anxiety the central theme in the neuroses, fear of the loss of bodily integrity symbolized by castration is usually integrated intrapsychically with the fear of the loss of self-approval, a fear of conscience, or as Rado termed it, "guilty fear." The following case illustrates some of these dynamics.

A couple consulted me because of an unconsummated marriage of five years. While the husband could achieve erections, albeit sometimes with difficulty, he would lose his erection every time he attempted to penetrate. His wife still loved him dearly but was in despair over the situation. Her husband was desperate as well. He felt hopeless about ever being able to achieve vaginal penetration. About a year before coming for help he had been very depressed, and the depression, anxiety, and fear of humiliation caused him to lose interest in sex with his wife. To prove his masculinity he began to have an extramarital affair. This proved to be intensely exciting, so he moved out of his home and lived with the other woman. Despite intense excitement and very firm erections, he would lose turgidity at the moment of penetration. After ten months, feeling more and more guilty about having deserted his wife, whom he greatly admired, he moved back to their home. Two months later they came to me for treatment.

I tried the couple-sensate-focus exercises as a diagnostic measure. I suspected that the husband would sabotage the treatment, and indeed this turned out to be true. He made every excuse to avoid the exercises. The futility of this approach led me to suggest analytic treatment for the husband. Over the period of a year he gradually began to improve. The story that gradually unfolded was his extraordinary erotic interest in large-breasted women; on the other hand, the only time in his life that he had successful intercourse was with a woman he described as "the most flat-chested woman I have ever seen." This led to a description of how, on many occasions prior to and around puberty, he had surreptitiously gone into his parents' bedroom, opened his mother's dresser, and masturbated while holding and fondling his mother's brassiere. As one might guess, his mother had very large breasts. The Oedipal impulses and associated guilty fear had their unfortunate culmination in the self-imposed punishment (symbolic self-castration to avoid actual castration) of impotence. His recovery was not uneventful. When he could achieve penetration, his penis became anesthetic. When that symptom disappeared, it was followed by retarded ejaculation. When the transference to the therapist was resolved and, in this instance, by a combination of life events rather than by interpretation, he became a very competent sexual partner. Three years later, he and his wife have become the parents of two children.

LEVELS OF SEXUAL FUNCTIONING

Money (17) divides sexual behavior into three phases: acceptive, proceptive, and conceptive. The acceptive phase involves the development of heterosocial skills, including the initiation of social relations with the opposite sex, the chain of social and interpersonal relations preceding sexual behavior, and the maintenance of heterosocial relationships. Biologists refer to these behaviors as *pair-bonding*. The proceptive phase includes sexual desire, excitement, orgasm, and resolution. The conceptive phase includes pregnancy, childbirth, and parenthood.

Inhibitions and symptom formation can occur at each of these levels. Pair bonding may be so ineffective that sexual behaviors are impossible, or if they are achieved, cannot be maintained. Inhibition of sexual desire is now the most common syndrome in women and the second most common in men. (At this level particularly, but really at all levels, one must be careful to consider the possibility of biogenic causes. Inhibition of sexual desire is found in diabetes and as a side effect of many drugs. Mental disorders as well, notably depression, affect sexual desire even more than sexual excitement or orgasm.) Inhibition or symptom formation at the level of orgasm creates either premature ejaculation or retarded ejaculation in men, and retarded or absent orgasm in women. (Premature orgasm in women is very rare). Coital anhedonia, even without actual anesthesia, does occur but is relatively rare. Dyspareunia and vaginismus are special afflictions of women, though on occasion men suffer from dyspareunia as well. Inhibition of the resolution phase is uncommon and generally reflects an emotional tuning out of the partner.

While the categories described above represent the tentative classification of DSM-3, when one returns to the writings of Freud one finds that our

DSM-3 Task Force on Sexual Dysfunctions has in essence reinvented the wheel. "The execution of the sex act presupposes a very complicated sequence of events, any one of which may be the locus of disturbance. The principal loci of inhibition in men are the following: a turning aside of libido at the initiation of the act (psychic unpleasure); absence of physical preparedness (nonerectability); abbreviation of the act (ejaculatio praecox) which may equally well be described as a positive symptom; suspension of the act before its natural culmination (absence of ejaculation); the nonoccurence of the psychic effect (of the pleasure sensation of orgasm). Other disturbances result from the association with the sexual function of specific conditions of a perverse or fetishistic character" (1).

Psychogenic maladaptations of pregnancy, childbirth, and parenthood, parts of the conceptive phase, are beyond the scope of this contribution, as are the paraphilias such as fetishism and exhibitionism, and the disorders we term "gender dysphoria" such as transsexualism.

CLASSIFICATION OF ANXIETIES

The demarcation of anxieties into separate categories for the purposes of classification has barely begun. DSM-3 lists phobic disorders of various types: panic disorder, obsessive-compulsive disorder, and generalized anxiety disorder (18). Of special interest is the differentiation between panic attacks and anticipatory anxiety. The latter, "apprehensive expectation," is almost always present in sexual dysfunctions, at least immediately prior and during sexual activity. On rare occasions one finds a patient with an extensive aversion toward sex, usually a female who describes a panic state that increases in intensity as vaginal penetration gets closer and closer. If her panic prevents penetration (such women report that they cannot even touch their vaginas, let alone permit stimulation by a partner), vaginismus may not be necessary as an unconscious means of preventing penetration.

Acute fear almost always accompanies rape. Except in rare cases, rape is a terribly painful experience, and for a majority of women, results in a disruption of their sexual lives, often leading to sexual dysfunction (19). The occurrence of orgasm during rape in previously preorgasmic women is rare; it occurs possibly because the woman feels a reduction of responsibility for sexual behavior and because the rape enacts masochistic rape fantasies. These reactions underscore the complexity of sexual psychophysiologic responses.

As a tentative scheme, it is possible to describe several different types of chronic anxiety: 1. as a cause of intrapsychic conflict—e.g., the desire for sexual pleasure in conflict with the fear of punishment for forbidden sexual pleasure ("guilty fear"); 2. as a consequence of intrapsychic conflict; 3. anticipatory anxiety without internal conflict; 4. associative anxiety in which sexual behavior is linked to another frightening event, generally regarded as a possible consequence of sex—e.g., fear of a heart attack in a post-coronary patient, fear of pregnancy, of venereal disease, and so forth.

OTHER AFFECTS

Guilt is a very frequent factor in sexual dysfunctions, but because guilt is almost always associated with the fear of punishment in a child and of humiliation in an adult, it has been listed above among the anxieties as "guilty fear."

Anger is also frequently implicated in sexual disorders, in preorgasmia and in vaginismus in the female and in potency problems in the male. Anger toward the spouse is an important ingredient of situational or "spouse only" dysfunction.

Depression can be regarded as an affect as well as a symptom or syndrome. When it occurs as a consequence of a sexual dysfunction, the cure of the sexual symptom will alleviate the depression. If depression is a causal factor, the therapist may wish to treat the depression first. The differentiation of depression as a cause or a consequence has to be made historically.

ENHANCEMENT OF SEXUAL AROUSAL

Additional proof that anxiety is the prime causative factor in sexual dysfunctions is derived from the results of therapeutic techniques that emphasize relaxation of tension. Muscle relaxation, systematic desensitization, rehearsal through role-playing, the reduction of demands for performance, the relaxation created by caressing and massaging, and the insistence on the absence of tension in carrying out the sensate-focus exercises, are all techniques of behavioral therapy carried out by sex therapists.

It would be helpful to therapists if other methods of sexual enhancement could be used in treatment. Clinical observations include the following as factors in enhancing sexual excitement: novelty, variety (of the partners or the sexual repertoire with the same partner), passionate responses of the partner, sharing emotions in a group, an "in love" feeling, and the vague "chemistry" associated with sexual interest, arousal, and excitement. Unconscious factors may be even more important than conscious ones in determining the attraction of one person for another.

The very factors that enhance sexual excitement, e.g., novelty and variety, may also produce enough anxiety to offset the excitement.

While love most often increases lust, in some individuals the two are separated (the so-called madonna-prostitute complex), so that lust is felt only for those partners who cannot be loved, usually someone who appears to be lower in the social scale or degraded in some fashion.

Aggression up to a point may enhance lust. Beyond this point it usually creates anxiety and a failure in performance. There are some people for whom extreme aggression (sadism, rape) is a necessary part of sexual arousal. Nevertheless, even most rapists have difficulty in penetration, or if they can penetrate, cannot ejaculate (20).

Recent examples of laboratory data related to enhancement of sexual excitement come from two sources: brain stimulation and psycho-endocrine studies of couples. Heath (9) demonstrated that electrical self-stimulation of the "pleasure center" of the brain in man will elicit orgasm, but only if the subject is in a sexually arousing situation. The context in which the experiment was conducted was crucial to the elicitation of sexual excitement and orgasm. Persky and coworkers (21) were able to show that a "husband's testosterone level peaks in an ordered fashion with respect to the female partner's menstrual cycle, and particularly to her day of ovulation. How the information necessary for this dyadic interaction is transmitted is not yet known."

INTEGRATIVE APPROACHES TO SEX THERAPY

Flexibility is the watchword of sex therapy. The sex therapist must be able to function at different levels of tasks and roles. At times the therapist is primarily an evaluator, at other times an educator, counselor, marital therapist, and psychotherapist. The sex therapist has to be able to shift from one role to another, as required by clinical circumstances. Sex therapy is serving as an integrative force in the entire field of psychotherapy. The process of combining and integrating behavioral therapy, psychotherapy, and marital therapy necessary in effective sex therapy is serving as a model for psychotherapy in general.

FUTURE RESEARCH DIRECTIONS

Data describing the psychophysiological processes in sexual functioning in normals have been described by a number of researchers. Increase in systolic and diastolic blood pressure and skin conductance are reported by all investigators (22,23,24). Heart rate increases during orgasm, but not during the excitement phase of the sexual response cycle. Increases in blood volume in the vagina and penis are sensitive and reliable measures of sexual arousal, but a still more valid indicator of sexual arousal in women seems to be vaginal pulse amplitude (25).

Studies have begun on psychophysiologic differences between functional and dysfunctional women. Wincze and his colleagues (26) found that anorgasmic women showed less vaginal vasocongestion during an erotic stimulus situation and that their diastolic blood pressure fell, rather than rose, in contrast to the normal control group. Helman (27,28) found that patterns

Table I. Management of sexual problems

	Roles and Tasks of Health Practitioners		
Evaluation of Sex Problem Level	Patient (Client) Need	Therapeutic Tasks	Therapeutic Roles
1. Unknown	To be understood	Active (creative) listening—i.e., understand and evaluate.	Evaluator-inquirer
2. Sexual ignorance	Sexual knowledge	Provide accurate information and suggest specific sexual behavior. Follow-up.	Sex educator
3. Sex discomfort dysfunction	Comfortable sexual functioning	If physician treats organic factors, reduce or remove discomfort dysfunction; make time-limited contract; suggest specific sexual behavior. Follow-up.	Sex educator-counselor; refer to helpful professional if own intervention is insufficient.
4. Interpersonal conflict and sex problem	Assistance with conflict leading to sexual dysfunction	Review, direct, restore bonding; make contract; suggest specific sexual behavior. Follow-up.	Sex educator-counselor and marital therapist; refer if indicated.
5. Sex problem and intrapsychic conflict	Explore internal conflicts and related interpersonal conflicts	Correlate internal conflicts with sex problem for perspective and resolution.	Sex educator-counselor and psychotherapist
6. All of above	Comfortable use of newly learned sex knowledge attitudes/skills	Recognizing hierarchy of patient needs to be addressed in rational brief treatment.	Sex educator-counselor, marital, and psychotherapist; sex therapist

of physiologic sexual arousal during various experimental conditions, including different types of erotic stimuli, were more similar than dissimilar when normal and dysfunctional subjects were compared, but that the absolute level of arousal across all conditions was somewhat lower in the clinical sample. Just as there often are discrepancies between recorded physiological responses to anxiety-provoking stimuli and subjective reports of anxiety, so are there differences between physiologic measures of sexual arousal and verbal reports of the degree of arousal. It may be that many women have an adequate physiologic response to erotic stimuli, but that these sensations are not fully conscious, and that this discrepancy is a significant factor in the failure to reach orgasm. As Heiman says, "At this point we have no clear idea of the extent to which the cognitive-affective experience is independent from the physiological experience of sexual arousal."

Future research will include: 1. an assessment of patterns of physiologic responses to erotic stimuli, comparing functional and dysfunctional persons; 2. studies contrasting physiologic response in different dysfunctions—e.g., premature ejaculation and retarded ejaculation; 3. studying in greater detail the differences between physiological and subjective responses to erotic stimuli; 4. exploring the factors that may enhance sexual responsibility; 5. additional studies contrasting the physiologic and subjective responses to dysphoric and pleasurable stimuli; 6. studying the psychophysiologic responses to treatment (pre- and post-treatment comparisons).

The dyadic interactional endocrine synchrony in normal couples should be compared with findings in sexually dysfunctional couples.

ACKNOWLEDGMENTS

This work was supported in part by USPHS Research Grant MH-08957.

References

1. Freud, S. *The Problem of Anxiety.* New York: Norton, 1936.
2. Rado, S. Emergency behavior. In P.H. Hoch and J. Zubin, eds., New York: Grune & Stratton, 1950.
3. Masters, W.H., and Johnson, V.E. *Human Sexual Inadequacy.* Boston: Little, Brown, 1970.
4. Kaplan, H. *The New Sex Therapy.* New York: Brunner/Mazel, 1974.
5. Lazarus, A.A., and Rosen, R.C. Behavioral therapy techniques in the treatment of sexual disorders. In J.K. Meyer, ed., *Clinical Management of Sexual Disorders.* Baltimore: Williams & Wilkins, 1976.
6. Derogatis, L.R. Psychological assessment of sexual disorders. In J.K. Meyer, ed., *Clinical Management of Sexual Disorders.* Baltimore: Williams & Wilkins, 1976.

7. Lief, H.I. Anxiety reaction. In A.M. Freedman, and H.I. Kaplan, eds., *Comprehensive Textbook of Psychiatry*, 1st ed. Baltimore: Williams & Wilkins, 1967.

8. Malmo, R.B. Physiological concomitants of emotion. In A.M. Freedman, and H.I. Kaplan, eds., *Comprehensive Textbook of Psychiatry*, 1st ed. Baltimore: Williams & Wilkins, 1967.

9. Heath, R.G. Pleasure and brain activity in man. *J. Nerv. Ment. Dis.* 154:3-17, 1972.

10. Cohen, H.D., Rosen, R.C., and Goldstein, L. Electroencephalographic laterality changes during human sexual orgasm. *Arch. Sex. Behav.* 5:189-199, 1976.

11. Herbert, J. The neuroendocrine basis of sexual behavior in primates. In J. Money and H. Musaph, eds., In *Handbook of Sexology*. Amsterdam: Excerpta Medica, 1977.

12. Everitt, B.J. Cerebral monoamines and sexual behavior. In J. Money and H. Musaph, eds., *Handbook of Sexology*. Amsterdam: Excerpta Medica, 1977.

13. Rose, R.M., et al. Androgen responses to stress. *Psychosom, Med.* 31 (5): 418-436, 1969.

14. Hoon, P.W., Wincze, J.P., and Hoon, E.F. A test of reciprocal inhibition: Are anxiety and sexual arousal in women mutually inhibitory? *J. Abnorm. Psychol.* 86 (1):65-74, 1978.

15. Fisher, C., Schiavi, R., Lear, H., et al. The assessment of nocturnal REM erection in the differential diagnosis of sexual impotence. *J. Sex. Marital Ther.* 1:277-289, 1975.

16. Karacan, I., Scott, F.B., Salis, P.J., et al. Nocturnal erections, differential diagnosis of impotence and diabetes. *Biol. Psychiat.* 12:373-380, 1977.

17. Money, J. Personal communication to Diagnostic Statistical Manual #3 Task Force on Psychosexual Disorders, 1977.

18. American Psychiatric Association. *Diagnostic and Statistical Manual of Mental Disorders*, 3rd ed. (Draft of January 15, 1978). R.L. Spitzer, Chairman, Task Force. Washington, D.C.: A.P.A. (in preparation).

19. Miller, W.R., Williams, A.M., and Bernstein, M.H. The impact of rape on marital and sexual adjustment. (Submitted to the *Arch. Gen. Psychiat.*)

20. Groth, N.A., and Burgess, A.W. Sexual dysfunction during rape. *New Eng. J. Med.* 297(14):764, 1977.

21. Persky, H., Lief, H.I., O'Brien, C.P., et al. Reproductive hormone levels and sexual behaviors of young couples during the menstrual cycle. In R. Gemme and C.C. Wheeler, eds., *Progress in Sexology*. New York: Plenum, 1977.

22. Masters, W.H., and Johnson, V.E. *Human Sexual Response*. Boston: Little, Brown, 1966.

23. Wenger, M.A., Averill, J.R., and Smith, D.D.B. Autonomic activity during sexual arousal. *Psychophysiol.* 4:468-477, 1968.

24. Hoon, P.W., Wincze, J.P., and Hoon, E.F. Physiological assessment of sexual arousal in women. *Psychophysiol.* 13:196-204, 1976.

25. Heiman, J.R. Uses of psychophysiology in the assessment and treatment of sexual dysfunction. In J. Lo Piccolo, and L. Lo Piccolo ed., New York: Plenum *The Handbook of Sex Therapy*. 1978.

26. Wincze, V., Hoon, E.F., and Hoon, P.W. A comparison of the physiological responsivity of normal and sexually dysfunctional women during exposure to erotic stimulus. *J. Psychosom. Res.* 20:40-50, 1976.

27. Heiman, J.R. Issues in the use of psychophysiology to assess female sexual dysfunction. *J. Sex. Marital Ther.* 2:197-204, 1976.

28. Heiman, J.R. A psychophysiological exploration of sexual arousal patterns in females and males. *Psychophysiol.* 14:266-274, 1977.

CHAPTER 22

Psychopharmacological Approaches to Treatment of Anxiety

Karl Rickels

Clinical Efficacy

A number of drugs have been utilized to treat anxiety, including barbiturates, such as phenobarbital and amobarbital, and antipsychotic agents, such as the phenothiazines. The category of drugs most commonly used in the treatment of anxiety has been referred to in the past as the minor tranquilizers, although this term is generally being replaced by the term "antianxiety agents."

Table 1 contains a listing of the currently utilized antianxiety agents. The substituted diol meprobamate is of considerable importance because of its historical significance as the first widely used modern antianxiety agent (1,2). Although meprobamate has fallen into some disfavor in recent years, it still appears to be an effective and reliable drug that is unfortunately prescribed much less frequently than it could be. Two newer agents of the benzodiazepine category, chlordiazepoxide and diazepam, have become the most popular agents in the treatment of anxiety today (3). In 1972, chlordiazepoxide and diazepam accounted for 49% of all psychotropic drug prescriptions written in the United States (4). These two drugs are clearly the most commonly used and the most popular of the antianxiety agents (5).

It is probably fair to say that clinicians in general will agree that the order of efficacy for these agents ranges from the barbiturates, through

Table 1. Minor tranquilizers (antianxiety drugs)

	Total Daily Dosage (mg), divided in . 2-4 doses
I. Substituted propane diols (glycol or glycerol derivatives)	
Meprobamate (Miltown, Equanil)	800-3200
Tybamate (Solacen)	750-3000
II. Benzodiazepines	
Chlordiazepoxide (Librium)	15-100
Diazepam (Valium)	5-60
Oxazepam (Serax)	30-120
Chlorazepate (Tranxene)	15-60
Prazepam (Verstran)	20-60
Lorazepam (Ativan)	2-6
III. Diphenylmethane antihistamines	
Hydroxyzine (Atarax, Vistaril)	100-400
IV. Miscellaneous compounds	
Chlormezanone (Trancopal)	200-800
V. Barbiturates	
Phenobarbital	60-150
Butabarbital (Butisol)	60-150

meprobamate, to the benzodiazepine derivatives, probably the most effective antianxiety agents today (6,7,8). Compounds such as hydroxyzine and chlormezanone generally appear closer to the barbiturates than to the benzodiazepines in regard to clinical efficacy.

Hydroxyzine, an antihistamine with sedative properties, has generally been found rather disappointing unless given in daily dosages of 400 mg/day, a regimen associated with marked sedation (9). Chlormezanone appears closer in clinical efficacy to the barbiturates than to the benzodiazepines (10), and tybamate seems effective only in rather severe neurotic disorders and is not very widely used (9). Oxazepam, another widely used benzodiazepine, because of its efficient absorption pattern and rapid metabolism to a psychopharmacologically inactive substance, may particularly be desirable in the treatment of the elderly in a daily dose of 45 mg/day, while higher daily dosages (60-120 mg/day) are needed in the treatment of the nonelderly adult anxious population (11,12). Chlorazepate is claimed to be equal in effect to diazepam, but to produce fewer side effects (13,14). Whether these findings can be confirmed, or will prove simply to be dosage related, has yet to be demonstrated. Prazepam, recently introduced (15,16), appears to be an effective anxiolytic even if given only at bedtime. Lorazepam, the most recently introduced benzodiazepine, also has definite anxiolytic properties even if sedative side effects in daily dosages of 3 mg or more may become quite troublesome for at least the mildly anxious patient (17).

Detailed information on the prescribing of anxiolytics within the United States is available from two recently conducted national surveys (4,5). Several major findings from these surveys are briefly noted here. First, a marked increase in the prescribing of anxiolytics occurred from 1964 to 1974. This increase was confined to the benzodiazepines and due primarily to diazepam; the prescribing of hydroxyzine, meprobamate, and phenobarbital held steady or declined slightly during this period. Indeed, by 1972, diazepam was the most frequently prescribed drug in the United States; its close analogue, chlordiazepoxide, was the third most often prescribed. Over 70 million prescriptions (half of all precriptions for psychotropic drugs) were written for these two agents at a cost of over $200 million, in 1972. Second, the majority of prescriptions for anxiolytics are written by nonpsychiatrists, and less than half of these prescriptions are dispensed to patients with a primary diagnosis of emotional as opposed to physical disorder. For example, according to a survey conducted in 1972, diazepam was prescribed by nonpsychiatrists for mental disorders in only 30% of patients. Third, comparable surveys of drug use in Europe have shown that the American rate of prevalence for minor tranquilizers and sedatives is about "average" for industrialized nations (5).

These current patterns of anxiolytic usage will no doubt be altered in the future by the introduction of effective new agents. A number of new benzodiazepines, not yet marketed in the U.S.A., are at present being studied actively.

A number of other drugs have been utilized in the treatment of anxiety, including antipsychotic agents (9) and some over-the-counter (OTC) preparations (18).

Phenothiazines or other antipsychotic drugs are used primarily in the treatment of prepsychotic patients and only infrequently in neurotic patients. In fact, in most anxiety conditions, these neuroleptics are generally prescribed only if such established antianxiety agents as meprobamate, chlordiazepoxide, or diazepam have proven ineffective. Even in the lower dosages used for neurotic patients, phenothiazines may produce disturbing side effects, including mild symptoms of akathisia or inner restlessness, thereby increasing rather than decreasing the patient's anxiety. In addition, long-term usage of these agents involves the danger of irreversible tardive dyskinesia.

A discussion of antianxiety agents would be remiss without some comparison of their short-term effectiveness to that of OTC sedatives. In a recently concluded two-week trial, Rickels and Hesbacher were able to show that the benzodiazepine derivative chlordiazepoxide (30 mg/day) was clearly more effective than either placebo, aspirin, or an OTC daytime sedative (18).

The latter three agents, in fact, produced rather similar and only small amounts of improvement. Even when treated for only two weeks, 60% of patients on chlordiazepoxide reported marked or moderate improvement. The lesson is clear; OTC daytime sedatives are no replacement for antianxiety agents.

Recently, there has been some interest in the possible role of beta-adrenergic blocking agents such as propranolol in the treatment of anxiety (19,20,21,22). The rationale for such use is that peripheral symptoms of physiological activation secondary to anxiety might be effectively diminished by these drugs. However, it is still too early in the phase of evaluation of the beta-adrenergic blocking agents in the treatment of anxiety to reach a sound judgment about their effectiveness in this area. While these agents do effect a demonstrable decrease in heart palpitations, which may or may not be related to anxiety, there is little direct evidence of their anxiolytic properties, and this investigator questions their utility in the treatment of anxiety.

Chlordiazepoxide, and even more so diazepam, have some degree of sedative-hypnotic effects, and can be so utilized for many patients, particularly when anxiety is a major cause of insomnia. Because of their extremely low suicide potential, benzodiazepines such as diazepam are of particular value as hypnotics for patients with agitated depression in whom the possibility of a suicide attempt is always a concern. Another benzodiazepine, flurazepam, is being promoted only as a hypnotic and is considered to be a rather effective agent in this condition (23). Finally, triazolam, an experimental benzodiazepine, has been shown to be a good hypnotic, and when administered at bedtime, to decrease neurotic symptomatology as measured by the Hopkins Symptom Checklist (24).

Clinical Safety

By far the most common and important side effects of all antianxiety agents, including the benzodiazepines, arise from their central nervous system depressant effects. Sedative side effects are commonly seen in the early phase of treatment and are usualy dose-related. With prolonged administration, side effects usually diminish. Patients should, however, be advised to exercise caution about driving or operating heavy machinery during the first few days of treatment.

More severe adverse drug effects such as hepatotoxicity or hematological disorders are rarely seen with the minor tranquilizers. Moreover, cross reactions with other drugs are quite uncommon. Although patients should be warned against mixing excessive amounts of alcohol and benzodiazepines, it seems that too much clinical importance has been attached to the dangers of combining alcohol, lightly consumed, with antianxiety agents taken as prescribed. One of the most important features of the benzodiazepines is their freedom from lethal toxicity in high dosages, giving them an extraordinarily low potential for successful use in suicide attempts unless taken together with excessive amounts of alcohol and/or sedative or narcotic drugs. There are no reported cases in the medical literature of deaths from overdosage of either chlordiazepoxide or diazepam alone, even though these drugs have been ingested in massive dosage (e.g., up to 1,850 mg for chlordiazepoxide) (25). The low suicide potential of these drugs, in addition to the general absence of serious side effects, makes them the safest and least toxic of all the psychotropic agents. The importance of a low suicide potential for a drug commonly used in a wide variety of psychiatric patients can hardly be overemphasized.

Most clinicians probably agree that compared to the benzodiazepines, the barbiturates produce more sedative side effects (26), are considerably more toxic, and are much more successful suicidal agents (27,28), and have a higher dependency and addiction potential. A final disadvantage of the barbiturates is that they stimulate microsomal liver enzymes and thus affect the drug metabolism of many other medications given concomitantly. Care must be used, therefore, in prescribing these agents to patients with concurrent medical conditions.

In view of these findings, there seems to be little reason to prescribe barbiturates when reduction of anxiety is the therapeutic goal.

In 1975, chlordiazepoxide and diazepam were placed on the restricted drug list by the Food and Drug Administration. This action reflects the growing concern about the addictive potential of these agents. Without doubt, there are cases of abuse of and addiction or habituation to benzodiazepines, especially on the part of individuals with addictive personalities. In several studies, patients treated with a high dose of benzodiazepines for prolonged periods and then abruptly switched to placebo subsequently developed withdrawal signs (29,30,31).

On the other hand, it should be pointed out that these withdrawal reactions do occur primarily in patients treated for long periods of time and usually with excessive daily dosages and when medication is stopped abruptly. Slow reduction of dosage can prevent such withdrawal reactions. Habituation has been reported in rare instances, but is still extremely uncommon.

Warnings concerning the abuse of various antianxiety agents continue to be issued despite clinical evidence of their relative safety (32). In the opinion of this investigator, it is time to dispel the myth that the unsuspecting housewife must be protected from the careless prescribing of dangerous drugs likely to produce lifelong addiction. The newer antianxiety agents, so widely prescribed by physicians, are simply not that dangerous and, indeed, have a low addiction potential. Also, extensive experience in the drug treatment of neurotic patients indicates that these individuals often take less, not more, medication than prescribed. To discourage the use of an effective agent because a very limited group of patients, such as heroin addicts or alcoholics, may misuse such a drug seems indefensible.

Furthermore, it seems that far too much importance is attached to warnings about the "psychological dependence" that patients may develop with antianxiety agents. Granting that some patients may come to use these agents as an occasional emotional crutch, is this necessarily harmful? Such dependency is clearly less expensive, and may even be less hazardous, than reliance on a physician's continued support (33). Freud's "psychoanalysis interminable" comes to mind. Dependent persons will simply depend on something or someone for support, and the taking of an occasional pill for emotional problems hardly seems cause for great concern.

General Comments

Antianxiety agents work symptomatically, not etiologically. They do not, for example, directly affect the psychodynamic and environmental factors responsible for emotional problems; they do not, at least in a direct sense, affect the basic personality attributes of the patient. By relieving the symptoms of anxiety and tension, however, these drugs may render a patient less miserable and better able to cope with intrapsychic and extrapsychic stress.

It certainly is important for the achievement of good therapeutic results that antianxiety agents be prescribed appropriately. The physician who prescribes these agents for the achievement of unobtainable goals rather than for symptomatic relief, or as a vehicle of rejection rather than within the context of a supportive relationship, will see only a few beneficial effects. In other words, drugs must be prescribed for the right reasons. Equally important for achieving good results is that the physician be knowledgeable about the antianxiety agents he uses. Even if precribed for the right reasons, the wrong agent, or the right agent given in the wrong treatment regimen, will not prove helpful to the patient.

While anxiolytic drug treatment does represent an appropriate first treatment approach for all anxious patients who have not responded to some supportive intervention, with patients who do not respond to pharmacological treatment in family practice being referred for psychiatric consultation, talking with a friend, a clergyman, or a physician is often of great help to many who suffer from anxiety, and in fact may be all that is needed by some, and particularly those who suffer from an acute or situational anxiety episode. More often, however, anxious patients need something more, that is they need additional pharmacological treatment at least for a limited period of time.

Drugs not only bring about change through their pharmacological effects, but also induce psychologically based improvement by serving as an indication to the patient of the doctor's knowledge and interest in him. In other words, the doctor helps, and this realization leads to psychological improvement (9).

A flexible approach based on the patient's initial needs is urged for antianxiety drug treatment. For example, antianxiety agents should be titrated for the individual patient, since drug plasma levels, assessed for the same dosages, may vary widely from patient to patient (34). Within this context, it should be noted that sedative side effects often decrease without dosage adjustment within a few weeks, allowing for dosage increase at this time in patients now showing initial improvement.

The choice of a specific antianxiety agent is largely empirical, and most physicians, quite understandably, initiate treatment with those agents most familiar to them.

Drug treatment should be employed only when warranted by the patient's degree of disability or discomfort, and should be primarily symptom-oriented. Duration of treatment should be influenced by duration of symptoms. Thus many acutely anxious patients may require treatment for only a few days or weeks, since their complaints are often short-lived and of a situational nature. With these acutely anxious patients, the main function of drug treatment is generally to mitigate the patient's acute discomfort until his anxiety attack runs its course. Short-term treatment, however, may well prove inadequate for more chronically anxious patients. It is likely that many chronically anxious patients are currently being treated inadequately and for too short a period of time.

Many anxious patients seem to need a more protracted course of pharmacologic treatment than is generally provided. For some, even a form of maintenance treatment similar to that of diabetics receiving insulin or hypertensive patients receiving antihypertensive medication may be necessary. This type of antianxiety treatment is frequently being provided in clinical practice, even if no research data are available to support or refute such a strategy. Other anxious patients may require such nondrug approaches, either alone or in combination with drug treatment, as family therapy, marriage counseling, or group or individual psychotherapy. Present findings suggest that this may be particularly appropriate for patients who are only mildly anxious, who are high in obsessive-compulsive symptoms and have difficulty coping with life's routine demands, and who have marked problems in their interpersonal relations.

The clinician should also consider whether or not some patients not responding well to antianxiety agents are actually latent depressives who might be better treated with antidepressants. It is a good practice to review the diagnosis of any patient who does not show signs of responding to anxiolytics within a reasonable period of time (roughly 2 to 4 weeks) in order to determine whether an underlying depression, a pseudo-neurotic schizophrenic or pan-neurotic illness, or some major characterologic problem has been overlooked.

Table 2. Predictors of improvement with anxiolytics

Physician Attributes

Warmth
Liking patient
Feeling comfortable with patient
Positive attitude toward drugs
Good prognosis

Patient Personality Characteristics

More verbal intelligence
More compliance
More realistic treatment goals
High ego strength
Low verbal hostility
Low acquiescence

Neurotic Psychopathology

More severe somatization
Less severe performance difficulty
Less severe interpersonal sensitivity
More severe anxiety
Less severe depression

Social Advantage

More education
Higher occupational level
Higher socioeconomic class
More marital stability

Treatment Orientation

Realizes problems are emotional rather than somatic
Expects drug treatment

Prior Treatment Characteristics

Treated with fewer prior psychiatric drugs
Better response to prior psychiatric drugs

Nonspecific Factors in Treatment Response

Clinical experience has indicated that drug response in anxiety is influenced by many factors above and beyond those associated with the pharmacological action of the medication the patient receives: improvement often occurs spontaneously; any effort at treatment, no matter how small, may produce at least some placebo response; and any doctor-patient contact may result in some change in clinical status (35,9).

The isolation of the most important nonspecific factors that influence drug treatment response in neurotic anxiety, and the evaluation of the nature and extent of their impact, represent a complex and challenging research undertaking.

A certain pattern of relationships between nonspecific factors and response to treatment with anxiolytics has emerged (36). Table 2 summarizes some of these relationships; it gives only those nonspecific factors that have been replicated rather consistently in research conducted by the author's research group or in research conducted by others.

Of particular interest is that such predictors as more realistic aspirations toward mental health, high ego strength, low hostility, and better social advantage are also good predictors for psychotherapy outcome (37).

Research on nonspecific factors suggest ways in which the physician can use anxiolytics more successfully. Thus, he may enhance a patient's chances of responding well to anxiolytics by such measures as adopting a warm and empathetic approach to the patient and seeking to instill realistic and positive treatment expectations in the patient. Presently available knowledge on nonspecific factors can also help the physician decide which of his patients are likely to respond well to anxiolytic treatment alone, and which probably require concomitant or alternative treatment.

Further research on nonspecific factors should go far toward enabling the physician to make more appropriate use of the anxiolytic agents in his armamentarium. It is strongly urged, then, that greater attention be directed toward specifying the impact of nonspecific factors on short-term as well as long-term anxiolytic treatment.

ACKNOWLEDGMENTS

This work was supported in part by USPHS Research Grant MH-08957.

REFERENCES

1. Berger, F.M. The similarities and differences between meprobamate and barbiturates. *Clin. Pharmacol. Ther.* 4:209-231, 1963.
2. Byck, R. Drugs and the treatment of psychiatric disorders, In L.S. Goodman and A. Gilman, eds., *The Pharmacological Basis of Therapeutics,* 5th ed. New York: Macmillan, 1975.

3. Balter, M.B., and Levine, J. The nature and extent of psychotropic drug usage in the United States. *Psychopharmacol. Bull.* 5:3-13, 1969.
4. Blackwell, B. Psychotropic drugs in use today: The rôle of diazepam in medical practice. *J.A.M.A.* 225:1637-1641, 1973.
5. Parry, H.J., Balter, M.B., Mellinger, G.D., et al. National patterns of psychotherapeutic drug use. *Arch. Gen. Psych.* 28:769-783, 1973.
6. Hesbacher, P.T., Rickels, K., Hutchinson, J., et al. Setting, patient, and doctor effects on drug response in neurotic patients: II. Differential improvement. *Psychopharmacol.* 18:209-226, 1970.
7. Cohen, J., Gomez, E., Hoell, N.L., et al. Diazepam and phenobarbital in the treatment of anxiety: A controlled multicenter study using physician and patient rating scales. *Curr. Ther. Res.* 20:184-193, 1976.
8. Lader, M.H., Bond, A.J., and James, D.C. Clinical comparison of anxiolytic drug therapy. *Psychol. Med.* 4:381-387, 1974.
9. Rickels, K. Antineurotic agents: Specific and non-specific effects. In D.H. Efron, J.O. Cole, J.Levine, and J.R. Wittenborn, eds., *Psychopharmacology: A Review of Progress, 1957-1967.* Washington, D.C.: Public Health Service Publication No. 1836, 1968.
10. Rickels, K., Pereira-Ogan, J.A., Case, W.G., et al.Chlormezanone in anxiety: A drug rediscovered? *Am. J. Psychiat.* 131:592-595, 1974.
11. Merlis, S., and Koepke, H.H. The use of oxazepam in elderly patients. *Dis. Nerv. Syst.* 36:27-29, 1975.
12. DeSilverio, R.V., Rickels, K., Raab, E., et al. Oxazepam and meprobamate in anxious neurotic outpatients. *J. Clin. Pharm.* 9:259-263, 1969.
13. Cooper, A.J., Magnus, R.V., Rose, M., et al. Controlled trial of dipotassium chlorazepate ("Tranxene") in anxiety. *Brit. J. Psychiat.* 123:475-476, 1973.
14. Dureman, I., and Norrman, B. Clinical and experimental comparison of diazepam, clorazepate and placebo. *Psychopharmacol.* 40:279-284, 1975.
15. Goldberg, H.L., and Finnerty, R.J. A double-blind study of prazepam vs. placebo in single doses in the treatment of anxiety. *Compr. Psychiat.* 18:147-156, 1977.
16. Rickels, K., Sablosky, H., Silverman, H., et al. Prazepam in anxiety: A controlled clinical trial. *Compr. Psychiat.* 18:239-249, 1977.
17. Rickels, K., Case, W.G., Chung, H.R., et al. Lorazepam and diazepam in anxious outpatients: A controlled study. *Int. Pharmacopsychiat.* 11:93-101, 1976.
18. Rickels, K., and Hesbacher, P.T. Over-the-counter daytime sedatives: A controlled study. *J.A.M.A.* 223:29-33, 1973.
19. Lader, M. The peripheral and central role of the catecholamines in the mechanisms of anxiety. *Int. Pharmacopsychiat.* 125-137, 1974.
20. McMillin, W.P. Oxprenolol in anxiety. *Lancet* 1:1193, 1973.
21. Tanna, V.T., Penningroth, R.P., and Woolson, R.F. Propranolol in the treatment of anxiety neurosis. *Compr. Psychiat.* 18:319-326, 1977.
22. Wheatley, D. Comparative effects of propranolol and chlordiazepoxide in anxiety states. *Brit. J. Psychiat.* 115:1411-1412, 1969.
23. Greneblatt, D.J., Shader, R.I., and Koch-Weser, J. Flurazepam hydrochloride. *Clin. Pharmacol. Ther.* 17:1-14, 1975.
24. Rickels, K., Gingrich, R.L., Morris, R.J., et al.Triazolam in insomniac family practice patients. *Clin. Pharmacol. Ther.* 18:315-324, 1975.
25. Jenner, F.A., and Parkin, D. A large overdose of chlordiazepoxide. *Lancet* 2:322-323, 1961.
26. Hesbacher, P.T., Rickels, K., Gordon, P.E., et al. Setting, patient and doctor effects on drug response in neurotic patients: I. Differential attrition, dosage deviation and side reaction responses to treatment. *Psychopharmacol.* 18:180-208, 1970.

27. Berger, F.M. The role of drugs in suicide. In L. Yochelson, ed., *Symposium on Suicide*. Washington, D.C.: George Washington University, 1967.

28. Hollister, L.E. Overdoses of psychotherapeutic drugs. *Clin. Pharmacol. Ther.* 7:142-146, 1966.

29. Covi, L., Lipman, R.S., Pattison, J.H., et al. Length of treatment with anxiolytic sedatives and response to their sudden withdrawal. *Acta Psychiat. Scand.* 49:51-64, 1973.

30. Hollister, L.E., and Glazener, F.S. Withdrawal reactions from meprobamate, alone and combined with promazine: A controlled study. *Psychopharmacol.* 1:336-341, 1960.

31. Hollister, L.E., Motzenbecker, F.P., and Degan, R.O. Withdrawal reactions from chlordiazepoxide ("Librium"). *Psychopharmacol.* 2:63-68, 1961.

32. Hollister, L.E. Valium: A discussion of current issues. *Psychosom.* 18:1-15, 1977.

33. Wheatley, D. *Psychopharmacology and Family Practice*. London: William Heinemann Medical Books, 1973.

34. Greenblatt, D.J., and Shader, R.I. *Benzodiazepines in Clinical Practice*. New York: Raven Press, 1974.

5. Uhlenhuth, E.H., Covi, L., and Lipman, R.S. Indications for minor tranquilizers in anxious outpatients. In P. Black, ed., *Drugs and the Brain: Papers on the Action, Use, and Abuse of Psychotropic Agents*. Baltimore: John Hopkins Press, 1969.

36. Rickels, K. Non-specific factors in drug treatment. In J.P. Brady, J. Mendels, M.T. Orne, and W. Rieger, eds., *Psychiatry: Areas of Promise and Advancement*. New York: Spectrum Press, 1976.

37. Luborsky, and L., Auerbach, A.H., Chandler, M., et al. Factors influencing the outcome of psychotherapy: A review of quantitative research. *Psychol. Bull.* 75:145-185, 1971.

CHAPTER 23

Beta-Adrenergic Blocking Agents in the Treatment of Anxiety

Ferris N. Pitts, Jr. and Robert Allen

There are numerous reports of the effectiveness of beta-adrenergic block-ing agents in the treatment of a wide range of anxiety symptoms in various clinical circumstances. Some of these are anecdotal case studies, some are reports of groups of patients treated in open trials, and others are results of various types of blind clinical pharmacological investigations. These studies differ so much in experimental design, patients studied, definitions of anxiety, types and dosages of beta-adrenergic blockers, and other variables that no two are strictly comparable. Most of these studies will be summarized in the following pages, and the interested reader can evaluate such factors as type of anxiety studied, method of analysis of results, qualifications to results, etc. The essential point to emphasize before proceeding with this review is that these studies have been reported from at least seven countries over a period of nearly fifteen years and *no negative report has ever been made*—that is, every study of beta-adrenergic blockade in the treatment of anxiety has found considerable improvement in symptoms consequent to the medication.

In 1965, three groups from three different countries reported anecdotal symptomatic benefit in anxiety from the use of propranolol. Besterman and Friedlander (1) described the alleviation of palpitations and tachycardia in 4 patients with effort syndrome and sinus tachycardia from a group of 56 patients with a wide variety of conditions treated with propranolol. Four patients with effort syndrome and sinus tachycardia were treated; all had complained of palpitation. In spite of sedation, casual pulse rates recorded in the outpatient clinic averaged 130,130,110, and 100 respectively. On treatment with propranolol the pulse rate slowed and averaged 85,80,87, and 70 respectively. Only one of the patients still noticed palpitation, and she found the symptom less marked. In one of these cases treatment was stopped and the heart rate then increased from 78 to 130. The slower rate was restored by further propranolol.

Nordenfelt (2) reported testing 12 patients with 5 mg IV propranolol; of these, "the remaining 3 patients sought medical advice for palpitations and were nervous and uneasy. Physical examinations and x-rays did not reveal any heart disease." The tachycardia before propranolol (pulses, respectively, 100, 95, and 110 recumbent; and 115, 110, and 130 erect) was corrected (pulses, respectively, 75, 70, and 80 recumbent; and 80, 85, and 95 erect) after 5 mg IV. The very slight T-wave depressions while recumbent, to which were added biphasic or negative T-deflection (only in leads III, II, and/or V_4) in the erect posture (which was the clinical reason for the test in these 3 neurotics), were completely cleared-absent in all 3 after the intravenous propranolol. The 3 neurotic "patients stated unanimously that they became calmer and experienced far less cardiac disturbance after the injection." Nordenfelt suggested that the neurotic manifestations and the slight EKG-cardiac changes were due to increased sympathetic tone and speculated that carefully selected neurotic patients would benefit from treatment with oral beta-receptor blocking agents.

Turner, Granville-Grossman, and Smart (3) reported that 5 mg IV propranolol (but not IV saline or 62.5 mg IV amytal) produced a significant reduction in tachycardia and discomfort in 8 patients with thyrotoxicosis and in 8 patients with anxiety neurosis.

In 1966, Granville-Grossman and Turner reported a systematic double-blind comparison of a week each on placebo and propranolol (with an Armitage closed sequential design) in the treatment of anxiety neurotics free of severe depression, schizophrenia, organic brain disease, heart disease, bronchial asthma, and others (4). Twenty mg propranolol four times per day was found to be significantly more effective than placebo in this short-term therapeutic design. "Only autonomically mediated symptoms were found to be significantly affected, suggesting that improvement was related to the known adrenergic Beta-receptor peripheral action of the drug."

In 1968, Suzman gave a preliminary report of an extensive systematic long-term therapeutic trial of propranolol in treatment of anxiety neurosis (5). Forty patients presenting with symptoms of anxiety of 1 month to 35 years' duration were studied before and during the administration of propranolol in the total daily dose of 40 to 160 mg, as well as during placebo substitution, for periods varying from 1 to 40 months. The report said that during propranolol therapy tachycardia was controlled, and the patients' multiform somatic symptoms were completely or partially relieved. Feelings of anxiety were allayed, particularly when they were primarily attributable to somatic symptoms, but to a lesser extent when obsessive, phobic, or depressive features were prominent. The orthostatic and hyperventilatory effects on the heart rate and ST-T changes were virtually eliminated. Notably, the patients' compelling tendency to overbreathe spontaneously under emotional stress was subdued, and moreover, the cerebral and peripheral effects of hypocapnia, formerly so readily induced by voluntary hyperventilation, were prevented or greatly lessened. During periods of placebo substitution, in all but five cases, the somatic symptoms recurred, accompanied by a recrudescence of the anxiety and the reappearance of the electrocardiographic changes. The relapse occurred within hours or after several days, with the same intensity as formerly in some patients but to a lesser extent in others. Suzman seemed to indicate a delayed resolution of central—psychologic—apprehensive anxiety and an immediate resolution of the cardiac and other somatic symptoms of anxiety. Only Suzman has reported continued treatment of anxiety neurotics with propranolol—he published a more complete study of 725 patients treated one to twelve years in 1976 (6). All other studies have been of short-term administration of propranolol, have found immediate improvement in somatic symptoms of anxiety and have usually been extrapolatively interpreted to show that propranolol has no effect on central-psychological anxiety, rather than (more precisely) little immediate effect on psychological anxiety.

In 1969, Wheatley reported a cooperative blind comparative treatment study conducted by general practitioners. The subjects were patients with acute and chronic anxiety neurosis (but no hypertension, asthma, hay fever, bronchitis, or pregnancy) (7). Thirty-five general practitioners treated 105 patients for 6 weeks with either 30 mg propranolol or 10 mg chlordiazepoxide three times a day, in double-blind randomized fashion, for 6 weeks. When the code was broken, it was learned that 54 patients had received chlordiazepoxide and 51 propranolol; there were very similar degrees of improvement in anxiety in the 2 groups, there were fewer side effects among those receiving propranolol, and there was more benefit to depression and sleep disturbance among those receiving chlordiazepoxide.

In 1968, Nordenfelt, Persson, and Redfors (8) reported on a randomized double-blind crossover trial of a propranolol analogue Alprenolol and placebo in 14 patients with "nervous heart complaints." In all patients heart disease, asthma, and other diseases had been ruled out. Complex exercise—cardiovascular function tests and interviews for symptom tabulation—were done before the drugs, after 2 weeks on 80 mg Alprenolol four times daily, and after 2 weeks on placebo. The authors emphasized that they considered their patient study groups an heterogeneous one: and consequently they were most cautious in avoiding making general conclusions. The symptoms tabulated, however, were those of anxiety neurosis (palpitations, chest pain, oppression, breathlessness, sweating, tremor, nervousness, dizziness, fatigue, headache, mild depression, gastrointestinal symptoms), and all were cleared or greatly improved (compared to placebo) with Alprenolol ($p < 0.00001$ per our X^2 assessment of their tabulated data). All 14 patients had relief of palpitations with Alprenolol, compared to 5 on placebo. In a global blind assessment 12 of the 14 had greatly preferred the Alprenolol to placebo on account of the marked reduction of symptoms. Of the 2 who preferred the placebo, one had experienced nausea with Alprenolol but had also noted clearing of tremor, vertigo, and palpitations. Another patient preferred placebo because of nausea with Alprenolol but had complete relief of symptoms and no side effects when, still blind, given a smaller dosage. (Nordenfelt, Persson, and Redfors counted a third patient a placebo preference who felt better during Alprenolol therapy but attributed this to resuming smoking.) The probability of this blind drug preference occurring by chance alone is less than 0.01 (our X^2 calculation). Additionally, heart rate during exercise and physical working capacity tended to improve to normal on Alprenolol as compared to pre-study and placebo assessments. Nordenfelt, Persson, and Redfors stated "it seems reasonable to assume that Beta-blocking agents can be valuable in the treatment of patients with nervous heart complaints."

In 1969, Frohlich, Tarazi and Dustan (9) reported the effectiveness of propranolol in the short-term treatment of "hyperdynamic beta-adrenergic circulatory state," a condition they had described and defined in 2 patients in 1966 (10). In brief, patients with hyperdynamic Beta-adrenergic circulatory state are characterized by: (a) symptoms characteristic of anxiety neurosis— "disturbing palpitations, chest discomfort, . . . rapid heart action associated with varying degrees of physical limitations, and . . . these symptoms persisted inordinately long following exertion"; (b) systolic and/or diastolic hypertension in most cases although 2 of 14 were normotensive at all times and 4 of 14 had only labile or episodic hypertension; (c) marked reported and observed activation of cardiac and other symptoms at times of great anxiety and/or physical exercise; (d) extraordinary sensitivity to infusion of the beta-adrenergic agonist isoproterenol (but not to Alpha-adrenergic agonists or control solutions) with excessive increase of heart rate and cardiac index as compared to both normal control subjects and other hypertensives, and with production of anxiety attacks ("almost uncontrollable hysterical outbursts"); (e) instantaneous response of isoproterenol-evoked signs and symptoms to the infusion of the Beta-adrenergic blocker propranolol (but not to placebo infusions); and (f) clearing or marked improvement of all symptoms and signs with daily ingestion of propranolol in individualized dosages (varying between 20 and 80 mg four times daily, usual dosage 40 mg four times daily) but not to placebo. Some of the comments of Frohlich, Tarazi, and Dustan at the end of their 1969 scientific report merit careful reading.

Patients with diseases such as thyrotoxicosis, pheochromocytoma, and porphyria were excluded. Increased sympathetic vasomotor outflow is identified as one explanation for the increased heart rate and emotional responses, and even hypertension; but the arterial pressure or vascular resistance responses to upright tilt, cold, Valsalva maneuver, levarterenol, and tyramine were normal and seemed to exclude this mechanism. Pressure responses following tyramine indicated normal catecholamine stores and release. Diminished parasympathetic activity seemed to be excluded by normal response of heart rate during the overshoot phase of the Valsalva maneuver, and to carotid sinus stimulation and ocular pressure. Tachycardia followed atropine. Having gone this far, however, the investigators must state that "until a short-acting parasympatholytic agent is available for more precise dose-response measurements and until more exact responses to atropine in the normotensive and hypertensive subject have been established, the interrelationship of parasympathetic and Beta-adrenergic functions remains speculative." . . . They go on to say that although several other groups noted amelioration of cardiac symptoms and anxiety with inhibition of Beta-adrenergic receptor activity and suggested that Beta-adrenergic stimulation may be the mechanism producing cardiac symptoms in certain anxious individuals, no attempt was made to reproduce anxiety and cardiac symptoms pharmacologically by Beta-stimulation. Frohlich, Tarazi, and Dustan believed that there was evidence for a syndrome of increased beta-adrenergic activity, but that afflicted patients did not constitute a homogeneous group comprising a single disease. Included among these patients were those who were normotensive or whose blood pressure elevation was sustained, labile, or episodic. Some were classified as "hypertensive" even though at the time of hemodynamic study arterial pressures were normal. Others considered to be hypertensive had pretreatment control blood pressure averages within the normal range, although at times pressure was significantly elevated. The investigators said that "the fact that most of these patients were hypertensive does not necessarily indicate that this syndrome occurs predominantly in hypertensive individuals; rather it probably reflects our investigative interest."

Bonn and Turner (11) demonstrated that D-propranolol, which has little or no Beta-blocking action, had no antianxiety action in a dosage of 40 mg four times a day with a double-blind sequential crossover design in 15 patients with marked anxiety symptoms in various psychiatric conditions.

Bonn, Turner, and Hicks (12) then used the Armitage closed sequential design in a double-blind drug-placebo study of practolol in a mixed group of outpatients whose "most prominent symptoms were attributable to anxiety. Patients whose symptoms were associated with severe depression, organic brain disease, or schizophrenia, or who had heart disease were excluded." Two anxiety rating scales were obtained before and after each of the two 14-

day experimental treatment periods. Patients received either 200 mg practolol or placebo twice daily for two weeks and then the other for a second 14 days. Plasma practolol levels demonstrated patient compliance. Some patients had side effects with practolol but not placebo: 5 patients experienced nausea not severe enough to cause cessation of drug trial; one patient noted reduced exercise tolerance but marked alleviation of anxiety symptoms; another patient (who had denied that she had an history of asthma as a child and had no attacks for 16 years since age 14) had an asthmatic attack on the practolol experimental sequence. After the first 8 patients had completed the trial, investigator's blind preferences for practolol over placebo were statistically significant ($p < 0.05$), and when the 15 subjects already in the study had completed the blind therapeutic sequences, all 15 were practolol preferences ($p < 0.01$). The authors noted that practolol appeared to block autonomic anxiety symptoms (palpitations, etc.) but not the psychological-apprehensive anxiety in the two-week trial. They noted that little practolol enters the central nervous system, further supporting their notion that Beta-adrenergic blocking agents act primarily on somatic (as opposed to psychic) aspects of anxiety. They qualified this concept, however, and noted that although practolol is supposed to have nearly pure Beta-receptor-blocking action, it nevertheless caused asthma in one of the patients on the experimental protocol.

Carlsson (13) in 1971, noted "hyperkinetic circulation" in alcoholics in the initial abstinence phase and reported "normal conditions were restored by 40 mg propranolol; even tension symptoms decreased." As a consequence of these findings Carlsson and Johansson (14) devised a propranolol-placebo comparison of the effects of propranolol on anxiety and other symptoms during the first 10-12 days of alcohol withdrawal. Patients were given an 8-day trial of 40 mg propranolol four times a day (or placebo); before and after the trial psychological questionnaires for tension (anxiety), depression, and dysphoria scales were obtained. The 18 propranolol subjects had significantly fewer anxiety-tension symptoms during treatment than did the 18 placebo patients; depression symptoms were not quite statistically significantly less in the propranolol group; dysphoric symptoms were not at all different between the two groups.

Gallant, Swanson, and Guerrero-Figueroa reported in 1973 (15) a double-blind random trial of propranolol in 10 patients and placebo in 10 patients. All were "hospitalized volunteer chronic alcoholic patients with the target syndrome of 'anxiety and tension.' All subjects were free of significant disabilities of the cardiovascular, renal, and hepatic systems. Psychotherapeutic drugs were discontinued for five days prior to initial doses of study drugs, and most recent exposure to alcohol was a minimum period of ten days prior to initiation of the study medication." Thus, all subjects had presumably completed alcoholic withdrawal prior to onset of the study. Patients were given propranolol (or equivalent placebo tablets) according to an incremental dosage schedule: 20 mg twice daily for seven days; then 20 mg four times daily for seven days; and finally, 40 mg three times daily for two weeks. Dosage was not increased if marked therapeutic and/or side effects appeared. A number of physiological, serological, and psychological measures were made. By the end of four weeks of treatment both the placebo and propranolol groups showed considerable improvement; no covariance measure of improvement of anxiety showed propranolol to be statistically more effective than placebo plus ward programs, but the blind investigator's global assessment of change showed the propranolol group to be significantly ($p<0.05$) more improved than the placebo group. The investigators pointed out that their study groups would have to be much larger than 10 subjects to show clear superiority of propranolol over placebo in a circumstance in which all subjects are improving considerably as a result of the natural history of maintained abstinence from alcohol abuse.

Linken reported clinical success with small amounts of propranolol (30-40 mg per day) treating the severe anxiety symptoms consequent to LSD ingestion in three patients (16).

McMillin performed a double-blind crossover one-week drug comparison of 80 mg practolol and 5 mg diazepam three times a day in tense, anxious, and frightened Belfast citizens caught in a civil war and found that both treatments resulted in considerable and similar improvement in symptoms, which recurred after medications were discontinued (17).

Forty mg of oxprenolol given before competitive jumping effectively inhibited emotional tachycardia and excessive tension in ski jumpers (18).

Brewer (19) reported such Beta-adrenergic blockade to alleviate-prevent the anxiety-tension state noted by many students (20) prior to major examinations.

Taggart, Carruthers, and Somerville (21) reported in 1973 that multiple cardiac manifestations and apprehensive anxiety associated with public speaking in susceptible individuals were prevented or markedly alleviated by a single oral dose of 40 mg oxprenolol one hour before; they concluded by suggesting "that Beta-blockade could be used to alleviate the unpleasant symptoms associated with speaking before an audience." Their data were obtained from 23 normal subjects and 7 subjects with coronary artery disease.

McMillin described in 1975 two further clinical studies of oxprenolol Beta-adrenergic blockade in the treatment of anxiety and tension states resulting from the environmental stresses of the Belfast, Northern Ireland, civil disorders (22). In the first, 10 patients completed a double-blind crossover comparison of 20 and 80 mg oxprenolol three times a day for a week; half of the patients were given 20 mg capsules the first week and half received the (identical in appearance) 80 mg capsules the first week. "The results from trial 1 showed a significant improvement with 80 mg of oxprenolol in tension ($p<0.05$), depression ($p<0.05$), and well-being ($p<0.01$) and a patient preference for the larger dose (8 patients vs. 1 patient; $p<0.04$).

One patient in trial 1 had no preference. On all the items except sleep, treatment was significantly more effective than pretreatment (anxiety and tension, $p < 0.001$; concentration and depression, $p\ 0.05$; well-being, $p < 0.01$)." In the second double-blind crossover trial, McMillin compared 80 mg oxprenolol to 5 mg diazepam three times a day for a week's treatment period for each. Again, half received the one drug for the first week and the other half the other drug the first week; again, the capsules were indistinguishable. "The results from trial 2 showed no significant difference between 5 mg diazepam and 80 mg of oxprenolol; this may be due to the small number of patients in the study. However, 5 mg of diazepam seemed to give better results in sleep while 80 mg of oxprenolol seemed to give better results in concentration. Treatment was significantly more effective than preteatment on all items (anxiety and tension, $p < 0.001$; sleep, concentration, depression, and well-being, $p < 0.01$)." McMillin stated that he believed Beta-adrenergic medications were useful in the treatment of anxiety and tension states in response to such mental stresses as speaking in public, driving in traffic, race car driving, or being present in the midst of civil disorder.

In 1973, Tyrer and Lader (23) reported on a double-blind crossover drug-placebo study of sotalol in the treatment of chronic anxiety of at least 6 months' duration in psychiatric outpatients free of other disease. Fourteen of 16 patients completed the Armitage closed sequential design of 2 weeks of placebo and 2 weeks of Beta-blocker. Sotalol was given in individualized dosages of 20 to 100 mg four times a day. "Significant drug-placebo differences were found for a number of clinical ratings, but for many of these there was discrepancy between patient and therapist." Investigator ratings produced more significant differences between sotalol and placebo than did subject ratings, apparently on account of a greater effect on somatic than psychological symptoms of anxiety during the 2-week trial.

Ramsey, Greer, and Bagley (24) described a double-blind attempt to assess the matter of somatic and/or psychologic-subjective-"central" anxiety symptom relief with propranolol. A two-week crossover drug-placebo design was used; propranolol dosage was 160 mg per day in 4 divided dosages; by randomization, 7 anxious neurotics and 7 thyrotoxic patients received propranolol first, and 7 anxious neurotics and 5 thyrotoxic patients received placebo first; clinical ratings of anxiety, IPAT Anxiety Scale Questionnaire scores, and several physiological measures of palmar skin conductance provided the pre-trial, inter-trial, and end-trial data. The authors were unable to solve the peripheral and/or central dilemma because of the uniformly good results and the small experimental samples. Their conclusions were "(1) Among patients with anxiety states, a significant reduction in anxiety, as measured by clinical ratings and by IPAT Scale scores, had occurred at the end of the trial irrespective of the order of administration of propranolol or placebo. (2) In patients with thyrotoxicosis, the administration of propranolol was significantly associated with a decrease in palmar skin conductance. (3)

No significant differences between propranolol and placebo were found with respect to clinical ratings or IPAT scores of anxiety in either diagnostic group."

Kellner and coworkers (25) compared one week of propranolol therapy to one week of placebo after a "practice week" on amobarbital in 22 chronically anxious outpatients using a double-blind crossover design. The dosage of amobarbital was 30 mg three times a day; the dosage of propranolol was self-selected beginning at 20 mg four times a day and increasing daily to symptom relief or a maximum of 40 mg four times a day; the dosage of placebo was similarly self-selected and started at one tablet four times a day and increasing to complete symptom relief or 8 tablets per day. Several observer and subjective rating scales were completed before and after each week of experimental treatment. When propranolol was compared to placebo, all measures of anxiety and somatic symptoms favored propranolol, with the differences reaching statistical significance for the Symptom Questionnaire. All measures of depression and inadequacy either were not different or tended toward negative correlation (placebo produced better results in depression than did propranolol). Kellner and coworkers felt that their results were not conclusive but stated "there was a trend and consistency of results which suggests that propranolol has short-term anti-anxiety effects."

Tyrer and Lader also used a one-week trial double-blind balanced crossover design in comparing response to placebo, diazepam and propranolol in 12 chronically anxious psychiatric out patients (26). Six of these patients had predominantly somatic and six had predominantly psychic (psychological) anxiety symptoms. Clinical ratings of anxiety were made separately by patient and psychiatrist after each week of experimental treatment. The dosages varied from 3 to 9 capsules per day (1 to 3 tablets three times per day). Patients received between 6 and 18 mg diazepam daily, and between 120 and 360 mg propranolol daily. Both diazepam and propranolol produced equal and marked improvement in the 6 patients with predominantly somatic anxiety as compared to placebo. Diazepam also produced marked relief of anxiety in the 6 patients with predominantly psychic anxiety (as compared to placebo), but propranolol did not. From these results, Tyrer and Lader concluded that diazepam is superior to propranolol in treatment of morbid anxiety, presumably because of its more general usefulness. "Nevertheless propranolol does have important clinical effects in somatically anxious patients. Its efficacy in this group is comparable to diazepam and its use is preferable because it rarely produces sedation, is very safe, and not prone to abuse."

Krishman (27) gave diazepam and oxprenolol to university students with pronounced pre-examination and examination anxiety symptoms in a double-blind study. Seventeen students received 2 mg diazepam twice a day, and 15 students took 40 mg oxprenolol twice a day for several days. Self-rating scales for anxiety and tension revealed improvement in symptoms in both groups, but neither drug was superior to the other. Six of seventeen students on diazepam overestimated the mark they would achieve on the exam and none did better than predicted. On oxprenolol, 5 students exceeded the predicted exam grade, 8 equaled it, and only 2 did worse than predicted. Krishman considered his results to show that diazepam increased confidence, perhaps unwarrantedly, while reducing anxiety. He further concluded that the more accurate predictions of achievement accompanying anxiety symptoms-relief with oxprenolol inidicated that β-adrenergic blockade does not interfere with the student's critical faculties. An alternative hypothesis that Beta-adrenergic blockade may enhance the concentrative powers of the severely anxious student was not considered by Krishman in his report (27).

Dr. J.R. Hawkings reported the results of treating 88 patients with various forms of severe anxiety with individualized dosages of Beta-adrenergic blocking drugs for at least 3 months in consultant psychiatric practice (28). He subdivided these 88 morbidly anxious patients into those with mental anxiety (N 16), phobic anxiety (N 17), anxiety with depression (N 13), and physical-somatic anxiety (N 42). Although individualized dosages ranged from 30 to 480 mg daily, the usual (majority of patients) dosage was 120 mg per day of propranolol or oxprenolol. Twenty-three of the 88 patients did not benefit, and the medication was stopped after 3 months; 18 benefited markedly and recovered, so that symptoms did not recur when the Beta-blocker was stopped; 41 continued Beta-blockers after 3 months because of clinical benefits. Improvement was assessed clinically and by statistical change in Hamilton Scales. Diagnostic subclassification of anxiety had predictive value only for those with physical-somatic anxiety; 93% (39 of 42) of these patients had satisfactory responses to treatment. Satisfactory responses to treatment with Beta-adrenergic blockers occurred regularly in the other anxiety subgroups after 3 months, also; 56% (9 of 16) of these with mental anxiety, 65% (11 of 17) of those with phobic anxiety, and 46% (6 of 13) of those with anxiety with depression responded satisfactorily to Beta-adrenergic blockers. Hawkings' reported experience seems to support the notion that propranolol and other Beta-blocking medications work well in a high percentage of anxiety states, whatever the predominance of somatic and/or mental-psychic-psychological symptoms, if the treatment is given for more than a week or two and the dosages are individualized to the point of clinical response.

Johnson, Singh, and Leeman (29) used an interesting and unusual double-blind research design for the comparison of diazepam, oxprenolol, and placebo in the treatment of anxiety states. Patients in an outpatient anxiety specialty clinic with primary clinical anxiety for not less than 3 weeks nor longer than 2 years, between the ages of 18 and 65, free of all other medical and psychiatric states, were given a week's trial on placebo. The placebo responders (5 of 38) were eliminated, and the remaining patients were blindly and randomly assigned to a 3-week individualized dosage treatment schedule with placebo, oxprenolol (80 mg caps), or diazepam (5 mg caps). The first week the dosage was one capsule three times a day, and in the second and third week dosage was individualized, with a minimum dose of one capsule and a maximum dosage of 7 capsules per day. The Hamilton Anxiety Scale and the Rapid Symptoms Checklist were used to evaluate changes in symptoms. Blood specimens were drawn weekly for measurement of diazepam and oxprenolol. Twenty-nine patients completed the protocol properly and were available for statistical analyses of covariance of group data. Thirteen patients received diazepam, 11 oxprenolol, and 5 placebo. After one week of treatment, diazepam had significantly reduced anxiety, as compared to both placebo and oxprenolol (which did not differ statistically although the direction of change was for improvement with oxprenolol). At the end of the three-week individualized trial, both diazepam and oxprenolol were associated with significantly reduced anxiety, as compared to placebo, and at this point diazepam and oxprenolol did not differ from one another.

Burrows, Davies, Fail, Poynton, and Stevenson (30) used both the Hamilton Anxiety Scale and an individualized Target Symptom Improvement Scale to measure improvement in a double-blind study design that was nearly identical to that of Johnson, Singh, and Leeman (29) described above. Sixty-two patients completed the 3-week individualized treatment schedules; 20 received placebo, 22 received oxprenolol, and 20 received diazepam; all three treatment groups were subdivided into the predominantly psychic and the predominantly somatic symptom anxiety groups. At the end of the three-week treatment trial, improvement was significantly greater in both the diazepam and oxprenolol groups than in the placebo group; there was no difference between diazepam and oxprenolol group improvement (except for observer-investigator preference) and there was no different group response to any of the treatments by the psychic and somatic subgroups.

Easton and Sherman (31) wrote of their experience in evaluating patients with anxiety states for the "hyperdynamic Beta-adrenergic circulatory state" described by Frohlich and associates (9,10). Easton and Sherman describe the production of severe anxiety attacks in 6 patients with such anxiety states by infusion of the pure Beta-adrenergic agonist, isoproterenol. The isoproterenol-induced anxiety attacks could be prevented and/or aborted by propranolol; treatment of these 6 patients with individualized daily doses of 60 to 320 mg per day virtually eliminated anxiety symptoms during a 4- to 24-month follow-up period.

Clearly, the studies summarized indicate that Beta-adrenergic blockade is an effective treatment for symptoms of anxiety. Beta-adrenergic blockers were consistently noted to be effective in relieving palpitations and tachycardia (1,2,3,5,8,9,12). In most reports they were significantly superior to placebo (4,8,12,14,15,25,29,30). Only in some instances when Beta-adrenergic blocking agents were given for two weeks or less was there no superiority to placebo (23,24,26). Studies comparing Beta-adrenergic blockers to benzodiazepines most often indicated equal efficacy (7,17,22,27, 29). Studies that found benzodiazepines superior were either based on a psychic anxiety versus somatic anxiety dichotomy (26), or on a finding after one week of treatment which did not exist at three weeks (29). Two reports indicated problems in concentration associated with benzodiazepines but not with Beta-adrenergic blocking agents (22,27), and others noted that there are fewer side effects associated with Beta-adrenergic blocking agents than with benzodiazepines (7,26).

Since Beta-adrenergic blocking agents specifically reduce the somatic symptoms of anxiety, produce no sedation, cause few side effects, and have no potential for abuse, they should be considered the treatment of choice for somatic anxiety. Moreover, the distinction between psychologic and somatic anxiety may be an unfortunate one. Anxiety neurosis, a syndrome which affects about 5% of the adult population, is characterized by cardiorespiratory anxiety symptoms as well as subjective anxiety (32,33). Indeed, these symptoms often lead the patient to an internist or family practitioner rather than to a psychiatrist (33). Our clinical experience, supported by the literature review, is that Beta-adrenergic blocking agents not only control somatic anxiety but also relieve psychologic anxiety after a period of three to six weeks.

Although dosages must be individualized, the usual therapeutic range of propranolol (the Beta-adrenergic blocking agent used in the U.S.) is between 40 and 160 mg/day. Dosage schedule is on a q.i.d. basis, since the biologic half-life is two to three hours. Because of the lag time before subjective anxiety symptoms are diminished, small dosages of benzodiazepines may be useful in the early phase of treatment.

REFERENCES

1. Besterman, E.M.M., and Friedlander, D.H. Clinical experiences with propranolol. *Postgrad. Med. J.* 41:526-535, 1965.
2. Nordenfelt, O. Orthostatic ECG changes and the adrenergic Beta-receptor blocking agent, propranolol (Inderal). *Acta Med Scand.* 178:393-401, 1965.
3. Turner, P., Granville-Grossman, K.L., and Smart, J.V. Effect of adrenergic receptor blockade on the tachycardia of thyrotoxicosis and anxiety state. *Lancet* 2:1316-1318, 1965.
4. Granville-Grossman, K.L., and Turner, P. The effect of propranolol on anxiety. *Lancet* 1:788-790, 1966.
5. Suzman, M.M. An evaluation of the effects of propranolol on the symptoms and electrocardiographic changes in patients with anxiety and the hyperventilation syndrome. *Ann. Int. Med.* 68:1194, 1968.
6. Suzman, M.M. Propranolol in the treatment of anxiety. *Postgrad. Med. J.* 52 (Suppl. 4):168-174, 1976.

7. Wheatley, D. Comparative effects of propranolol and chlordiazepoxide in anxiety states. *Br. J. Psychiat.* 115:1411-1412, 1969.
8. Nordenfelt, I., Persson, S., and Redfors, A. Effect of a new Beta-blocking agent, H 56/28, on nervous heart complaints. *Acta Med. Scand.* 184:465-471, 1968.
9. Frohlich, E.D., Tarazi, R.C., and Dustan, H.P. Hyperdynamic Beta-adrenergic circulatory state. *Arch. Int. med.* 123:1-7, 1969.
10. Frohlich, E.D., Dustan, H.p., and Page, I. Hyperdynamic Beta-adrenergic circulatory state. *Arch. Int. Med.* 117:614-619, 1966.
11. Bonn, J.A., and Turner, P. D-propranolol and anxiety. *Lancet* 1:1355-1356, 1971.
12. Bonn, J.A., Turner, P., and Hicks, D. Beta-adrenergic-receptor blockade with practolol in treatment of anxiety. *Lancet* 1:814-815, 1972.
13. Carlsson, C. Haemodynamic studies in alcoholics in the withdrawal phase. *Int. J. Clin. Pharmacol. Therap. Toxicol.* 3(Supp.):61-63, 1971.
14. Carlsson, C., and Johansson, T. The psychological effects of propranolol in the abstinence phase of chronic alcoholics. *Brit. J. Psychiat.* 119:605-606, 1971.
15. Gallant, D.M., Swanson, W.C., and Guerrero-Figueroa, R. A controlled evaluation of propranolol in chronic alcoholic patients presenting the symptomatology of anxiety and tension. *J. Clin. Pharmacol.* 13:41-43, 1973.
16. Linken, A. Propranolol for L.S.D.-induced anxiety states. *Lancet* 2:1039-1040, 1971.
17. McMillin, W.P. Oxprenolol in anxiety. *Lancet* 1:1193, 1973.
18. Imhof, P.R., Blatter, K., Fuccella, L.M., et al. Beta-blockade and emotional tachycardia, radiotelemetric investigations in ski jumpers. *J. Appl. Physiol.* 27:366-369, 1969.
19. Brewer, C. Beneficial effect of Beta-adrenergic blockade on "exam nerves." *Lancet* 2:435, 1972.
20. Pitts, F.N., Winokur, G., and Stewart, M.A. Psychiatric syndromes, anxiety symptoms and responses to stress in medical students. *Am. J. Psychiat.* 118:333-340, 1961.
21. Taggart, P., Carruthers, M., and Somerville, W. Electrocardiogram, plasma catecholamines and lipids, and their modification by oxprenolol when speaking before an audience. *Lancet* 2:341-346, 1973.
22. McMillin, W.P. Oxprenolol in the treatment of anxiety due to environmental stress. *Am. J. Psychiat.* 132:965-968, 1975.
23. Tyrer, P.J., and Lader, M.H. Effects of beta-adrenergic blockade with sotalol in chronic anxiety. *Clin. Pharmacol. Therapeutics* 14:418-426, 1973.
24. Ramsey, I., Greer, S., and Bagley, C. Propranolol in neurotic and thyrotoxic anxiety. *Br. J. Psychiat.* 122:555-560, 1973.
25. Kellner, R., Collins, A.C., Shulman, R.S., and Pathak, D. The short-term antianxiety effects of propranolol HCl. *J. Clin. Pharmacol.* 5:301-304, 1974.
26. Tyrer, P.J., and Lader, M.H. Response to propranolol and diazepam in somatic and psychic anxiety. *Br. Med. J.* 2:14-16, 1974.
27. Krishman, G. Oxprenolol in the treatment of examination nerves. *Scottish Med. J.* 20:288-289, 1975.
28. Hawkings, J.R. Clinical experience with Beta-blockers in consultant psychiatric practice. *Scottish Med. J.* 20:294-297, 1975.
29. Johnson, G., Singh, B., and Leeman, M. Controlled evaluation of the Beta-adrenoceptor blocking drug oxprenolol in anxiety. *Med. J. Aust.* 1:909-912, 1976.
30. Burrows, G.D., Davies, B., Fail, L., Poynton, C., and Stevenson, H. A placebo controlled trial of diazepam and oxprenolol for anxiety. *Psychopharmacol.* 50:177-179, 1976.
31. Easton, J.D., and Sherman, D.G. Somatic anxiety attacks and propranolol. *Arch. Neurol.* (Chicago) 33:689-691, 1976.

32. Cohen, M., and White, P. Life situations, emotions, and neurocirculatory asthenia (anxiety neurosis, neurasthenia, effort syndrome). *Assoc. Res. Nerv. Dis. Proc.* 29:832-869, 1950.

33. Woodruff, R.A., Goodwin, D.W., and Guze, S.B. *Psychiatric Diagnosis.* New York: Oxford University Press, 1974.

CHAPTER 24

Benzodiazepine Antianxiety Agents: Pharamcokinetic Similarities and Differences

David J. Greenblatt and Richard I. Shader

Numerous benzodiazepine derivates are now available for the treatment of anxiety in clinical practice. While the class of drugs as a whole is unquestionably effective in anxiolytic therapy (1,2), it is often difficult for the clinician to make a rational choice among the available derivatives within the class. Indeed, animal studies suggest that all benzodiazepines have similar sedative, antianxiety, muscle-relaxant, and anticonvulsant properties. However, despite the closely similar neuropharmacologic effects of the various benzodiazepines, the drugs may have quite different patterns of absorption, distribution, biotransformation, and elimination by the human body (3,4) (Table 1). These pharmacokinetic differences can in turn lead to differences in clinical action. This article outlines some important pharmacokinetic properties of benzodiazepine anxiolytics, with emphasis on clinical implications of kinetic differences among drugs.

LONG-ACTING BENZODIAZEPINES

One major group of benzodiazepine anxiolytics are the long-acting compounds (Table 1). The derivatives now available in this category are chlordiazepoxide (Librium), diazepam (Valium), clorazepate (Tranxene, Azene), and prazepam (Verstran). Flurazepam (Dalmane), although market-

Table 1. Pharmacokinetic summary of benzodiazepine derivatives

Parent compound	Parent compound present in blood?	Active metabolites present in blood	Effective duration of clinical action (due to parent compound and/or active metabolites)
LONG-ACTING GROUP			
Chlordiazepoxide	Yes	Desmethylchlordiazepoxide Demoxepam (Desmethyldiazepam) (Oxazepam)	Long
Diazepam	Yes	Desmethyldiazepam	Long
Clorazepate	No [b]	Desmethyldiazepam	Long
Prazepam	No [b]	Desmethyldiazepam	Long
Flurazepam	No [b]	Desalkylflurazepam (N-hydroxyethyl-flurazepam)	Long
SHORTER-ACTING GROUP			
Oxazepam	Yes	None	Short
Temazepam	Yes	None	Short
Triazolam	Yes	(? 1-Hydroxymethyl triazolam)	Short
Lorazepam	Yes	None	Intermediate
Bromazepam	Yes	(? 3-Hydroxybromazepam)	Intermediate

a: Parentheses indicate less important metabolites or those of uncertain significance.
b: Relatively small amounts of parent compound may be detected for a short period after dosing.

ed as a hypnotic, has pharmacokinetic and probably clinical characteristics identical to the long-acting anxiolytics. Flunitrazepam (Rohypnol), under testing primarily as a hypnotic, may also fall in the long-acting category, although its kinetic properties are not well established (5).

The benzodiazepines in this group have a long duration of clinical action because the drug itself, and / or metabolic products which have pharmacologic activity, are slowly eliminated from the body. In clinical practice this means that a once-a-day therapy is quite feasible because active compounds persist in the blood throughout the day. Furthermore, the drugs will accumulate when given on a multiple-dose basis. That is, the total amount of drug in the body, the concentration in blood, and perhaps the clinical response will change over time as the drug accumulates to a so-called steady state. When therapy is abruptly terminated, the long-acting compounds are not immediately eliminated; instead, the drugs or their active metabolites persist in the blood and the body for many days or even weeks, creating what Dr. Leo Hollister and others have called a built-in tapering-off effect. This probably explains why problems following abrupt withdrawal are seldom seen with drugs such as diazepam. When withdrawal symptoms do occur, they tend to appear many days after drug discontinuation.

Chlordiazepoxide

Chlordiazepoxide, the first of the benzodiazepines, is undergoing a "rediscovery" simply because it is now available as a generic compound and often can be obtained at reduced cost. The metabolic pathway of chlordiazepoxide exemplifies the complexities in metabolism of these long-acting agents (Fig. 1). Chlordiazepoxide is transformed by the human liver into a succession of active metabolic products formed by the stepwise modification of the molecule (6,7). The final metabolic product is oxazepam, and its immediate precursor is desmethyldiazepam. An understanding of desmethyldiazepam is essential to understanding of the long-acting benzodiazepines, since it is a metabolite of chlordiazepoxide as well as of diazepam, prazepam, and chlorazepate. It also is a metabolite of several experimental benzodiazepines, including medazepam, halazepam, and ketazolam. All of these derivatives at some time or another become desmethyldiazepam, making it an extremely important metabolic product. In any case, the net clinical action of chlordiazepoxide is attributable in some complex way to the combined action of the parent compound and any of its active metabolites that may be present.

Examination of the blood level curve for a subject who took 50 mg of chlordiazepoxide once daily at bedtime indicates why the compound is suitable as a once-a-day antianxiety agent (Fig. 2). Concentrations of the parent compound are maximal just after the dose, thereby promoting the onset of sleep, then decline throughout the 24-hour period until the next dose

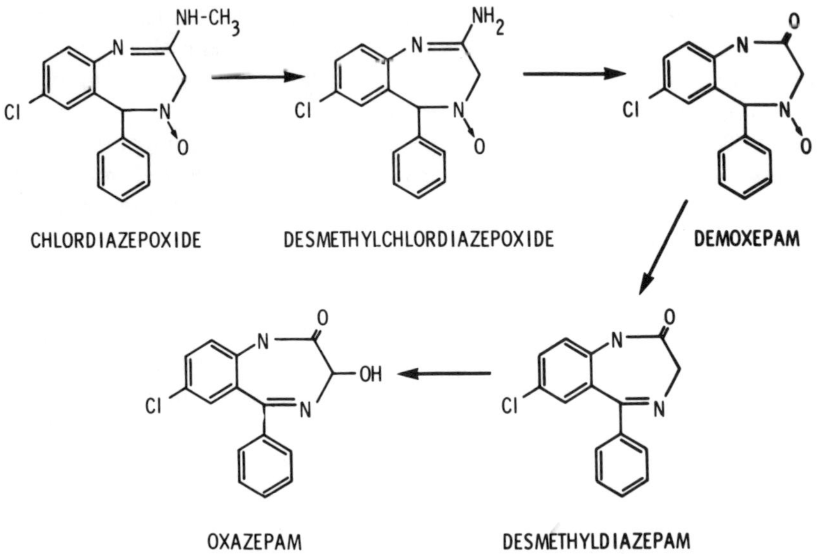

Fig. 1. Major metabolic pathway of chlordiazepoxide in humans.

CHLORDIAZEPOXIDE   DESMETHYLCHLORDIAZEPOXIDE   DEMOXEPAM

OXAZEPAM   DESMETHYLDIAZEPAM

is given. Yet there is gradual accumulation and a rather consistent blood level of the active metabolic products throughout the day, even though the parent drug is only given every 24 hours. Thus the once-daily dose contributes to sleep at night, and the persistence of the drug and its metabolites throughout the day can contribute to the antianxiety effects throughout the 24-hour period. Finally, when the drug is abruptly terminated, there is persistence in the blood for many days of either the parent compound or its active metabolites (8,9).

Several factors can influence the pharmacokinetics and probably the clinical response to chlordiazepoxide. One such factor is age. There is abundant clinical experience to show that elderly individuals are more sensitive to the central depressant and perhaps the therapeutic effects of benzodiazepine derivatives (10-12), and of psychopharmacologic agents in general. Pharmacokinetic changes accompanying the aging process could explain some of these changes in clinical effects. As the human organism ages, even if good health persists and no disease processes are active or detectable, the efficiency of drug metabolism tends to decline, and foreign compounds are not eliminated as readily or rapidly (13). A study of chlordiazepoxide clearance in young versus elderly males, all of whom were healthy, indicated that elimination of the drug was greatly slowed in the elderly subjects (14). This means that the clinical effects of a single dose probably would persist longer, and there would be more drug accumulation during multiple-dose therapy in the elderly. Such kinetic changes could partly account for why the

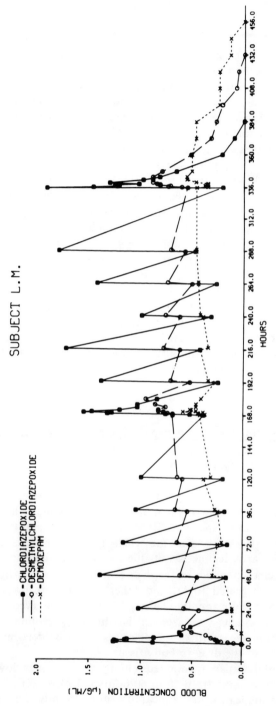

Fig. 2. A healthy volunteer subject ingested 50 mg of chlordiazepoxide hydrochloride by mouth every 24 hours for 15 consecutive days. Venous blood samples were drawn just prior to and 1.5 hours after the dose on each day of therapy. On days 1, 8, and 15, numerous samples were drawn over the 24-hour dosage interval. Finally, samples were drawn every 12 hours for 5 days after the last dose, which was given on day 15 (hour 336). No samples were drawn on days 7 and 14 (hours 144 and 312). Concentrations of chlordiazepoxide and two of its metabolites were determined in all whole-blood samples. Note the differing rates of accumulation of the parent compound and its two metabolites, as well as the slow elimination following the final dose (reprinted from reference 8, with permission).

elderly seem to be more sensitive to chlordiazepoxide (10). Thus the age of the patient should be carefully considered when benzodiazepine therapy is planned and the clinical response assessed.

Since all benzodiazepines are metabolized by the liver, it is not surprising that the presence of cirrhosis, acute hepatitis, or other hepatocellular disease may influence the disposition of these drugs. Clearance of chlordiazepoxide is substantially impaired in patients with cirrhosis (6,15). Chlordiazepoxide as well as other benzodiazepines should be given with caution to such patients, although they generally are a very safe class of compounds.

It is traditionally taught that intramuscular (IM) injection of drugs leads to rapid and reliable clinical effects. In fact, IM injection may be the worst mode of administration for many drugs (16). This is not surprising if one looks at the solubility characteristics of such compounds as chlordiazepoxide, diazepam, phenytoin, digoxin, or quinidine—they are not soluble in aqueous media at physiologic pH. Therefore, they probably precipitate at the site of injection, are slowly redissolved, and therefore are very slowly absorbed. In clinical terms, IM injection of such drugs can lead to unreliable, erratic pharmacologic effects. Slow absorption of IM chlordiazepoxide (17-19) and diazepam (20-22) has been documented in several studies. We recommend that these compounds be given by intravenous infusion rather than IM injection when parenteral administration is clinically indicated.

Diazepam

Diazepam, the most popular of the benzodiazepine derivatives, also falls into the long-acting category. The major metabolic pathway in humans involves removal of the N-methyl group to form desmethyldiazepam (Fig. 3). If one administers diazepam orally to a human subject, peak blood levels are reached very quickly due to rapid absorption from the gastrointestinal tract (23-25). These rapidly achieved high levels in blood may cause the feeling of mild euphoria, relaxation, and "spaciness" that many persons report after taking diazepam orally. After peak levels are reached, concentrations then fall quite rapidly. This early decline is not due to drug elimination, but rather to the chemical characteristics of the drug which make it very lipid-soluble. Diazepam is distributed to fat and other tissues, causing it to disappear from the blood quite rapidly. This is commonly observed with lipid-soluble compounds such as diazepam having large volumes of distribution—the duration of action of a single dose may be determined primarily by distribution of the drug to body tissues.

After distribution of diazepam is complete, elimination proceeds slowly, with a half-life generally ranging from 20 to 60 hours (23,24,26-28). Thus, although the action of a single dose may appear to wear off rapidly, this is not due to elimination—the drug is still in the body but is distributed differently

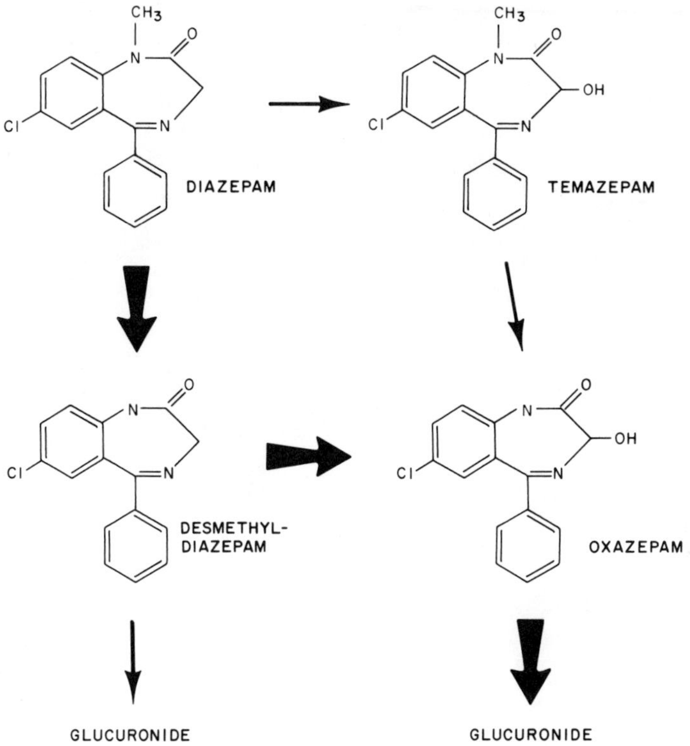

Fig. 3. Major metabolic pathway of diazepam in humans.

and will accumulate during multiple dosing. Furthermore, elimination of the parent compound is mirrored by formation of desmethyldiazepam, which will also accumulate during multiple dosage.

During long-term therapy it is perfectly reasonable to give diazepam on a once-daily basis, since active compounds will persist in the body throughout the day. Accumulation of the drug in the blood usually takes 5 to 14 days to be complete, at which time the so-called steady state is reached and there is no further accumulation (24,26,29,30). Desmethyldiazepam, the pharmacologically active metabolite, also accumulates, and both compounds contribute to clinical activity. Abrupt termination seldom leads to withdrawal syndromes because of slow elimination of the drug and its metabolite, which may persist for days or weeks after termination of therapy (Fig. 4).

As in the case of chlordiazepoxide, the clearance of diazepam is impaired in patients with liver disease (27,28). The effect of age on diazepam clearance is equivocal (27), although elderly persons appear to be more sensitive to the drug (10).

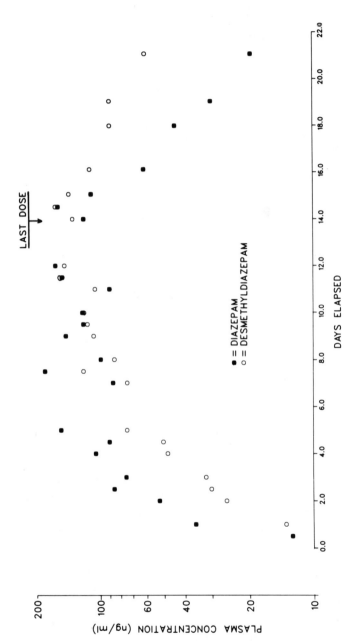

Fig. 4. A healthy volunteer subject ingested 2.5 mg of diazepam every 12 hours for 15 consecutive days. Multiple plasma specimens, always obtained just prior to each dose, were analyzed for concentrations of diazepam and its major metabolite, desmethyldiazepam. Note the extensive accumulation of both compounds, as well as the slow elimination following the final dose.

Clorazepate and Prazepam—Precursors of Desmethyldiazepam

Clorazepate and prazepam are termed "prodrugs"—that is, drug precursors. Both compounds are transformed to desmethyldiazepam prior to reaching the systemic circulation. In the case of clorazepate, conversion probably occurs in the acidic medium of the stomach, where desmethyldiazepam is formed by hydrolysis and decarboxylation (31,32). Desmethyldiazepam is by far the predominant compound in blood and probably accounts for the clinical action of the drug. Elimination of desmethyldiazepam is very slow—its half-life can exceed 100 hours in some persons. For this reason, extensive accumulation of desmethyldiazepam occurs during multiple-dose therapy with clorazepate (33,34). As with diazepam, clorazepate is quite suitable for once-daily administration as an antianxiety agent.

The kinetic behavior of prazepam is very similar. Transformation to desmethyldiazepam by dealkylation of the large cyclopropylmethyl substituent probably occurs during the first pass through the liver. Other metabolites (3-hydroxyprazepam and oxazepam) are found in urine, but only as inactive glucuronide conjugates (35). The pharmacologic activity of the drug is attributable to desmethyldiazepam, making prazepam another long-acting compound that can be given once daily.

Flurazepam

Although marketed as a hypnotic (36,37), the kinetic properties of flurazepam make it essentially identical to the long-acting benzodiazepine anxiolytics—in particular, to prazepam. Flurazepam, like prazepam, undergoes removal of a large alkyl side-chain substituent during the first pass through the liver (38). The major metabolic product is desalkylflurazepam, which has a very long elimination half-life similar to that of desmethyldiazepam. Desalkylflurazepam accumulates extensively during multiple-dose therapy with flurazepam (39) (Fig. 5). Undoubtedly flurazepam could serve as a once-a-day anxiolytic.

SHORTER-ACTING BENZODIAZEPINES

Two shorter-acting benzodiazepines, oxazepam and lorazepam, are currently available (Fig. 6), and others are being tested. This group of compounds differs from the long-acting derivatives. Active metabolites need not be considered because the metabolic products are pharmacologically inactive. In the case of oxazepam and its congener lorazepam, the metabolic pathway proceeds by conjugation to glucuronic acid, at the site of the 3-hydroxy substituent, yielding a pharmacologically inactive water-soluble product that is excreted in the urine. Furthermore, these drugs have a shorter

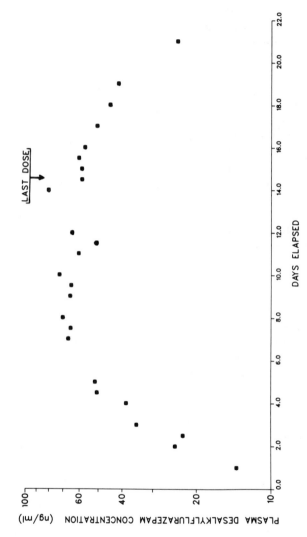

Fig. 5. A healthy volunteer subject ingested 15 mg of flurazepam nightly for 15 consecutive nights. Multiple plasma samples were obtained, always 12 to 24 hours after the most recent dose. Samples were also obtained for 7 days after the last dose. Concentrations of desalkylflurazepam, the primary active compound appearing in blood, were determined in all plasma samples. Note the slow and extensive accumulation of desalkylflurazepam, as well as its persistence following termination of therapy.

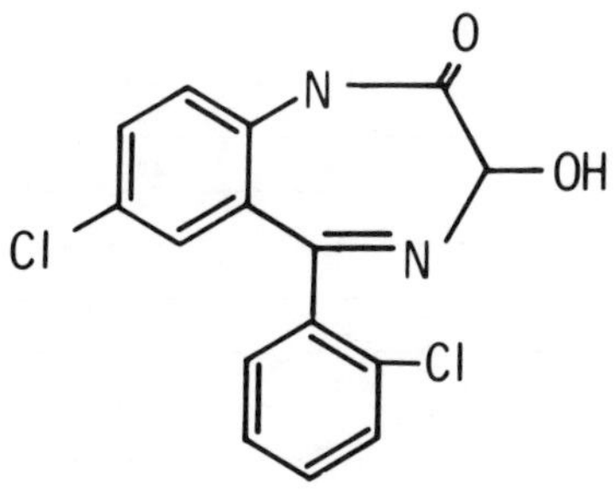

LORAZEPAM 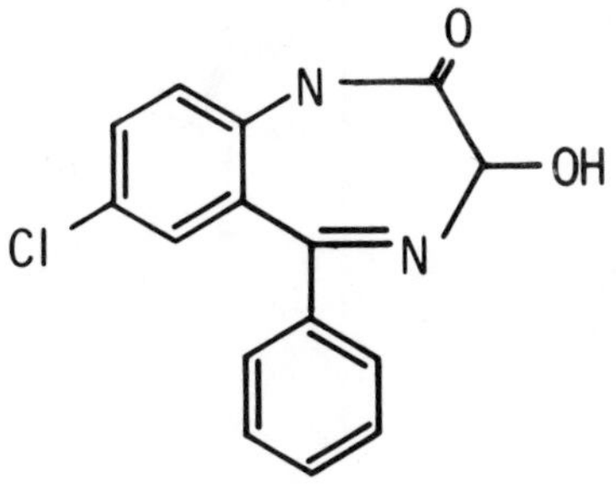   OXAZEPAM

Fig. 6. Structural formulas of lorazepam and oxazepam.

duration of action and shorter half-life, and they do not accumulate extensively when given repeatedly.

Oxazepam

Oxazepam is a short-acting compound, with a half-life somewhere between 5 and 10 hours (4,40-42). A single dose is largely eliminated within 24 hours. During multiple-dose therapy there is very little accumulation, so that 3 or 4 daily doses are usually necessary to maintain adequate blood levels.

Preliminary results suggest that the clearance of oxazepam, unlike that of chlordiazepoxide and diazepam, is not altered by the presence of liver disease (42). The same study also indicates that age does not seem to influence oxazepam clearance (42). Further studies of this important problem are needed.

Lorazepam

Lorazepam has a slightly longer half-life of between 10 and 20 hours (43-45). Kinetics of this compound have been extensively studied following intravenous, IM, and oral administration (Fig. 7). Lorazepam absorption is rapid and 80% to 100% complete after oral as well as IM dosage. During multiple-dose therapy, there is less extensive and more rapid accumulation of lorazepam than of the long-acting benzodiazepines. In a study in our laboratory, lorazepam accumulation was complete after 3 days of therapy as opposed to 10 days to 2 weeks with diazepam (Fig. 8). The steady-state concentration was maintained as the drug continued to be given; accumulation was not extensive. After termination of therapy, elimination was complete within a few days.

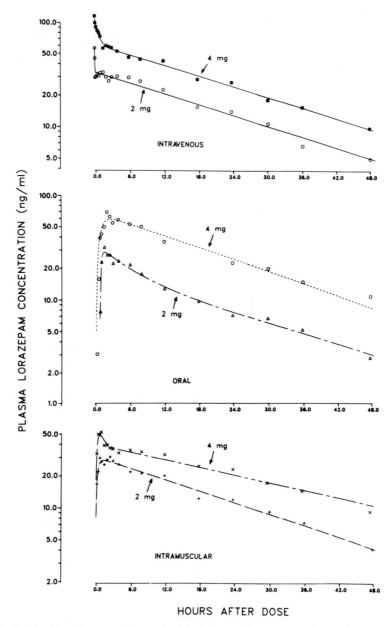

Fig. 7. A healthy volunteer subject received single doses of lorazepam on six occasions, separated by at least one week. Routes of administration were: intravenous, oral, and intramuscular, with 2- and 4-mg doses given by each route. Plasma lorazepam concentrations and computer-determined pharmacokinetic functions are shown following each mode of administration. The elimination half-life is approximately 18 hours, regardless of how the drug was administered. Absorption of both oral and intramuscular lorazepam was 80% to 100% complete.

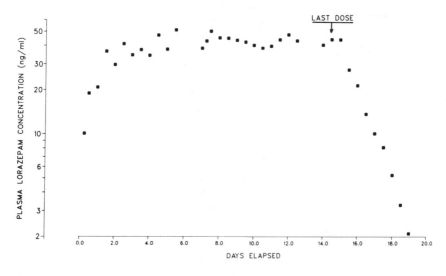

Fig. 8. A healthy volunteer subject received 3 mg of lorazepam daily in divided doses for 15 consecutive days. Plasma lorazepam concentrations were determined in multiple samples, always drawn prior to a dose. Note that in comparison with multiple-dose therapy with diazepam (Fig. 4) or flurazepam (Fig. 5), accumulation of lorazepam is more rapid and less extensive. Elimination is essentially complete within a few days of termination of therapy.

Other Shorter-Acting Benzodiazepines

Several other compounds of this category are undergoing clinical trials. Bromazepam, like lorazepam, has an elimination half-life between 10 and 20 hours (46). However, the quantitative importance and pharmacologic activity of its metabolites (in particular, 3-hydroxybromazepam) are not established. Temazepam (3-hydroxydiazepam), a metabolite of diazepam, has a short half-life similar to that of oxazepam (47). Temazepam has been used both as a hypnotic (48,49) and an anxiolytic (50). Finally, triazolam, a triazolobenzo-diazepine hypnotic (51), itself has a short half-life, but the kinetics and clinical importance of its metabolites are not yet established (52).

COMMENT

Understanding of pharmacokinetic differences among benzodiazepines can assist physicians in choosing the right drug to meet a particular clinical need, in selecting the proper dose and dosage schedule, and in anticipating and avoiding episodes of drug ineffectiveness and toxicity. However, pharmacokinetics do not provide a complete understanding of anxiolytic drug action, because individuals differ unpredictably in clinical response to such drugs. Clinical judgment and careful monitoring is still the cornerstone of successful anxiolytic drug therapy.

ACKNOWLEDGEMENTS

We are grateful for the collaboration and assistance of Jerold S. Harmatz, Kate Franke, Ann Werner, Marcia D. Allen, Dr. Stuart M. MacLeod, Dr. Edward M. Sellers, and Dr. Dean S. MacLaughlin. Dr. MacLaughlin is supported by Grant GM-23430 from the U.S. Public Health Service, to the Boston Collaborative Drug Surveillance Program.

This research was supported in part by Grant MH-12279 from the U.S. Public Health Service, and by Grant 77-611 from the Foundations' Fund for Research in Psychiatry.

REFERENCES

1. Greenblatt, D.J., and Shader, R.I. *Benzodiazepines in Clinical Practice.* New York: Raven Press, 1974.
2. Greneblatt, D.J., and Shader, R.I. Pharmacotherapy of anxiety with benzodiaze-pines and β-adrenergic blockers. In M.A. Lipton, A. DiMascio, and K.F. Killam, eds., *Psychopharmacology: A Generation of Progress.* New York: Raven Press, 1978.
3. Shader, R.I., and Greenblatt, D.J. Clinical implications of benzodiazepine pharmacokinetics. *Am. J. Psychiat.* 134:652-656, 1977.
4. Grenblatt, D.J., Shader, R.I., and Koch-Weser, J. Pharmacokinetics in clinical medicine: oxazepam versus other benzodiazepines. *Dis. Nerv. Syst.* 36(5):6-13, 1975.
5. Haefelfinger, P. Determination of nanogram amounts of primary aromatic amines and nitro compounds in blood and plasma. *J. Chromatogr.* 111:323-329, 1975.
6. Greenblatt, D.J., Shader, R.I., MacLeod, S.M., and Sellers, E.M. Clinical pharmokinetics of chlordiazepoxide. *Clin. Pharmacokin.* 3:381-394, 1978.
7. Greenblatt, D.J., Shader, R.I., Franke, K., MacLaughlin, D.S., Ransil,B.J., and Koch-Weser, J. Kinetics of intravenous chlordiazepoxide: Sex differences in drug distribution. *Clin. Pharmacol. Ther.* 22:893-903, 1977.
8. Greenblatt, D.J., Shader, R.I., Franke, K., and Harmatz, J.S. Pharmacokinetics of chlordiazepoxide and metabolites following single and multiple oral doses. *Int. J. Clin. Pharmacol. Biopharm.* 16: 486-493, 1978.
9. Boxenbaum, H.G., Geitner, K.A., Jack, M.L.,Dixon, W.R., and Kaplan, S.A. Pharmacokinetic and biopharmaceutic profile of chlordiazepoxide HCI in healthy subjects: multiple-dose oral administration. *J. Pharmacokin. Biopharm.* 5:25-39, 1977.

10. Boston Collaborative Drug Surveillance Program. Clinical depression of the central nervous system due to diazepam and chlordiazepoxide in relation to cigarette smoking and age. *New Eng. J. Med.* 288:277-280, 1973.
11. Greenblatt, D.J., Allen, M.D., and Shader, R.I. Toxicity of high-dose flurazepam in the elderly. *Clin. Pharmacol. Ther.* 21:355-361, 1977.
12. Greenblatt, D.J., and Allen M.D. Toxicity of nitrazepam in the elderly: A report from the Boston Collaborative Drug Surveillance Program. *Brit. J. Clin. Pharmacol.* 5:407-413, 1978.
13. Crooks, J., OMalley, K., and Stevenson, I.H. Pharmacokinetics in the elderly. *Clin. Pharmacokin.* 1:280-296, 1976.
14. Shader, R.I., Greenblatt,t D.J., Harmatz, J.S., Franke, K., and Koch-Weser, J. Absorption and disposition of chlordiazepoxide in young and elderly male volunteers. *J. Clin. Pharmacol.* 17:709-718, 1977.
15. Sellers, E.M., MacLeod, S.M., Greenblatt, D.J., and Giles, H.G. Influence of disulfiram and disease on benzodiazepine disposition. *Clin. Pharmacol. Ther.* 21:117, 1977.
16. Greenblatt, D.J., and Koch-Weser, J. Intramuscular injection of drugs. *New Eng. J. Med.* 295:542-546, 1976.
17. Boxenbaum, H.G., Geitner, K.A., Jack, M.L., et al. Pharmacokinetic and biopharmaceutic profile of chlordiazepoxide HCI in healthy subjects: Single-dose studies by the intravenous, intramuscular, and oral routes. *J. Pharmacokin. Biopharm.* 5:3-23, 1977.
18. Greenblatt, D.J., Shader, R.I., Koch-Weser, J., and Franke, K. Slow absorption of intramuscular chlordiazepoxide. *New Eng. J. Med.* 291:1116-1118, 1974.
19. Greenblatt, D.J., Shader, R.I., MacLeod, S.M., Sellers, E.M., Franke, K., and Giles, H.G. Absorption of oral and intramuscular chlordiazepoxide. *Eur. J. Clin. Pharmacol.* 13267-274, 1978.
20. Hillestad, L., Hansen, T., Melsom, H., and Drivenes, A. Diazepam metabolism in normal man. I. Serum concentrations and clinical effects after intravenous, intramuscular, and oral administration. *Clin. Pharmacol. Ther.* 16:479-484, 1974.
21. Assaf, R.A.E., Dundee, J.W., and Gamble, J.A.S. The influence of the route of administration on the clinical action of diazepam. *Anaesthesia* 30;152-158, 1975.
22. Gamble, J.A.S., Dundee, J.W., and Assaf, R.A.E. Plasma diazepam levels after single dose oral and intramuscular administration. *Anaesthesia* 30:164-169, 1975.
23. Mandelli, M., Tognoni, G., and Garattini, S. Clinical pharmacokinetics of diazepam. *Clin. Pharmacokin.* 3:72-91, 1978.
24. Kaplan, S.A., Jack, M.L., Alexander, K., and Weinfeld, R.E. Pharmacokinetic profile of diazepam in man following single intravenous and oral and chronic oral administrations. *J. Pharm. Sci.* 62:1789-1796, 1973.
25. Greenblatt, D.J., Shader, R.I., Weinberger, D.R., Allen, M.D., and MacLaughlin, D.S. Effect of a cocktail on diazepam absorption. *Psychopharmacol.* 57:199-203, 1978.
26. Klotz, U., Antonin, K.H., and Bieck, P.R. Comparison of the pharmacokinetics of diazepam after single and subchronic doses. *Eur. J. Clin. Pharmacol.* 10:121-126, 1976.
27. Klotz, U., Avant, G.R., Hoyumpa, A., Schenker, S., and Wilkinson, G.R. The effects of age and liver disease on the disposition and elimination of diazepam in adult man. *J. Clin. Invest.* 55:347-359, 1975.
28. Andreasen, P.B., Hendel, J.,Greisen, G., and Hvidberg, E.F. Pharmacokinetics of diazepam in disordered liver function. *Eur. J. Clin. Pharmacol.* 10:115-120, 1976.

29. Hillestad, L., Hansen, T., and Melsom, H. Diazepam metabolism in normal man. II. Serum concentrations and clinical effect after oral administration and cumulation. *Clin. Pharmacol. Ther.* 1:485-489, 1974.

30. Eatman, F.B., Colburn, W.A., Boxenbaum, H.G., et al. Pharmacokinetics of diazepam following multiple-dose oral administration to healthy human subjects. *J. Pharmacokin. Biopharm.* 5:481-494, 1977.

31. Chun, A.H.C., Carrigan, P.J., Hoffman, D.J., Kershner, R.P., and Stuart, J.D. Effect of antacid on absorption of clorazepate. *Clin. Pharmacol. Ther.* 22:329-335, 1977.

32. Greenblatt, D.J. Determination of desmethyldiazepam in plasma by electron-capture GLC: application to pharmacokinetic studies of clorazepate. *J. Pharm. Sci.* 67:427-429, 1978.

33. Carrigan, P.J., Chao, G.C., Barker, W.M., Hoffman, D.J., and Chun, A.H.C. Steady-state bioavailability of two clorazepate dipotassium dosage forms. *J. Clin. Pharmacol.* 17:18-28, 1977.

34. Post, C., Lindgren, S., Bertler, A., and Malmgren, H. Pharmacokinetics of N-desmethyldiazepam in healthy volunteers after single daily doses of dipotassium clorazepate. *Psychopharmacol.* 53:105-109, 1977.

35. DiCarlo, F.J., Viau, J-P., Eps, J-E., and Haynes, L.J. Biotransformation of prazepam by man. *Ann. N.Y. Acad. Sci.* 179:487-492, 1971.

36. Greenblatt, D.J., Shader, R.I., and Koch-Weser, J. Flurazepam hydrochloride. *Clin. Pharmacol. Ther.* 17:1-14, 1975.

37. Greenblatt, D.J., Shader, R.I., and Koch-Weser, J. Flurazepam hydrochloride, a benzodiazepine hypnotic. *Ann. Intern. Med.* 83:237-241, 1975.

38. deSilva, J.A.F., Bekersky, I., and Puglisi, C.V. Spectrofluorodensitometric determination of flurazepam and its major metabolite in blood. *J. Pharm. Sci.* 63:1837-1841, 1974.

39. Kaplan, S.A., deSilva, J.A.F., Jack, M.L., et al. Blood level profile in man following chronic oral administration of flurazepam hydrochloride. *J. Pharm. Sci.* 62:1932-1935, 1973.

40. Alvan, G., and Vessman, J. Pharmacokinetics of oxazepam in healthy volunteers. *Acta Pharmacol. Toxicol.* 40 (Suppl. 1):40-51, 1977.

41. Melander, A., Danielson, K., Vessman, J., and Wahlin, E. Bioavailability of oxazepam: Absence of influence of food intake. *Acta Pharmacol. Toxicol.* 40:584-588, 1977.

42. Shull, H.J., Jr., Wilkinson, G.R., Johnson, R., and Schenker, S. Normal disposition of oxazepam in acute viral hepatitis and cirrhosis. *Ann. Intern. Med.* 84:420-425, 1976.

43. Greenblatt, D.J., Schillings, R.T., Kyriakopoulos, A.A., et al. Clinical pharmacokinetics of lorazepam. I. Absorption and disposition of oral ^{14}C-lorazepam. *Clin. Pharmacol. Ther.* 20:329-341, 1976.

44. Greenblatt, D.J., Joyce, T.H., Comer, W.H., et al. Clinical pharmacokinetics of lorazepam. II. Intramuscular injection. *Clin. Pharmacol. Ther.* 21:222-230, 1977.

45. Verbeeck, R., Tjandramaga, T.B., Verberckmoes, R., and DeSchepper, P.J. Biotransformation and excretion of lorazepam in patients with chronic renal failure. *Brit. J. Clin. Pharmacol.* 3:1033-1039, 1976.

46. Kaplan, S.A., Jack, M.L., Weinfeld, R.E., et al. Biopharmaceutical and clinical pharmacokinetic profile of bromazepam. *J. Pharmacokin. Biopharm.* 4:1-16, 1976.

47. Fuccella, L.M., Bolcioni, G., Tamassia, V., Ferrario, F., and Tognoni, G. Human pharmacokinetics and bioavailability of temazepam administered in soft gelatin capsules. *Eur. J. Clin. Pharmacol.* 12:383-386, 1977.

48. Fowler, L.K. Temazepam (Euhypnos) as a hypnotic: A twelve-week trial in generla practice. *J. Int. Med. Res.* 5:295-296, 1977.
49. Fowler, L.K. Temazepam (Euhypnos) as a hypnotic: A twelve-week trial in general practice. *J. Int. Med. Res.* 5:297-300, 1977.
50. Sarteschi, P., Cassano, G.B., Castrogiovanni, P., Placidi, G.F., and Sacchetti, G. Major and minor tranquilizers in the treatment of anxiety states. *Arzneim. Forsch.* 22:93-97, 1972.
51. Rickels, K., Gingrich, R.L., Jr., Morris, R.J., et al. Triazolam in insomniac family practice patients. *Clin. Pharmacol. Ther.* 18:315-324, 1975.
52. Eberts, F.S., Jr. Comparative metabolism of triazolam, a new sedative-hypnotic, in rat, dog and man. *Pharmacologist* 14:196, 1974.

CHAPTER 25

Behavior Analysis and the Elimination of Anxiety Response Habits

Joseph Wolpe

Inappropriate anxiety is an essential constituent of most neuroses. No patient can be said to be recovered from a neurosis as long as he continues to a substantial degree to have habits of responding with anxiety to situations in which it is not appropriate—i.e. situations that contain no real threat. It is therefore obviously important that our therapeutic armamentarium include methods that can reliably and lastingly diminish and, in the last resort, eliminate anxiety response habits. Behavior therapy embodies a considerable number of such methods.

The Anxiety Core of Neuroses

Though behaviorists do not often see eye to eye with Freud, they agree with him in regarding anxiety as central to the neuroses—a point which has been lost on many of his followers. There are, of course, many neuroses in which the role of anxiety is obvious. This is clearly the case with patients with phobias and the much larger group afflicted by interpersonal fears of various kinds—for example, fears of criticism or rejection. In some of these cases there is also pervasive anxiety (which is generally rather inappropriately referred to as free-floating anxiety). However, in a great number of other cases, anxiety does not figure in the presenting complaint. For example, it is not very likely for anxiety initially to be mentioned in cases of sexual inadequacy—such as the common cases of "impotence" or "frigidity." The same applies to obsessive-compulsive neuroses, reactive depression, psychosomatic states, stuttering, and antisocial habit patterns like kleptomania, exhibitionism, and pedophilia.

In the great majority of these and other clinical presentations, behavior analysis shows anxiety nonetheless to be at the very center of things. For example, the stutterer, upon questioning, will tell you that he speaks perfectly fluently under certain circumstances, as when he is with members of his immediate family—so that clearly there is no intrinsic flaw in the speech mechanism. Stuttering only appears in specifiable social situations that vary from case to case; a common context being the presence of strangers. Further analysis reveals that strangers elicit anxiety quantitatively related to such factors as the degree of strangeness, the number of strangers, their age, their sex, their authority status, and their manifest attitudes. The severity of the stutter is invariably related to the intensity of anxiety elicited by the situations—in this case those involving strangers. Since this is so, it is not surprising that in a great many stutterers, all that has to be done to overcome the disability is to decondition the patient so that the relevant stimuli no longer arouse anxiety in him. Similarly, the deconditioning of anxiety is usually found to be the key to the successful treatment of psychosomatic states, obsessive-compulsive neuroses, and the other syndromes mentioned above (1,2,3).

Behavior Therapy

Behavior therapy consists of the applications of experimentally established principles of learning to the purpose of overcoming unadaptive habits. As discussed above, with respect to the neuroses, the crucial habit is generally anxiety. It will be helpful briefly to describe the experimental paradigm from which most of the current methods for breaking anxiety response habits have emerged.

Experimental neuroses, conditions that are remarkably similar to those that appear in the clinic, can easily be produced in cats, dogs, sheep, and other animals. The essential procedure is to elicit very intense anxiety in the animal repeatedly in a constant situation. The two basic ways of eliciting such anxiety are the administration of noxious stimulation (1,4,5,6) or the subjection of the animal to a situation of intense conflict (4). The elicitation of anxiety in a constant location results in that location acquiring a rising titer of anxiety conditioning. For example, in my own experiments (1,6), I found that when cats repeatedly received a non-tissue-damaging high-voltage, low-amperage electrical stimulus in a small cage, that cage acquired the capacity to evoke strong anxiety continuously after, on the average, 10 shocks had been administered. Although the administration of shocks then ceased, the anxiety-evoking power of the experimental cage continued indefinitely, even if the animal was reexposed to the cage many times and should logically have learned that there was no more "danger." Lesser measures of anxiety were observed on the floor of the experimental room, and in other rooms in proportion to their resemblance to the experimental room. An interesting observation was that neurotic animals, starved for 24-48 hours, would not, in the experimental cage, eat food dropped in front of their noses. This shows the power of neurotic anxiety to inhibit adaptive function; and is parallel to what is found in many cases of anorexia nervosa. Anxiety is also the usual cause of sexual inadequacy and may also impair performance at work or in other settings—for example, if the person is made anxious by authority figures or merely by being looked at.

The experimental neuroses were overcome by offering the animals food in situations where anxiety was not strong enough to inhibit eating: in a room that remotely resembled the experimental room. Repeated eating overcame that anxiety, and the same thing happened in other rooms up the scale, and finally in the experimental cage.

The demonstration of the power of a competing response to break anxiety response habits was subsequently extended to human neurotic cases in a large number of ways. It was found, for example, that the counteranxiety effects of relaxation responses could be used to overcome a wide variety of anxiety response habits—notably through the technique known as systematic desensitization; sexual responses were similarly used in cases of impotence; and the expression of legitimate anger and other appropriate emotions in overcoming timidity (1,2).

Behavior Analysis

In order to be able to make intelligent use of the available methods, it is necessary to have precise information about the stimuli or stimulus chains that lead to the triggering of the behavior that is to be eliminated. This information-gathering is called *behavior analysis*. The first interview begins by asking the patient to state his major behavioral problems, and an attempt is made to establish the originating circumstances of each. The course of each problem is traced through the years, careful consideration being given to any circumstances that may have ameliorated or exacerbated it. Finally, the stimuli currently controlling the anxiety responses are analyzed. The historical information not only gives perspective, but may also throw light on the stimulus complexes presently relevant to the patient's problems.

When all the presenting complaints have been explored as far as possible, the therapist turns to the patient's background. He questions him about his early home life—how he perceived his parents through his childhood; whether they were kind and interested; whether they meted out punishment fairly or unfairly, and in what manner; how the parents related to each other;

how much religious training they gave him, and to what extent he is still influenced by it. How did he get on with his siblings? Did he have any childhood fears or nervous habits?

His educational life is the next topic: whether he liked school, how he fared as a student, how easily he made friends and close friends, and whether any of his teachers or fellow students were sources of fear or tension. At what age did he leave school? Did he continue his education or take a job? How did he get on functionally and with people in each educational and occupational setting?

The background history concludes with a systematic inquiry into the patient's love life, beginning with his first awareness of sexual feelings and continuing with later experiences in sequence. Did he masturbate, and was this associated with fear or guilt? At what age did he begin heterosexual or homosexual relationships? When and with whom did he have emotionally important relationships? In each case, one ascertains what attracted him to his partner, and how they got on together, socially as well as sexually. Love and emotional warmth are given as much attention as sexual behavior per se.

A survey of the patient's present social situation follows the history, with special attention to interpersonal difficulties. *A characteristic feature of all behavioristic questioning is the stress-reducing attitude of the therapist.* He is not merely nonjudgmental, but positively countercritical.

After the history-taking, the patient is routinely given two questionnaires-the Willoughby Neuroticism Schedule, which contains 25 questions relevant to neurotic behavior, and a Fear Survey Schedule of 108 sources of neurotic fear (2). Both of these are answered on a 5-point scale. The total Willoughby score is a useful index of the general range and severity of neurotic reactions, with emphasis on social neuroticism. High-scoring responses to particular questions provide grounds for detailed probing. For example, if the patient indicates that he is easily hurt by criticism, the therapist must ascertain how the distress is related to the character of the criticism and to its personal sources. The Fear Survey Schedule often discloses areas of neurotic sensitivity that history-taking misses—for example, anxiety at ideas of possible homosexuality, at taking responsibility, or at medical orders.

As stated above, therapeutic strategy is shaped by the findings of behavior analysis. Assertiveness training, systematic desensitization, or both, are very commonly indicated, as is the use of sexual arousal for deconditioning anxiety responsible for inadequate sexual responding, notably in many cases of premature ejaculation. It cannot be too strongly stressed that strategies are not mechanically dictated by broad diagnoses but are carefully adjusted to the requirements of the particular case (1,2).

In many cases, the initial behavior analysis provides a sufficient basis for effective therapy. In others, new information emerges in later sessions that changes the direction of therapy. Lack of progress with particular procedures

is always a strong reason for reassessment. For example, when desensitization using imaginary scenes progresses poorly, it may be because the patient has little or no anxiety when he imagines situations that he fears, or it may be that the hierarchy content is off target. An example of the latter is the agoraphobic who does not respond to desensitization to increasing distances from home; and in whom reassessment reveals that the real fear is of a heart attack. Separation from home is prominent in the patient's mind because it makes help less accessible.

Although the great bulk of neurotic anxiety reactions are a matter of the conditioning of autonomic responses, a considerable number of others are attributable to misinformation. The patient falsely *believes* that a particular thing, animal, or situation is dangerous. For example, there is the person who fears elevators because he believes that there is a paucity of air in an elevator, and that if it gets stuck he will suffocate. The elevator arouses the false idea, and that is what produces anxiety. To have anxiety in an elevator because of this idea is objectively inappropriate because one really is not going to die of suffocation in an elevator. To have anxiety at the idea of dying is not inappropriate; what is inappropriate is to attribute a danger of death to being in an elevator.

A skilled behavior analysis must distinguish between cases based on misconceptions and those due to emotional conditioning, for the treatment is quite different. Where the fear is due to wrong information, the therapeutic task is to correct it—informing the patient, and if necessary, showing him that the elevator has air holes. Once the patient's thinking is corrected, nothing else needs to be done.

Two Examples Illustrating the Importance of Behavior Analysis

Mrs. A represented a case in which wrong information was of central importance. For ten years she had constantly been in a fluctuating state of depression, with frequent spells of desperation that often culminated in tantrums. During the entire period she had been undergoing psychoanalysis without any benefit. Questioning revealed that the basis for her depressions was her inability to have coital orgasms. This, she had been led to believe, was because there was something inherently wrong with her. The disability gave her an excruciating sense of inferiority, so that, for example, if at a party her husband engaged in conversation with any other woman, no matter how unattractive, she would feel intensely jealous, for her thought would be "No matter what else, at least she does not have my terrible affliction." In the course of the first three sessions we established that her coital inhibition was associated with a fear of trusting anybody. This had originated with her father habitually doing things behind her back. For example, one day without saying a word the father had had her beloved dog destroyed. This was typical of a large number of acts. She could have an orgasm by masturbation *while alone;* but she could not have one coitally, nor could she have one by masturbation if her husband was watching because she had the feeling that the orgasm was a particularly intimate and private event that entailed the risk of betrayal if it were witnessed. From the moment it was clear to her that this was the basis of her trouble she never had another depression. Of course, it remained necessary to enable her to have orgasms coitally, which was accomplished by desensitizing her to images of herself in her bedroom masturbating to orgasm while her husband was visiting at a house five doors away, and subsequently closer and closer. Eventually, she could, without anxiety, imagine her husband watching her masturbate to orgasm; that was the bridge to coital orgasms. However, the central issue of Mrs. A's case lay in the terrible emotional state that arose from her negative self-evaluation. Just changing that faulty cognition was the most important part of the treatment. Recovery has now been sustained for seven years.

In the case of Mrs. B, although the neurosis had a clear basis in misconception, correcting it was not enough. Five years previously, a few weeks after Mrs. B. had given birth to her second child, she had two or three very transient attacks of dizziness. When she reported these to a friend at a party, the latter commented, "Oh yes, I know about those; they are very common after childbirth, and they often lead to committing suicide." This "information" threw Mrs. B. into a persistent state of dread. Psychiatrists she consulted added fuel to her fears. For example, one told her that the situation was indeed serious and could only be cured by delving into her early childhood; and a second said that she was only trying to get attention and should receive electroconvulsive therapy! As time went on, she became increasingly incapacitated until she could not go anywhere on her own. Although by the end of our second therapeutic session she fully accepted the baselessness of her long-continued fear of "cracking up," this was not sufficient to overcome her fears, since many sensations, situations, and thoughts had become autonomously conditioned to anxiety over the years, and a program of systematic desensitization was necessary.

The Results of Behavior Therapy

As is well-known (7,8), practitioners of almost all modes of psychotherapy can count upon between 40% and 50% of their cases either recovering or improving markedly. This appears to be a generally constant figure, so that the recovery rates cannot be attributed to the specific methods but to some process that is common to all of them. It is likely (9) that the common process depends upon the nonanxious emotional responses that therapists evoke in a large proportion of their patients. Therefore, unless the therapeutic system can obtain marked improvement in a percentage of patients significantly greater than the common baseline of 50-60%, it can not be claimed that the methods specific to the system have any efficacy. Up to now, behavior therapy has been unique in that, in skilled hands, it produces recoveries and marked improvements in 80-90%. without relapse or symptom substitution (10).

REFERENCES

1. Wolpe, J. *Psychotherapy by Reciprocal Inhibition.* Stanford: Stanford University Press, 1958.
2. Wolpe, J. *The Practice of Behavior Therapy,* 2nd ed. New York: Pergamon, 1973.
3. Wolpe, J. *Theme and Variations: A Behavior Therapy Casebook.* New York: Pergamon, 1976.
4. Pavlov, I.P. *Conditioned Reflexes.* Trans. G.V. Anrep. New York: Liverhigt, 1927.
5. Masserman, J.H. *Behavior and Neurosis.* Chicago: University of Chicago Press, 1943.
6. Wolpe, J. Experimental neurosis as learned behavior. *Brit. J. Psychol.* 43:243-268, 1952.
7. Knight, R.P. Evaluation of the results of psychoanalytic therapy. *Am. J. Psychiat.* 98:434, 1941.
8. Eysenck, H.J. The effects of psychotherapy: An evaluation. *J. Consult. Clin. Psychol.* 16:319, 1952.
9. Wolpe, J. Behavior therapy in complex neurotic states. *Brit. J. Psychiat.* 100:28-34, 1964.
10. American Psychiatric Association Task Force Report No. 5: *Behavior Therapy in Psychiatry.* Washington, D.C., 1973.

CHAPTER 26

Anxiety States and Short-Term Psychotherapy

Jorge de la Torre

Anxiety is endemic to our time and culture, the distinctive mood of our era (1). Everyone at one time or another experiences anxiety. The intense dysphoria that accompanies anxiety leads many individuals to do anything to find relief, even consult a psychiatrist. In many such cases with heightened motivation short-term psychotherapy can produce remarkable results. Not infrequently the pain that the patient experiences is translated into asking the doctor to provide a concrete treatment that rapidly, if not magically, will do away with the pain. For the doctor to withstand such demands and proceed with psychotherapy requires a sense of conviction regarding the psychopathology of anxiety and familiarity with the technique and indications of short-term psychotherapy.

Laughlin has defined anxiety in a way that will offer a practical working concept for this paper. "Anxiety is the apprehensive tension or uneasiness which stems from the subjective anticipation of impending danger, in which the source is largely unknown or unrecognized" (2). Like many other authors he differentiates fear from anxiety, the former having to do with an external, undefinable source usually with greater unconscious components. Such a differentiation, not always dynamically well delineated, is clinically useful (3). Fear calls for some external change, anxiety for some internal one.

It is assumed for the purpose of this paper that the reader is acquainted with some of the analytic concepts regarding anxiety, specifically with Freud's late ideas defining four different sources of anxiety: loss of the object, loss of the love of the object, fear of castration, and anxiety derived from the superego (4,5). According to the prevalent source, differing emphasis will be placed on the short-term psychotherapy and variations in the technique will be called for.

Although emphasis is placed on the pathological manifestations of anxiety, which bring patients for treatment, we should not forget that anxiety is a normal manifestation in the repertoire of an individual's emotions, and as Zetzel (6) has demonstrated, the incapacity to experience anxiety at different developmental points indicates a poor prognosis.

Short-Term Psychotherapy

Throughout the years, analysts have attempted to shorten the time of treatment without sacrificing the quality of the results (7,8,9,10). Either determined by theoretical conviction, by chance, or by external limitations, a growing body of knowledge has accumulated supporting the notion that psychoanalytic principles can be utilized to obtain remarkable results in a short period of time (11).

Particularly in the last two decades, there has been a proliferation of such efforts that have given a great deal of momentum to the understanding, application, and effectiveness of short-term psychotherapy. Most significant has been the work of David Malan (12,13) and his group at the Tavistock Clinic, with its very rich clinical considerations and disciplined research efforts, which have been followed by the work of many others, such as Balint (14), Sifneos (15), Bellack (16), Mann (17), and Wolberg (18), and a host of other contemporary analysts.

From outside of the psychoanalytic field, the understanding of crisis states from a social and general system vantage has also advanced our understanding of short-term psychotherapy. The work of Caplan (19), Rapoport (20), and Lindemann (21) has been seminal to the knowledge which is now taken for granted about the conceptual definition, progression, and resolution of crisis. All these authors have stressed that although a crisis, a superlative state of anxiety, is painful, there is a particular flexibility of the ego that can lead to significant therapeutic gains.

Short-term psychotherapy in the context of this paper should be understood as lasting anywhere from between a few and some twenty sessions. The appointments, usually on a weekly basis, are conducted in a "therapeutic ambience." The general interviewing technique is geared to allow and help the patient to develop some of his important dynamic themes—hence the necessity of greater activity on the part of the therapist, without confusing it with a question-and-answer model of a traditional review of systems. A common expectation is shared by patient and therapist regarding the length of the therapeutic process, which is to be measured in weeks rather than in months or years. Most patients who profit from short-term psychotherapy are of at least average intelligence, with the capacity to express themselves adequately; they harbor the notion that there is some psychological reason for their problems, and believe that talking therapy will be helpful.

The Issue of Diagnosis

The ubiquitousness of anxiety among psychiatric patients demands a careful assessment and diagnosis. The transitory anxiety in a well-compensated individual differs considerably from the intense anxiety that heralds psychotic decompensation. Both situations require different kinds of interventions and will have different prognostic outcomes.

It is assumed that before considering short-term psychotherapy for a patient suffering form anxiety, the clinician is satisfied in having ruled out such nonpsychiatric conditions as hyperthyroidism or other systemic conditions that can produce anxiety symptoms. He has also ruled out the possibility of a psychiatric condition for which short-term psychotherapy is not an effective treatment, such as chronic brain syndrome, withdrawal symptoms, agitated depression, or schizophrenia. The fine-tuning diagnosis (22), which includes a consideration of the patient's psychological assets and liabilities as they are operative and required in psychotherapy, should be completed before short-term psychotherapy is initiated. Intelligence, motivation, capacity for insight, strength of the secondary gains, general level of personality integration, and capacity for object relations must all be carefully assessed if the therapist is to approach his work adequately prepared.

In the treatment of anxiety three different modalities of short-term psychotherapy can be distinguished: 1. *crisis intervention;* 2. *nonspecific short-term psychotherapy;* and 3. *specific short-term psychotherapy.* With the help of clinical vignettes, the management of anxiety using each of these treatment modalities will be described.

1. Crisis Intervention

Crisis intervention is a brief treatment process dealing with an acute state of imbalance in an overloaded ego exhausted in its coping resources. In a crisis, the individual experiences a sudden and marked regression with accompanying paralysis of his capacity to properly assess reality and to make adequate choices. Crises are characterized by an intense sense of helplessness and inadequacy. The term "crisis" is reserved for extreme circumstances, rather than for any kind of acute anxiety episode (23). In order to counteract such feelings, the individual jumps into impulsive thoughtless action. The patient in a genuine state of crisis will easily surrender to poor judgment and make irreversible decisions with deleterious results that will last long after the crisis has been overcome. It is generally accepted that crises have a self-limited duration, and within approximately six weeks some resolution is brought about. The resolution might leave the individual at his previous state of organization, at a lower level of organization, or at a higher one, in which case the crisis has become a growing experience assimilated into the ego. A clinical vignette might illustrate psychotherapy in a state of crisis.

The Real Estate Lady

The patient, a petite brunette in her late thirties, has been an active and successful businesswoman after she moved to a new city about a year before. She bought a real estate business with which she was making slow but consistent progress.

When she came to the first interview, accompanied by a friend with whom she stayed for the previous two days, she appeared less attractive than she actually was because of her expression of fear and perplexity and her noticeable agitation. Her speech was pressured, and although a thought disorder was not detected, her anxiety made it difficult at times to follow her stream of thought. Frequently she would ask the therapist for reassurance. She felt unsure of herself, could not concentrate or make decisions, was sleepless at night, and could only think of selling her business and going back home to the parents.

Her present state of anxiety had been triggered when she learned, a few days before, that one of her female associates in the firm was leaving. She was somewhat puzzled by her reaction, as she did not feel particularly close to that woman.

In the initial session she was firmly advised to delay any drastic decision until she had the opportunity to talk more about her plans. She was very appreciative that an appointment was scheduled for two days later. The therapist mainly listened and suggested that in a few days she might look at her problems differently.

In the second appointment she reported and appeared to be feeling better. Since her first visit she had taken certain steps in order to clarify the reality of her present situation: she met with her lawyer, had a conference with her accountant, and called some other business friends, breaking the "helpless cycle." She commented that she felt reassured that the therapist was willing to see her even sooner if necessary. She then was able to give more of a history: most significant was her relationship with her father. Her father praised her independence, but at the same time tried to undercut it at every opportunity. Her move to the city was related to her counterphobic tendency in doing what she feared most. She wanted very much to prove to her father that she was independent and thereby to obtain his recognition and praise. The leaving of her associate had restimulated her strong dependency, and she thought seriously of returning to her parents' home.

In the next two sessions as the anxiety diminished she understood her fear of emotionally severing some of the final infantile ties with her original family should she become completely independent as the established owner of her own business.

Separations were always painful for the patient; she had received individual psychotherapy in the past precisely in connection with being separated from her husband. The departure of her associate on the anniversary of her own move, and the loss of an older figure upon whom she had always sensed she could rely, had triggered the present episode.

She wanted, by the fifth session, to continue treatment for a long and undetermined period of time, although she had become asymptomatic. This was explained as another manifestation of her dependency and avoidance of being on her own. For a few days there was a mild resurgence of the anxiety, which iniated termination of treatment. Termination took two additional appointments spaced at three-week intervals.

Comments. The case of the real estate lady clearly illustrates how the intensity of anxiety during a crisis can impel an individual to take action impulsively and regress markedly from a previous hard-won battle. In this case, the patient's intelligence, her previous treatment, her ability to work psychologically, and her intact ego were all favorable factors in allowing the treatment to proceed with rapid results.

When dealing with a state of crisis the first few sessions require that the therapist allow himself to be used as a buffer for the patient's anxiety. Directly confronting some of the patient's magic expectations before a potentially sustaining relationship is established will tax an already overburdened ego with unnecessary demands for therapeutic work. The placebo effect, usually in operation in all therapeutic first interviews, is even more significant in the first session with the patient in a crisis state, when he is most susceptible to psychological influence (24). It is important that the therapist assure the patient that he is available, that he is willing to work with the patient, and that he is not contaminated by the patient's anxiety.

This particular case was responsive to psychological work. In patients with less substantial internal resources, one must be prepared to utilize outside contributions, perhaps by inviting a relative to one of the interviews or by including him in the treatment plan. Frequency of appointments should be tailored to the patient's need. An appointment for less than the customary length of the session might prove to be more effective. The use of antianxiety medication is helpful particularly if one can discontinue it before the treatment ends, with the understanding that the medication is an ancillary measure that will make the patient more accessible to the psychotherapeutic process. Many patients who get relief from an anxiolytic drug tend to return to it any time that anxiety subsequently arises, and can become habituated while impairing the progress of their own maturational growth.

2. Non-specific Short-Term Psychotherapy

Nonspecific short-term treatment is probably the commonest form of brief psychotherapy practiced. It is called nonspecific because no particular or specific dynamic focus emerges quickly and clearly. Some authors refer to the modality as "anxiety suppressing" (25). It is essentially comparable to long-term supportive psychotherapy, but practiced in a much briefer period of time.

The method of such treatment is to endure with the patient his psychological dysfunction, supplementing certain areas of ego deficit, reinforcing some particular defense mechanism, or acting as a more benevolent superego figure. This psychotherapy is accomplished by cathartic ventilation, the reassurance that a figure in authority is on one's side, and the therapist's clarification, explanation, or advice. The patient needs a certain degree of motivation to resolve the particular conflictive situation that causes anxiety, although not necessarily motivation to obtain insight or understanding. The treatment is conducted under the impetus of a positive transference that remains undisturbed; a certain degree of dependency on the figure of the therapist develops and remains to some extent after termination.

While there is not a clear dynamic focus in evidence, there is a clear boundary of the patient's problem and a definite wish to resolve it. This is what makes these patients good candidates for short-term nonspecific psychotherapy rather than long-term psychotherapy. Some of these patients accomplish remarkable changes in their behavior, which could be understood either as "transference cures" or "flights into health," which the therapist permits to remain undisturbed and sometimes even tends to reinforce. Many of these patients become great propagandists for psychotherapy and for the particular therapist, which indicates the remainder of idealization. It is among these patients that the greatest danger exists for "interminable" therapy in which the rewards of the dependency long outweigh the benefit of the treatment. Usually this treatment does not reach beyond the conscious ego and manipulation of the transference (rather than the environment) is utilized.

The therapeutic consequences of such treatment should not be underestimated. It is postulated that mechanisms similar to those which Horwitz (26) has described regarding the efficacy of "supportive" psychotherapy operate in these cases. That is, if the patient experiences a high level of anxiety, then there is a certain predisposition to experience the therapist as a good object, and a corrective emotional experience ensues, with therapeutic reverberations that can be very significant.

The Medieval Knight

A successful engineer in his early fifties became extremely anxious following a fire in one of his factories. His anxiety was manifested by intense feelings of apprehension and somatic preoccupations. Because of the reality of his physical symptoms, related to the absorption of the fumes and for which a clear treatment had not been found, his preoccupation with bodily functions was not completely unjustified. Over a period of weeks and months he had developed a pattern of going from specialist to specialist, asking for different opinions until they would cancel one another out. His life revolved largely around a large metropolitan medical facility. His weight changed, his concentration became affected, and his general performance in the family began to show signs of strain. Socially he was extremely restricted, since he had no time left to spend with former associates or friends, while all his energy was devoted to the pursuit of his medical well-being. When he first came to therapy he brought with him a very thick folder containing reports of many medical tests, consultations, and previous hospitalizations. He came ready to prove his case, and his thick folder was the evidence that all his problems were *only* of physical origin.

This man had a satisfactory previous adjustment; he had been very successful professionally and had accumulated a significant amount of wealth. He had an unusually optimistic and sometimes naive outlook on life and had secretly entertained the fantasy of being a medieval knight, idealizing himself as virtuous, loyal, generous, fair, and very much admired by others.

He had always seen his father, now dead for a few years, as a very admirable person, and his relationship to him had been most rewarding. He rapidly developed a marked positive transference and commented on the therapist's patience, wisdom, and interest. He added that he felt he was in good hands and idealized the therapist in the same manner that he had previously idealized his father.

After the first two or three sessions the patient began to accept the psychological components of his behavior; by avoiding a confrontation with his present limitations and with the necessity of making new arrangements and modifications in his professional and personal life, he protected his self-esteem. He was neither taking the chance of meeting new situations nor facing the fact he was no longer exactly as he had once been. Early in therapy he was first able to acknowledge anger at having been an innocent victim of an accident, which he had previously completely denied. The anger was followed by fear and sadness.

The therapist avoided uncovering the patient's tendency to idealize male figures or the possible latent homosexual overtones. His tendency to handle angry feelings at the expense of reaction formation was likewise carefully bypassed, as were the narcissistic components in his personality.

After thirteen sessions the patient was symptomatically free, and his visits to doctors had decreased to a much more realistic and acceptable level. His social and vocational life was resumed within the natural limitations of his present condition. Idealization of the therapist continued in considerably diminished form, and the patient did not abuse the open-ended invitation to return should there be any need for it.

384   DE LA TORRE

Although this patient did not develop any particular insight into his difficulties, he was able to obtain a fresh understanding of his problems, which allowed him to continue and to pick up where he had left off.

Comments. The medieval knight illustrates a short-term therapy process that was successful in its limited goal. The patient did not develop any particular kind of insight other than some fresh understanding of a contemporary and particular episode in his life. The therapist was carefully maintaining a positive transference without exploring it or any negative elements in the relationship. The treatment was centered on a present and conscious situation, to which the therapist carefully adhered. The goal of the treatment was to help the patient reconstitute his previous defensive constellation, with which he was satisfied. Initial reinforcement of his feelings of victimization and acceptance of his emotional turmoil offered an alternative explanation to his behavior. Subsequently the possibility of mastering his situation with some intellectual understanding as well as denial of some of his basic longing constituted the core of therapy.

The use of "selective neglect" in choosing the areas and depth of work in consonance with the objective of treatment, suggested by Pumpian-Mindlin (27), seemed particularly relevant in this case.

It is noteworthy to mention that many general practitioners, medical students, and para-professionals can be quite successful in practicing this kind of treatment. If the patient is appropriate for this treatment modality, interest, dedication, and good intentions seem to go a long way even without a great deal of technical astuteness or sophistication.

3. Specific Short-Term Psychotherapy

Specific short-term psychotherapy is the most ambitious form of short-term treatment. It requires that a "focus" (12,13,14,15,17) emerges rapidly in the interaction with the patient. A focus is a dynamically important area of work connecting the patient's present problem with some infantile conflicts that appear of equal importance to both patient and therapist. As the patient acquires insight regarding a particular central conflict, psychological changes occur that might lead to concomitant structural modification. This form of psychotherapy is the most controversial and the most demanding of both patient and therapist. Patients who benefit from short-term psychotherapy are generally those who could profit from psychoanalysis. The therapist, on the other hand, needs the familiarity and experience with dynamics that is gained only after years of practicing long-term therapy. The temptation in many such cases is for the therapist and patient to collude in a fanciful work of rationalization in which both parties feel very satisfied for different reasons: the therapist because of his ambitious achievement, the patient because of the success of his resistance.

Presently it is not possible to establish a more accurate prognostication about which patient could successfully be treated with this kind of therapy rather than with insight producing long-term treatment. Wolberg (18) has gone as far as to recommend this kind of treatment initially and to go on with another long-term kind of psychotherapy only if it proves to be insufficient.

Malan has demonstrated that with these patients the "triangle of insight" can be accomplished in a few sessions (12,13). The present conflict is relived in the here and now of the transference and connected to its genetic roots. There is little doubt that agreement between the therapist and the patient in clearly establishing a focus of work is a necessary condition for successful outcome. In this treatment the therapist does not avoid the negative transference but brings it into exploration while he maintains a position of relative neutrality.

The Ugly Duckling

A man who had experienced pronounced restlessness, irritability, short temper, and recent fear of losing control and becoming violent toward his wife and small child finally accepted, with great skepticism, the family's advice to see a psychiatrist. His eating, drinking, and smoking habits had markedly increased. He constantly felt as if he were walking through a mine field. He felt very jumpy, ready to explode. He spent the first interview trying to project a picture of himself as very normal. However, by the end of that interview he was, in contrast to his initial attitude, very enthusiastic about coming back for further appointments.

The patient was doing well in his job as a manager of one of his family's businesses. He was born in Europe, had traveled extensively, and had lived in different countries during his childhood. He was nevertheless simple and unaffected rather than cosmopolitan in his outlook.

During the second interview he showed a remarkable and unexpected amount of psychological curiosity and capacity to reflect. It was also greatly surprising to learn that this well-mannered, somewhat overweight and tranquil-looking man had spent most of his adolescence struggling with anger, fights, and violence. He belonged to a gang in a metropolitan city, and his favorite activity was to go around picking fights, mainly with other gangs over territorial issues. Drugs and even sex were secondary to fighting. In addition he was an accomplished wrestler, weight lifter, and judo expert. In spite of his upper-middle-class position he had always identified with the underdog.

I suggested to him the analogy (28) of a small country surrounded by enemies. The country had to spend a great part of its budget on protecting itself from potential enemies, but many years later, when there were no longer enemies around, continued to spend a large portion of its budget on weapons and military equipment. It was later revealed that this was the turning point in the patient's therapeutic progress. In the next few sessions he was able to relate that metaphor to his own life; he had been very small and skinny as a child and was pushed around by the other boys, particularly when he moved to a new school, something that happened often during his early years. He also felt emotionally disadvantaged because he thought he had been adopted and that his natural mother didn't love him. His aggression was thus delineated as a clear defensive maneuver against his own passivity, and being hyper-masculine was a defense against being "too feminine." He had to prove himself time and again. He felt very envious of the relationship of his wife and small infant child. He wanted to be in a similar passive position, but his dependent longing triggered off defensive aggressive fantasies. This situation was further complicated by the fact that he was toying with the idea of starting his own firm, to which his father was firmly opposed.

Comments. The case of the "ugly duckling" helps to demonstrate the importance of several different technical aspects in a specific short-term psychotherapy:

a. the establishment of a dynamic focus. The link between the patient's fear of losing control, his use of activity to counteract passivity (and his feminine unacceptable longings) around Oedipal aggression and competition with the fear of symbolic castration, emerged very early in the therapy. This focus was easily shared by both therapist and patient.

b. the patient's particular psychological aptitude to work with and communicate psychological aspects of his life, which in these cases is always remarkable.

c. the patient's readiness for the therapeutic work is acknowledged by many short-term therapists as being of determining importance (the "ripe plum"). Such "ripeness" could be a function of the considerable psychological work the patient has accomplished before the initial appointment (one could speculate if the initial working through of many defensive operations, so time-consuming in long-term therapy, is not already accomplished to a great extent by the patient on his own).

d. the correlation between increased motivation as the dynamic focus becomes established appeared quite clear in this case. According to Malan (13), such correlation has a significant prognostic indication for successful cases.

Acquiring insight as a link between present and transferential situations vis-a-vis infantile ones, with the therapist maintaining a position of limited neutrality, differentiates the specific from the nonspecific short-term psychotherapy.

Concluding Remarks

Anxiety is a frequent complaint of psychiatric outpatients and is often successfully treated with short-term psychotherapy. I have tried to suggest with clinical vignettes the various techniques possible in dealing with patients presenting manifestations of anxiety in different forms and for whom the objectives of the treatment differed greatly.

The case of the real estate lady illustrated the intensity and potential disruption of a crisis. The need for immediate support, flexibility, accommodation to the patient's need, and reinforcement of her own unimpaired ego was accomplished, and she was able to acquire better understanding of her problem, emerging from the crisis in a stronger and more mature position than before.

In contrast, the case of the "medieval knight," although it did not present the disruptive acuteness of the previous case, was well on the way to becoming a chronic case with a great deal of somatization; the patient was gradually developing a system to deal with these feelings of anxiety at the expense of the subjective acceptance of his emotions.

Finally, the "ugly duckling" demonstrates the discovery of an unanticipated capacity to do psychological work that was very well utilized by the patient. The insight he acquired extended over many different areas and reached back into some unanticipated infantile roots.

If there is any formal and clear division of the three types of brief therapy in the preceding pages, it is only for the sake of illustrative clarity. The overlapping of different interventions is the rule, rather than the exception.

REFERENCES

1. Bellak, L. *Overload: The New Human Condition. New York:* Human Sciences Press.
2. Laughlin, H.P. *The Neuroses.* Washington, D.C.: Butterworth, 1967.
3. A. Freeman and H. Kaplan, eds., *Comprehensive Textbook of Psychiatry.* Baltimore: Williams & Wilkins, 1967.
4. Freud, S. (1895). *Standard Edition,* Vol. III. London: Hogarth.
5. Freud, S. (1926). *Inhibition, Symptom and Anxiety,* Vol. XX.
6. Zetzel, E. *The Capacity for Emotional Growth, Anxiety and the Capacity to Beat It.* 1949.
7. Sterba, R. A case of brief psychotherapy by Sigmund Freud. *Psychoanal. Rev.* 38:75-80, 1951.
8. Ferenczi, S., and Rank, O. *Development of Psychoanalysis.* Nervous and Mental Disease Monograph Series, No. 40. New York and Washington: Nervous and Mental Disease Pub. Co., 1925.
9. Alexander, F., and French, T.M. *Psychoanalytic Therapy.* New York: Ronald Press 1946.
10. Knight, R.P. Psychotherapy in acute paranoid schizophrenia with successful outcome: A case report. *Bull. Menninger Clinic* 34:97-105, 1939.
11. de la Torre, J. Brief encounters: general and technical psychoanalytic considerations. *Psychiatry* 41(2) 1978.
12. Malan, D.H. *A Study of Brief Psychotherapy.* New York: Plenum, 1963.
13. Malan, D.H. *The Frontier of Brief Psychotherapy.* New York: Plenum, 1976.

14. Balint, M., Ornstein, P.H., and Balint, E. *Focal Psychotherapy*. Philadelphia: Lippincott, 1972.
15. Sifneos, P.E. *Short-Term Psychotherapy and Emotional Crisis*. Cambridge, Mass.: Harvard University Press, 1972.
16. Bellack, L., and Small, L. *Emergency Therapy and Brief Psychotherapy*. New York: Grune & Stratton, 1965.
17. Mann, J. *Time-Limited Psychotherapy*. Cambridge, Mass.: Harvard University Press, 1973.
18. Wolberg, L.R., ed. *Short-Term Psychotherapy*. New York: Grune & Stratton, 1965.
19. Caplan, G. *An Approach to Community Mental Health*. New York: Grune & Stratton, 1961.
20. Rappoport, L. The state of crisis: Some theoretical considerations. *Soc. Sci. Rev.* 36(2):211-217, 1962.
21. Lindemann, E. Symptomatology and management of acute grief. *Am. J. Psychiat.* 101:141-148, 1944.
22. Fisher, S. Primun non nocere: Too much of a good thing? *Sem. Psychiat.* 1(4):1969.
23. de la Torre, J. Outpatient services: A present perspective. *Bull. Menninger Clinic* 37(6):581-597, 1972.
24. Strupp, H.H. *Psychotherapy: Clinical, Research and Theoretical Issues*. New York: Jason Aronson, 1973.
25. Sifneos, P.E. Two different kinds of psychotherapy of short duration. *Am. J. Psychiat.* 123:1069, 1967.
26. Horwitz, L. *Clinical Prediction in Psychotherapy*. New York: Jason Aronson, 1974.
27. Pumpian-Mindlin, E. Considerations in the selection of patients for short-term psychotherapy. *Am. J. Psychother.* 7:641-652, 1953.
28. de la Torre, J. The therapist tells a story: A technique in brief psychotherapy. *Bull. Menninger Clinic* 36(6):609-616, 1972.

CHAPTER 27

Hypnotic Procedures in Treatment of Anxiety

Fred H. Frankel

Before the consideration of the use of hypnosis or hypnotic procedures in the treatment of anxiety, the term "hypnosis" will be discussed. No one can refute that there are several aspects of this fascinating area of human behavior which remain ambiguous, but in a field where many of the concepts are as yet only minimally understod we must in practice take a firm hold of what we do know, rather than linger with and emphasize what we do not. Twenty years from now we might have revised our position in the light of information not yet discovered, but at this time the data persuade us to regard the event of hypnosis in a specific light.

This chapter will first touch on erroneous or inadequate assertions about hypnosis, and then after a description of a hypnotic procedure will present a practical understanding of the event and a few of its characteristics. That will acquaint the reader, even though very briefly, with what might be called the evolving basic science of the subject. A few clinical vignettes will follow, succeeded by a consideration of what other therapeutic factors in those clinical cases might have been operative.

Erroneous or Inadequate Assertions about Hypnosis

We are reminded, as we proceed, that much of the information which enables us to evaluate the legendary characteristics of hypnosis has

389

accumulated from the findings in the laboratories of experimental psychology. The clinical literature, though rich, has for the most part failed to separate hypnosis from much that takes place in the clinical context even without hypnosis, and observers are frequently left pondering the extent of the role of hypnosis in a specific case, and the part that might have been played by other factors such as placebo and relaxation.

Perhaps because of the unusual subjective experiences that can occur in hypnosis, or possibly as a result of Mesmer's original dramatization (1) of the uncanny role of the hypnotist (or magnetizer as he was called two centuries ago when Mesmer first drew the attention of medical science to animal magnetism), the effects of hypnosis have often been coupled with the supernatural or the quasi-magical. Furthermore, assertions are still frequently heard about hypnotists being able to exercise control over the actions of subjects against their will; about a subject, in some way because of the hypnotist, being able in hypnosis to transcend his normal physiological limits; or about hypnosis being a form of sleep. More recently, in attempts to explain hypnosis in terms more suited to the language of modern psychology, phrases and metaphors have been loosely introduced, ascribing hypnotic behavior to the direct expression of the unconscious, a term that is in itself complicated and not readily understood.

Some of these assertions border on the truth, but none reflect it fully. It can be firmly stated that there is nothing supernatural or essentially mystical or magical about hypnosis. Furthermore, there is little evidence that hypnotized subjects can outstrip their maximal performance, either mentally or physically, because of the hypnosis. On the contrary, there *is* evidence to support the assertion that a well-motivated, physically healthy person can, for example, suspend himself between two chairs by his head and his heels (2) (a performance not infrequently included in stage demonstrations of hypnosis) *without* the use of hypnosis. Regarding control, in the routine clinical context that concerns us here, the clinician does not and cannot control the actions or experiences of the patient with hypnosis any more than the patient will permit him to control them. Experience will readily prove that any attempts to have the patient follow instructions that he is unwilling to follow will lead to embarrassing results, noncompliance with the suggestion, or even waking from the trance in anger.

Hypnosis is neither a form of sleep nor a stage leading to sleep, and electroencephalographic tracings in hypnosis display no similarity to those of sleep (3). Furthermore, there has been no objective measurement of any physiological change in the body that is uniquely associated with hypnosis. Blood pressure, heart rate, and other variables might alter in hypnosis, but apparently in no way distinguishably from the alterations that might occur with progressive relaxation, transcendental meditation, yoga, and other related practices (4). The presence of hypnosis is diagnosed primarily from the description of the subjective experiences of the patient, and not from what he does or demonstrates physiologically. What then is hypnosis? Before attempting the answer, let us consider an episode of hypnosis.

Description of Hypnosis

Typically the operator sits at the side of the patient's bed, facing him, or sits opposite or alongside him in the office. When possible, the induction procedure should be preceded by conversation and interaction that encourages the development of a comfortable clinical relationship. A medical history and a psychiatric evaluation should have been completed; the topic of hypnosis, including the patient's previous experience of it, should have been discussed. For an enriching experience of hypnosis to occur, the patient should trust the physician and be willing to undergo hypnosis. The physician should be sensitive, observant, and supportive. Not all patients are hypnotizable, but most, under appropriate circumstances, can respond to the simpler suggestions.

The induction procedure can be one of many types ranging from asking the patient to close his eyes and think of a peaceful scene to having the patient gaze at a spot on his hand, a shiny object, or a swinging pendulum until his eyelids become heavy and close. The object is to lead him carefully but confidently to redistribute his attention so as to withdraw it from his general surroundings and focus it on a circumscribed area. Meanwhile he is encouraged to relax and let happen what will happen. This induction procedure is sometimes followed or even replaced by what are described as deepening techniques. The patient is directed to imagine himself descending gradually on an elevator or staircase, or drifting on a boat past a slowly shifting landscape. Counting forward or backward is another deepening or induction technique. Throughout the procedure the physician fosters the illusion by offering his comments in a slow, repetitive, and persuasive monotone, exhorting the patient to feel relaxed and calm, or to imagine himself floating or drifting.

After a period generally lasting from one to several minutes, the physician introduces ideas of a motor or sensory kind. He suggests to the patient, for example, that as he concentrates on the feelings in his fingers and his hand, the small muscles in his fingers will begin to twitch and his hand and forearm will begin to feel light. They will eventually feel so light that they will lift up off the armrest of the chair, and continually floating upward, will ultimately reach the side of his face. The physician might add the comment that the higher the hand floats, the deeper the hypnosis will become, and the deeper the hypnosis, the higher the hand will float. He adds, too, that when the hand reaches the side of the face the patient will be deeply hypnotized.

When this point is reached and the hand and arm have "levitated," the physician assumes that the patient is hypnotized and then adds whatever other suggestions are appropriate to the situation.

Before leaving the induction procedure and the introductory phase, it should be emphasized that the initial procedures can be as simple or as complicated as the physician prefers them to be. They can be delivered with a dramatic flourish or offered very simply. The use of gadgets such as shiny objects, spinning disks, and metronomes is not recommended. The simpler the procedure, the better. Although the type of suggestions and their sequence is left to the physician's preference, a useful principle is to proceed from the suggestions that are easily experienced to those that are more difficult. Success in the early stages enhances the likelihood of success with the suggestions that follow (5). As twitching movements in the small muscles of the fingers and the hand are more readily experienced than levitation of the hand and forearm, the suggestion of the small movements and sensations should precede the other. Failure to experience suggestions that are offered early in the hypnotizing procedure tends to interfere with the progress. Exhortatory comments are made as the patient advances step by step.

Returning now to the point at which the physician considers his patient to be hypnotized, we can briefly examine one or two of the several options that are available to him. If the purpose of the procedure is to reassure a dental patient and induce dental analgesia, for example, the dentist encourages the patient whose hand is still near his face to concentrate on the feelings in his fingers, to imagine numb and tingling feelings intensify in his fingertips, and then to feel the numb and tingling feelings drain from his fingers into his face and teeth, which will then be surrounded and permeated by the numbness (6). He is then advised that the numb sensation will screen out any hurt or pain from the dental procedures that are about to begin. For the relief of pain in other sites, transferring the numb feeling from the fingertips to other parts of the body is readily accomplished by suggesting that the hand can move to touch the appropriate areas.

If the purpose of the exercise is to induce and establish relaxed and calm feelings throughout the body, these are accentuated in the suggestions, and vivid images of tranquil scenes, real or imagined, are encouraged. The colorful picture of a rose garden, a scene from a mountaintop overlooking a valley, or a wheatfield are but a few examples. In this way, attention is diverted from the experience of anxiety by the presentation of a well-defined alternative for the patient to concentrate on.

These events mentioned in the description of hypnosis are not intended as an exhaustive survey of the experiences possible in hypnosis, but include a sufficiently varied number to reflect the innovative clinical uses that can evolve. Before termination of the hypnosis, with, for example, an instruction to open the eyes and be wide awake, continued feelings of well-being are suggested by the hypnotist, as is the return of the usual sensation and control in the levitated arm or other part of the body in which altered sensations were encouraged, unless persistence of the tingling, for example, is preferable.

A Working Definition of Hypnosis, and Some of Its Characteristics

We can now consider a working definition of hypnosis, and a few of its characteristics. Hypnosis is an event developed in the Western world involving an operator and a subject, and dependent for its occurrence on the *trance capacity* of the subject, his or her *motivation* to be hypnotized, and the *relationship* between the subject and the operator (7). When these are appropriate, the subject can be guided or directed to experience reality differently. This altered state of awareness includes the essential aspect of the hypnotic trance, which is the presence of altered or distorted perceptions.

In addition, the event might be associated with an ability to tolerate logical inconsistencies, an unusual performance of memory such as amnesia or hypermnesia if these are suggested, and a poorly understood psychosomatic interaction when this is encouraged, such as a rise in the temperature of the skin, dramatic improvement in a skin disease (8), or reduction in blood pressure.

The definition explains for us how some well-motivated subjects who have a marked capacity for the trance experience hypnosis in a way that is qualitatively different from that of the subjects who are well motivated but have only minimal trance capacity. For instance, the latter group might experience the relaxation and warm feelings of a positive kind, but will not be capable of altering their perceptions to any extent. Truly hypnotizable subjects, when they are well motivated and comfortable in their relationship with the operator, will be capable of the whole experience—namely, the relaxation and the calm, the warmth of the relationship, *and* an appreciation of the altered perception, such as the tingling or the sweet taste or the perfumed smell, depending on what has been suggested to them.

It can be realized from the comments thus far, if the reader had not previously known it, that hypnotic responsivity is neither universally nor equally distributed. The data (9) strongly support the view that responsivity is a stable attribute; that a small percentage of people (2-5%) are very highly responsive; that 25-30% are minimally responsive; and that the test scores of the others fall on a bell-shaped curve. Stated another way, almost all subjects can relax and feel comfortable in response to an induction procedure, but only some will achieve hypnosis and experience altered perceptions. What effect does this have on the clinical use of hypnotic techniques?

Clinical Exercise

Let us briefly consider a few clinical situations which illustrate the specific benefits of an essentially hypnotic event, or the therapeutic effect of the hypnotic induction procedure. These are not synonymous.

Case 1: A 20-year-old man was carried down a ski slope, having sustained a fracture of the tibia. He was shocked, cold, in pain, and fearful. He was taken to an encouraging and confident physician in a nearby town who readily assured him that he had treated countless numbers of similar cases successfully, and that the chances of a full recovery of the use of his limb were extremely good. The physician then used a hypnotic induction procedure, claiming to prefer natural methods of pain relief to chemical analgesics. He then talked to the patient encouragingly of entering a state of relaxed calm in which the pain in the limb would give way to a tingling or heavy feeling at the fracture site, which would screen out the hurt from the pain.

Case 2: The next case was that of a woman in her mid-thirties, unduly anxious about the prospect of abdominal surgery. She was visited the previous evening by her anesthesiologist, who spent time with her eliciting her fears and expressing an understanding of them; he reassured her of the relative safety of the procedure scheduled for the next day, and of the fact that he would be present in the operating room to greet her on her arrival there. He then used a hypnotic induction procedure to induce a state of calm, and added beneficial suggestions about her feeling fine both before and after surgery; she was told that postoperatively she would void urine comfortably shortly after she wakened, that she would develop an interest in eating, and that she would enjoy her food. He also instructed her in self-hypnosis procedures, confidently anticipating that she would be able to apply them herself efficiently both pre- and post-operatively, and that she would thereby obtain relief, comfort, and a sense of relaxation. She chose the view from the mountain top as the calm and tranquil scene of her imagination, and was encouraged to experience, as vividly as she could, the colors, the sounds, the cool breeze, and the subtle fragrance in the air.

Case 3: A third case was that of a 59-year-old man who was suddenly stricken with a myocardial infarct, and although ready for discharge home after a few weeks was immobilized by his anxiety about separating from the protective environment of the hospital; he feared this would leave him exposed and vulnerable to further and more serious heart attacks. He was understandably concerned about the necessary readjustments in his life, and despite reassurances from his physicians that innumerable victims of heart disease go out of the hospital to lead full and healthy lives for many years, he continued to be somewhat depressed, and his anxiety failed to improve. Ultimately the decision was made to have his case evaluated by the liaison psychiatrist.

The psychiatric encounter commenced with attention directed to his concerns and anxieties; he disclosed that two cousins of an age similar to his had died within recent years from myocardial infarcts. He was told that his anxiety was perfectly understandable, and his preoccupation with the problem and his sense of insecurity were discussed at length with him. He was then told that if he could be calmer and more relaxed about the problem, difficult as that might be, it would be to the advantage of his health. It was explained that hypnosis was especially useful in the attainment of a relaxed frame of mind, and that people could readily learn to hypnotize themselves into calm, comfortable, and tranquil states.

After a simple induction procedure he was encouraged to consider the fact that his health had been satisfactory for years, that he could look forward to a rapid healing process, and that in all probability he would enjoy many years of a healthy and productive life. He was then taught to use a self-hypnotic induction procedure aimed at achieving a state of calm in which he could feel his confidence cautiously expanding as his heart grew stronger.

Discussion

In none of these cases was the hypnotizability of the patients of major concern. It was not even assessed. Great emphasis was placed by the hypnotist, however, on establishing a sound rapport with the patients, recognizing and discussing their anxieties with them, and encouraging them to relax and to expect that whatever clinical methods he used would be of benefit to them. Their interest in participating in the treatment programs was encouraged, they were gently persuaded to permit themselves to relax and enjoy a calm feeling, and they were taught, when appropriate, to practice self-induced hypnosis. These steps, in addition to paving the way to hypnosis for some, also probably led to relaxation and the placebo response for all.

Were we to examine the clinical encounters closely, including the final outcome, we still might have difficulty knowing the nature of the effective therapeutic principle in each case. Traditionally, physicians invoke the power of the placebo very much more often than they realize; and we know that when patients relax, their anxiety diminishes and they tolerate pain more effectively. To what extent, we might ask, could relaxation or the placebo response have been primarily responsible for the therapeutic benefit in each of these cases, and to what extent did hypnosis account for it.

We do *not* yet know whether hypnosis per se—namely, altered or distorted perception—actually did take place in any one of them. We *do* know that although hypnotic induction procedures were used, we cannot be confident that the event of hypnosis followed, because not all individuals are capable of it. We would need to question the patients about their *subjective* experiences to know whether perceptual alterations had indeed taken place, before we could label the event as hypnosis.

However, we *also* know that they all were capable of experiencing some or all of the following: a deep sense of relaxation and calm; a comfortable and trusting feeling about the physician and the expectation that the procedures used by him would be of benefit to them; and a shift of attention from the painful or fearsome circumstance to the tranquil or pleasantly absorbing imaginary scene of their choosing. The therapeutic principles that might well have been effective then were those of relaxation or lessened anxiety, the placebo effect, or a shift in attention. These can all result from the use of hypnotic induction procedures to the same extent that they can occur in many other circumstances—without constituting an event of hypnosis. It will be noticed from the title of this paper that we are concerned not only with hypnosis but also with hypnotic procedures in the treatment of anxiety. One might well ask where, in these cases, does the essential difference lie. We believe it is this: If the tingling at the fracture site is actually experienced, or if the mountaintop and the breeze and the fragrance are so vividly imagined as to seem real, it can be assumed that hypnosis has occurred. We can then expect an *even greater therapeutic effect* than that accomplished through relaxation and placebo alone. The assumption that hypnosis had occurred would be justified if good hypnotic responsivity on a standardized rating scale was obtained; such rating scales do exist and are reliable (10,11,12). Furthermore, the hand levitation response and measure of dissociation in the Hypnotic Induction Profile (13) provide a rapid, approximate index of the subject's likely responsivity.

If perception can voluntarily be altered by the patient, he might be assisted further to alleviate his symptoms by actively substituting mild discomfort for the severe pain, smelling the fragrance of the mountain air, or even altering his sense of time and thus experiencing the painful periods as brief and the periods of relief as prolonged. These additional therapeutic moves are possible only if the patient is a good hypnotic subject.

The effects of relaxation, the placebo, and a shift in attention occur, as already indicated, under many other circumstances. Clearly, the therapeutic effect of a good bedside manner or clinical presence (not always encouraged by our exclusively technological orientation in many medical schools) becomes operative precisely because that behavior encourages confidence, relaxation, the expectation of a cure, and a lessening of anxiety. Former generations of physicians were confident of its effectiveness. We might well ask whether in fact we understand the situation today any better than they did then; we probably do. Whether we use a standard hypnotic procedure or cultivate a bedside manner of high caliber, we can alleviate anxiety to some extent in almost all patients by means of relaxation, placebo, and a shift in attention, In patients who are good hypnotic subjects, however, we will accomplish noticeably more if we help them to achieve the hypnotic trance, and thereby enable them to add to their relief by altering their perceptions.

REFERENCES

1. Ellenberger, H.F. *The Discovery of the Unconscious: The History and Evolution of Dynamic Psychiatry.* New York: Basic Books, 1970.
2. Collins, J.K. Muscular endurance in normal and hypnotic states: A study of suggested catalepsy. Honors thesis, Department of Psychology, University of Sydney, 1961.

3. Evans, F.J. Hypnosis and sleep: Techniques for exploring cognitive activity during sleep. In E. Fromm and R.E. Shor, eds., *Hypnosis: Research Developments and Perspectives.* Chicago: Aldine-Atherton, 1972.
4. Benson, H., Beary, J.F., and Carol, M.P. The relaxation response. *Psychiatry* 37:37-46, 1974.
5. Weitzenhoffer, A.M. *General Techniques of Hypnotism.* New York: Grune & Stratton, 1957.
6. Owens, H.E. Hypnosis and psychotherapy in dentistry: Five case histories. *Int. J. Clin. Exp. Hypnosis* 18:181-193, 1970.
7. Shor, R.E. Three dimensions of hypnotic depth. *Int. J. Clin. Exp. Hypnosis* 10:23-38, 1962.
8. Frankel, F.H., and Misch, R.C. Hypnosis in a case of long-standing psoriasis in a person with character problems. *Int. J. Clin. Exp. Hypnosis* 21:121-130, 1973.
9. Hilgard, E.R. *Hypnotic Susceptibility.* New York: Harcourt Brace & World, 1965.
10. Weitzenhoffer, A.M., and Hllgard, E.R. *Stanford Hypnotic Susceptibility Scale, Forms A and B.* Palo Alto, Calif.: Consulting Psychologists Press, 1959.
11. Morgan, A.H., and Hilgard, J.R. The Stanford hypnotic clinical scale. Appendix in E.R. Hilgard and J.R. Hilgard, *Hypnosis in the Relief of Pain.* Los Altos, Calif: William Kaufmann, 1975.
12. Shor, R.E., and Orne, E.C. The Harvard group scale of Hypnotic Susceptibility, Form A. Palo Alto, Calif: Consulting Psychologists Press, 1962.
13. Spiegel, H., and Bridger, A.A. *Manual for Hypnotic Induction Profile: Eye-roll Levitation Method.* New York: Soni Medica, 1970.

Index

calcium, 130, 131, 132, 134, 135, 209, 241, 245, 247, 248
cannabis, 245
carbamates, 245
carbohydrate tolerance, 169
cardiac arrest, 115
cardiac index, 209, 340
cardiac neuroses, 20, 21
carditis, rheumatic, 33
cardiorespiratory anxiety symptoms, 348
cardiovascular function, 3, 127, 169
carotid sinus stimulation, 341
castration anxiety, 253, 255, 272, 273, 290, 291, 317, 318, 378, 386
catatonia, 117
catecholamine, 46, 153, 155, 156, 168, 178, 179, 186, 207, 208, 209, 341
catharsis, 36, 38
cell glycogen, 169
central nervous system (CNS), 3, 45, 107, 113, 117, 154, 164, 170, 171, 172, 174, 182, 184, 212, 237, 238, 247, 312, 342
cerebellum, 164
cerebral cortex, 154
cerebrospinal fluid, 169
cerulo-cortical norepinephrine psthways, 174
character disorders, 35, 105, 186
Character Disorder cluster, 69
chlorazepate, 326
chlordiazepoxide, 173, 174, 325, 327, 328, 329, 339, 351, 353, 354, 356, 357, 361
chlormezanone, 326
chlorothalidone, 215
chlorpromazine, 175, 176, 240
chronic brain syndrome, 379
cingulate gyrus, 154
cirrhosis, 356
clonidine, 159, 161, 164, 171, 176, 180, 187
clorazepate, 351, 353, 359
cognition, 43, 107, 119
cold pressor (CP) test, 118
colliculi, 155
coma, 207, 208, 240
combat fatigue, 54
compensatory responses, 60, 61, 120
competitive Beta-adrenergic blocking drugs, 136
compulsive behavior, 106
conditioning, 147, 148, 149, 186, 347
conflict, 54, 145, 265, 312, 370, 384, 385
confusion, 207
conscience, 99, 101, 252

conversion reaction, 106, 255
convulsions, 20
cortex, insular, 155
cortical activation, 62
cortical inhibition, 238
cortical norepinephrine turnover, 174
cortisol, 168, 208
countertransference, 40
couple-sensate-focus, 317
courtship displays, 147
crisis, 378, 379, 380, 381, 387
cyclopromethyl, 359

Da Costa's syndrome, 21, 127, 129
danger, 94, 104, 237
dealkylation, 359
decarboxylation, 359
decathexis, 293
decompensation, 379
deconditioning, 370, 372
defenselessness, 308
defense mechanisms, 37, 38, 39, 44, 53, 80, 82, 104, 106, 257, 258, 301, 386
delirium, 240
delta activity (EEG), 240
delta sleep, 214, 215
delusion formation, 257
denial, 104, 105, 289
dependence, 301
dependency, 95, 100, 291, 381
depersonalization, 83
depression, 1, 24, 27, 43, 45, 47, 68, 79–84, 86–89, 106, 129, 130, 135, 142, 143, 145, 147, 168–170, 175, 178, 186, 208, 209, 212, 218, 221, 222, 226, 228, 229, 230, 234, 238, 258, 274, 276, 292, 317, 318, 320, 338, 339, 341, 343–345, 374
deprivation, 301
desalkylflurazepam, 359
desensitization, 108, 315, 320, 372, 374
desmethyldiazepam, 353, 356, 357, 359
despair, 143
desynchronization, 240, 245, 247, 248
deterministic conceptual frame, 262
development, 94, 95, 96, 97, 99, 100, 103, 106, 108, 263, 264, 272
deviant behavior, 309
DeVries' Inventory of 13 MMPI items, 81
dextroamphetamine, 240
dextrose-in-saline, 133
diabetes, 318, 331
diacetylmorphine, 245

labile personality, 186
lactate, 30, 128, 130–136, 169, 184, 209, 240, 241, 245, 247, 248
learned helplessness, 147, 148
levarterenol, 341
libido, 51, 252, 253, 255, 261, 311, 314, 319
Librium, 351
limbic forebrain, 180, 183
limbic system, 113, 114
lithium, 88
liver, 136, 208, 353, 356, 357, 359, 361
locus coeruleus, 155–159, 161, 163, 164, 166, 169, 171, 172, 174, 175, 177–187
lorazepam 327, 359, 361, 363
loss 45, 47, 82, 101, 103, 104, 106, 143, 272, 274, 276, 293, 294, 295, 296, 313, 317

Madonna-Prostitute complex, 320
mania, 178, 245
M. arctoides, 157, 159
marijuana, 173, 245
masochism, 289, 290
medazepam, 353
meditation, 182, 245, 390
medulla, 155, 183
Mellaril, 108
memory, 32, 38, 45, 52, 182
menarche, 100
meprobamate, 173, 178, 215, 325, 327
metabolism, 142, 326, 329, 353
methacholine, 238
methadone, 68, 245
methionine enkephalin, 165
MHPG, 156, 159, 168
mianserin, 247
migraine, 176
Miller-Magaro cluster, 69
Minimal Brain Dysfunction (MBD), 107, 186
MMPI, 81, 213, 215, 216, 218, 221, 231
monoamine oxidase inhibitors, 136, 173, 175, 176, 245
mood, 3, 205, 214, 215, 222, 377
morphine, 165, 175, 187
motivation, 113, 114, 115, 144-146
Multiple Affect Adjective Check List, 3
muscarinic receptors, 176
muscle relaxants, 173

naloxone, 165
narcissism, 96
narcoleptic, 117
narcosis anxiety, 291

negativism, 96, 101, 106
neonate, 263
neural autonomic activation, 116
neurasthenia, 20, 21, 24, 26, 27, 39, 40, 87, 127, 129, 252
neurocirculatory asthenia, 87, 127, 129
neuroleptics, 36, 148, 149, 176, 177, 327
neurosis, 8, 13, 22, 24, 25, 27, 34, 35, 51–53, 62, 74, 83, 84, 105, 135, 142, 143, 145, 148, 184, 232, 238, 239, 253, 272, 284, 288, 369–371, 389
neurotic depression, 30, 83
Neuroticism Scale of the Eysenck Personality Inventory, 232
neurotransmitters, 148, 179, 184, 312
nightmares, 2, 97, 108
nociceptive information, 185
nocturnal penile tumescence, 315
noradrenergic-anxiety hypothesis, 154
noradrenergic systems, 154, 166, 167, 172, 173, 175, 180, 183, 186, 187
norepinephrine, 46, 61, 63, 117, 127, 135, 136, 153–156, 159, 165, 168–172, 175, 176, 178, 179, 184–186
"not me," 265
nucleus locus coeruleus, 154

Observer Rating, 5, 135
obsessive-compulsive neurosis, 26, 30, 84, 85, 130, 136, 255, 319, 331, 370
ocular pressure, 341
Oedipal issues, 273, 274, 277, 283, 284, 291, 317, 318
opiate agonists, 176
opiate receptors, 174, 176
opiates, 173, 175, 187
organic brain syndrome (OBS), 43, 47, 338, 341
orgasm, 117, 316–319, 321
oxazepam, 252, 326, 359, 361, 364
oxprenolol, 173, 343, 344, 345, 346, 347

pain, 79, 87, 119, 171, 178, 180, 182, 186, 266, 291–293
pair-bonding, 318
palmar skin conductance, 344
palpitations, 128, 170, 207, 337, 338, 340, 347
panic, 5, 20, 80, 88, 176, 238, 256, 282, 294, 295, 319
pan-neurotic illness, 331
paralysis, 256
paranoia, 80, 257, 266, 302